Understanding FDDI

For my wife and best friend Sue
and
my children Samantha and Luke

Understanding FDDI
A 100Mbps solution for today's corporate LANs

Andrew Mills
Advanced Micro Devices (UK) Ltd

Prentice Hall
New York London Toronto Sydney Tokyo Singapore

First published 1995 by
Prentice Hall International (UK) Limited
Campus 400, Maylands Avenue
Hemel Hempstead
Hertfordshire, HP2 7EZ
A division of
Simon & Schuster International Group

Printed and bound in Great Britain by
Redwood Books Limited, Trowbridge, Wiltshire

Library of Congress Cataloging-in-Publication Data

Mills, Andrew.
Understanding FDDI : a 100Mbps solution for today's corporate LANs / Andrew Mills.
p. cm.
Includes bibliographical references and index.
ISBN 0-13-219973-4
1. Local area networks (Computer networks) 2. Fiber Distributed Data Interface (Computer network standard) I. Title.
TK5105.7.M56 1995
004.6 ' 8–dc20 94-24703
CIP

British Library Cataloguing in Publication Data

A catalogue record for this book is available from the British Library

ISBN 0-13-219973-4

1 2 3 4 5 99 98 97 96 95

Contents

Preface

This is a book about the 100 Mbps local area network, FDDI. The capabilities, performance and maturity of FDDI has helped it to become the most sturdy backbone network to date. From its resilient optical fibre to lower-cost unshielded twisted pair implementations, it covers a wide variety and breadth of applications from mainframes to the humble personal computer.

FDDI has undergone a number of changes in the last few years, and has also seen new competition from technologies such as Fast Ethernet (100Base-T, 100Base-VG/ANYLAN) and 155 Mbps ATM. Many have asked if both the painstakingly slow standardisation processes, and this new competition will see FDDI diminish as a viable market solution. People have a right to be concerned. After all, FDDI has not exactly taken over from the well-established base of Ethernet or Token Ring installations. However, times are changing rapidly. Newer applications, network-ready desktop operating systems are placing a great strain on some networks that are primed for upgrade.

So why FDDI? Why not ATM or Fast Ethernet? The answer is quite simple. FDDI is a network for today. It is mature, well tested for interoperability, and many problems have been ironed out by its usage for over seven years. All these other solutions have a great proving period to go through. Yes, technologies like ATM will certainly prove to be a good solution once the total picture has been put together across the wide area. This is not expected to happen until the late 1990s. This is why FDDI and its derivative TPDDI will be successful over the next few years, as it meets the objectives of most of these new applications as shown in this book, without the heavy risk associated with a brand new technology.

True, FDDI will probably never reach the installed base of Ethernet or Token Ring, but it is a very important evolutionary process en route to higher-speed networking and communications in the local area. Just as importantly, it has helped us to understand that reaching the level where a networking standard is truly multivendor interoperable (i.e. an end user has a high degree of confidence that it will work seamlessly with that of another vendor) is not the easiest thing in the world. FDDI has taken many years to reach a level that most other standards cannot not even come close to. For instance, what other standards-based, widely available LAN can boast an integral, comprehensive management capability that can automatically handle network topology changes (reconfigurations) and provide the necessary visibility to the outside world to illustrate what has happened in a well-defined, consistent manner? Other networks are seeing this only now, as management and reliability become ever more important.

This is the reason for this book. FDDI has a large enough installed base, and is the most available open standard there is today, and will be for some time. Whereas all the other 100 Mbps networks are in development, FDDI has just approached maturity, which is what end users need, not new bells and whistles, not yet another competing, confusing technology, that essentially provides the same end result. FDDI has got what it takes to implement a reliable, high-speed backbone and desktop network today, without having to wait until the other embryonic technologies have even got the stage where they are widely available from multiple sources.

What I have tried to do in the following chapters is to present FDDI technology in an easy to understand, logical format. Note that throughout, the term FDDI is used to refer to both the optical and copper variants, as only the physical media changes. From time to time, I have also used the term TPDDI to refer to the newer ANSI copper FDDI standard. I have started with some basic drivers in the end user marketplace, moving onto the technology itself, and then onto the implementations and applications of FDDI products.

The following is a summary of the chapter contents.

Chapter 1: Developments in the LAN This chapter concentrates on the most recent developments in the LAN and computing world. Client/server computing and the emerging networked multimedia applications are discussed, as these are driving the need for high speed, more fault tolerant LANs. A brief overview of the standards that specify LANs and their operation is given.

Chapter 2: FDDI Networks This serves as a basic introduction to FDDI, the standards, station and equipment types, installation and cabling, and finally an overview of the specific implementations of FDDI and its copper cabling derivatives.

Chapter 3: FDDI Connections An introduction is given to the methods used by FDDI to transport raw data '1's and '0's around the network. Schemes for encoding and decoding data for both fibre- and copper-based cabling are described. A summary is given of the various cabling options available for use in an FDDI networking environment.

Chapter 4: FDDI Data Transmission and Reception Once the basic concepts of FDDI networks have been understood, Chapter 4 will explain in detail how data is transported and managed on an FDDI ring. A detailed description of the timed token protocol at the heart of FDDI is given, along with a detailed example of the transmission and reception process.

Chapter 5: Station and Network Initialisation The initialisation of an FDDI station and the network ring is described from a logical viewpoint, from the moment a station is switched on, to the point where the ring becomes fully operational.

Chapter 6: Network Reconfiguration and Fault Recovery The ability of FDDI to recover from network operational and cabling faults is unfolded, ending with practical methods for producing fault tolerant installations. The managment processes described in both Chapter 5 and 6 are based on the latest FDDI Station Management specification, v 7.3.

Chapter 7: Management of FDDI Nodes FDDI has a large section of its standards documents devoted to management of individual stations and the FDDI ring. As well as covering the built-in mechanism provided by FDDI's SMT, some of the broader aspects, such as management within an SNMP environment, are covered.

Chapter 8: Implementations and Products FDDI has come a long way in terms of its applications and available products. Without going into too much specific detail, enough information is provided for a network implementor to be able to understand the requirements of the products they are looking for. In particular, some of the larger vendors' products are covered as examples of some of the FDDI equipment that is available today.

Chapter 9: Applications It is always useful to understand where FDDI products are used. Chapter 9 explains the rationale behind moving towards an FDDI based solution, covering specific examples and case studies, in order to show how FDDI is being applied today.

As many different standards are sited, a complete listing is included in the Bibliography for reference rather than within the chapters themselves.

Acknowledgements

I would like to thank the following people for the part they played in the production of this book: Mike 'SG' King for finding the publisher for me, and fooling me into thinking I could write a book; Viki Williams of Prentice Hall (UK) who gave me the chance to try; Steve Scott of Prentice Hall for helping me to produce the final copy; Mark Smith and Nick Thorpe for their valuable comments on the early manuscripts; finally, my wife Sue for enduring many lonely nights of soap operas!

CHAPTER 1

Developments in local area networking

Local area networks, or LANs, are becoming a necessary part of today's business computer systems, allowing a cost-effective means of communication between everything from simple desktop computers and peripherals, to large mainframes or distributed server systems. As the need grows to connect more devices to a LAN, and in turn connect LANs together, a computer network needs to be capable of adequately managing and detecting fault conditions in order to maintain a consistent service to the end users. The Fiber Distributed Data Interface, or FDDI as it is commonly known, has an important role to play in the way LANs are expanded to cope with these demands.

It is currently estimated that there are over 60 million LAN interfaces installed in the world today (IDC, 1994), and this is expected to grow at an average rate of 20 per cent, well into the latter half of the 1990s. The vast majority of these are based on Ethernet and Token Ring, with Ethernet owning greater than 50 per cent of the installed base. As existing LANs on their own cannot cope with this increase in most cases, it comes as no surprise that there is a large market for high-speed networks, such as FDDI. More than 1 million FDDI adapters a year are expected to ship by 1997, with connection charges decreasing rapidly. FDDI on its own is not expected to solve all networking problems of the future, so many newer technologies such as Asynchronous Transfer Mode (ATM), and also faster versions of Ethernet are expected to emerge. However, FDDI is the only technology mature enough today to tackle most of the communication needs, having been through a significant proving period of nearly ten years. Microsoft went through the processes of upgrading their backbone to FDDI technology due to the increasing demands placed on their Ethernet backbone, leading to its eventual flooding. This overload was brought on by the increases in processing power at the desktop level, the need for a central access to servers (though still physically distributed across campus) and the demand for faster network response times.

Another important aspect of growth is the effect on the decisions made by a network implementor and manager. Though technology often presents many exciting opportunities for us to try out new ways of implementing networks, the investment in existing infrastructures is often far too great to consider anything that involves a global replacement of network services or equipment. For this reason, the vast majority of LANs evolve over time, with minimal changes incurred at each stage of upgrade in order to preserve the status quo where possible. It is for this reason we see technologies like switched LANs being successful as they enhance performance whilst maintaining the investment in end station LAN interfaces.

Factors Driving Change

As well as growth in the number of LAN nodes, new applications and advances in technology are responsible for many changes in the way networks are implemented or developed. As the number of nodes increase, the main impact is in the area of data flow and fault management. Most of this can be accomplished using many of the internetworking devices available, and a high-speed backbone technology. New applications, more often than not, demand a change in the LAN technology itself. For example, multimedia applications demand a more predictable network response time, or higher transmission rates, not met by many existing network installations. Technological advances, such as those found in transmission line driver semiconductors, have also allowed lower-cost cabling to be used where previously they were too unreliable as a communications cable. Switching technology has also been introduced to the common LAN technologies as semiconductor advances permit a low enough cost point to be achieved.

Technology Advancements

The saying, *'the only constant in this world is change'* is especially true for technology. Regular software upgrades to a desktop PC are a way of life, as are hardware changes (motherboard upgrades) as product lifecycles get much shorter, and processor technology continues to develop.

Since the inception of Ethernet, computers have come from a performance level of no more than a few Mips (million instructions per second), to a few 10s or even 100s of Mips. In all this time, Ethernet has remained at 10 Mbps, fast enough in the earlier days for the highest-performance computers to rarely get anywhere near this input/output rate. Today, even an average desktop computer is capable of saturating a 10 Mbps Ethernet or 16 Mbps Token Ring LAN, though everyday applications are only just surfacing to take advantage of this. FDDI for this reason runs at 100 Mbps, enabling it to easily carry the payload of a single high-performance workstation, and also that of many lower-rate LANs when used as a backbone. Obviously, the faster the data rate, the better, but costs increase rapidly as rates exceed 100 Mbps, as other factors such as cabling types and maximum radius come into play, making overall installation and operation difficult.

Increased computer power brings new applications, some never conceived until such power became available. For example, many personal computer operating systems now come complete with integral networking, a feature only found in workstation class computers previously. Networking as a standard feature allows software developers to make use of the standard interfaces provided without having to write their own drivers. This is helped further by the inclusion of some LAN network interface devices directly on the motherboard of desktop PCs.

Networked Multimedia

Networked multimedia is the term applied to the transport of audio-visual and associated traffic across the LAN. Examples of applications that are classed within the networked multimedia umbrella include video conferencing and remote interactive working, playback of real-time video clips from a networked video server, and the transfer of large amounts of bit-mapped graphics data, such as medical X-ray or photographic images (Figure 1.1). The end points may be on the same LAN, or over a WAN gateway or router to another site, either national or international. An example of a local application includes interative CD-ROM software for browsing through an encyclopaedia, where the CD-ROM(s) is on a central server. An application that

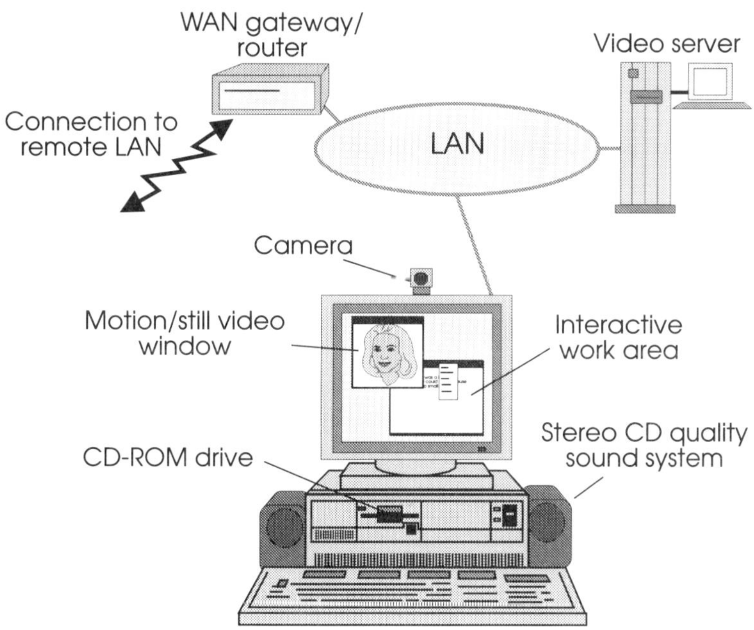

Figure 1.1 *Networked Multimedia PC*

allows communication on a wider scale is interactive working (shared whiteboard) over the LAN and/or WAN, sometimes using video conferencing.

The demands placed on the LAN by multimedia are not so much bandwidth intensive (though too many multimedia related transmissions can easily swamp a LAN), but are more related to latency and jitter. This is discussed in more detail in Chapter 8. Again, the increased loading created by these applications creates the need for careful planning and balancing. High-speed networks, such as FDDI, can greatly assist in meeting the demands of networked multimedia.

Adoption of Client/Server Architectures

Another significant factor of change has been the migration of many mainframe computer network environments to a client/server architecture, where the traditional data processing departments give way to a more decentralised approach. Many newer computer systems are implemented using a number of lower powered computers instead of one large central mainframe, connected by a LAN (Figure 1.2). This is frequently referred to as *downsizing*. Fragmenting the computer system in this manner demands a high level of fault tolerence in the communications channels set up between the smaller servers. Furthermore, mainframe systems typically hold large amounts of information that many users may wish to access, often at the same time. In a downsized computer network, large portions of the database are normally downloaded to a desktop PC and processed locally rather than on the mainframe itself. One such example in a sales environment, is the access of customer order entries (historical data) via a desktop PC, graphically displayed using a spreadsheet application. As the tools become ever easier to use, the ability to process centrally stored data at the desktop will continue to increase, and the amount of LAN traffic along with it.

The political implications are that the end user has more influence than ever over the traffic type, flow and complexity over a network, all of which have placed higher management, performance and reliability demands on the LAN. Networks such as FDDI have been designed specifically to meet these growing demands. The technical implications are that a new generation of server PCs and their interconnections must meet the same fault tolerence requirements as their mainframe predecessors, requiring a robust networking technology at the critical points in the LAN.

Aggregate vs. Total Bandwidth

Although maximum or burst data rate on a LAN is important, the most important factor is the *aggregate* data bandwidth. Ethernet's 10 or Token Ring's 16 Mbps is more than adequate for most applications, even compressed packet video data as is being demonstrated by a number of products in the marketplace. For example, compressed full-frame NTSC or PAL video can be transmitted across a communications channel using only 2 Mbps of bandwidth. The problem is that this

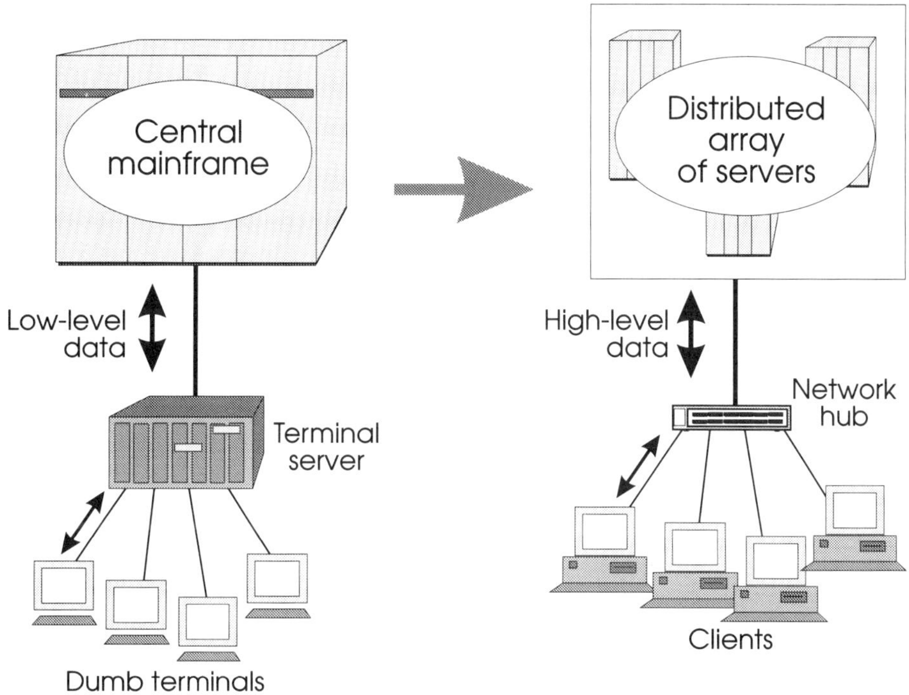

Figure 1.2 *Migration to client/server*

bandwidth is usually shared between a number of end stations, and there is a delay in getting access to the network determined by the current activity on the LAN. For this reason, packet-switched LANs, such as switched Ethernet, Token Ring and even FDDI, were developed to increase the overall throughput of the network. This is accomplished whilst keeping the communications data rate the same, e.g. 10 Mbps for Ethernet or 100 Mbps for FDDI. What this means is that in a standard shared LAN, only a single station in a segment can transmit at any one time, whereas switched versions allow many stations to be transmitting at a time. This may be to different end points, or to the same end point through a higher speed pipe. Switched Ethernet with an FDDI link to a server cluster is one example. Though end stations are only communicating at 10 Mbps, theoretically up to ten stations in a switched environment can communicate over an FDDI pipe to a server simultaneously, increasing the overall throughput of the network to 100 Mbps as opposed to just 10 Mbps if the server was on Ethernet. The benefit to the end user is that the end stations still retain their existing 10 Mbps interface.

Switched operation is described in more detail later, and in Chapter 7. Combining lower-speed switching LANs with that of a high-performance backbone can greatly enhance the overall bandwidth and response of a network.

LAN Developments

Due to the number of changes that have taken place in LAN architectures, it is worth summarising the most significant changes that have taken place so far. These are summarised in Figure 1.3.

These start with the change of physical networks to a predominantly *star-wired* or *mesh* topologies, driven mainly by the adoption of structured cabling standards for telecommunications and data communications wiring in buildings. The shift in cabling structures allowed the development of *intelligent* and *workgroup* hubs, which reside at the wiring centres of most of today's networks.

As the popularity of the star-wired structure grew, the importance of network management grew. Though management was by no means new to the world of networking, it was only usually an afterthought, bolted onto an existing network once the need for it arose. Star-wiring, with intelligent hubs at the central wiring points, made management an easy, and readily available feature of any network. The level of management chosen could be varied according to the users' needs. As there were many common approaches to management, the standards bodies soon produced standards to cover both the transport aspects of management information, and the types and classes of the managed objects themselves. In many cases, along with management, came security. The ability of a network manager to control who gains access to the network and through which port has become very important as more mission-critical and sensitive data are added to the LAN.

Another important development was the migration to segmented backplanes within intelligent hubs, where a *collapsed* backbone could be implemented, with several Ethernet, Token Ring or FDDI networks coexisting on the same physical backplane. Such an architecture resulted in the wider usage of bridges and routers integrated into the hub itself. The advantages of such an evolution is the improvements in management, traffic monitoring and control, and, of course, cost of internetworking equipment.

Structured Cabling

One of the most significant trends in recent years is a migration of most, if not all data communications wiring to a predominantly star-wired or mesh topology. A number of factors have led to such a change.

- As the number of nodes and end users grow, the ability to manage and control the network became more difficult, particularly in shared physical media technologies such as 10Base-2 Ethernet.
- The need for easier wiring and network topology changes, caused by users moving location more frequently.

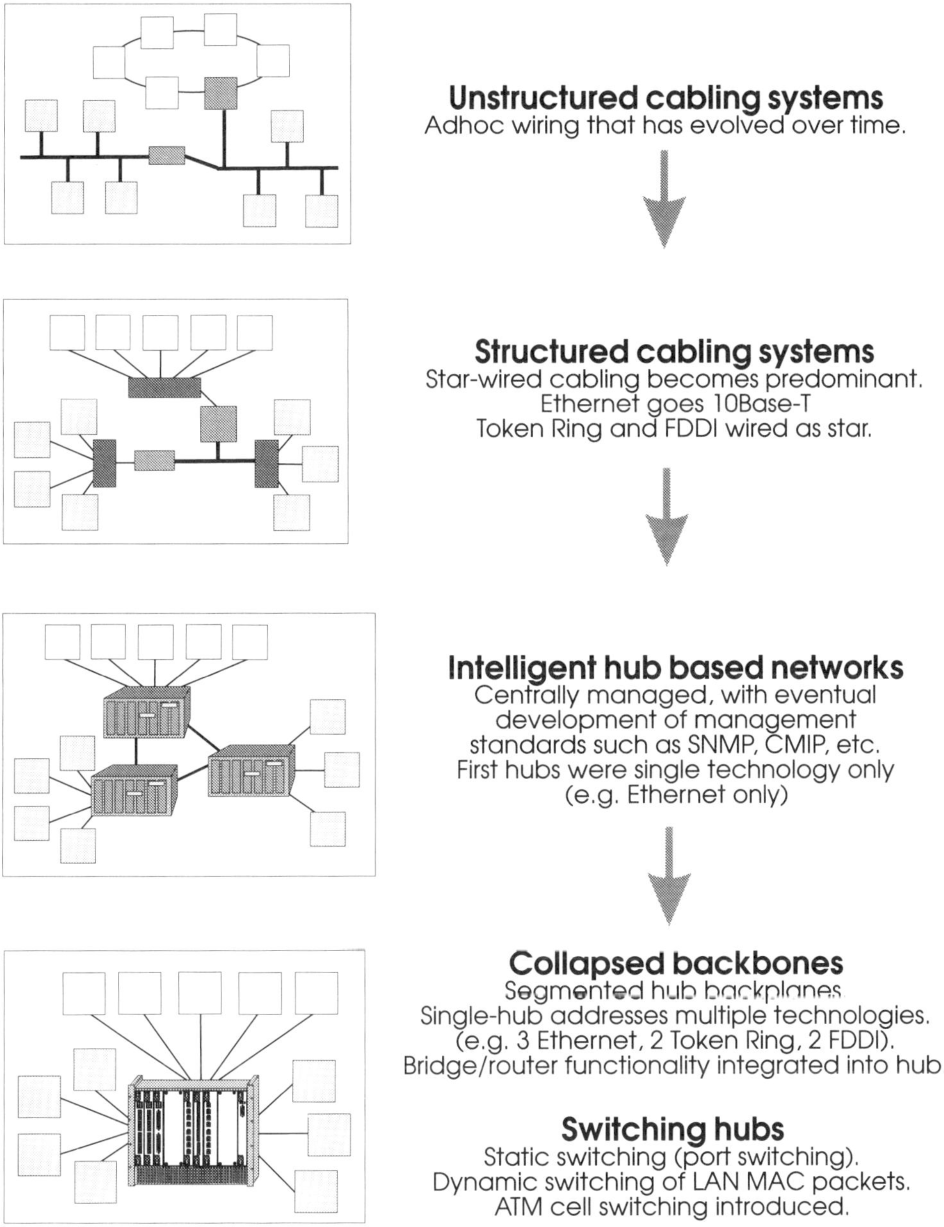

Figure 1.3 *Evolution of LAN architectures*

- The need to utilise the same wiring structure as the telephone network on the premises, and even the same cabling.
- The need to protect investments in hardware installation and removal costs, allowing a cabling lifetime of at least 5-10 years.

The EIA/TIA (Electronics Industries Association/Telecommunication Industry Association) 568 standard was put together in order to standardise on the way cables are installed into a building for new cabling installations, along with the basic cable types and characteristics. It was aimed specifically at the office environment as opposed to the more stringent industrial environment, handlling issues to campus level wiring. Its design goal was to provide a wiring lifetime of at least ten years. This ten years is intended to cover any possible technology changes that may occur (i.e. faster networks), and also allow networking physical standards to have a standard to adhere to instead of creating new cabling standards to fit the LAN. Other standards organisations, such as ISO and CENELEC, base their work around this standard, covering additional aspects such as designing and implementing cabling schemes, cable and apparatus installation, and so on. The AT&T Systimax Premises Distribution System (PDS) is an example of a structured cabling system.

In particular, the EIA/TIA 568 standard covers the following:

- Wiring topology options
- Maximum segment cable distances
- Physical media options
- Physical characteristics
- Connector types and pin assignments

The preferred topology is a star network. Figure 1.4 illustrates a generalised situation and preferred cabling scheme. The cabling is broken down into two main areas, namely the horizontal and vertical riser/campus links. For the vertical riser (typically the backbone cable), cabling can include optical fibre, unshielded twisted pair (UTP), or shielded twisted pair (STP), and coaxial cable. Vertical and campus maximum cabling distances vary according to the technology, and can be anywhere from 500 m upwards. For the horizontal wiring, 90 m of cabling is recommended, and is usually UTP in most modern installations. For this reason, most modern LAN driver electronics are designed to meet a distance requirement of 100 m over UTP under specific electrical interference conditions.

Valid cable types include the following:

- Four pair 100 Ohm UTP
- Two pair 150 Ohm STP
- 50 Ohm coax
- 62.5/125 μm optical fibre

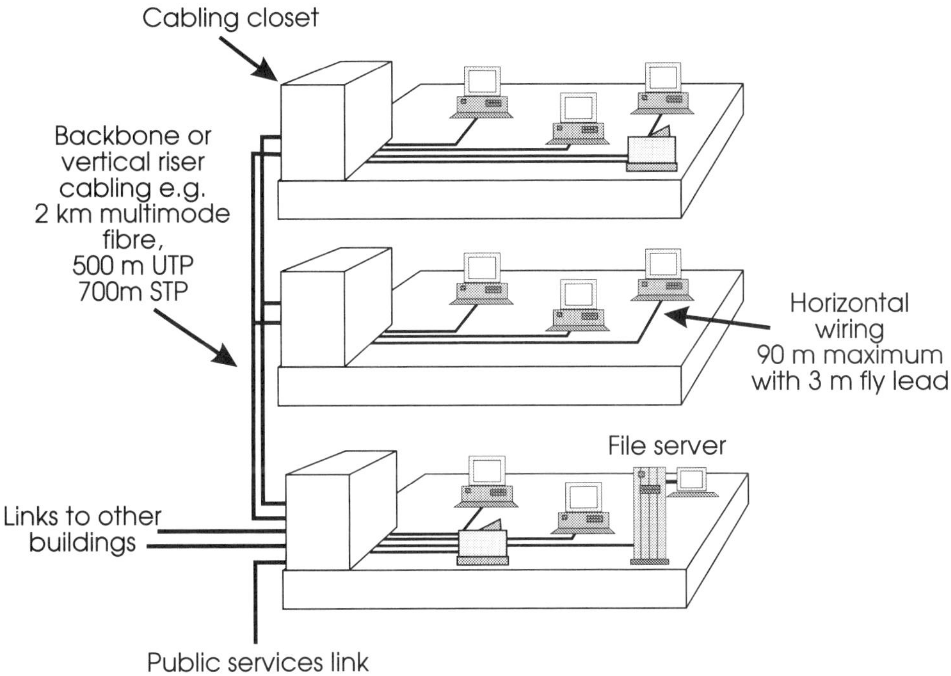

Figure 1.4 *EIA/TIA 568 structured wiring standard*

Out of the available cable types, twisted pair is by far the most common in the world today, with an estimated installed base of greater than 75 per cent. This is expected to increase, and not decrease over time. The installed base of coax is expected to decrease over time as a result, with longer-distance connections being made with optical fibre.

The cabling closet (Figure 1.5) has become the central point for most of today's networks, with all of the required electronics and connectors being housed in a 19 in. rack-based system. For security purposes, the main networking equipment and patch bay connections are housed behind a closed door under lock and key to prevent unauthorised changes. By going to the wiring closet, a network administrator can easily change the port an end user is connected to on the main central networking hub device using the patch leads. More sophisticated systems exist that allow automatic routing of the patch panel connections (i.e. an electronic patch bay). The next evolution allows the networking hub to change the routing of physical ports onto a particular network segment or service (sometimes referred to as *port mobility*).

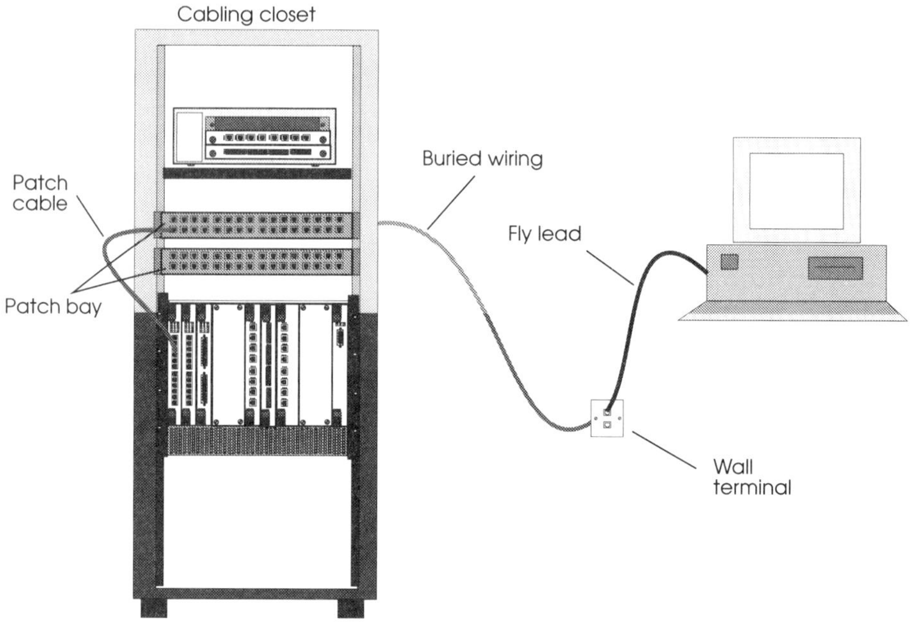

Figure 1.5 *Typical wiring closet arrangement*

Impact of Cabling on LAN Technology

The use of a particular set of cable types of known characteristics allows the LAN technologies to be assured of a more stable environment as far as transmission line drivers are concerned. In particular, it allows standard semiconductor components to be reliably manufactured and tested to known environments.

One example can be found within 10 Mbps Ethernet/IEEE 802.3 networks. The development of star-wired networks has allowed the 10Base-T standard to emerge. Originally developed by Synoptics under their own brand name, it was later modified, and made an official extension to the 802.3 standard by the IEEE committee. It has since been adopted by many manufacturers to become the most dominant Ethernet implementation in the world. 10Base-T Ethernet uses 100 Ohm UTP wiring, restricted to 100 m maximum distance, and unlike its previous cousins, 10Base-2 (Cheapernet) and 10Base-5 (Thick Ethernet), is based on point-to-point cabling (Figure 1.6).

The 4 and 16 Mbps Token Ring has been developed around a star-wired topology even though it is a ring based network (Figure 1.7), with the central wiring concentrator being upgraded more recently to enable active, as opposed to passive, connections. There are a number of benefits to using an active connection in a concentrator. Firstly, the electrical or optical signal is regenerated, and secondly, the management on a node by node basis is greatly enhanced to the extent that it is possible automatically to detect and shut down excessively noisy links on a port-by-port basis. FDDI and TPDDI, as we shall see later, are often wired in this fashion, again driven by the widespread advantages of star wiring.

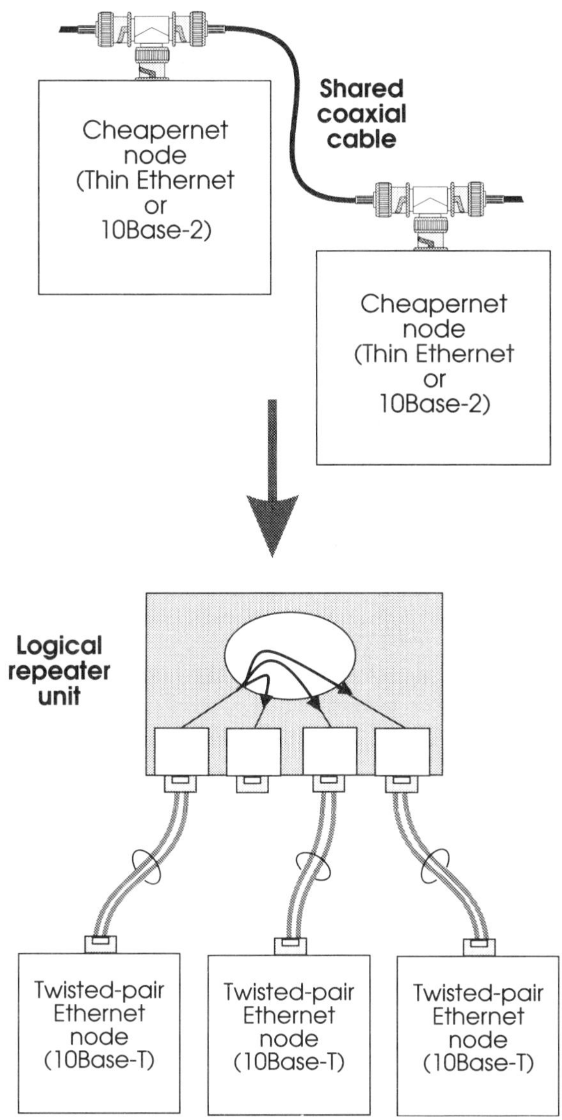

Figure 1.6 *Ethernet/IEEE 802.3 migration to star-wired 10Base-T*

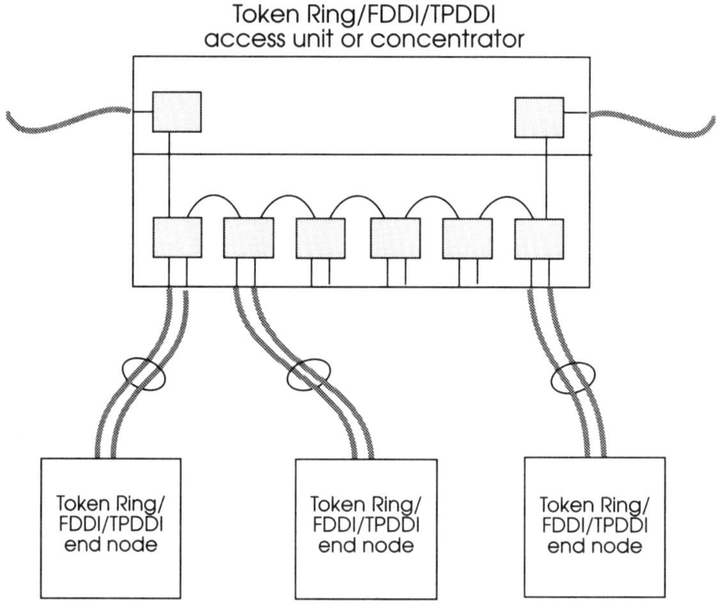

Figure 1.7 *Star-wiring of ring topology networks*

Another significant impact on LANs is the speed at which data can be transferred across the wire. There was a time when it was thought impossible to transfer more than a few megabits per second over an unshielded twisted pair, later proved wrong by the introduction of 10Base-T Ethernet. It is now possible to transfer data at a rate of 100 Mbps over UTP as in TPDDI, and this is expected to increase further to 155 Mbps in coming years.

The Evolution of Intelligent Hubs

The intelligent hub (Figure 1.8) has come to be one of the most important components of LANs, especially in the larger corporate networks, and has evolved in a number of important stages. The first implementations of the intelligent hub were not so intelligent, and were usually dedicated to one particular network type or technology, with a single backplane. Hubs have advanced significantly since then, and have become the main workhorse of the network.

The main stages of its development from a LAN perspective (though not fully comprehensive) were summarised in Figure 1.3, and are as follows:

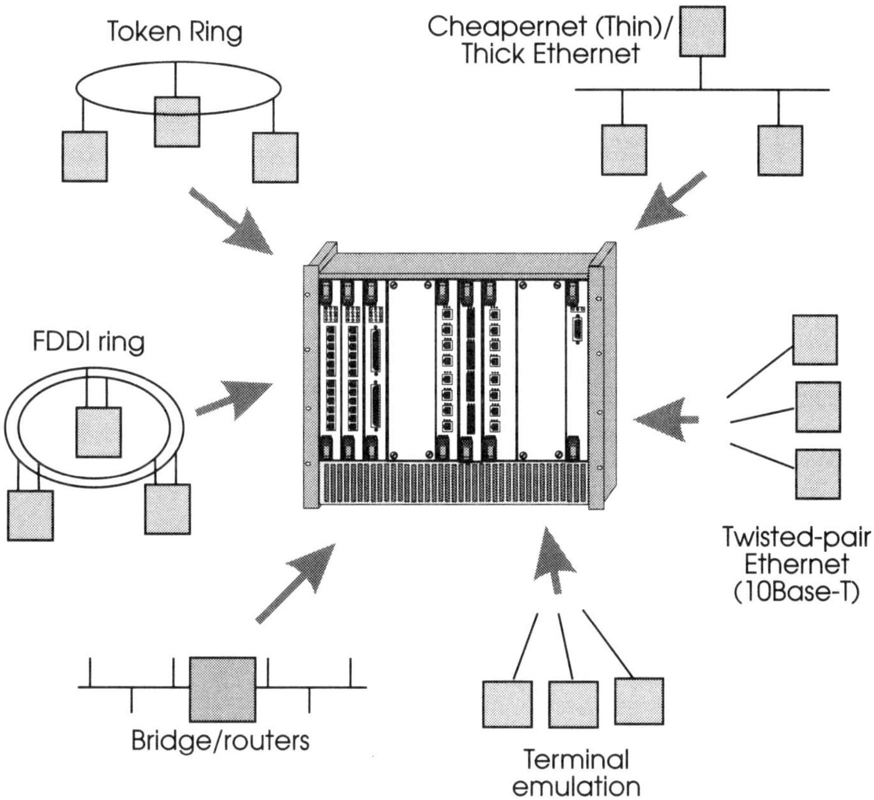

Figure 1.8 *The Intelligent Hub*

- Provision for more than one networking technology (typically Ethernet, Token Ring and FDDI).
- Incorporation of management features, security etc., in order to allow better control and monitoring of the network.
- Capability to partition hub backplane into multiple segments.
- Migration to *collapsed backbone*, where a number of separate LAN segments and types could coexist on segmented backplane as opposed to individual LANs and bridge/router boxes.
- Addition of *static port switching*, where individual ports could be steered into a particular segment remotely from a network management station.
- Eventual migration to full *dynamic switching* of data packets to any port, allowing simultaneous transmissions between end stations as opposed to them having to wait for the shared medium to become free.

Increasingly, there are intelligent hubs that have packet- or cell-based switching backplanes, with a dedicated switch and controller that can cope with a total capacity in the order of gigabits (10^9) per second data transfer rates. Ethernet, Token Ring and FDDI LANs are connected into the switching *fabric* via the appropriate bridge/router module or interface. The advent of switching, and in particular technologies such as ATM, is leading to the creation of virtual networks, where real hardwired networks no longer exist, except inside the backplane of a hub, or as a virtual connection across a mixed LAN and WAN environment.

Developments in the WAN

Another important development is in the area of remote office connectivity, where remote LANs are connected into a central corporate network via the wide area network (WAN). It is beyond the scope of this book to explore the different technologies available, but one of the important developments is again that of ATM within the Broadband-ISDN umbrella. *En route* to a global ATM standard, other technologies such as Frame Relay and SMDS (Switched Multimegabit Data Services) are being offered as a replacement for the traditional X.25 leased line WAN links between remote sites. All of these services are becoming more cost effective, and provide a significant increase in network performance across the WAN.

High-Speed Networking

The development of networks based around intelligent hubs has placed an increased demand on the traffic loading between each of the hubs in a network. There may be anything from two to a few tens of hubs that need interconnecting. This interconnection must be seamless to the end users and devices, and ideally must not impact on the overall performance of the network. Distributed computing and *downsizing* has led to many servers instead of a single one, which need to be accessed by each hub in a centralised manner. This type of scenario calls for a high-speed backbone LAN, or super LAN, that is capable of carrying the traffic of many different networking types and protocols in a clean and consistent fashion. One of the key requisites for this kind of LAN is that it is a multivendor, interoperable LAN, as many new devices may wish to be attached at some stage in the future.

Enter FDDI, the Fiber Distributed Data Interface. FDDI was designed as a high-speed backend and backbone network, and due to its ANSI standards backing has become the *de facto* LAN backbone standard. Its extensive management and robustness has made it an ideal candidate for the job, and due to the distances it can cover, has also provided a vehicle for implementing private metropolitan area networks (MANs). It has been used extensively to date in installations that require a common backbone technology for Ethernet and Token Ring LANs, and adopted by leading systems vendors such as DEC and IBM, and many of the internetworking vendors.

The main applications for high-speed LANs are the following:

- Backbone – a LAN of LANs, internetworking many slower LANs, consisting overall of several hundreds of users.
- High-speed links to key networking components, such as a server or mainframe, usually connected directly to the backbone LAN.
- File transfer intensive workgroup applications, typically large image-based files (few megabytes upwards), e.g. medical imaging, CAD/CAM.
- Multimedia applications, where large amounts of time-critical data need to be transported in a short space of time.

High-Speed Backend Networks

FDDI was originally intended to be a high-speed backend network for interconnecting mainframe class computers and their peripherals. However, it was quickly established that a much higher aggregate bandwidth would be required to service the requirements of the newer generations of applications.

For this reason, a number of schemes have been, and are being, developed for this purpose. These include IBM's 200 Mbaud ESCON (Enterprise System Connection Architecture), and the ANSI Fibre Channel networks. The main feature of these networks is that they are high-speed serial channel oriented, with data rates ranging from the low 100s of megabits/sec up to the gigabit/sec level. As they are based on many concurrent channels, the total networking bandwidth is very scalable, and limited only by the centralised switching fabrics and point-to-point link data rates. Backend networks are specifically targeted at applications, such as mainframes, that require a very large aggregate bandwidth restricted to a few nodes, as opposed to the shared bandwidth of a local area networking technology. They are also typically restricted to a single protocol environment.

Network Access Mechanisms

The two main network access methods in use today are Ethernet/IEEE 802.3's collision-based (referred to as CSMA/CD – Carrier Sense Multiple Access with Collision Detection) and Token Ring/FDDI's token access based mechanisms. In addition, a new breed of LANs is emerging based on switching of packets or cells of information, migrating technology traditionally found in the WAN (e.g. X.25, frame relay and ATM) into a LAN environment. These form the basis of Switched Ethernet,

Token Ring and FDDI all of which retain the same technology and MAC layer protocols, but apply switching to the hub portion of the LAN.

Ethernet/IEEE 802.3 CSMA/CD Networks

The CSMA/CD access mechanism is based on a common or shared cable mechanism (10Base-2/5 Thin and Thick Ethernet) or a logical repeater structure (10Base-T – twisted-pair Ethernet). The IEEE 802.3 standard is practically identical (hence used interchangeably) to Ethernet, being based on the original Ethernet LAN developed by Xerox, DEC and Intel. Ethernet has a maximum data transfer rate of 10 Mbps.

In the case of the common wire approach (Thin/Cheapernet or Thick Ethernet), each station attaches to the same physical cable via a special transceiver that allows the Ethernet controller to listen to the wire to see if any other station is currently using the wire for transmission purposes (carrier sense), and if all is clear, commences transmission. If two stations start transmitting at the same time (Figure 1.9), having both individually determined it is safe to go, the transceiver detects that a collision has occurred (two stations attempt to drive the line, changing the electrical characteristics), and the controller jams the line for a while before backing off for a random period of time. This random time is specially defined by the IEEE standard (a process referred to as 'truncated binary exponential backoff'). The station then retries several times before reporting its failure to higher-layer processes.

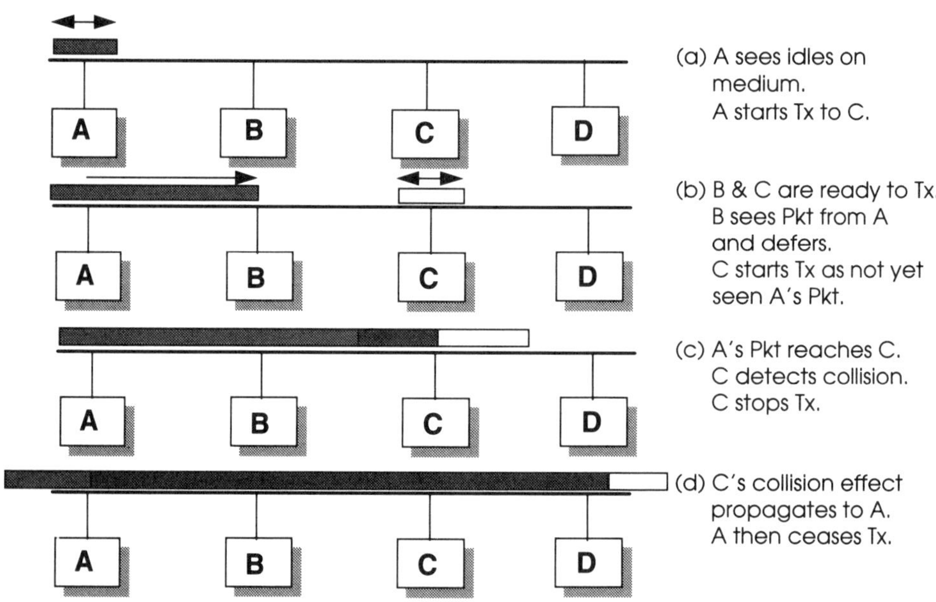

Figure 1.9 *CSMA/CD principle for Thin and Thick Ethernet/IEEE 802.3*

For the twisted-pair, star-wired approach of Twisted Pair Ethernet, or 10Base-T, the same principle is applied, but this time each station has a point-to-point link (i.e. no other stations share the same physical wire) with a central repeater unit. As illustrated in Figure 1.6, two signal paths now exist, a send and return, and the incoming data at the repeater end is repeated to all the other ports. If activity occurs on two or more ports at once (i.e. a *logical* collision as opposed to an *electrical* one), the repeater detects this, and jams the signal transmission on all links in order to instigate the backoff and retry algorithm in the transmitting end stations. Due to the fact that only a single point-to-point link ever exists in a 10Base-T network, the number of isolation transformers are less, and the electrical requirements less stringent.

Token Ring and FDDI Networks

Token Ring/IEEE 802.5 networks originate from IBM's work in LANs in the late 1970s and early 1980s. The Token Ring standards have since been extended from the original 4 Mbps specification to include 16 Mbps operation, the use of lower-cost cabling (UTP) and connectors, and also a mechanism for early token release to improve performance. FDDI and derivative networks such as TPDDI (Twisted Pair Data Distributed Interface), have their roots in Token Ring. Many of the concepts and features were derived directly from the original Token Ring standard, but suitably enhanced to provide adequate performance at the 100 Mbps data rate. Work soon started on FDDI after Token Ring networks appeared in the early 1980s, and a stable set of core standards was achieved by the early 1990s. Additional work has since led to the specification of other transmission cable types (such as twisted pair, low-cost fibre), allowing lower-cost implementations of FDDI than the original optical fibre only standard.

Both Token Ring and FDDI are based on the token access method described in simplistic terms in Figure 1.10. One other standards-based network called Token Bus (IEEE 802.4) also uses a token-passing technique, but is not discussed here. The basic principle (described for FDDI in more detail in Chapter 2) is relatively straightforward for all token access networks. A special control frame circulates around the network from station to station, referred to as the *token* frame. Only one token is allowed to exist on the network at any one time. Any station wishing to transmit a frame of any type cannot do so until the token has first been received by the station, and captured (i.e. not passed on). Obviously, the network must be configured into a ring topology for the token to circulate continuously around each of the stations. Each station is said to *repeat* the token if it simply passes it from its *input port* to its *output port*, connecting to different stations *upstream* and *downstream* respectively. Once the token has been captured, the station can then transmit a data or control frame onto the ring via its output port. This is repeated by each of the stations that are not the intended recipients, and copied in the local data buffer by the destination station(s) when the data frame arrives.

With a ring-based architecture comes the requirement that a logical closed loop data path must always be present for the network to function correctly, otherwise the token will 'fall off the end of the path'! It is easy to see how this is achieved for a network wired in a physical ring, where a cable goes from station to station, and is looped back to the first one at the end. For a star-wired topology, the logical ring must be created inside the wiring concentrator device itself (Figure 1.11). In Token Ring terminology, the ring extension from the wiring concentrator to the end station is termed a *lobe*.

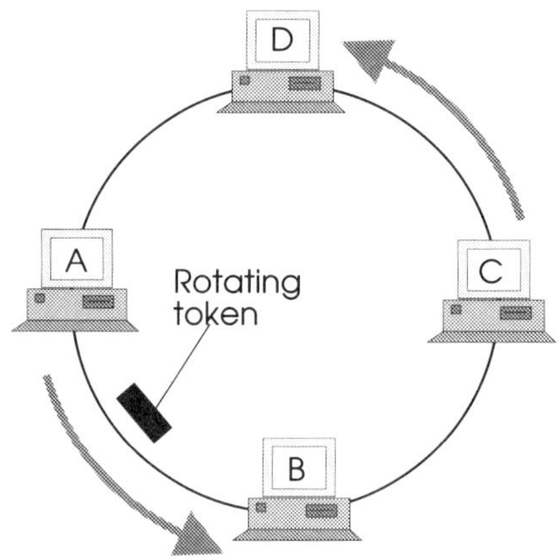

(a) Token circulates ring, being repeated by all stations until captured for transmission purposes

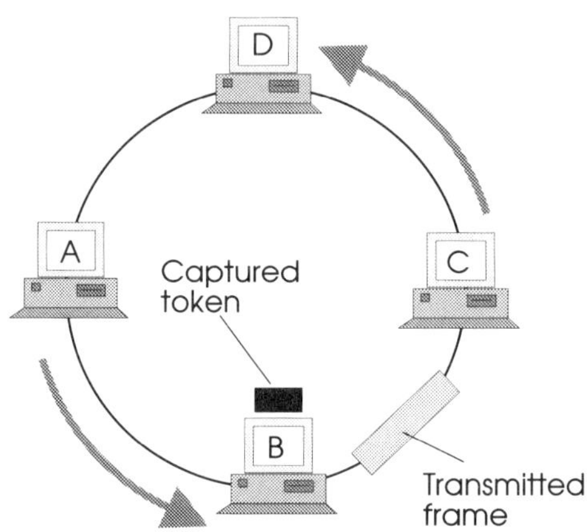

(b) Token captured by station B, and a data frame transmitted onto the ring. No other station may transmit frames whilst another is holding the token – only receive, or repeat.

Figure 1.10 *Token access principle*

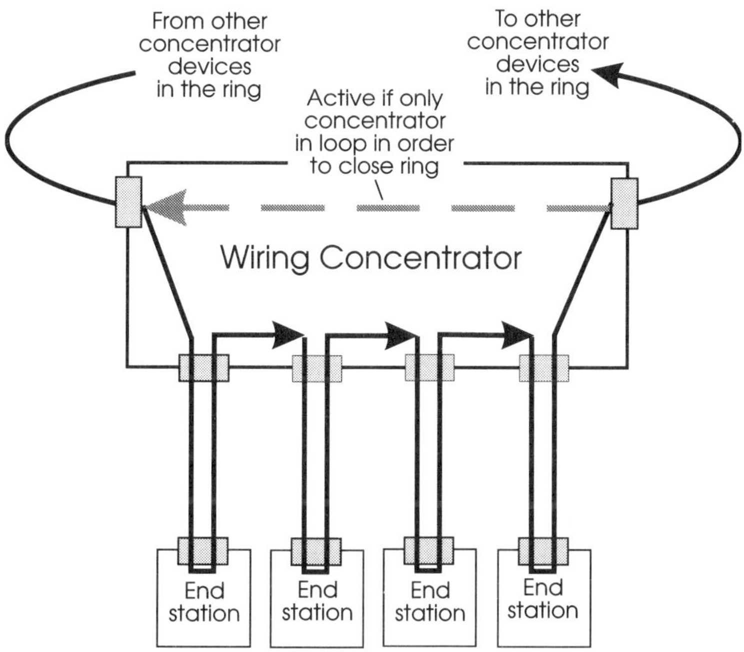

Figure 1.11 *Logical ring in a physical star cabling system*

One of the reasons why Ethernet/IEEE 802.3 networks have become so popular, even more so than Token Ring, is due to the low-cost of the hardware needed to implement the Ethernet protocols and transmission. As a rough guide, in hardware terms only, end adapter cards for Token Ring can be as much as 2.5 times that of Ethernet, due to the added complexity of the interface devices. FDDI adapters vary according to their performance and complexity (single or dual); typically, copper versions are roughly 8–10 times the cost of an Ethernet card – but of course provide far greater performance.

Packet- or Cell-Switched Networks

As there are significant growths in switched-based networks, it is worth spending a little time looking at the mechanisms used. FDDI finds its way into switched applications as we shall see in later chapters.

As pointed out earlier, there are basically two types of LAN switching, and these are not to be confused. The first type is *static* switching, where individual ports may be set up to connect to a specific LAN segment. In the world of Ethernet, the term *port mobility* or *group segmentation* is sometimes used to describe the process of steering a particular port into a specific *collision domain* (i.e. a specific Ethernet segment). Any number of users may also be in that domain. For example, the marketing department may be on one segment or domain, and the engineering on another in order to keep the two 'virtual networks' separate. The benefit is that the IS manager may remotely (via an SNMP management console for example) 'switch' a user to another LAN segment without having to pay a visit to the wiring closet.

The second type of switching, and the more relevant to us, is *dynamic* switching. This involves 'on the fly' switching of data packets or data cells by examining specific addressing or routing information in the data packet or cell's header field. Hence, for ANSI/IEEE 802 frame formats, this involves the destination and source address fields. For ATM networks, virtual channels and paths, identified by specific identifiers in the header of the cell, are used to switch or route data cells through a switch fabric. This dynamic switching technique is also at the heart of the backend networks discussed earlier.

The basic principle is as follows (Figure 1.12). Consider a central point to which a number of stations are connected (e.g. a wiring concentrator or hub). An incoming data packet/cell's header is examined at the port it arrives as soon as the address/routing information portion has been input. An internal lookup table is then examined to see which output port the packet/cell should be directed to. As soon as this is known, the data is forwarded as soon as possible to that port. In a similar fashion, data arriving on any of the other ports are processed simultaneously.

For an IEEE- or ANSI-based LAN such as Ethernet, this is basically a multi-port bridge with the ability to start forwarding packets before the entire packet is read in. This is referred to as a *cut through* bridging in some cases. This architecture assumes a prior knowledge of which port the end station is on. For IEEE/ANSI networks, the switching hub will initially learn this over time by monitoring transmissions, or using discovery techniques. In ATM networks, a *virtual connection* is first set up using a specific protocol, based on the ITU Q.931/93B/2931 standards. The destination port

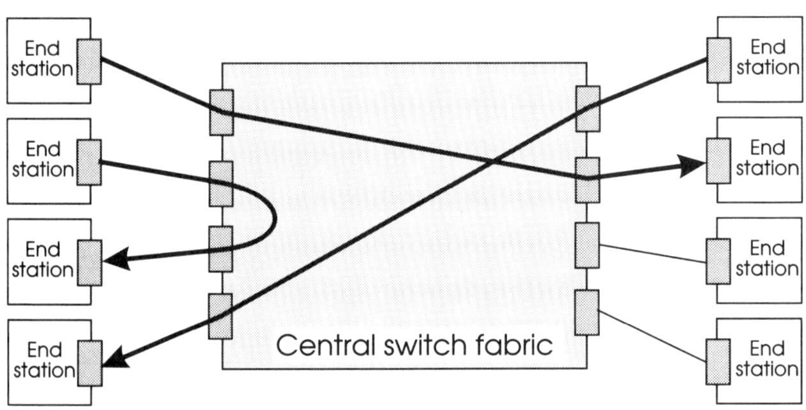

Figure 1.12 *Switching LANs*

may also be an entire network segment containing many end stations. It may also be of a different technology, hence a conversion must first take place to the other format. For this reason, switch architectures vary considerably. A switch also has to deal with the situation where there are multiple destinations, or the destination port is unavailable. Various schemes (such as internal buffering) exist to deal with this situation.

Dynamic switching also brings another feature not found in standard mainstream LAN implementations, namely full duplex operation, i.e. the ability to pass data in both directions at once. The advantages of such a feature have yet to be fully exploited, but can lead to performance advantages, for instance overlapped data packet acknowledgements, or in video conferencing applications, the video streams may be passed in both directions at once.

A Brief Look at Standards and Protocols

The two main standards bodies that are of interest in the field of local area networking, are the American National Standards Institute (ANSI) and Institute of Electrical and Electronic Engineers (IEEE). ANSI were responsible for the development of the FDDI standards, and the IEEE are responsible for some of the broader issues regarding local area networking standardisation, along with specific standards such as the IEEE 802 series (which includes Ethernet and Token Ring). An important organisation that takes many of the ANSI and IEEE standards to form the basis of a more international standard is ISO (International Organisation for Standardisation). For example, the ISO 8802.3 standard is equivalent to the IEEE 802.3, and the ISO 9314 is equivalent to the ANSI FDDI standard. In 1979 ISO introduced their famous OSI seven-layer model (OSI – Open Standards Interconnect), which is frequently used to describe the various structures and layers encountered in the makeup of LAN products and services.

OSI Seven Layer Model

The OSI model breaks the end to end communication process into seven key areas or *layers*, each of which are summarised in Table 1.1.

The main purpose of the model is to provide a framework in which to describe and understand the various components that make up a complete communications stack. The various layers defined allow the general problem of communication between two or many end points to be categorised into known functions. For example, the point at which the data is compressed or encrypted within a protocol stack would normally occur at what is referred to as the *presentation* layer, and not somewhere like the *data link* layer. Cabling and connector specifications can be found in the physical layer, and so on. In general, layers 1–3 provide a general framework for the underlying network services, and are where the LAN specific technology definitions can be placed, such as the Ethernet, Token Ring and FDDI standards. Layer 4 provides the basic interface

Table 1.1 *OSI seven layer model description*

	Layer	Purpose
7	Application	Interface to user/equipment, containing application specific protocols e.g. terminal emulation, file transfers, electronic mail, etc.
6	Presentation	Concerned with syntax and semantics of information e.g. standard encoding schemes, data compression, data encryption.
5	Session	Establishes sessions between different machines. Dialogue control. High level token management. Synchronisation during transfers.
4	Transport	Provides a network technology independent interface to the session layer, ensuring delivery in the correct sequence to the corresponding session layer at the other end. Sets up specific link or links if more than one route required to another computer. Establishment of network layer service type. Multiplexing of several message streams into a single channel. Host flow control.
3	Network	Routing of data packets from source to destination. Congestion control. Usage accounting for billing purposes. Handling of heterogeneous networks, packet size translation, etc. Usually more relevant in point-to-point networks, where end points can be reached by many routes.
2	Data link	Creation of data frames for error free transmission and creating and recognising appropriate frame boundaries presented to and received from the physical layer. Handles lost, damaged and duplicate frames. Flow regulation and error handling.
1	Physical	Transmission of stream of raw bits over a communications channel. Transmission line voltage levels, pulse widths, timing, connector characteristics.

between the network services and users of the network. Layers 5–7 are concerned with how the data is presented and interpreted by the end user or application.

What the model allows in the context of this book is the placement of the various functional elements of FDDI into the appropriate layer. Further, it clearly defines an interface mechanism that FDDI uses to describe its interaction with the layers above it. The mapping of the FDDI standards and related functions into the OSI 7 layer model is described in more detail in Chapter 2. The lower two layers – the data link layer and the physical layer – are the most important in the description of LAN technologies, all other layers being a function of the computer or equipment that the FDDI interface is contained within. In the case of the physical layer this means the physical dimensions of the optical fibre MIC connector, copper DB9 or RJ45 connector, the required shape of the optical or electrical waveform travelling across the cable, encoding of the data bits on the wire, and so on. The data link layer is concerned more with the reliable transfer of data. This means that the appropriate FDDI-specific portion of this layer must form the data presented to it by the higher layers into well-defined frames with the appropriate error-checking mechanism for reliable transmission to another FDDI station across the physical layer.

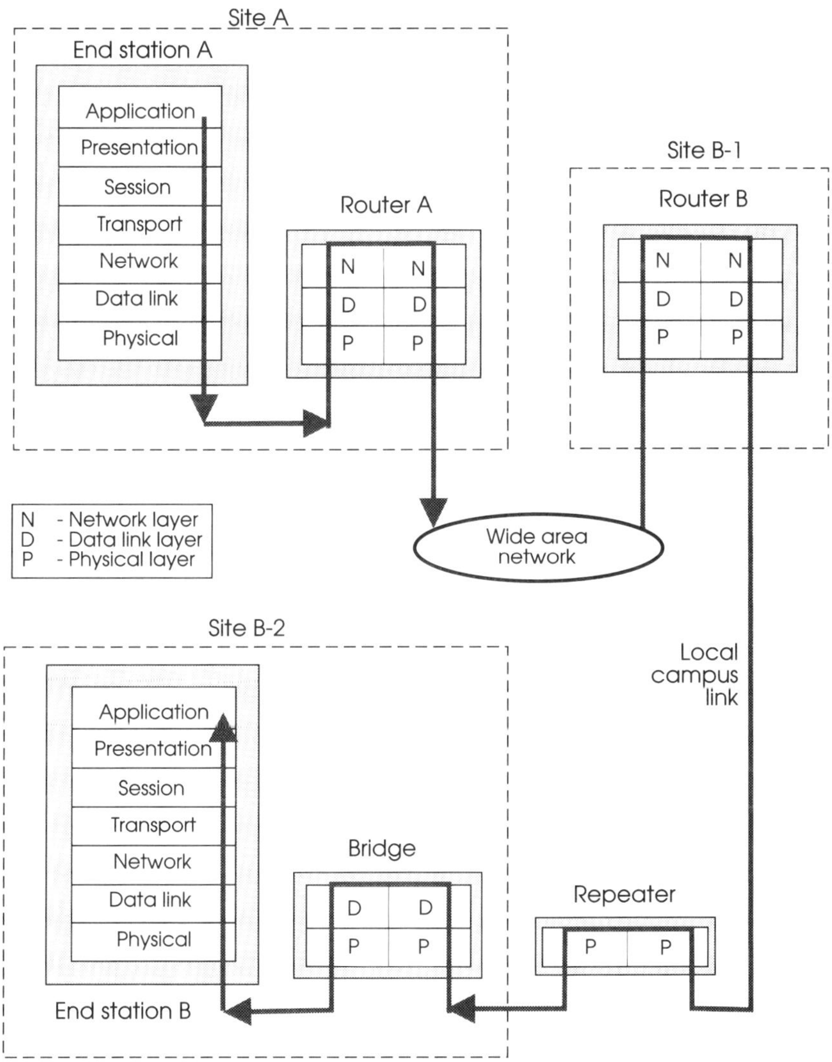

Figure 1.13 *Internetworking components and OSI model*

One benefit of the OSI model comes to light when classifying the functionality of various networking devices. For example, a repeater device only acts at the physical layer, a bridge acts at the data link layer, and a router acts at the network layer. Figure 1.13 illustrates how the OSI model applies to each of the internetworking functions. At the simplest level, a repeater device only acts at the physical layer as its job is to repeat signals without altering the information or higher-layer data structure in any way. This is consistent with the fact that repeaters are used to extend particular segments of a LAN connection as we shall see in later chapters.

Bridges act at the data link and physical layers. Instead of repeating the signal out of another port without examiniation or modification, it examines the MAC layer address of the incoming data stream and makes decisions as to where, or what, should happen to the data frame. As the bridge deals with information at the data link layer only, it cannot make decisions as to what type of information in the data field can or cannot be accepted, or passed on, as this is a network layer function. It can, however, convert from one compatible LAN type to another, e.g. from Ethernet to FDDI and vice versa. Any 'routing' decisions that are made in a bridge are purely from a MAC address viewpoint.

The router goes one step further than the bridge, and examines the actual content of the data frames and can make decisions as to where the packet should go based on additional routing information, protocol type, priority levels and so on. A further device, not shown, is a gateway that acts at layers above the networking layer. Examination of the seven layer descriptions in Table 1.1 reveals that gateways can effectively do many more things, such as translations between protocols and networking environments.

Figure 1.13 illustrates a typical path a communication between two end stations, *A* and *B*, may take, both connected to LANs. In this case, the application running on *A* sends data to a compatible application running on *B*. As *B* is at a different site, the packet has to pass through two routers connected across a WAN, one at each site. *B* is at a different building to where the router is, so the data packet passes through a repeater (as the distance of the communcations medium is exceeded) before being connected through a bridge onto the appropriate LAN segment.

IEEE 802 Standards

The IEEE 802 set of standards are the most relevant to the area of local area networking. They provide a common approach to the definition of all the IEEE standard LANs, and also for ANSI's FDDI, as well as addressing issues such as MAC layer bridging between 802 networks, management and architectural considerations.

The 802 standards map into the lower two layers of the OSI model as shown in Figure 1.14, but divide the data link layer into a further two sub-layers, the Logical Link Control (LLC) sub-layer, and the Medium Access Control (MAC) sub-layer. The LLC provides common interface to all the 802.x standards, such as 802.3 (Ethernet) and 802.5 (Token Ring), and is used by the FDDI standards as the interface to its

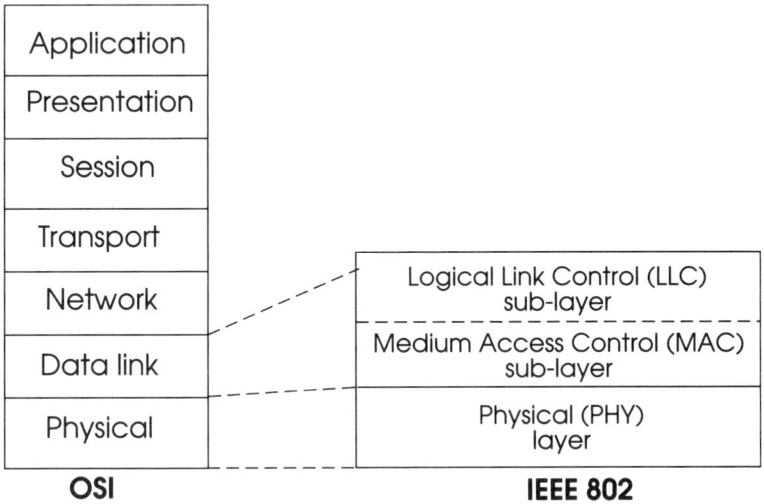

Figure 1.14 *ISO's OSI seven-layer model and IEEE 802 layers*

higher layers. LLC also provides a common, network-independent interface to higher-level protocols such as the OSI network layer X.25 protocols, or the IETF IP protocol.

Some of the main IEEE standards are illustrated in Figure 1.15 (there are additional ones not listed here under development). From the figure we see that standards such as 802.3 (Ethernet) and 802.5 (Token Ring) are defined at the MAC and PHY levels, and the higher-layer protocol that the MAC interfaces to is the LLC sub-layer. A specific LLC protocol is defined, that allows the transport of data to another peer LLC layer in a destination station. In Chapter 4 we will see how FDDI, for example, carries LLC frames between two end stations.

LLC (IEEE 802.2) defines three types of data transfer services as follows:

- *Type 1* Unacknowledged, connectionless services, which are datagram like, supporting point-to-point, multi-point and broadcast. This is the basic type used by Ethernet and FDDI.
- *Type 2* Connection-oriented services. Logical connections, providing a sequence control mechanism, error control and acknowledgements (similar to HDLC).This is the basic type used by Token Ring.
- *Type 3* Acknowledged connectionless services. Datagram service, with point-to-point acknowledgements, but no prior logical connections setup.

Four different classes of stations are also defined. Class I supports type 1, class II, types 1 and 2, class III, types 1 and 3, and class 4 all types (1, 2 and 3). The LLC layer provides an important link between the various IEEE LAN technologies, especially in transparent bridging applications, where the LLC is the common interface. LLC is also

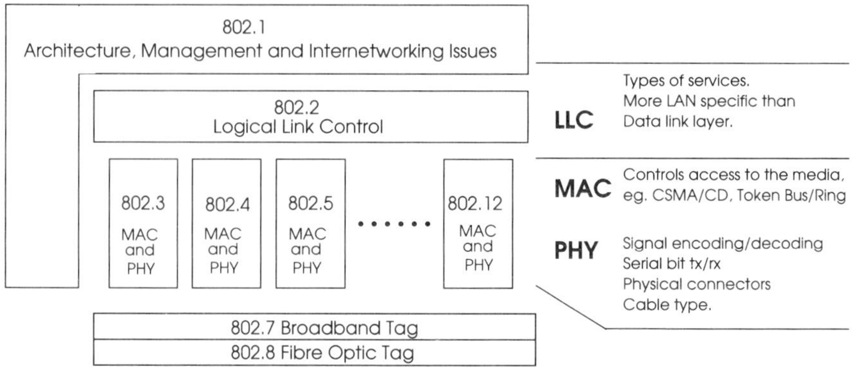

Figure 1.15 *IEEE 802 family of standards*
(Source: IEEE 802 standards documents)

utilsed as the data link layer for other protocols, such as Novell's IPX, Internet's TCP/IP and so on.

Internet Protocols

A whole suite of protocols and associated applications exist, based on the TCP/IP (Transmission Control Protocol/Internet Protocol). These were developed by the US Government's Defense Advanced Research Projects Agency (DARPA). TCP/IP is in many ways in direct competition to the OSI standards, as it is based on a different set of rules and standards. Due to its wide installed base, and wealth of adopters and specifications, it has maintained a strong hold in both the WAN and LAN community. The widely used Internet is based on these protocols. The total layers up to application level of the protocol suite (referred to as the DoD protocol suite) are illustrated in Figure 1.16, next to the equivalent OSI layers.

It is under this umbrella that other standards for management, such as Simple Network Management Network Protocol (SNMP) and their derivatives, exist. All the standards under the suite are referenced by Request For Comment (RFC) documents, each of which define a particular portion of the protocol, or extensions. RFCs are freely available to those who have access to the Internet either by email or via File Transfer Protocol (FTP) facilities. Developments are always underway to add newer facilities to the Internet suite of specifications. For example, the Multicast Backbone (MBONE), an Internet facility for carrying real-time voice and data, addresses multicast (one-to-many) transmissions for carrying live video and audio data streams over the Internet via special MBONE bridges and translaters. New protocols such as the RTP, or Real-time Transport Protocol (and associated RTP Control Protocol, RTCP), implement schemes for carrying such data types.

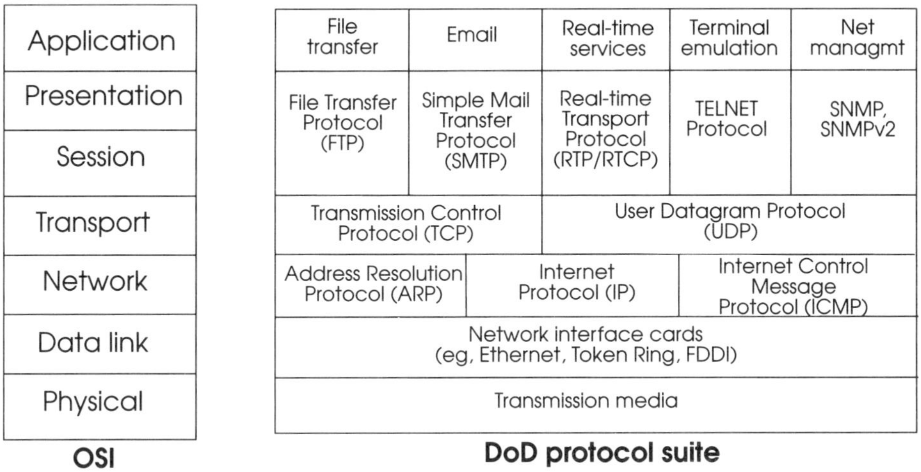

Figure 1.16 *US Department of Defense protocol stack*

Many corporate backbones are based on TCP/IP, with management implemented using SNMP compatible protocols. TCP/IP serves the needs of most corporations, large and small, and hence has maintained a healthy existence, being incorporated into many network operating systems as a standard. Readers are referred to Black (1992) for additional information on TCP/IP and its related protocols.

Summary

LANs are constantly changing and evolving. When they first appeared, the cabling was often unstructured, but subsequently developed into a structured, star-wired system in accordance with international wiring standards. This change was necessary due to the increasing management problem brought about the large increase in LAN usage. Processing power and new applications are also driving the changes in LANs. Specific applications include client/server computer systems and networked multimedia. Intelligent hubs have formed the heart of most LANs, enabling better management and fault monitoring. Finally, networks are defined by a set of open international standards that ensure multiple vendors' products can work reliably together, and ensure a consistent approach to LAN implementation and development.

CHAPTER 2

FDDI Networks

Fiber Data Distributed Interface (the American spelling is used for fibre) local area networks have been in existence since around 1987. FDDI was first discussed in ANSI as early as 1982 within a discussion group set up to look at higher-speed networking issues. Like so many LAN standards, it has evolved from its original inception to include many features and applications that were never anticipated. In its very early days, its main purpose was to provide a high-speed backend network, e.g linking peripherals to a mainframe or high-speed server. Since then, it has evolved to become the main backbone LAN technology. LANs such as FDDI, Token Ring and Ethernet provide the open systems networking capabilities of any computer system, enabling multiple independent vendors to build products with a high degree of interoperability.

The set of ANSI/ISO documents that make up the FDDI family of standards have, like the technology itself, evolved over time. The first standards to be completed were the important MAC and PHY layer standards, followed by various lower-cost cabling options (PMD extensions) and a fuller Station Management standard. In fact, it took six years from the time of the first approved document from ANSI (1987) to the stabilising of the Station Management (SMT) document (the final one of the core set of standards). In the early days, much of the work was carried over from the IEEE 802.5 work for Token Ring, hence FDDI can be classed as a kind of *super-set* of Token Ring, with some significant differences.

The ANSI/ISO FDDI Standards

The ANSI/ISO set of standards that make up the core of the FDDI standard are divided up as follows:

- Physical Medium Dependent (PMD: ANSI/ISO 9314-3)
- Physical Layer Protocol (PHY: ANSI/ISO 9314-1)

- Media Access Control (MAC: ANSI/ISO 9314-2)
- Station Management (SMT: ANSI standard rev 7.3, not ISO at time of writing)

The above standards make up the core of the current FDDI standards. The realtionship between these specifications and the OSI seven-layer model is shown in Figure 2.1.

As it was envisaged that there would be a number of different cable types, FDDI divides the OSI physical layer into the PMD and PHY sub-layers. Hence, we have one PHY standard that remains unchanged in FDDI, i.e. is common to all PMD sub-layers, and covers both fibre and copper physical medium options. Within the PMD sub-layer, the shape of the electrical or optical pulse is defined, and also the types of connectors that are used to connect to the FDDI equipment, i.e. is specific to the medium being used. Several PMD specifications exist that cover multimode fibre, single-mode fibre, low-cost fibre and twisted pair copper.

The PHY standard describes the formation of a NRZI (non-return to zero, invert on ones) serial bit stream, from a 4B5B encoded 5 bit *symbol* derived from 4 bit 'chunks' of the raw low-level transmission data. As we shall see in Chapter 3, this serial symbol stream allows special control symbols to be transmitted across the physical media that cannot be confused with data information. Clock recovery (synchronisation with the incoming data stream) is covered in this portion of the standard. Specific 'line states' of special significance are also defined at this level, such as QLS (quiet line state: no signal/light level being received from far transmitter), or ILS (idle line state:

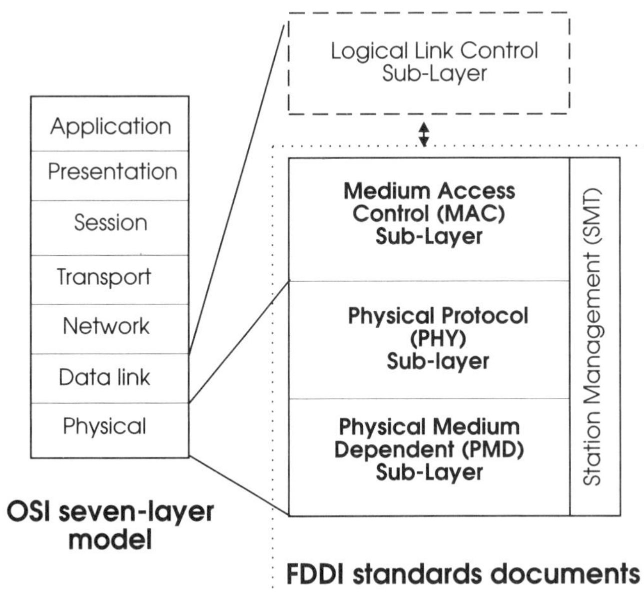

Figure 2.1 *Core FDDI standards*

connection alive, but not being used).

The MAC standard specifies how the various frame types are built up, including normal data frames, the token frame, management specific frames and so on. Maximum and minimum lengths for the frames are defined, along with methods of error checking, the timed token access protocol, destination/source addressing and the various operational modes and conditions. Initialisation of the network operating parameters (via the claim and beaconing mechanisms) is also described.

SMT is the largest of the FDDI standards, and has come through many iterations to its final ANSI version of 7.3. SMT describes all areas associated with the management of the MAC, PHY and PMD entities within an FDDI station. In particular, the FDDI management information base (MIB) is defined, along with management-specific frame types and protocols. The complete initialisation, error monitoring and fault recovery processes are defined. These allow an FDDI station to perform with a high degree of reliability within a network.

Additional standards (some still at draft level) exist in the ANSI FDDI standards group, and include the following:

- Physical Layer Protocol – 2 (PHY-2)
- Media Access Control – 2 (MAC-2)
- Hybrid Ring Control (HRC)
- Station Management – 2 (SMT-2)

These are largely related to a development of FDDI, referred to as FDDI-II, designed to carry isochronous data services. Isochronous is defined as 'occurring at the same time' or 'occupying equal time', and in this context means the capability to carry data within well-defined, guaranteed time slots. This caters for time-sensitive data such as voice or video that need regular transmissions to maintain the continuity of the communication. For example, if voice data being sent over the network was held up along the way, the other end would not receive a constant stream, and the voice would be garbled.

Much of the work on these new standards is still being carried out to solidify these specifications, and are thus not included in this book. The HRC details a method for carrying both packet- and circuit-switched data (125 μs cycles) on the same FDDI ring, with the option of operating in a backwards compatibility mode with existing FDDI installations. However, when FDDI-II circuit-switched services are required, the network is no longer FDDI compatible. It is the opinion of this author, and many others in the networking industry, that FDDI-II will not become a widely implemented standard, especially in light of the fact that emerging networks such as ATM address circuit-switched or isochronous services far better. The MAC-2 and PHY-2 are basically maintenance releases of the existing MAC and PHY standards, which also include the newer FDDI-II specifics. The original FDDI MAC operation is referred to as the *basic* mode of operation in these standards, and the FDDI-II mode as the *hybrid* mode.

ANSI also looked at follow-on architectures for FDDI (referred to as FFOL – FDDI

Follow On LAN), taking the data rates of FDDI up to the gigabit region, with integral data-, packet-, and circuit-switched features. Most of this work has lost its momentum, and most industry resources appear to be concentrated on developing ATM as the basis of future networking standards.

Other Related Standards

As the usage of FDDI-based backbone networks has grown, the requirement to connect other networks in a standard fashion has also become important. As bridging IEEE 802 networks over FDDI was a key application area, the IEEE 802 standards committee produced a supplement to their 802.1D standard on MAC layer bridging that includes aspects of transparent bridging between FDDI networks, and also between 802 and FDDI. The standard is referred to as the 802.1I supplement, and is now included as part of the IEEE 802.1D publication.

In the Internet world of TCP/IP, RFC (Request For Comment) 1188 outlines the transport of IP traffic over FDDI networks using the 802.2 LCC type 1 frames.

Main Features of FDDI Networks

FDDI provides data transfer rates of 100 Mbps, compared with standard Ethernet and Token Ring rates of 10 and 4/16 Mbps respectively (Table 2.1). Its primary cabling

Table 2.1 *Top-level comparison of FDDI, Token Ring and Ethernet*

LAN	Maximum serial data rate (Mbps)	Maximum frame bytes	Access control	Cabling options
FDDI ISO 9314	100	4500	Token Ring	Single-mode fibre Multimode fibre UTP/STP twisted pair
Token Ring IEEE 802.5	4 or 16	17800/65635*	Token Ring	Fibre Coax STP/UTP twisted pair
Ethernet IEEE 802.3	10	1518	CSMA/CD (bus/star)	Fibre Coax UTP/STP twisted pair

* Depedent on the total number of stations, timing constraints, cable lengths and so on.

scheme uses multimode optical fibre allowing it to achieve inter-node distances of up to 2 km. Other cabling options introduced since the original multimode fibre specification include single-mode fibre (40 km), copper twisted pair (unshielded and shielded to 100 m) and low-cost multimode fibre (500 m). In addition, mapping of FDDI onto the wide area networking standard SONET is also defined for the PMD layer, providing a mechanism for directly extending an FDDI ring over the WAN.

As outlined in Chapter 1, FDDI is based on a token-passing scheme, where network devices are connected in a logical ring, with a special circulating token frame and associated protocol, governing access to the shared 100 Mbps bandwidth. All the definitions and default values specified in the FDDI standards provide for a total of 1000 physical connections (which translates to a maximum of 500 stations), and a total overall fibre path length of 200 km, though these figures are not absolute. The actual number of stations or the distances covered may actually be greater or lesser, depending on the delay characteristics of the overall installation, and for this reason, a careful analysis is sometimes necessary to ensure that all the necessary parameters are met. If for any reason, the minimum and maximum parameters are not adhered to, this could result in the incorrect operation of the token access protocol.

Topologies

The physical network topology of FDDI can be either a ring, a star or a mesh. In a dual-ring configuration, no active concentrator devices are required, though the physical cabling may still be that of a star by the use of a passive optical patch panel. The cabling for the physical ring is based on a *dual-ring*, also referred to as the *trunk ring* consisting of two fibre ring paths. One ring, the main data-carrying ring, is referred to as the *primary*, the second as the *secondary*. The secondary acts as a backup in case of a primary ring failure, and can also be used as another ring for data transmissions if necessary, as it is totally separate from the primary. This provides up to 200 Mbps total bandwidth over the dual-ring.

If for any reason a failure occurs between two nodes, then data is *wrapped* back around onto the secondary ring at the stations either side of the break as we shall see later. For this reason, the dual-rings are referred to as *counter-rotating*, as they effectively have opposite data flow directions. A second optional reconfiguration policy (i.e. not always supported by all stations) is available referred to as *global hold*, which allows the data traffic to be completely switched to the other available fault-free ring if necessary. If the secondary was being used for data transmissions as well as the primary, then under fault conditions, the two rings collapse into a common primary ring, the total data rate dropping back to 100 Mbps.

In general, the topology of an FDDI network can be described as a *ring of trees* (Figure 2.2), as a number of tree networks can be spawned off the main trunk ring. In a tree-only network, the end station types are single attachment only, interconnected by concentrator units, which themselves are only single attachment or *null* attachment units (Figure 2.3). As explained in Chapter 1, there are many advantages to using a tree

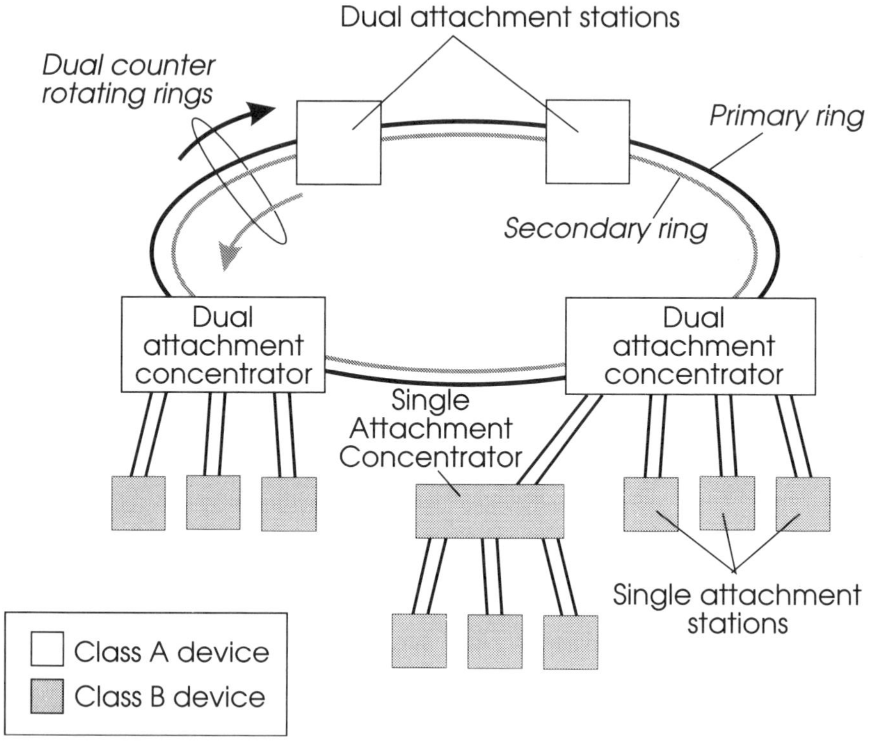

Figure 2.2 *General FDDI network structure – the 'ring of trees'*

(referred to as a star) vs. a ring wiring topology. FDDI also allows a mesh topology to be implemented (Figure 2.4), based on redundant links in certain critical arms of the tree.

FDDI Device Types

Stations either connect directly to the dual-ring (i.e. dual attached), and have an interface to both the primary and the secondary, or they connect into a concentrator device with a single link (i.e. single attached). These two types of network devices are broadly categorised into class A and class B devices respectively. Both stations and concentrators adopt the *dual attachment* or *single attachment* prefix depending on their capabilities. Hence a dual-ring station is referred to as a *dual attachment station* (DAS), a station connected via a single link to a concentrator a *single attachment station* (SAS) and so on.

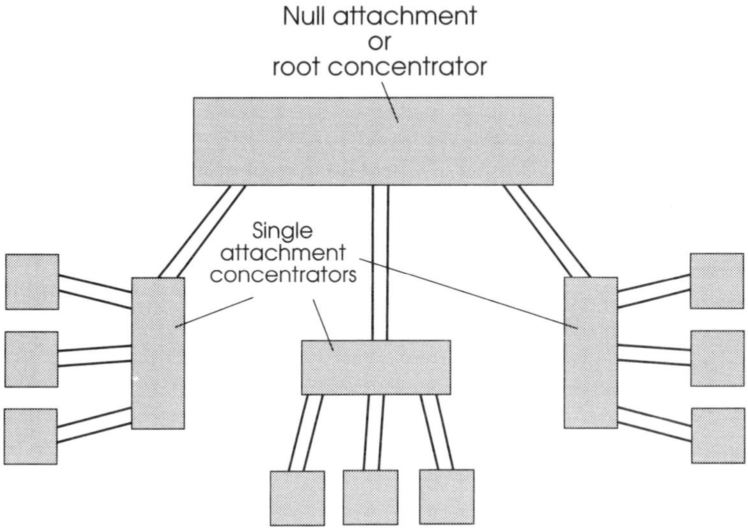

Figure 2.3 *FDDI tree topology*

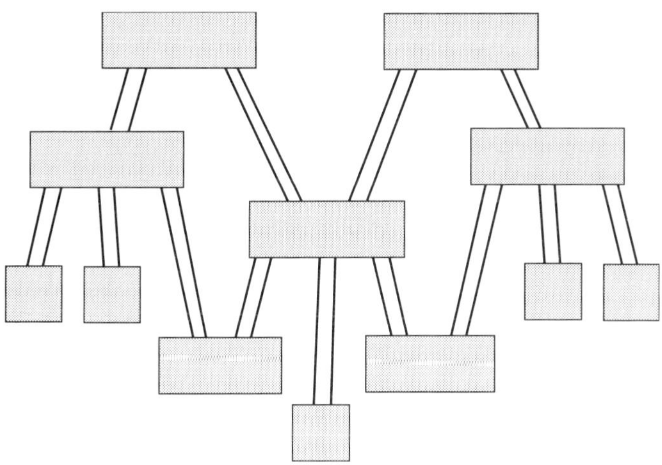

Figure 2.4 *FDDI mesh topology*

Dual Attachment Stations (DASs)

Dual attachment stations have two ports (Figure 2.5), referred to as simply port A and port B. Each port can carry data in two directions (i.e. bidirectional), though in normal operation, only a single direction is used. In a dual-ring, the A port connects to a B port of an *upstream* neighbouring station, and the B port to a *downstream*

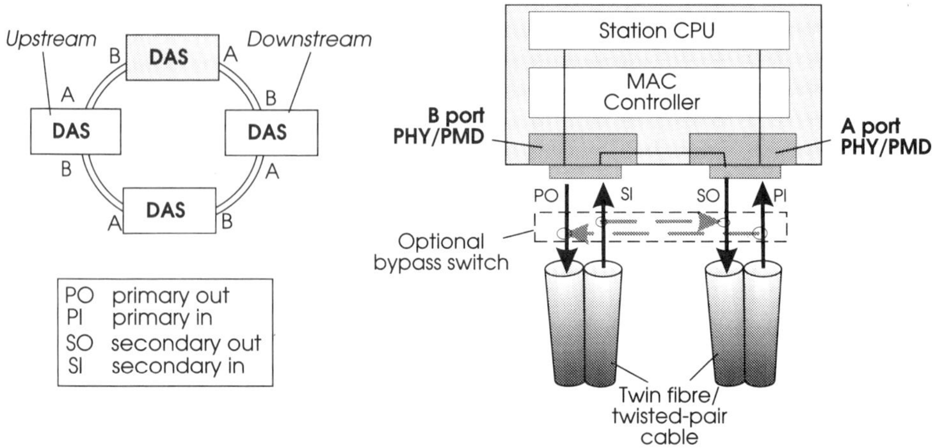

Figure 2.5 *Dual attachment station (DAS)*

neighbouring station. Both cables carry the primary and secondary rings, with the A port receiving serial data on the *primary in (PI)*, the B port transmitting serial data on the *primary out (PO)*. When the secondary ring is active, A transmits on the *secondary out (SO)* and B receives on the *secondary in (SI)*.

The DAS nodes operate in a number of modes, depending on the current configuration status of the ring. *THRU* is the normal mode for the station, receiving a serial data stream on the A.PI port, and repeating/transmitting a serial data stream on the B.PO port. In either the *WRAP_A* or *WRAP_B* modes, as the names suggest, serial data is routed in and out of the same port, with the MAC usually still in the path of the data stream. Hence, whenever an A port has wrapped on a station in the dual-ring, data is rerouted back onto the secondary ring in the opposite direction. In the case of a B wrapping, data is rerouted back off the secondary ring, onto the primary. By wrapping an A port at one end of the DAS chain, and wrapping a B port at the other end, a complete ring is maintained. This process is examined in more detail later.

Also shown in Figure 2.5 is an optional bypass switch that allows a station to fail or cease network operation without causing a break in the ring. The number of such devices in a ring is limited, due to the signal losses they can incur.

Dual Attachment Concentrators (DACs)

The primary function of a concentrator is to extend the primary, and sometimes secondary, rings down into the tree. They do this via M, or *master* ports, which provide a single attachment capability for a single station, which may itself be a concentrator. The primary ring is extended to each of the M ports, via an internal path,

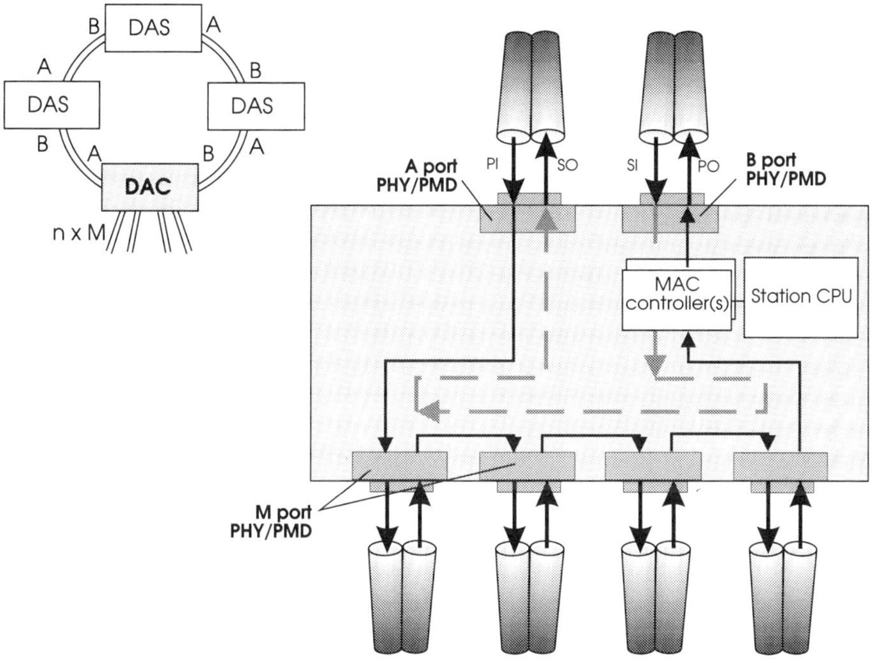

Figure 2.6 *Dual attachment concentrator*

referred to as the *primary path*. Internal routing elements at each M port 'junction' enable any of the M ports to be internally bypassed, thus isolating a failed or inactive arm of the tree from the primary path, and hence from token/data flow (Figure 2.6).

DACs come in varying levels of complexity, the simplest only extending the primary ring, and the more complex extending *both* rings down into the tree. If both rings can be extended, then the concentrator will have a *secondary path* as well as a primary. The routing elements may then connect the M ports on an individual basis onto either of the paths. It is also common to find a third, or *local path*, which is utilized for creating a local FDDI ring down a particular arm of the tree. This has the benefit of testing any new connections before bringing them on-line to the main primary ring. Due to the larger number of path combinations within a DAC than within a simple DAS, specific types of *WRAP* conditions are defined, namely *concatenated* wraps (*C_WRAP_A* or *C_WRAP_B*) and a condition called *WRAP_AB*. The first ensures that the secondary path inside the concentrator gets included in the primary data path following an A or B port wrap condition. The other simply extends the secondary ring down onto the secondary path, and thus down on into the tree if an M port is connected to this path. Each of these conditions will be examined more thoroughly in Chapter 4.

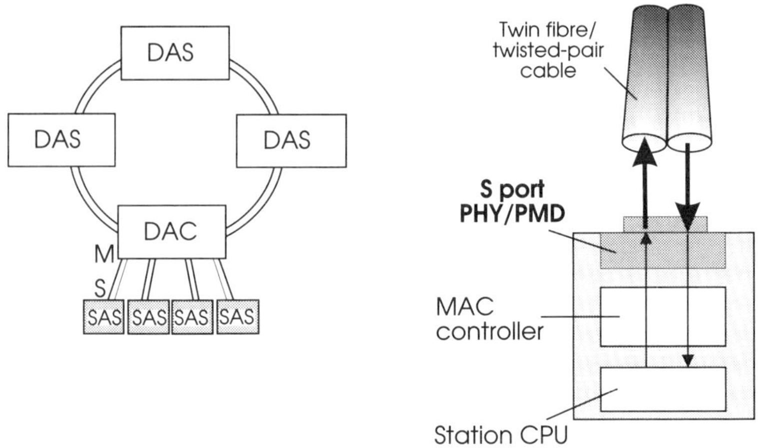

Figure 2.7 *Single attachment station (SAS)*

Single Attachment Stations (SASs)

The simplest form of station is the *single attachment station*, or SAS for short (Figure 2.7). A single fibre or copper pair allows the serial transmission and reception of data out of and into the station via a *slave*, or *S* port. S port characteristics are defined by the PHY and PMD portions of the FDDI standards. This type of connection is the most widely used interface to end workstations or personal computers. S ports almost always connect to concentrator M ports, though it is possible for it to connect to other port types as we shall see later. Data is recovered off the incoming data link, and is automatically repeated out onto the output link, and also received by the CPU if the data stream is identified as for this station. The exact rules governing data receive and transmit processes are described in Chapter 4.

Single/Null Attachment Concentrators (SACs/NACs)

The two other concentrator types that exist are very similar internally to the DAC architecture, except that the A and B ports are replaced with a single S port (SAC) and a NAC has no root connection at all (Figure 2.8). These type of concentrators are used only in the tree portion of the network. Any additional paths to the primary in this case provide a means of creating totally separate FDDI rings down different arms of the tree. This results in a segmented FDDI network, that will need some form of filtering bridge device to allow them to intercommunicate. A concentrator tree topology that can handle segmentation of FDDI rings can be a very flexible architecture, in that it allows specific groups of users or bridged LANs to be confined to a particular segment.

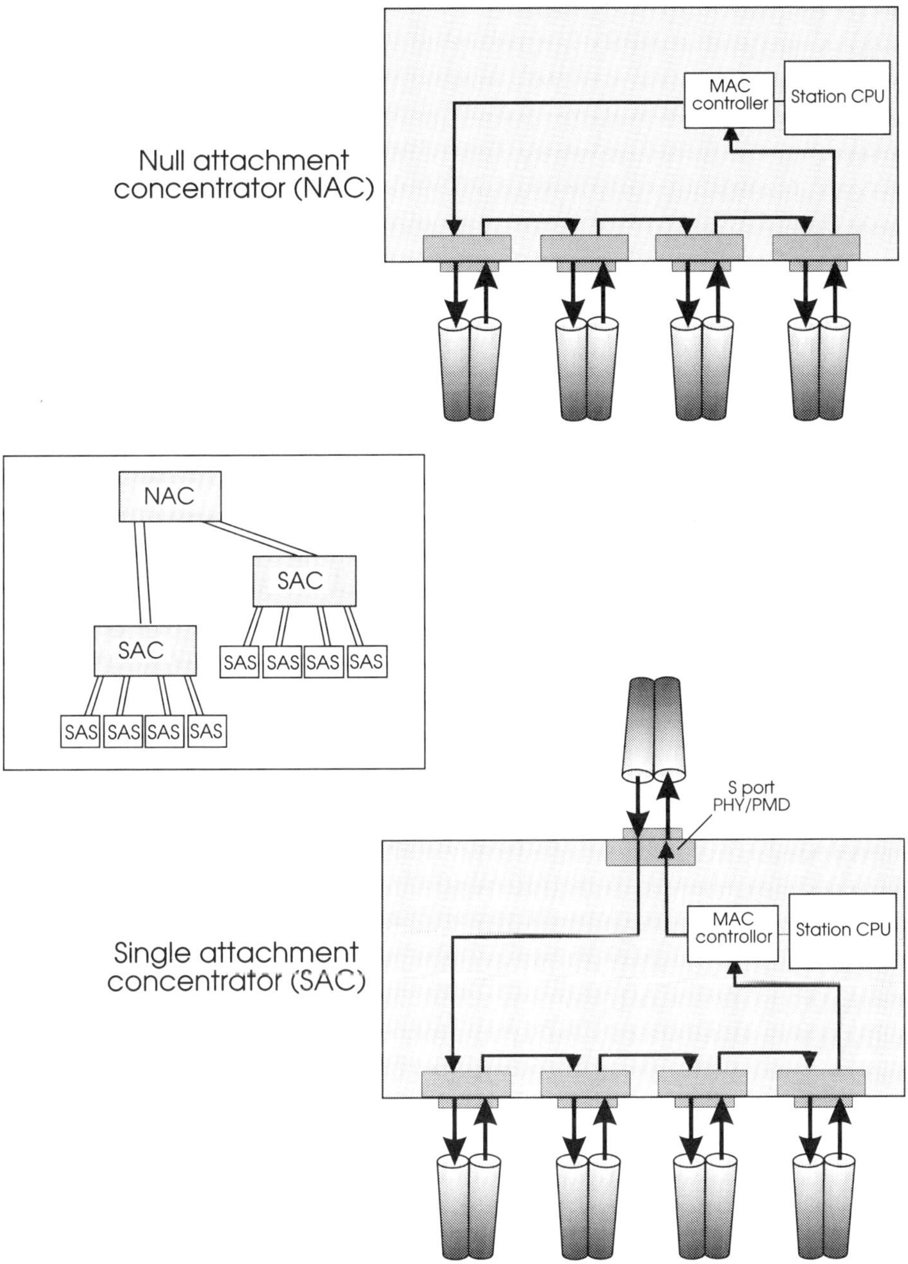

Figure 2.8 *Single/Null Attachment Concentrators*

Dual-Homing Station (DHS)

In a mesh topology, both the A and B ports of a dual attachment device (e.g. a DAS or DAC) connect to concentrator M ports, with the A port only being active when the B port is inactive. This leads to the mesh topology of Figure 2.4, and is a common configuration of FDDI networks where dual-ring cabling or equipment is a non-preferred solution. The operation of DHS is described in more detail in Chapter 6.

FDDI Bridge/Routers

The most common devices found in FDDI networks include bridges, routers and gateways, linking either FDDI segments together, or other network types into a common FDDI backbone. Similar hybrid device types include *brouters, ridges*, etc. These function as any other DAS or SAS, with a few minor operational differences.

A number of modifications to the FDDI MAC stripping protocol (Chapters 4 and 8) are necessary to ensure the smooth operation of bridges on the ring. For example, in a translational bridge, the source station that originated the frame is not actually resident on the FDDI ring, and in most cases neither is the destination station. As many of FDDI's rules for maintaining the ring are based on the fact that source and destination stations are resident on the ring itself, this means that its standard rules cannot apply. Hence, a slightly modified form of operation at the MAC layer is introduced in FDDI bridges to ensure that no orphaned frames are left circulating the ring, and also that multiple copies of the same frame are not sent onto the destination LANs. As the format of the IEEE address differs across some LAN types (bit ordering in the byte), this also has to be taken into consideration. Many of the aspects related to bridging are discussed in more detail in Chapter 8.

In most cases, a high-performance processor and/or dedicated hardware bridging engine is used to achieve a fast transfer rate from one network type to the other. Early types of FDDI bridges implemented an *encapsulation* technique for bridging non-FDDI LANs. This takes the native non-FDDI frame, and simply encapsulates it within an FDDI frame's information field (Figure 2.9). This gets over the problems associated with translating the IEEE addresses, and the FDDI MAC layer frame stripping processes, as the ring sees valid FDDI station addresses. As the destination LAN is of the same type, the FDDI bridge at the destination LAN point simply 'unwraps' the original frame, and retransmits it in its original form onto the destination LAN. Like all bridge architectures, this assumes a learning process whereby all the non-FDDI LAN end station addresses are determined from prior transmissions from the appropriate stations and LANs.

Encapsulation is based on vendor proprietary techniques as opposed to standards, thus limiting the bridge types to a single vendor. Furthermore performance is not always that good as encapsulation adds an overhead to the size of the original data packet. A more recent type of bridge is *translational*, and conforms to the IEEE 802.1D/I MAC bridging standards. In particular, these cover the aspects of translating

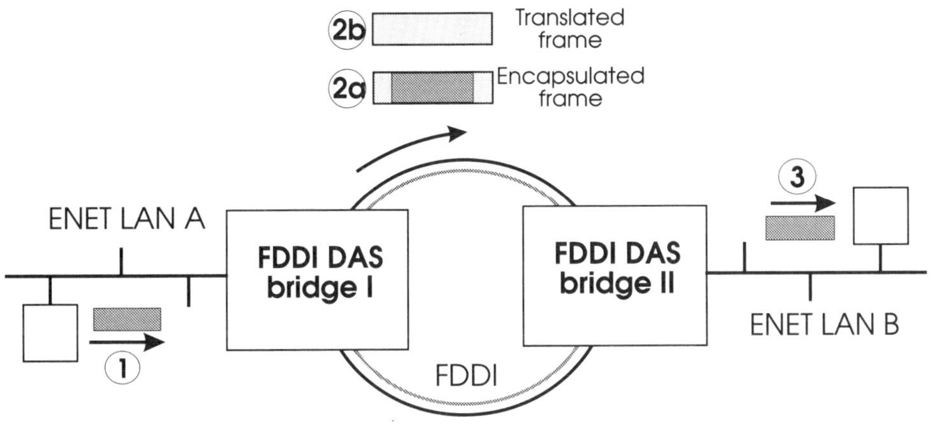

Figure 2.9 *Ethernet to FDDI to Ethernet bridging*

802 frames (including FDDI in 802.1I) between the LANs, and define the *spanning tree* algorithm and protocol for determining the best route through a number of LAN bridges where they exist. Finally, *source routing* bridges are common when bridging Token Ring LANs, though standards are not yet readily available that define a non-vendor specific approach, again tying the end user in to a particular bridge vendor.

Figure 2.9 illustrates the processes that take place within FDDI for both encapsulating and translating bridges. Note that though standalone bridges are shown, it is more common for the bridge function to be integrated into an intelligent hub in a wiring closet as discussed in Chapter 1.

Number of MACs

FDDI allows any station to have more than one MAC layer controller. The main purpose of a MAC in any station is to enable it to extract data from, and transmit data to the network ring. It is also feasible that a station or node may have no MAC at all. For example, in a low-cost workgroup environment, a simple NAC or SAC may only use physical layer devices, acting basically as a repeater node. The MAC and associated CPU may only be required if specific management features are needed to remotely manage the concentrator, e.g. by an SNMP management process. In many cases, it is desirable to have a MAC in a concentrator, if only for low-level management and simple diagnostics purposes. It is a general rule that a MAC should always be present in class A stations, i.e. those on the dual-ring.

At the other end of the scale, a station may have two or even three MAC devices in order to receive and transmit data onto the network. For example, a station acting as a LAN analyser may wish to monitor both the traffic on the primary and the secondary rings independently. This way it can determine the reconfiguration state of the network, and also possibly utilize the secondary ring to pass diagnostics information along to another dual MAC station on the ring. A concentrator can quite often employ three MAC devices, one attached to the primary ring, another to the secondary and a third acting as a *roving* MAC that can be configured internally to perform extended diagnostics on specific M port(s) that have been taken 'off line'. The benefit of this is that the whole ring is not disrupted while testing of particular links and network segments take place, as the third MAC, along with station(s) connected off the M port(s), form their own independent network ring.

Finally, an FDDI bridge/router device may include multiple MACs in order to provide FDDI ring segmentation, or connection to multiple types of other networks (i.e. a multiport bridge/router).

Token Access Protocol Overview

As described earlier, FDDI uses a token access protocol. A token is a special frame type that each station recognises by a control field present in the header of every frame. When a station sees a token, it does one of two things. It either passes it along to the next station downstream, i.e. *repeats* the token, or it effectively takes it off the ring, by *capturing* it. The rules that govern whether a station is allowed to capture the token at all, and how long it may hold onto it, are detailed in Chapter 4. Once a station has captured the token, it may then transmit data *frames* onto the ring. As soon as it has completed transmitting all queued data frames (or been timed out by a token timer), the station releases the token, immediately after the current or last transmitted frame. For those familiar with Token Ring, this is similar to the more recent addition to the 802.5 standard, and is known as *early token release*. The token continues circulating until captured by another station on the ring.

The path followed by a token through a ring and tree topology is illustrated in Figure 2.10. In this case, the secondary ring, shown as the inside path in the ring section, carries no data traffic and is a redundant ring. The concentrator device extends the primary ring down to the single attached nodes as we saw earlier.

As described in Chapter 4, when a station transmits information, it may address it to a specific station, to a number of stations within a particular address group, or even broadcast it to all stations on the network. Each station recognises when a particular data frame is addressed to itself, and as the data passes itself on the ring, makes a copy of it in its internal buffer (i.e. receives it). A special indicator is set at the end of the data frame to indicate to the originating station that the recipient had copied the data successfully (or not as the case may be). The data frame continues around the network until it arrives back at the originator, who then *strips* it off the ring.

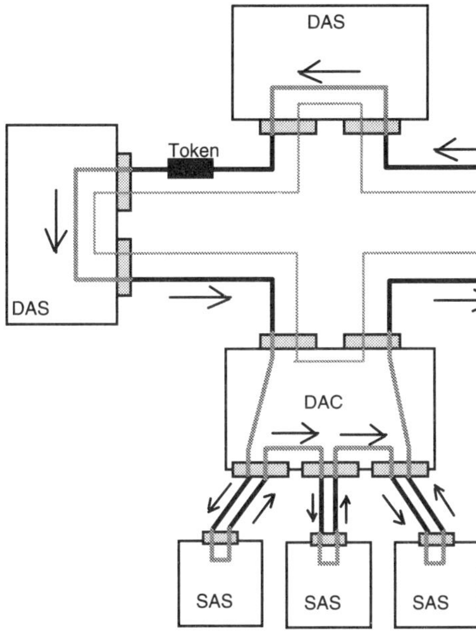

Figure 2.10 *Token and frame data path for normal configuration*

Ring Reconfiguration

As we have seen, FDDI has a number of built-in features that allow for faults in the network to be automatically detected, and the token and data to be rerouted via a backup path. This is a very important feature of FDDI, especially as optical fibre cables can travel great distances, typically underground on long hauls, and are not always immediately accessible for repair.

Figure 2.11 illustrates two possible places where the network cables, when broken, cause the network to halt operation temporarily, and then reconfigure around the broken links. In the dual-ring, whenever a break occurs, as we saw earlier, the stations either side of the break detect the fault condition. Their ports upstream and downstream of the failure points enter a *wrap* configuration so as to reroute the data back around onto and off the secondary ring. The two stations DAS 1 and DAS 3 may still communicate, but now the data has to travel back along the secondary ring from DAS 3, to DAS 1, through the DAC and DAS 2. Note that the SAS stations are not affected by the break on dual-ring (other than having to re-initialise), as the concentrator just routes its secondary in to its secondary out. The second break point illustrated between the DAC and a SAS results in the latter being cut off completely, and the data being rerouted by the concentrator with the effect of bypassing the faulty link.

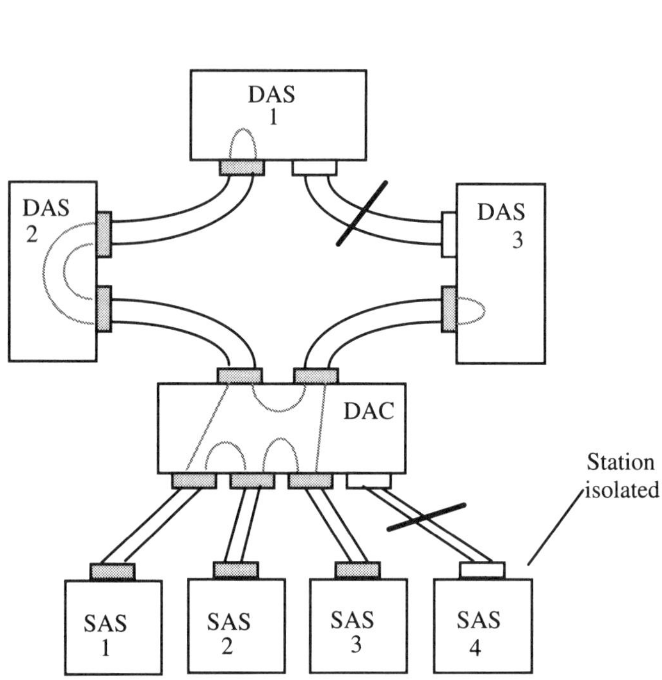

Figure 2.11 *Network reconfiguration on main ring and concentrator trees*

If for any reason any of the links are restored, then the ring automatically reconfigures back to normal. Of course, it is not always cable breaks that result in a station or stations becoming isolated from the network. Powering a station down results in the same processes (except that the ring wraps in a different place).

Figure 2.12 illustrates the alternative fault redundant scheme that may be employed using dual-homing stations and a mesh topology. In a standard tree topology using only concentrators and single attachment devices, when a cable fault develops, the single attached device is isolated. Dual-homing replaces critical arms of the tree with a dual-homed device that attaches to two M ports, either on the same or different concentrators. FDDI's built-in intialisation processes ensure that only one port of the dual-homed station is ever active, the B port taking precedence over the A port. Hence, a non-fault condition leads to the B port being the active connection as shown in Figure 2.12(a), the A port only becoming active when a fault develops with the B port connection as shown in Figure 2.12(b). Hence, a dual-homed connection allows a second path to be utilized if the primary connection fails, preventing the isolation problem associated with the single attachment devices.

Chapter 6 takes a closer look at the fault recovery mechanisms for both of the dual-ring and dual-homing cases.

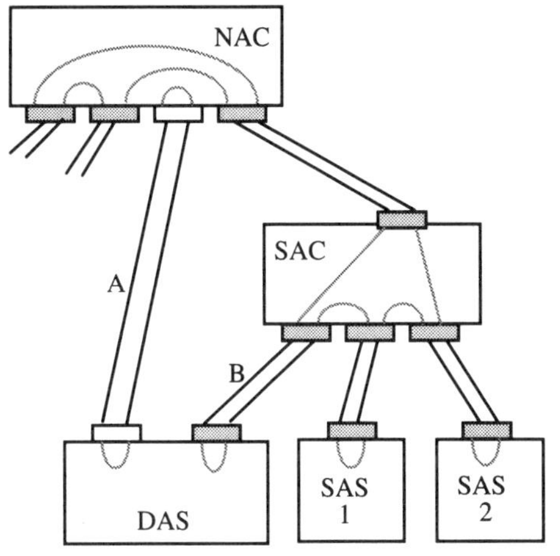

(a) Default Configuration with link A not configured into network

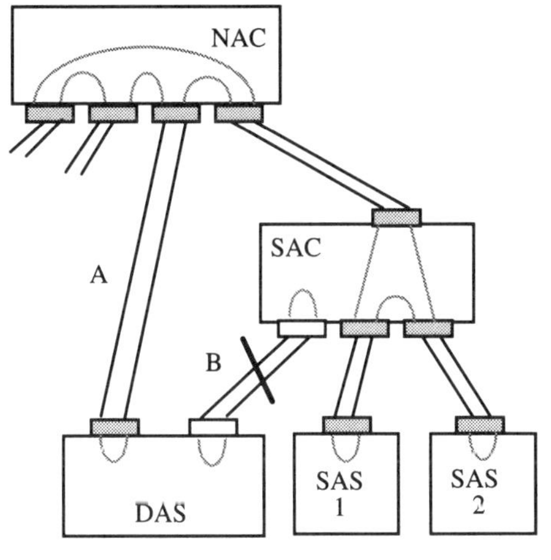

(b) Link B has broken, network reconfigures and uses A

Figure 2.12 *Network reconfiguration with dual-homing stations*

Placement of Stations

A number of important aspects that affect where stations are placed in terms of the dual-ring or tree comc out of the reconfiguration process. For example, it is no good putting stations on the dual-ring that are constantly powering up or down, as this leads to unnecessary reconfigurations of the ring. This is even more important where the dual-ring is the main backbone.

It is for this reason that only critical stations are put onto the dual-ring, e.g. mainframes, which are rarely powered off, or bridge/routing devices. In many installations, the only devices attached to the dual-ring at all are DACs, with all end equipment and peripherals connected as either dual-homed devices (Figure 2.4) or simply as single attached. Hence, it is quite common for critical dual-ring stations to have optical bypass switches to maintain the dual-ring topology when powered down.

A general rule in FDDI networks is to keep the number of dual-ring nodes low, and limited to critical components as described. A good reason for this is because it is very easy to create a fragmented ring due to more than one link failure. Two or more such breaks on the dual-ring can result in an important device being isolated from all the others. For instance, the stations shown in Figure 2.13 have been divided up into two separate rings by only two cable link failures, one consisting of stations A–C, and the other of D–H. If H was the server, then the top segment would be completely isolated from it.

This is one of the reasons that mesh topologies have become important, and are often used in FDDI installations, as they allow greater control over the way a network can fail. *Dual-homing stations* (DHSs) have a redundant or backup link (the A port connection) tied into a totally different concentrator on the dual-ring, for example. This means that if the concentrator attached via the B port of the DHS fails, or powers down, the DHS still has access via its A port connection (Figure 2.12). One of the benefits of the way FDDI handles this situation over similar schemes (Token Ring for example), is that the reconfiguration is totally automatic and transparent to the end user, occurring at the physical layer only. The main difference seen by the individual FDDI stations is a (probable) change in its nearest neighbour's address.

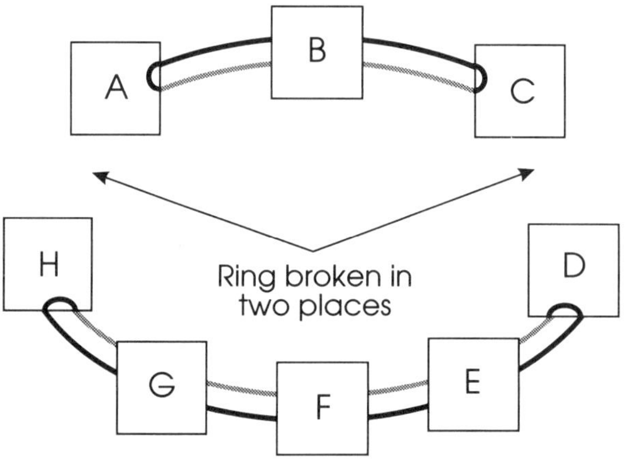

Figure 2.13 *Dual-ring fragmentation*

Less critical stations (with respect to the overall operation of the network health) are best placed on the network as a SAS, as this both keeps the cost of the interface hardware down, and has a lesser impact on the network when switched on or off.

Other FDDI-Compatible Networks

In Chapter 3, we look at the various cabling options that may be used in FDDI installations, as defined by the FDDI standards, along with the appropriate transmission schemes. The cable options include multimode and single-mode optical fibre, unshielded twisted pair (UTP) and shielded twisted pair (STP). Wide area extension is possible through the SONET PMD specification.

Whilst standards efforts were on-going to produce alternative, lower-cost cable options to the standard multimode fibre the standard specified, other non-standard copper transmission schemes were proposed. Some of these were successfully implemented in many installations, whereas others were more for technology demonstration purposes. The most popoular are summarized as follows.

Green Book STP Specification

The *Green Book* standard was an interim shielded twisted pair copper variant of FDDI, based on IBM Type 1/2 150 Ohm STP cable. Supporting companies included Advanced Micro Devices Inc., Chipcom Corporation, Digital Equipment Corp., Motorola Inc. and Synoptics Communications Inc. A document was produced (coloured green, hence the name of the standard!), and was really a demonstrator for FDDI technology over copper wiring. It was designed to match the physical connector and cabling structure of Token Ring (i.e. STP and shielded 9-pin D-type connector). The main benefit of this scheme was to show how existing VLSI components could be utilized, with only a few additional electrical components to support copper wiring. As copper wiring and installations at the time were significantly cheaper than fibre, this attracted a lot of attention. The specification targeted the single attachment connections only, and was not really suitable for dual-ring implementations which were assumed to remain as fibre.

Shielded Distributed Data Interface – SDDI

IBM introduced an early copper-based implementation for FDDI, referred to as Shielded Distributed Data Interface (SDDI). SDDI is in many ways similar to the Green Book standard above, and supported by a great deal more companies (eleven) including many Token Ring players. The same team of companies as above, along with IBM, were responsible for the main development of SDDI, with many more companies joining in at a later stage. The Green Book and SDDI proposals are not interoperable, even though they are very similar. In all cases, the companies expressed that TPDDI products would be chosen for support in the long term. SDDI has an added advantage over TPDDI in that it can also be used in the dual-ring. IBM still support both standards today, but TPDDI in the long term will be the preferred solution for copper wiring. Cable type supported by SDDI includes the IBM Cabling System Type 1, 2, 6 or 9.

100Base-T Specification

This was perhaps the most confusing of all the pre-ANSI standard copper offerings, as it uses a terminology normally reserved for IEEE 802.3 (Ethernet) installations. It is not to be confused with other efforts in the IEEE 802.3 area, aimed at providing a 100 Mbps Ethernet solution. It was a proposal put forward by National Semiconductor and Cabletron as a possible solution for FDDI over UTP and STP (the others only tackled STP). ANSI's TP-PMD working group eventually abandoned 100Base-T in favour of a different scheme based around Crescendo's CDDI.

Copper Distributed Data Interface – CDDI

Copper Distributed Data Interface (CDDI) is the name given by Crescendo Communications Inc. to its copper FDDI offering. CDDI is the popular name given to copper variants of FDDI, before the more recent term TPDDI (or FDDI/TP) was applied. It used a modified encoding scheme (i.e. non 4B5B) which allowed 100 Mbps data rates to be achieved over 100 m of datagrade level 5 UTP cable as well as STP. This scheme, as it forms the basis of the ANSI TP-PMD standard, is described in more detail in Chapter 3.

TPDDI, TP-PMD and FDDI/TP Specifications

Twisted Pair Data Distributed Interface (TPDDI) is the loose term applied throughout this book to refer to the ANSI standard TP-PMD version of FDDI. TPDDI was derived from Crescendo's CDDI product technology, and modified to achieve an interoperable standard. The final version of TP-PMD was set in early 1994, once all the related electromagnetic interference (EMI) and electrical signal interfacing issues were resolved. TP-PMD will form the basis of all standards-based copper FDDI networks, since it has been defined by ANSI and is standards-based. All other copper versions are likely to be superseded by this standard. The standard uses an multilevel encoding scheme called MLT-3, with a scrambling function, to achieve the necessary operating requirements over datagrade level 5 UTP and Type 1 and 2 STP cabling (Chapter 3).

FDDI Products

Products supporting FDDI networks fall into the following broad categories :

- Adapter cards – workstation to mainframe
- Intelligent hub modules
- Dedicated workgroup concentrators
- Bridge/routers
- LAN analysers

As FDDI technology has matured quite considerably, there are a wide range of interoperable products available to end users, thanks to interoperability test houses such as the Advanced Networking Test Centre (ANTC), Sunnyvale, California. To show their interoperability status, many products have been tested at such centres, and will carry a form of identification indicating that they have been adequately tested against a number of different vendor's products (and passed of course). Most FDDI vendors will be (or have at some time been) members of the ANTC.

Chapter 8 looks at FDDI product implementations, and specific product types from the main networking companies.

Vendor-Specific Versions of FDDI

Most vendors refer to their products as being FDDI compatible, and use this term globally to apply to both their fibre- and copper-based products. However, SDDI is one example where this differs for IBM and their early copper offerings. Madge Networks announced their earlier FDDI adapter card products under the banner Fast Token Ring (FTR), as they are traditionally a Token Ring vendor and felt it appropriate to aim their products at the Token Ring upgrade market. All Madge's FTR products are 100 per cent FDDI compatible.

Summary

FDDI standards are made up of four core documents: Physical Medium Dependent (PMD), Physical Layer Protocol (PHY), Medium Access Control (MAC) and Station Management (SMT). Multiple PMD documents exist to cover additional cabling types, and others are available that cover extensions to the basic FDDI standards (FDDI II).

FDDI networks operate at 100 Mbps data transfer rates, and are implemented as a dual-ring-of-trees topology, with point-to-point connections between stations forming a ring for data to travel around. Two different station classes are defined: Class A – those that connect to the dual-ring (dual attachment stations), and Class B – those that connect to a concentrator tree. The main station types encountered are dual attachment stations (DAS), single attachment stations (SAS), and dual, single and null attachment concentrators (DAC, SAC and NAC).

Network access is controlled using a token access mechanism, where stations need to capture the token before being allowed to transmit data onto the network. An automatic fault recovery mechanism gives FDDI networks a high degree of fault tolerance.

CHAPTER 3

FDDI Connections

In this chapter, various aspects of data bit transmissions are examined in order to understand how FDDI stations handle the transport of the physical data '1's and '0's and control information between neighbouring stations. The methods FDDI uses to encode and transmit data bytes are examined without any particular attention being paid to the actual content of the data stream itself. FDDI frames, and their control, are examined in Chapter 4. Cabling options are also summarised, along with the rules that govern which neighbouring station ports may be connected together.

Though it is often convenient to describe the operations involved in terms of the FDDI standards, frequent references are made to how they are implemented in real hardware terms to better aid understanding.

FDDI Point-to-Point Connections

FDDI stations communicate with their neighbour(s) via dedicated point-to-point cables. Each station port has a transmit and receive cable associated with every connection, allowing a station to communicate bidirectionally with its immediate neighbour. Figure 3.1 illustrates the transmit and receive portions that we will be describing in the following sections between two stations. To simplify explanations, the corresponding receiver and transmitter sections in the opposite directions are omitted.

As can be seen from Figure 3.1, the raw data bytes are not simply serialised and transmitted one bit at a time over the cable to the neighbouring station. The data bytes are firstly encoded, and the output data bit stream adapted to add clocking information that allows the receiver to recover the data correctly. The encoded data is passed to the Physical Medium Dependent (PMD) part of the interface as a serial data bit stream. In just about all implementations that exist today using standard custom VLSI devices, the serial data is interfaced to the physical medium interface using pseudo-ECL (or

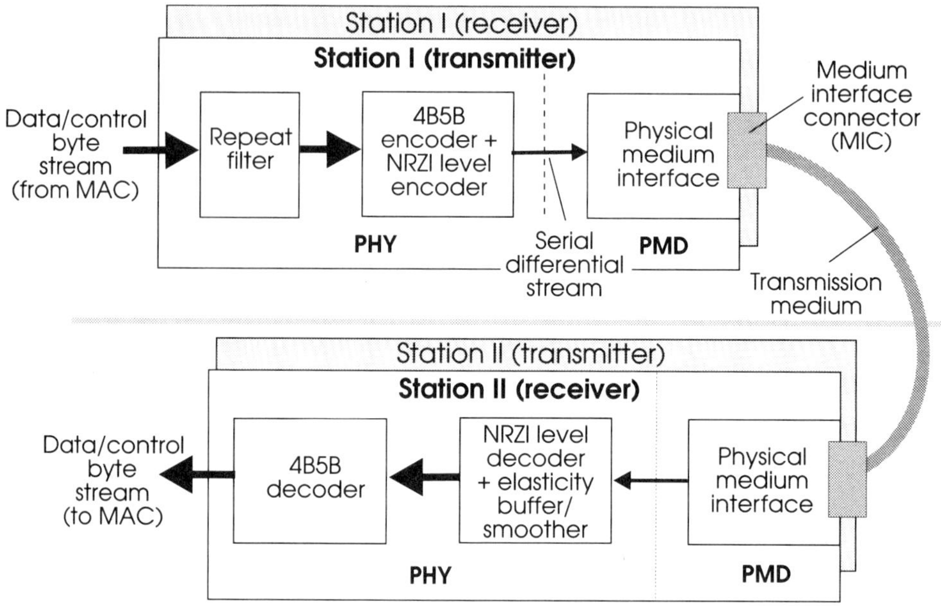

Figure 3.1 *Transmit and receive processes during byte transfers*

PECL) differential signals. The physical medium interface may be an optical data converter or copper cabling interface module.

FDDI stations transmit information across the cable using a special encoded serial data stream that allows the raw data '1's and '0's to be received correctly by the receiving end. Though the data is transmitted serially, one bit at a time, the data passing across the cable is often described in terms of data *symbols*, consisting a group of five serial data bits. The presence of a stream of similar types of symbols can lead to a particular *line state*, indicating the current status of the transmission across the cable. Each of these particular aspects of the serial transmission process is described in more detail in the following sections.

Encoding Schemes

Encoding, among other things, provides a mechanism for transmitting raw data '1's and '0's across the cable, at the same time providing synchronisation or clocking information. Without the clocking information, the receiving station would not know when or where the transmitted data bit was positioned within the incoming signal. The advantage of combining the clocking and data information allows a single point-to-point connection to be used, without the need for a dedicated clock line.

LANs such as Ethernet and Token Ring use a scheme called *Manchester encoding* to encode both the data and clocking information. This encoding method uses either a positive or negative going transition in the transmitted signal to represent a data '0' or '1' respectively. For example, in Ethernet, the desired data rate is 10 Mbps, requiring a clock running at twice this rate, i.e. 20 MHz, as shown in Figure 3.2. The *efficiency* of this scheme when described as the ratio of the bit rate to the clock rate, is 50 per cent. At the receiving end, a clock-recovery *phase-locked loop* (PLL) is used to keep the local clock it is using to recover the raw data bits, synchronised with the clocking information within the received signal. The benefit of manchester encoding is that a transition occurs every bit time, whether a '0' or a '1', enabling a simple clock recovery scheme to be used. For this reason, the scheme can be though of as 'clock-rich'.

Manchester encoding, though perfectly adequate for Ethernet and Token Ring, is not optimal for FDDI's 100 Mbps data rate. If we were to apply it to FDDI, then a 200 MHz reference clock would be needed, making implementation difficult and costly. Also, 200 MHz would be outside the 2 km limit between stations needed for multi-mode optical fibre. Thus a different encoding scheme is required that allows a lower clocking rate to be used, while maintaining the 100 Mbps data transfer rate.

FDDI's 4B5B NRZI Encoding Scheme

FDDI uses an encoding scheme that allows it to transmit at 100 Mbps, utilising only a 125 MHz timing reference. The approach is twofold. Firstly, a NRZI (non-return to zero, invert on ones) encoding is used to represent the bits on the transmission line. Secondly, the data bytes and any control information prior to serialisation for transmission across the line, is encoded into symbol pairs in a 4B5B format which we will define later. Figure 3.3 illustrates the process.

The NRZI coding represents a '1' with a transition (either positive or negative) from the current line level, and a '0' as no transition. Thus, a high number of '1's leads to high clocking, and a high number of '0's leads to low clocking on the line. Converting

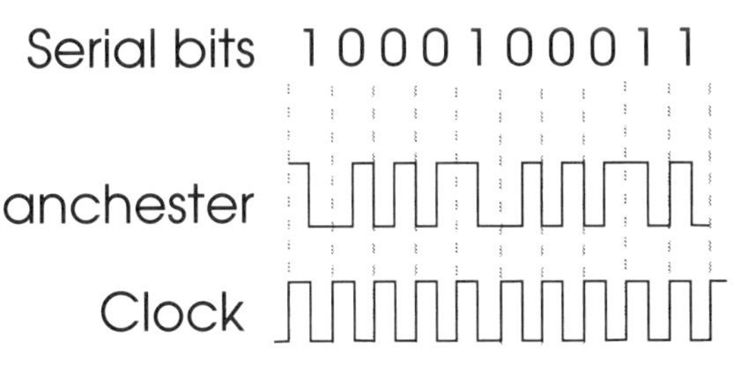

Figure 3.2 *Ethernet and Token Ring Manchester encoding*

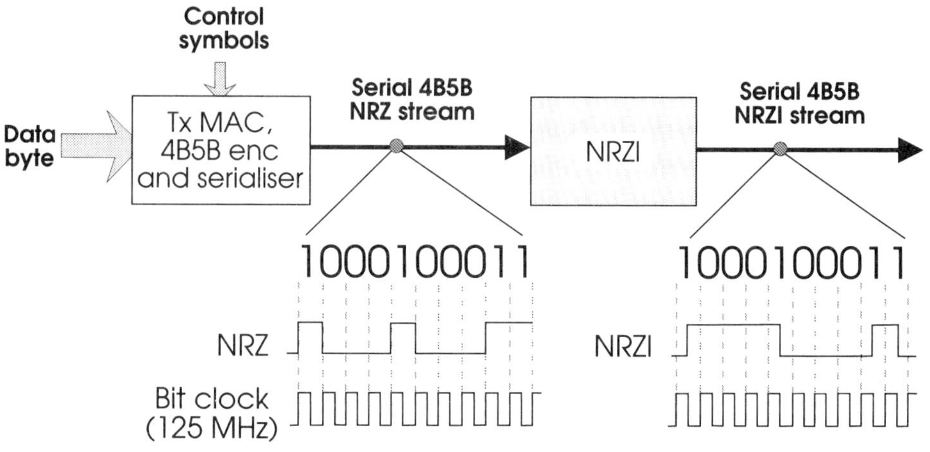

Figure 3.3 *FDDI Encoding using 4B5B and NRZI*

to NRZI, however, is not good enough on its own. For example, if there were only ever '0's transmitted, then the receiver's PLL would not see any transitions, and would have a tendency to drift out of synchronisation with the incoming signal. As this situation can never be prevented (i.e. the user's data can never be guaranteed to have no long strings of '0'), an additional encoding prior to NRZI is needed. This encoding must ensure that long strings of '0's do not occur, regardless of the original data stream. The coding used is called 4B5B, and solves the synchronisation problem by changing every nibble (4 bits) into a 5 bit code before serialisation and NRZI encoding. The nature of the 4 to 5 bit encoding (hence the name 4B5B) is such that no more than three consecutive '0's ever occur in the bit stream before a '1' causes a transition to occur. As there are effectively 10 bits for every original 8 bits transmitted, the resultant clock rate is 125 MHz (80 per cent efficient), enabling the station-to-station distance objectives of FDDI to be met.

Table 3.1 lists the 5 bit codes that are generated from the original 4 bits of data and are referred to as *symbols*. The 5 bits allows 32 possible bit combinations, 16 of which are used to represent the 4 data bits, and the remaining ones used as special control symbols, e.g. to indicate the start of a frame. For example, the 11000 and 10001 codes, referred to as J and K respectively, are reserved for the start of an FDDI frame. Symbols are generally paired together, hence the number of symbols in an entire frame will always be an even number up to maximum of 9000 as we shall see later.

Figure 3.4 illustrates the data flow process involved in the transmission and reception of control symbols and data bytes. The top part of the diagram shows how the transmit MAC forms the unencoded information or control bytes into pairs, in this case, JK (control) and D3 (data). These are tagged with special bits, as shown, to indicate to the 4B5B encoder which are control and data. The coding indicated for the J and K is that commonly found in many VLSI implementations of FDDI interfaces.

Table 3.1 *FDDI symbols*

Symbol name	Encoded binary value	Usage in FDDI	Symbol name	Encoded binary value	Usage in FDDI
0	11110	Data symbol 0	Q	00000	Quiet line state
1	01001	Data symbol 1	I	11111	Idle line state, preamble
2	10100	Data symbol 2	H	00100	Halt line state
3	10101	Data symbol 3	J	11000	First part of frame start delimiter
4	01010	Data symbol 4	K	10001	Second part of frame start delimiter
5	01011	Data symbol 5	T	01101	Terminates data stream
6	01110	Data symbol 6	R	00111	Reset symbol
7	01111	Data symbol 7	S	11001	Set symbol
8	10010	Data symbol 8	V	00011	Violation symbol
9	10011	Data symbol 9	V	00101	Violation symbol
10 (A)	10110	Data symbol 10 (A)	V	00110	Violation symbol
11 (B)	10111	Data symbol 11 (B)	V	01100	Violation symbol
12 (C)	11010	Data symbol 12 (C)	V or H	00001	Violation on Tx, Halt on Rx
13 (D)	11011	Data symbol 13 (D)	V or H	00010	Violation on Tx, Halt on Rx
14 (E)	11100	Data symbol 14 (E)	V or H	01000	Violation on Tx, Halt on Rx
15 (F)	11101	Data symbol 15 (F)	V or H	10000	Violation on Tx, Halt on Rx

Once the symbol-pairs have passed through the 4B5B encoder, creating the actual bit patterns that will be sent across the cable, these are serialised and transmitted in the NRZI format described above. The lower part of the diagram illustrates the reverse process.

The encoding of the control symbols is carefully chosen to produce either unique, or distinguishable NRZI waveforms on the transmission medium. For instance, the JK symbol pair is used at the start of every frame, and produces a partial pattern 100010001 which is not produced by any valid user-data stream, thus making it easier to detect.

Baseline Wander

A commonly encountered term in FDDI is *baseline wander*. This is the term used to describe the effect of a drift in the DC component from the mid-signal point of the transmitted AC data signal (the NRZI transitions). This is caused when the average AC signal, over a reasonable period of time, is non-zero. For example, in manchester encoded signals, the average signal is zero (i.e. on average, the signal spends as much

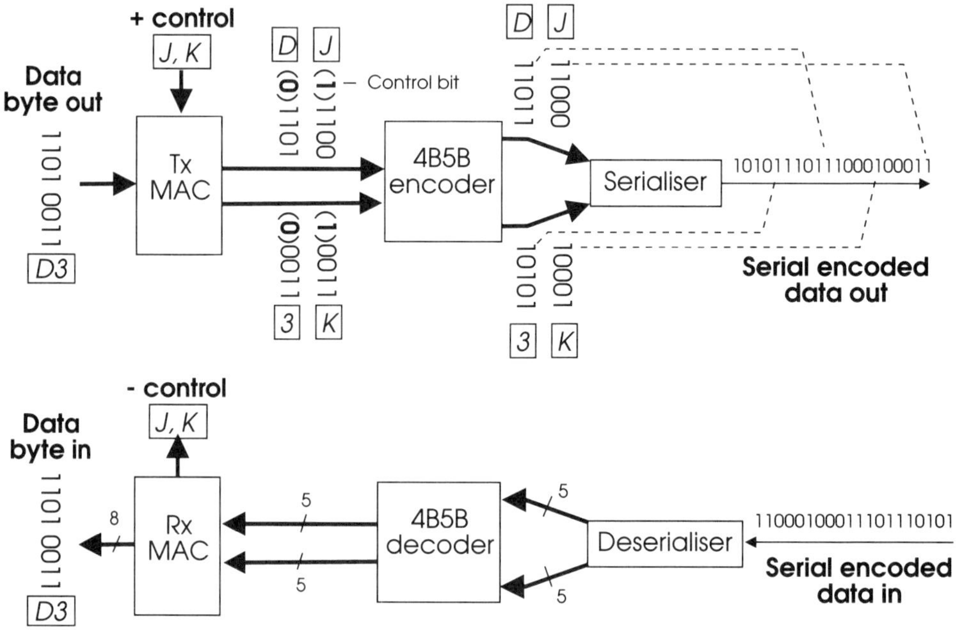

Figure 3.4 *FDDI 4B5B data encoding*

time high as it does low), and is said to be DC balanced. For FDDI, the 4B5B NRZI coding produces a transition only when there is a '1', with a maximum of three consecutive '0's (which produce no transitions). In the worst case, this produces a ±10 per cent deviation in the DC component of the transmitted AC signal. This is an important design consideration for the receiver portions of stations.

Line States

A stream of symbols results in a particular *line state*, which indicates the current condition or state of the point-to-point data-link connecting two stations. Line states are also used during the signalling process to a neighbouring port when initialising fault finding, and during synchronisation of the data scramblers in TP-PMD copper cable variants. Their usage will become clearer in following sections and chapters.

The line states and their meaning are summarised in Table 3.2. Many of the line states are not covered in this chapter, but have more relevance in later chapters where the node initialisation and fault recovery processes are described in more detail. Note that the NRZI encoding of these line states produces regular square-wave patterns with the frequencies as shown. As idles are encoded as 11111, ILS produces the maximum possible frequency, i.e. 62.5 MHz, for an FDDI 4B5B encoded bit stream.

Table 3.2 *Line states*

Line State Name	Usage	NRZI
QLS - Quiet Line State	Continuous stream of Q symbols, indicating either absence of a physical connection, or used during the port initialisation process (see Chapter 4)	No change in signal levels (0 Hz)
MLS - Master Line State	Continuous stream of alternating H and Q symbols (HQ or QH), used by the port initialisation process and during TRACE function	One transition every 10th bit (6.25 MHz)
HLS - Halt Line State	Continuous H symbols received, used in the port initialisation process	One transition every bit (12.5 MHz)
ILS - Idle Line State	Continuous stream of I symbols, used to establish and maintain clock synchronisation, and during initialisation and normal operation of network to separate data frames. Indicates physical connection is present when there is no network activity.	One transition every bit (62.5 MHz)
ALS - Active Line State	Active during a valid data frame sequence	Random (user data dependent)
NLS - Noise Line State	Indicates noisy input stream of invalid symbols or line conditions	Random (noise dependent)

Encoding for Twisted Pair Copper Cabling

The standard 4B5B NRZI encoded bit stream, when directly transmitted across copper cabling, does not meet either the EMI, or the distance requirements of UTP-5 (unshielded twisted pair category 5) cabling. It is, however, acceptable for STP, and is in fact used by IBM's SDDI solution, running over IBM type 1 or 2 cable. For UTP-5, in order to achieve both the 100 m distance objective, and to meet world-wide emission standards, a different encoding scheme must be implemented to lower the maximum transmitted frequency (62.5 MHz with 4B5B NRZI) to within acceptable limits.

The encoding scheme chosen for twisted pair cabling, specified in the TP-PMD FDDI standard, takes a threefold approach. Firstly, instead of NRZI's two-signal level scheme, a similar three-level encoding scheme is used, called MLT-3 (sometimes referred to as NRZI-3). Secondly, in addition to MLT-3 encoding, a data *stream cipher scrambler* is used to help further reduce the energy spectrum peaks present in the resultant data bit stream. Finally, at the receive end of the wire, an adaptive equaliser circuit is used to help adapt the receiver response to differing lengths of cable, as the MLT-3 and data scrambling do not produce a waveform with consistent characteristics across all possible lengths.

Figure 3.5 illustrates the functional blocks relative to the 4B5B NRZI encoders. As

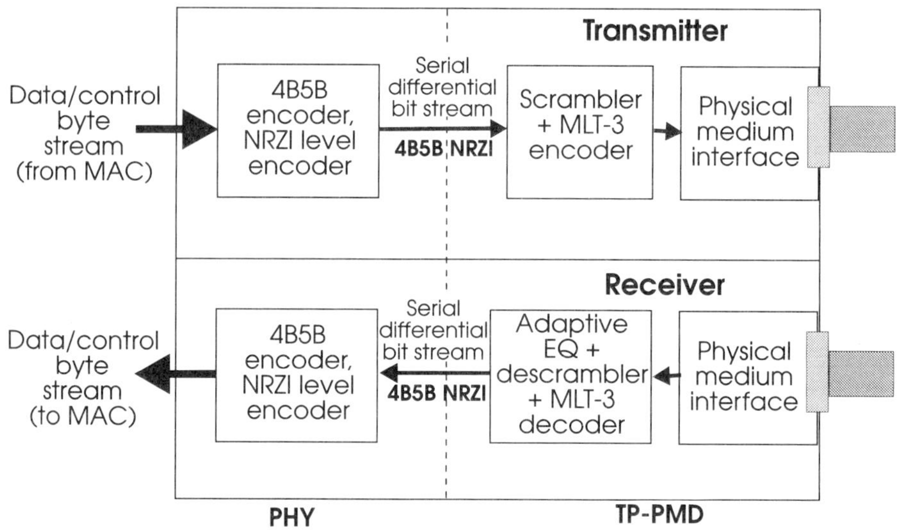

Figure 3.5 *TP-PMD scrambler, MLT-3 and adaptive EQ functions*

the standard specifying the new encoding and transmission schemes is at PMD level, strictly speaking, the new encoding is applied after the PHY layer 4B5B NRZI interface. However, as the order of the NRZI and scrambler functions is not important (as the data gets converted to MLT-3 anyway), it is possible to integrate in hardware the 4B5B and scrambler functions, as found in some VLSI components. This helps reduce the cost of adding the scrambler function at the PMD interface level. Figure 3.6 illustrates a commonly used implementation.

MLT-3 Encoding

MLT-3 uses three levels to encode the binary digits as they are passed across the twisted pair cable. It is similar to NRZI in that it contains the same number of transitions by only changing level when a '1' is to be transmitted. The scheme works by making a positive (or negative) transition to the next signal level out of three, every time a '1' occurs in the serial bit stream. The direction of the transition (positive or negative) depends on the both the current level, and the direction of the last transition. When either the high or low signal level is attained, then at the next '1', the transition direction reverses. At the receiving station, a '1' is recognised by any transition within a bit slot time, otherwise a '0' is interpreted. Figure 3.7 illustrates the process for a particular bit stream.

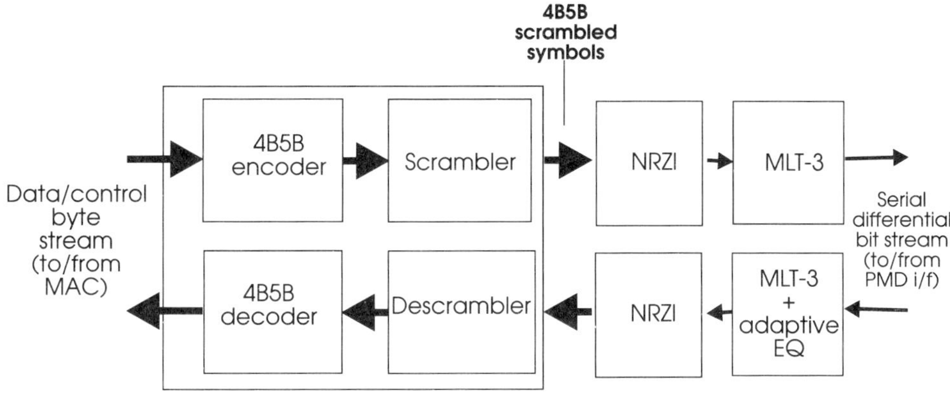

Figure 3.6 *4B5B and scrambler VLSI integration*

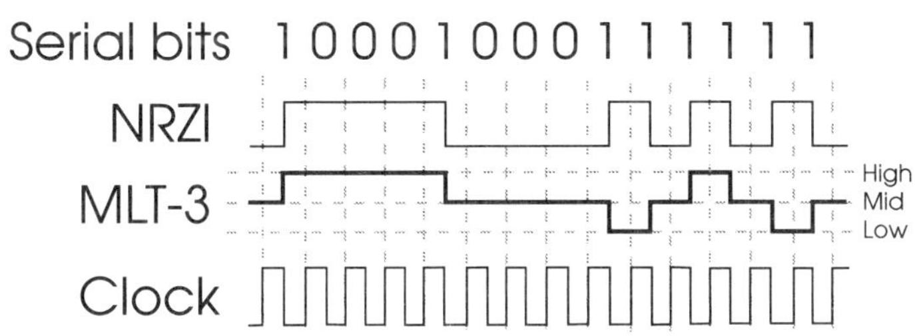

Figure 3.7 *MLT-3 encoding example*

From Figure 3.7, we see that when there are a string of '1's, the maximum frequency is attained. However, this time the waveform has a period of 4 bits, instead of 2, as in the NRZI example above it. This means that the maximum fundamental frequency is 125 MHz/4, i.e. 31.25 MHz, thus lowering the highest frequency component of the data bit stream. This is one of the main reasons that the MLT-3 encoding allows the distance requirements of unshielded twisted pair to be met.

Stream Cipher Scrambler

MLT-3 on its own is not enough to achieve compliance with world-wide radio frequency (RF) emission specifications. As you would expect, unshielded copper cabling radiates significantly more RF energy than its shielded counterpart, STP, and optical fibre. By utilising a data stream cipher scrambler, the energy peaks within the MLT-3 encoded streams can be decreased, resulting in further reductions in RF emissions.

Scrambling refers to the modification of the 4B5B serial data stream, by the addition of a random component. This random component is then removed at the receiving end to re-create the original data bit stream (Figure 3.8). The random bit generator function is based on the polynomial, $x^{11} + x^9$. Figure 3.9 illustrates how the scrambled bit sequence is generated using a shift register and performing a Boolean exclusive-OR (XOR) of the random bit and the data bit to be scrambled (the Boolean XOR function performs a single bit add). The shift register runs at the bit transmission rate, and the random bit itself is fed back into the input of the shift register.

In order for the scrambling to work properly, both the transmitting scrambler and the receiving descrambler must be synchronised in order to reconstruct the original data stream. Synchronisation is accomplished using the FDDI line states (ILS, MLS, QLS or HLS) that produce predictable patterns in the scrambled data stream. The receiving station can detect this, and lock its descrambler so that it contains the same bit values as the scrambler (on the basis that it is known to have scrambled the known detected line state). Once the descrambler is synchronised, its random bit stream may be

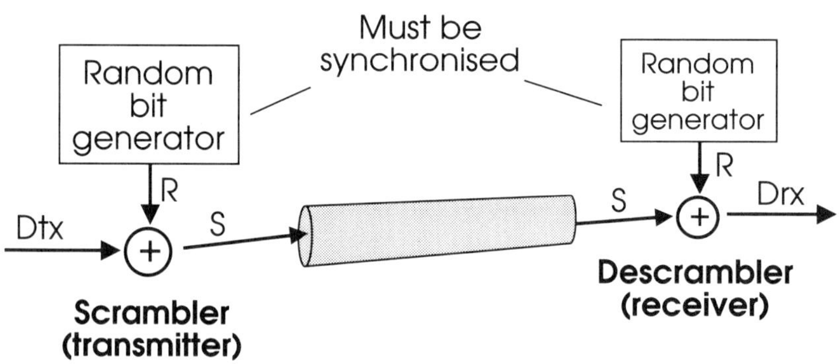

Figure 3.8 *TP-PMD stream cipher scrambling*

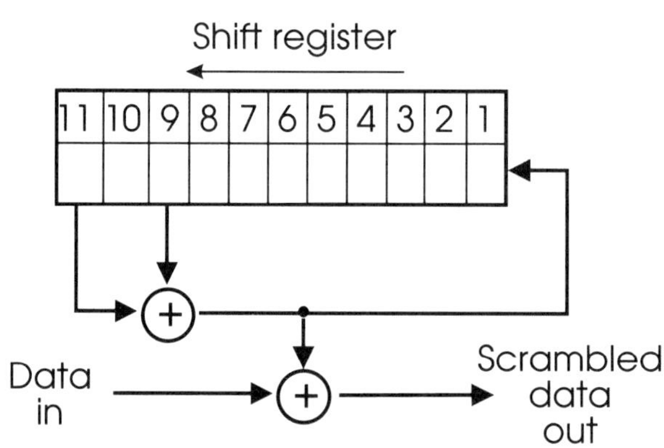

Figure 3.9 *Stream-Cipher Scrambler*

XORed with the scrambled data to reproduce the original before passing onto the 4B5B encoder for final reconstruction. The whole reason this is possible is because the basic property of the Boolean XOR (⊕) function is that data XORed with itself, produces a zero result.

To illustrate this, from Figure 3.8, we see that

$$S = Dtx \oplus R$$
$$Drx = S \oplus R$$

where

S = scrambled bit
R = random bit
Dtx = original data bit
Drx = recovered data bit.

Hence, substituting for S in Drx,

$$Drx = (Dtx \oplus R) \oplus R$$

As R XORed with itself is zero, then as required

$$Drx = Dtx \oplus 0 = Dtx$$

i.e. the descrambled data is the same as that before scrambling at the transmitter end.

Though we have described the scrambler as a bit level function, in the VLSI integration example shown in Figure 3.6, a parallel version of the scrambler (symbol wide) is implemented. The principle is exactly the same, except that scrambled 4B5B symbols are produced before being serialised and NRZI/MLT-3 encoded. The only reason NRZI is still present, even though it has been made redundant by the MLT-3 encoding, is because the same VLSI device(s) is used to support both schemes, with standard TP-PMD modules supporting NRZI to MLT-3 conversion.

Elasticity Buffer, Smoother and Repeat Filters

As every station has its own local clock, there will always be a slight difference between the local clock frequency of the transmitting station, and that of the receiving station. Further, as the clocks are totally independent, the chances are that they can be completely out of phase. What this means is that there is a slight timing difference between the incoming recovered clock, and the local clock within the receiver of the station.

For this purpose an *elasticity buffer* is implemented within the receiver portion of the station, which is a FIFO (first in, first out) based temporary storage for the incoming recovered bit stream. As shown in Figure 3.1 earlier, the elasticity buffer is placed before the 4B5B encoding function in the receiver's PHY logic. The buffer compensates for the difference between the transmit and receive clock frequencies by clocking data into the FIFO at the recovered clock rate (derived by the PLL from the incoming data), and out of the FIFO at the station's local receive clock rate (Figure 3.10). Most hardware VLSI implementations perform this function at symbol-pair level at the byte clock rate (12.5 MHz).

Inbetween frame transmissions, the FIFO's input pointer is repositioned to the centre of the FIFO as a drift can occur in either direction. Certain rules govern cases where this may not occur, such as an incorrect number of inter-frame symbols being detected. As FDDI specifications call for a local clock crystal accuracy of 50 p.p.m. (parts per million), then for a maximum FDDI frame size of 9000 symbols (thus 45,000 bits), a possible 4.5 bit (45,000 bits $\times$ 50 $\times$ 10^{-6} $\times$ 2) difference can occur. This assumes both station clocks are out by +50 and −50 p.p.m. respectively (hence the factor of 2). To cater for a drift in either direction, then at least 9 bits are in theory needed for an elasticity buffer. In practice, a larger size is used (as many as 80 bits) to cater for differences beyond 50 p.p.m.

An additional function incorporated into the elasticity buffer is a *smoother* function. The smoother adds or deletes idle symbols in the received data stream when an inadequate number or surplus number of idles are detected between frames. Most smoother implementations attempt to maintain at least seven idle symbol pairs (fourteen idles) between back-to-back frame transmissions. The reason for the smoother is because the inter-frame gap can be shortened by multiple elasticity buffers to the point where the frame is no longer valid, and is rejected. This can be caused by either an underflow or overflow of the buffer(s) around the station ring as the elasticity buffer is not required to recentre its input pointer when inter-frame gaps of less than four symbols are encountered, for example.

The *repeat filter* is a function incorporated into the transmission portion of the

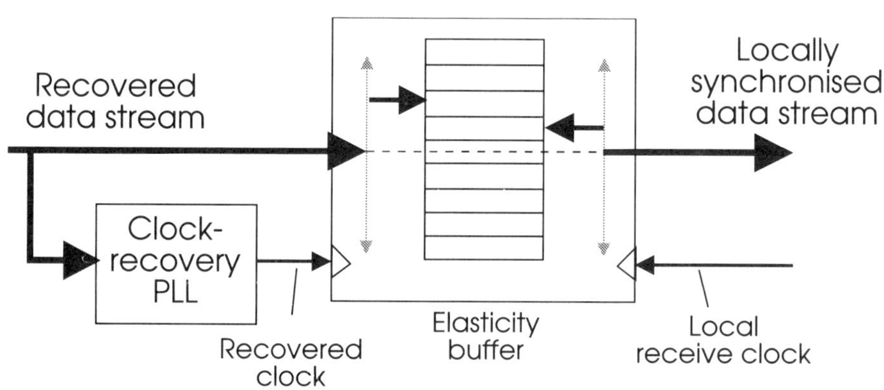

Figure 3.10 *Elasticity buffer*

station's PHY, and prevents, in the absence of a MAC, the propagation of invalid symbols (4B5B code violations – Table 3.1) or line states. Normally, as a MAC is present on the repeat data path between the receive and transmit ports, this function is not necessary. However, in MAC-less concentrators, or in single MAC DAS stations where no MAC is on the secondary data path, this function must be carried out by the repeat filter. The filter changes any invalid symbols into idles. If these occur in the middle of a frame, then four halt symbols are transmitted first, before commencing with transmitting idles. These idles are continually transmitted until the next valid start of frame is seen. The frame in this case is said to be *truncated*, and is counted as a lost frame by the next downstream station MAC in its internal error counters.

Many station implementations incorporate a *gobble-byte* feature within the repeater filter. After detection of a frame fragment or truncated frame (detected by idles appearing before the end of frame), as the fragment is repeated, the last two non-idle symbols are converted to idles, i.e. they are 'gobbled up'. After passing through several stations with this feature, the fragment is converted completely to idles (though this is not the normal mechanism for removing frame fragments as we shall see in Chapter 4).

Link Detection

In all cable media types used by FDDI, a means of detecting that the signal received from the neighbouring station is adequate, and usable, is required. This function is called *signal detect*. The power levels being received are constantly monitored to ensure that a minimum power threshold is detected. In the case of optical fibre, this is a minimum light power level, and in copper cabling schemes, a minimum differential signal strength. At the PMD level, a control signal is fed back to the PHY layer to indicate that the PMD is functioning correctly, and receiving a sensible signal.

Cable continuity is something more commonly encountered in copper-based PMD implementations. A scheme is used that allows the station's receiver to detect if both cables running to the neighbour make a complete round trip. A DC path is set up along both the transmit and receive cable, such that a DC component is only detected if the complete round trip connection is made. Obviously, the transmitter and receiver circuits at the far end must be DC coupled for this occur.

Cabling and Transmission Options

The number of cabling and transmission options offered by FDDI are detailed by separate PMD standards documents, and cover a variety of options: multimode fibre, single-mode fibre, low-cost fibre, twisted pair copper cabling, and FDDI extension over a SONET/SDH based WAN.

Multimode Optical Fibre (MMF-PMD)

This was the first PMD proposed for FDDI, and is probably one of the most common optical fibres. The optical wavelength of the light-emitting diode (LED) is 1300 nm. The maximum distance for this type of cable is 2 km. A special MIC (media interface connector) is defined for MMF, incorporating a mechanical keying mechanism to ensure the correct ports are interconnected (Figure 3.11). The fibre type used is the 62.5/125 μm (core/cladding dimensions). Alternative fibre options for MMF include the lower cost 50/125 μm with a slightly higher loss per km than the above (around 4 dB/km vs. 3 dB/km). Some buildings already have this type of cable available. Another option is to use 85/125 μm fibre.

Single-Mode Optical Fibre (SMF-PMD)

Single-mode fibre was introduced to allow distances of 40–60 km (depending on the category of fibre used). The light wavelength is again 1300 nm. An almost identical MIC to that for MMF is used, the only difference being the tighter design tolerances and the keying mechanism preventing accidental connection to MMF. SMF-PMD specifies the use of 8–10/125 μm core/cladding fibre. The various options for the cable

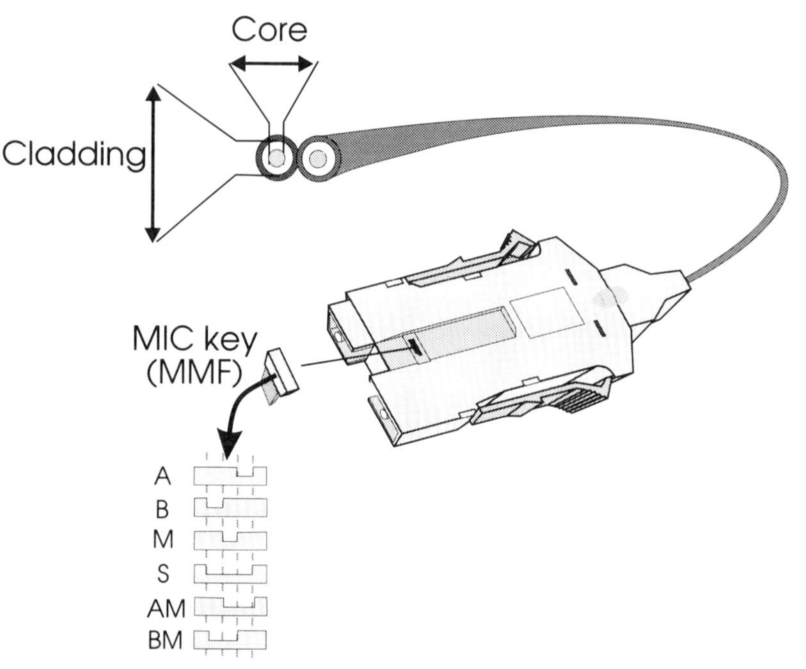

Figure 3.11 *MMF optical fibre cabling and MIC connectors*

relate to the loss characteristics, and for SMF are typically less than 0.5 dB/km.

Low-Cost Fibre (LCF-PMD)

LCF specifies the use of fibre in the range 62.5/125–200/230 μm, though the 200/230 μm fibre tends to be used in most cases as the optical transceivers can be more expensive using the larger diameter fibres. LCF is intended to provide lower cost optical fibre connections than the standard MMF for lengths of up to 500 m. The main saving in cost over the standard MMF option is in fact in the transceiver eletronics and not the cable, and so the name 'low-cost fibre' is perhaps a little misleading.

A LCF-MIC is defined, again only capable of plugging into a compatible LCF socket. This is based around two simplex, SC or optionally ST connectors. The overall cost reduction associated with this type of cable can be from 30 per cent over conventional MMF, depending on the cable and optical component manufacturer.

Twisted Pair Copper (TP-PMD)

TP-PMD specifies the use of datagrade category 5 100 Ohm unshielded twisted pair (UTP), and Type 1/2 150 Ohm shielded twisted pair (STP). Distances of up to 100 m are catered for using UTP, meeting with the EIA/TIA 568 recommendations for structured cabling. Datagrade 5 cabling (also known as *supertwist UTP*; EIA/TIA TSB 36 – Technical Systems Bulletin Additional Cable Specification for UTP Cables, November 1991) is a high quality twist UTP, designed specifically to carry data rates up to 100 Mbps. Two types of connector are specified: an RJ45 connector for UTP (the same as for IEEE 802.x networks) and a 9-pin D-type connector for STP (Figure 3.12). Due to the 100 Mbps line rate, shielded connectors play an important role in helping to meet the strict electrical and electromagnetic interference requirements. In addition, the MLT-3 line encoding scheme is used, in combination with a stream cipher scrambler as outlined earlier. The change in data signal encoding is in order to reduce the electromagnetic emissions to within standards, and to make the signal more suitable for transmission over UTP.

SONET Physical layer Mapping (SPM)

The SONET (synchronous optical network) physical medium option provides a mechanism for extending the FDDI ring over the public WAN. The nearest SONET rate to cater for the FDDI 100 Mbps (125 Mbaud actual line bit rate due to 4B5B encoding) is 155.52 Mbps (STS3c). Note this scheme is not the same as using a remote bridging method to connect FDDI rings, as it actually extends the ring itself. This means that the delay characteristics of the FDDI ring is affected, along with the token

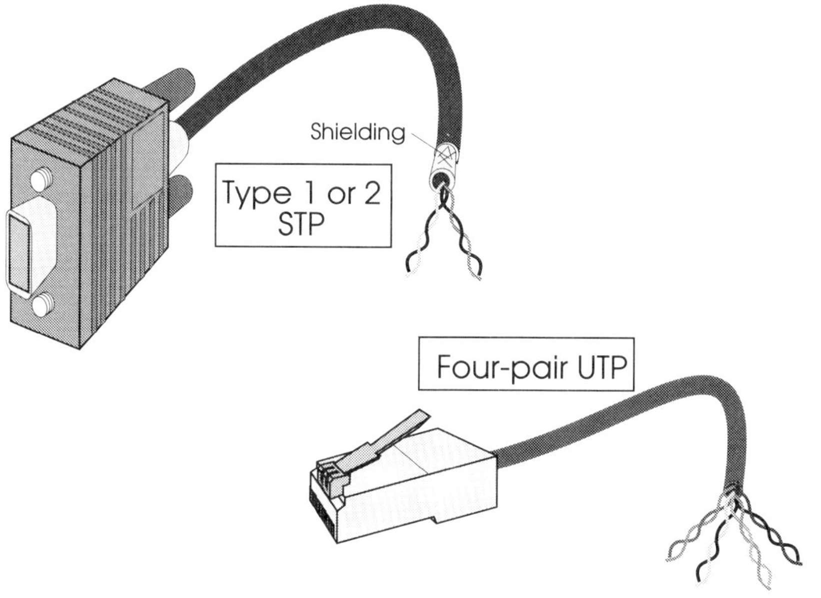

Figure 3.12 *UTP and STP copper cabling and connectors*

rotation time, and so on.

Other Cable Types

Some vendors supply alternative cable types; DEC, for example, provide coax support for their FDDI products. Most of these options are usually designed to fit in with the vendor's own cabling schemes (such as DEC's DEC-Connect in this case).

There is also work ongoing to provide support for FDDI data rates over level 3 UTP, which has a lower-quality twist than with datagrade level 5, and is much lower in cost. The benefit is that this type of cable is widely installed, especially in the United States, and is already being used by many Ethernet 10Base-T networks across the world, as well as being widely used as telephone wiring.

Station Connection Rules

Due to the ring topology, and dual-ring connections, care must be exercised when interconnecting FDDI stations. A mechanical keying mechanism ensures that the connectors themselves only mate with the appropriate receptacle, ensuring that an A port connects to a B port of another station for example. However, accidents do happen, and installations do get the odd cabling problems, even if the greatest care is taken. Chapter 6 takes a more detailed look at the way FDDI automatically reconfigures its port connections in response to connection problems, and the undesirable topologies that can be created by incorrect wiring. Here we will take a look at the specific rules that define undesirable connections between ports.

Port-to-Port Rules

Port connections in FDDI follow set rules. These define which port type may be connected together, and under what circumstances. For example, in a ring of dual attachment stations, A–B and B–A are valid connections, whereas A–A or B–B connections create problems with the network topology and station communication capabilities. Figure 3.13 summarises the port-to-port connection rules, and Tables 3.3 and 3.4 summarise which ports may be connected, and under what circumstances.

A low-level signalling scheme is used when a station initialises itself in the ring (see Chapter 5). This occurs before any tokens have been circulated, and as each station is coming up onto the ring. As each port is effectively a bidirectional link to its neighbour port, it is able to communicate with this port. In a normal set-up, an A port would expect to find a B port at the other end of its link. For a dual-homed node, both the A and B port would expect to find an M port at the other end of their respective links. Based on the capabilities or *connection policy* of the station, the connection may

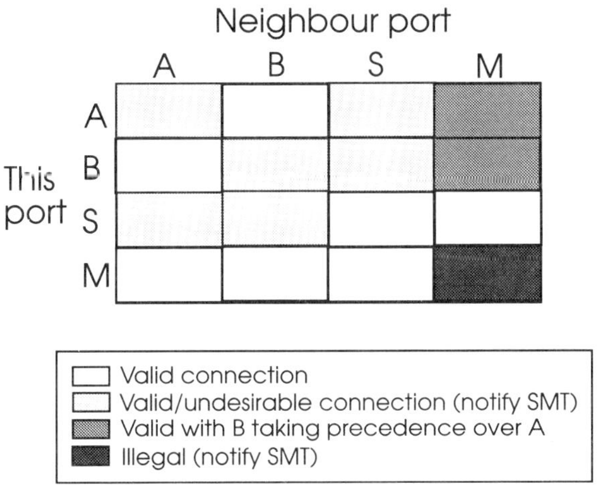

Figure 3.13 *Port-to-port connection rules/preferences*

either be accepted or rejected during this communication. Hence a standard DAS would probably only allow A–B and B–A connections, and allow the A–A and B–B connections in order not to cause a *WRAP* condition whilst the appropriate notification is carried out of the incorrect wiring (e.g. a message is flashed up on the user console of the station, or the network manager console). A lot will depend on the internal architecture of the station, and whether it is able to transmit and receive frames under such circumstances. A high-end DAS may even be able to correct the situation temporarily by reconfiguring the A port to be a B port, and vice versa. An example of a connection that would be rejected is an M–M, as a *tree of rings* topology would be created, an illegal FDDI topology.

Table 3.3 *DAS/DAC/DHS A and B port connection rules*

Port–Port	Rules and Actions
A–B and B–A	Connections valid and accepted, the port status set to *peer*, and the station enters a *THRU* mode of operation
A–M and B–M	Connections allowed if this station supports dual homing. The A–M connection is withheld by the A port in favour of the B port connection, which is allowed (i.e. during the low-level signalling, A–M is rejected and B–M is accepted). Port is status set to *tree*. *THRU* mode of operation is disabled.
A–S or B–S	Connection is possible, but undesirable. If allowed to proceed, will result in the dual-ring being *WRAP*ed by the S port, hence the appropriate management authority is to be notified. Port status is set to *peer*.
A–A or B–B	This results in a twisted primary and secondary ring (see later), and usually are accepted but the appropriate management authority notified. Port status is set to *peer*.
A–M and B–A	Dependent on the policy of the station, this set-up may or may not be accepted. If the station accepts the B–A (port status = *peer*), and not the A–M, it effectively *WRAP*s the ring at its B port. If the B–A is not accepted, it will cause a main ring *WRAP* at the next station anyway, and the station gets into the ring as a dual-homed station would via its concentrator connection. Obviously, this situation needs to be resolved by rectifying the wiring fault in order to restore the dual primary ring. The A port status would be set to *tree* under these circumstances.

Table 3.4 *SAS/SAC/NAC S and M port connection rules*

Port–Port	Rules and Actions
S–M and M–S	Valid concentrator tree connection, and ports connect and status set to *tree*.
S–S	Valid connection (though not always the one wanted), creating a single ring of two slave stations. Port status set to *peer*.
M–M	Illegal, creating a tree of rings topology. Connection rejected by both ends. Port status remains set to *none*.
S–A or S–B	Allowed connection, but is undesirable as it creates a wrapped dual-ring (if the other station is on the dual-ring, that is). If the other station's A or B port is connected to an M port (i.e. a tree connection), whether this station actually gets configured into the ring depends on the policy of the other station, i.e. if A–M and B–S is allowed. Ultimately, this situation will need rectifying.

FDDI Installations

Where to use each type of cabling depends on the user's requirements and available cable types that already exist at the time of the network installation.

Figure 3.14 illustrates the possible options available in a general campus environment. The use of optical fibre is predominant in most FDDI backbone installations due to the higher levels of security and longer distances required. Determining the best solution for an end customer is highly dependent on the type of installation they have or require. FDDI installations generally follow these guidelines:

- *End equipment to wiring closet (mainly horizontal).* For less than 100 m, datagrade level 5 UTP and Type 1/2 STP (TP) is typically used to keep the overall costs to a minimum, and also because many installations have this cabling already installed. This also keeps the cost of the end station interfaces to a minimum. Low-cost fibre (LCF) can be utilised where distances of between 100 m and 500 m are required, or if preferred the standard multimode fibre (MMF). SMF may be utilised in extremely large, flat buildings, and in situations where the immunity to EMI of fibre is a benefit (e.g. a car production line). It is possible to extend both single attach and dual attach links to the end equipment using a star-wired arrangement.

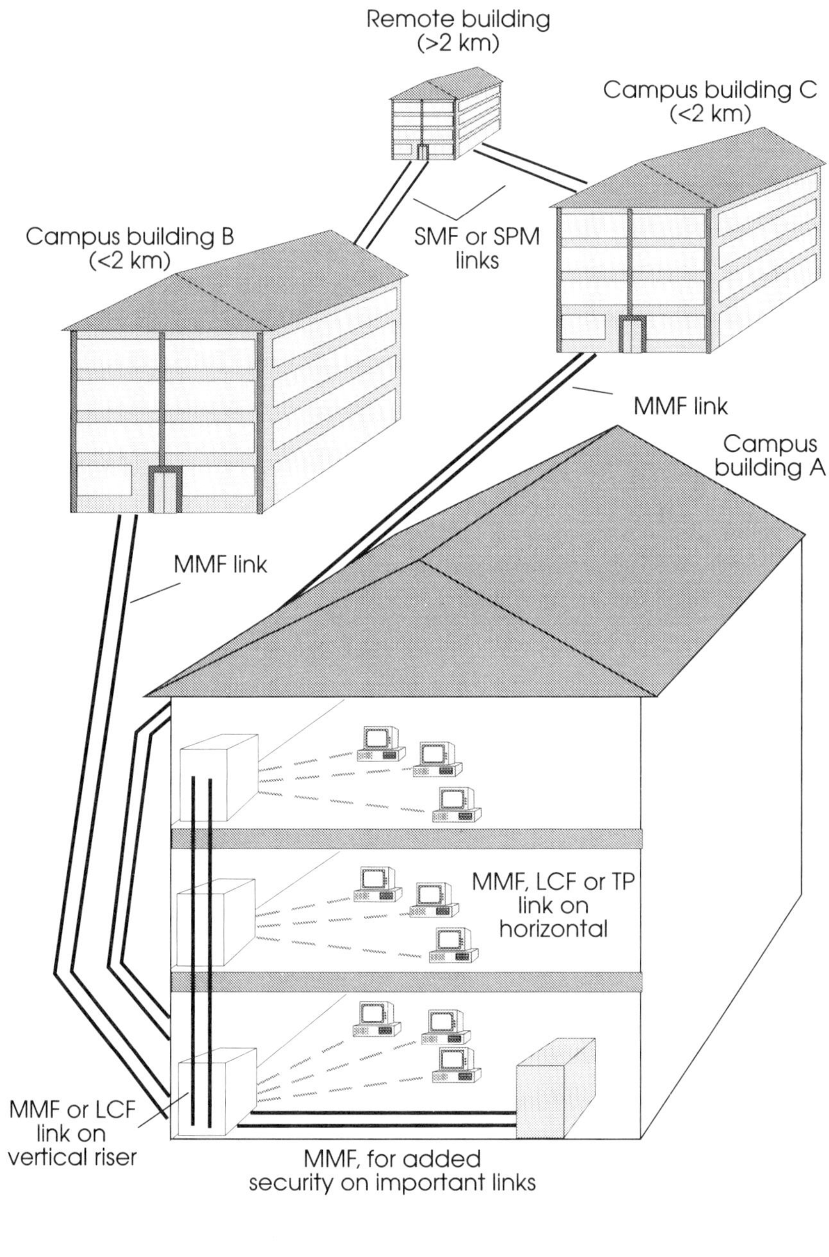

Figure 3.14 *FDDI cabling installation options*

- *Inter-wiring closet (e.g. vertical riser).* Where more than a single wiring closet is employed in a network, optical fibre is generally used as the interconnecting medium. Standard MMF is typically used in these instances, possibly LCF.

- *Building to building (campus).* Due to the potentially large distances involved, different earth potentials, and the possible susceptibility to interference and trouble caused by difficult routing of cabling, MMF and SMF fibre is normally employed. Many FDDI products offer the capability to configure one port of a dual attach station or concentrator to one particular type, and the other to something different. For example, it may be useful to connect MMF to the A port, as this is a relatively short link, and SMF to the B port, as this links to a much further station (>2 km). In Figure 3.14, campus building B may use this technique if the remote building is within reach of a SMF link.

- *Remote site.* Sites within 40 km can typically use the SMF method of interconnection, though a lot depends on the access rights for the cabling, and so on. It may even be possible to utilise a third party's network or cabling. One such scheme was proposed around a section of London's M25 motorway for example. If it is necessary to go out over the WAN to the remote site, then it is usual to use a remote bridge linking the two sites over a leased 2 Mbps line for instance. If much greater performance is required, then the SPM (SONET/SDH) mechanism could be used to extend the ring directly to the other site. This can be a very costly exercise however, not only in terms of end equipment, and the impact on network transit delay has to be closely examined.

Summary

FDDI uses a 4B5B NRZI encoding scheme to transmit raw data '1's and '0's between stations, along with clocking information so that the neighbouring station can recover the data properly. Whilst this scheme is adequate for optical fibre, and some forms of shielded copper cabling, it is not suitable for unshielded twisted pair (UTP). For the datagrade unshielded twisted pair (UTP-5) and shielded twisted pair (STP) cabling options specified by FDDI's TP-PMD standard (TPDDI), a different encoding scheme is used to transit raw data bits: MLT-3, with data scrambling and adaptive equalisation. This is necessary to meet the 100 m distance requirement, and to minimise RF emissions that would otherwise prevent it from meeting world-wide EMI restrictions.

Cabling options available for FDDI installations include multimode optical fibre for distances of 2 km between stations, and single-mode fibre for distances of up to 40–60 km. Low-cost fibre and UTP-5/STP copper cabling options are also available for shorter cable runs of up to 500 m or 100 m respectively. Wide area expansion of FDDI rings is also possible using a SONET PMD interface.

CHAPTER 4

Frame Transmission and Reception

In this chapter, we will take a look at how FDDI data frames are made up, and how they are handled by each of the stations on the network at the MAC layer level. Chapters 5 and 6 will look in more detail at the initialisation and management aspects. Here we will concentrate on how the various frames are transported around the ring, how they start and terminate, how the frame types are identified, and also look more closely at the token control mechanism. An example of frame transmission on a simple FDDI ring is illustrated, describing the various mechanisms that take place on the ring and within the stations themselves, including the operation of the station timers. Finally, a brief explanation of how the higher layer software interfaces to FDDI's MAC layer is given.

Basic Data Types

The basic types of traffic that exists on an operational FDDI ring are *data frames*, *frame fragments*, *idle symbols* and the *token frame*. The role of each of these will be outlined using a basic model for a station, and an example FDDI data communication. Each type of frame has a special structure that is identified by a specific field within each frame. Every station in the network uses these specific fields to process the incoming frame it receives. As the station has to perform these decisions at the 100 Mbps rate the information enters the station, most of the decisions have to be performed by dedicated hardware in the station, usually within custom semiconductor devices.

In addition to the standard traffic types, leftovers of the frame transmission and reception process also circulate the ring. The formation of these unwanted fragments, truncated tokens, etc., and their automatic removal from the ring, is explained later within the simple example used to explain the exchange of frames between stations in a ring.

Protocol Data Units

The FDDI MAC layer has two fundamental types of *protocol data units* or PDUs: *tokens* and *frames* (Figure 4.1). The frame data structure is the basic means of data transportation around the network, and has a maximum size of 9000 symbols. There are a number of basic frame types defined by a frame control field within the frame itself. Types of frames include *Medium Access Control* (MAC) frames (e.g. claim and beacon type frames used in the ring initialisation process), *Logical Link Control* (LLC) frames used for normal data transmissions from upper layers, *Station Management* (SMT) frames for passing of management information, *implementor-specific* frames defined by the system designer, and *void* frames used in special circumstances such as bridge applications.

A *preamble* (PA) always precedes a valid token or frame to allow the receiver to synchronise with the incoming data stream, and must consist of a minimum of 16 idle (I) symbols. The *start delimiter* (SD) indicates the start of the frame and consists of a J symbol followed by a K symbol, or a 'JK' symbol pair. The *frame control* (FC) field is 2 symbols wide and defines the type of frame – whether it is a MAC frame, SMT frame and so on. The FC also defines the length of the source and destination addresses which follow, i.e. 16 or 48 bits (4 or 12 symbols). Following the two address fields (which indicate simply where on the ring the data came from and is going to), is the information field which is a variable length field, with a maximum size of around 4478 bytes. This carries higher-layer information, including end-user data. At the end

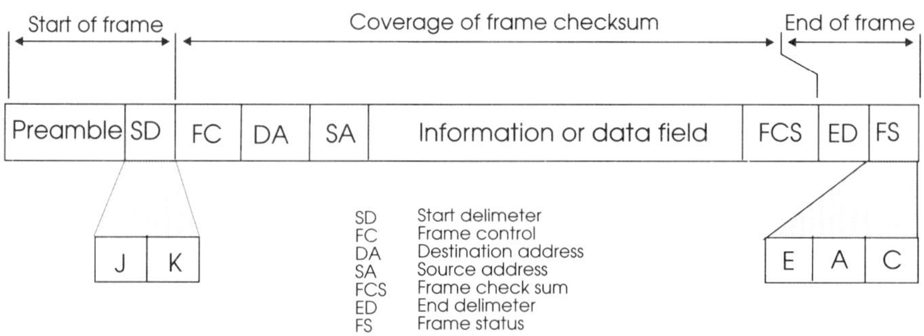

(a) MAC frame

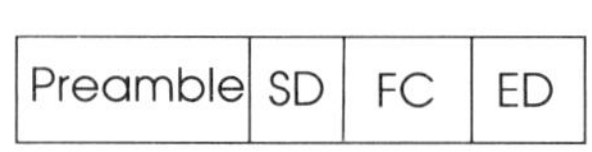

(b)Token frame

Figure 4.1 *The FDDI token and frame PDUs*

of the data portion of the frame, a 32 bit (8 symbols) *frame checksum* (FCS) follows, which is a CRC value based on the preceding frame data. The *end delimiter* (ED) consists of a single T symbol, marking the end of the data portion of the frame. Finally, a *frame status* (FS) indicates, using three symbol fields, the status of the frame – *frame error* (E), *address recognised* (A) and *frame copied* (C) indicators. In each of the three fields, a *reset* (R) or *set* (S) control symbol is used to indicate the appropriate state. For example, an R in the frame error field, E, indicates that no frame error was detected by the last station that received the frame. The usage of the three indicators will become more apparent later as we look at the frame transmission and reception process. A complete FDDI frame must never exceed the maximum allowed 9000 symbols (4500 bytes or octets).

Frame Type Identification

The type of FDDI frame, be it a token, a normal data frame, a special management or control frame, is identified by the FC field of the PDU. The FC is the first field to be read into the station after the starting delimiter. The various control fields of the FC are illustrated in Figure 4.2. The FC is also used to identify the type of service (asynchronous or synchronous), and format of the address fields (16 or 48 bits).

The C (class) and L (address length) bits (or flags) depend on the overall network application and protocol requirements. C identifies the class of service, i.e. *asynchronous* or *synchronous*. The main difference between the two types of service is

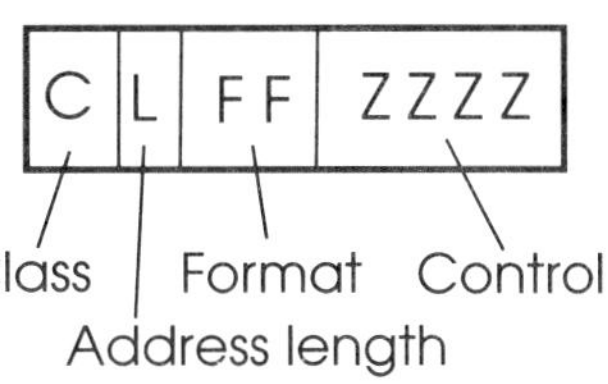

CLFF	ZZZZ	PDU type
0x00	0000	Void frame
1000	0000	Non-restricted token
1100	0000	Restricted token
0L00	0001–1111	SMT frame
1L00	0001–1111	MAC frame
CL01	r000–r111	LLC frame
CL10	r000–r111	Implementor frame
CL11	rrrr	Reserved for future use

x, don't care; r, reserved.

Figure 4.2 *Frame control (FC) field*

that the latter guarantees a station can transmit on every token rotation, the former only when unused bandwidth is available. Asynchronous is the most used service, and is like that of other IEEE 802 LANs. The synchronous service is a useful feature for transmitting time-sensitive data, as network access is more predictable than with asynchronous, i.e. data can be transmitted within reasonably accurate time intervals irrespective of network loading. If C is set to a binary zero (0), then the frame is asynchronous, otherwise a one (1) indicates synchronous.

The 'L' control bit signifies 16 or 48 bit address usage in the following destination and source address fields. In most commercial networks today, 48 bit addressing is the only scheme used, and it is likely that 16 bit addresses will be removed from the IEEE/ANSI standards altogether. The address space is controlled by the IEEE, with ranges allocated to manufacturers, as explained below.

The bits in the FC allow for a number of frame types, even implementor-specific frames, permitting individual manufacturers to send special control frames to their equipment. The main frame types are Token, SMT, MAC and LLC. LLC frames are used for normal data transmission, and originate from the sub-level above MAC in the data link layer (Figure 2.1). The MAC level frames are used during the initialisation or error recovery processes of the MAC layer. Void frames are used in bridge applications, e.g. as a method of cleaning up the network of any *orphaned frames* that may exist due to a station's exit from the ring.

So, taking the most commonly used frame type as an example, an LLC frame carrying asynchronous data will have an FC field *0L01 rppp*, where the *ppp* indicates the asynchronous priority level (000 for lowest, 111 for highest). A synchronous LLC frame would have an FC field *1L01 rrrr* (the reserved bits *rrrr* set as *0000*).

Frame Destination and Source Addressing

The format of the address fields is based on the IEEE address format. These are administered by the IEEE, and any company wishing to use a block of numbers must apply to the IEEE for them. This ensures a strict control over which stations can be assigned what addresses, and that every individual global IEEE address used in the world is unique. As mentioned before, 16 bit addresses are rarely used nowadays.

Figure 4.3 illustrates the most significant bit (MSB) format of the 16 and 48 bit destination address frames. In both the 16 and 48 format, the first bit of the destination address field is a control bit that identifies whether the address is intended for a single specific station, or a group of stations. If the I/G bit is a 0, then it signifies that this is an individual address. If it is set to a 1, then the address is to a group of stations, and is generally called a *multicast* address. It is also possible for a station to broadcast its frame to every station on the network using a *broadcast address* of all 1s. If the address consists of nothing but zeros then the address is a *null address*, and is of course recognised by no one. Source addresses have the I/G bit set to '0' under normal circumstances, except in some bridging applications where this bit may be set to '1'.

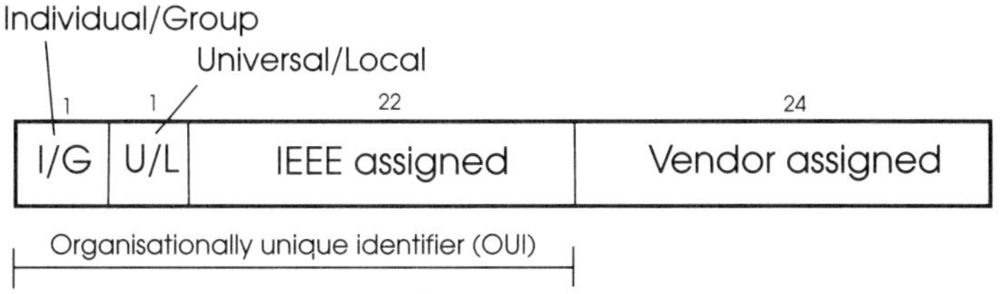

(a) 48 bit address format

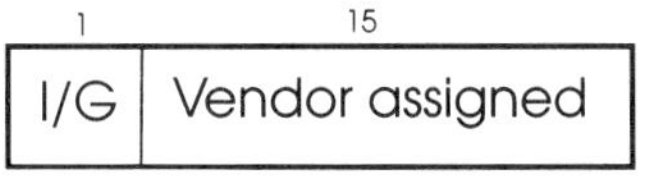

(b) 16 bit address format (no longer used by IEEE compatible LANs)

Figure 4.3 *Destination address (DA) format*

In the case of the 48 bit address format, a second control bit (U/L) is used to indicate if the remaining 46 bits are a locally administered address (= 1) or universally assigned by the IEEE (= 0). In the case of the locally administered address, this is only usually applicable to the local network, and is assigned by the local network administrator. The global address is uniquely assigned to each individual station in the world, with this assignment being controlled by the IEEE. With 46 bits available, then, 2^{46} ($\sim 7 \times 10^{13}$) possible combinations exist, allowing every station connected to a LAN in the world to have a unique number that can allow it to be addressed individually, even if the other station is on a different kind of IEEE-based network. Companies usually acquire IEEE addresses in blocks of 2^{24} addresses, and thus construct the individual addresses out of a 3 byte vendor-specific code, the *organisationally unique identifier* (OUI). The remaining bits are free to be assigned by the individual vendor. Typically, larger networking companies take out many of these blocks, and can have many OUIs assigned to them.

The addressing representation used above assumes a most significant *bit*, most significant *byte* format (referred to in later sections as the MSB format). Hence, the most significant bit of the address is the I/G multicast bit. FDDI uses this format as its transmission scheme is based on most significant bit transmitted first. In other standards such as Ethernet/IEEE 802.3 and Token Bus (802.4), a different format is used as they use a least significant bit transmitted first scheme on an octet (byte) by octet basis. This is generally an issue when bridging onto FDDI LANs. This other format is referred to as *canonical*. For example, an MSB address '04:43:27:63:72:10' would have the bits reversed in each of its octets to give a canonical representation of '20-C2-E4-C6-4E-08', where hexadecimal representation of the bytes is used in both cases.

The Information Field

This field is used to transmit the information carried by the frame, and may consist of any number of symbols from 0 to a maximum limited by the total number of symbols allowed in any FDDI frame (including 4 symbols of the preamble, the end delimiter and frame status), i.e. 9000. The maximum number of symbols allowed in the information field thus depends on how many are left over after the other fields are taken into consideration. Table 4.1 summarises the total number of symbols required before considering those left over for the information field. From Table 4.1, we see that in a 48 bit addressing mode, there can be 8956 symbols used for carrying actual data, assuming the standard minimum length FS field. This equates to 4478 bytes of data, as each symbol carries a nibble (4 bits) of data.

The contents of the information field of the frame depends on the type of frame it is. For example, when carrying MAC control data (indicated by the FC field), a total of 8 symbols (or 4 *octets*) are used to carry the control information as illustrated in Figure 4.4. For an LLC frame, which is used to carry data to and from the higher level protocols, the data field can carry up to the maximum capacity of the frame, i.e. 4478 bytes.

The Frame Checksum

An essential part of the overall frame structure is the frame checksum (FCS), which gives the receiving stations some assurance that the frame was not corrupted in transit. Of course, not every checksum scheme is foolproof, but at least it significantly reduces the chance of errored frames being interpreted as valid, and incorrectly passed to the LLC layer as a good frame.

The checksum itself is an 8 symbol (4 byte) value derived from the frame control

Table 4.1 *MAC frame overhead symbols*

No. of Symbols	**16 bit Addressing**	**48 bit Addressing**
Preamble (PA)	4	4
Start Delimiter (SD)	2	2
Frame Control (FC)	2	2
Destination Address (DA)	4	12
Source Address (SA)	4	12
Frame Checksum (FCS)	8	8
End Delimiter (ED)	1	1
Frame Status (FS)	3+	3+
Total	**28**	**44**

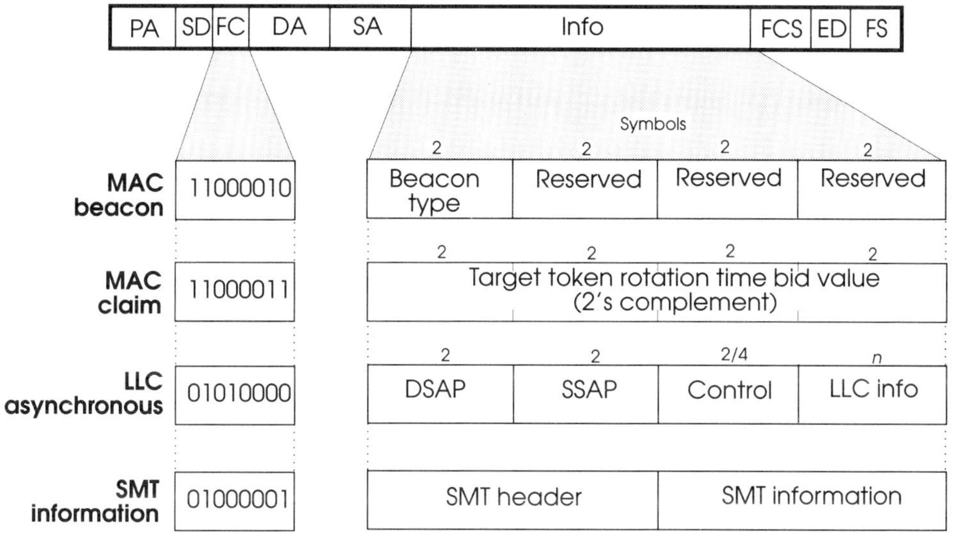

Figure 4.4 *Example contents of information field of frame*

field of the frame, right through to, and including, the FCS field itself. The FCS is calculated on the fly, i.e. whilst the data is being transmitted out of the station. This means that the job is performed in hardware as opposed to software. As every station receives and repeats the frame, it performs a check by recalculating the checksum, and comparing it to the FCS field in the frame as it passes through (or is copied by) the station. If a mismatch occurs, then the error (E) symbol in the frame status field is set from R to S. If the station was copying the frame into memory, it may still retain the frame, or opt to have it automatically flushed out of its memory, depending on the hardware configuration used.

End of Frame Delimiter and Status

The final part of any frame or token is the end delimiter (ED). In the case of frames, an additional frame status field is appended.

For the token, the ED is simply two consecutive terminate (T) symbols, making up an even number of symbols (figure 4.5b). A frame, however, has only a single T as part of its ED. This is followed by the frame status symbols, EAC, *errored frame*, *address recognised* and *frame copied* (Figure 4.5a). In each of these symbol fields, either a *reset* (R) or *set* (S) indicates the appropriate condition for the frame. These first three symbols are mandatory, and their function will be explained in more detail as we look at data transmission within a station. It is also possible, but not used a great deal, to have additional status symbols that are implementor defined. Even if other

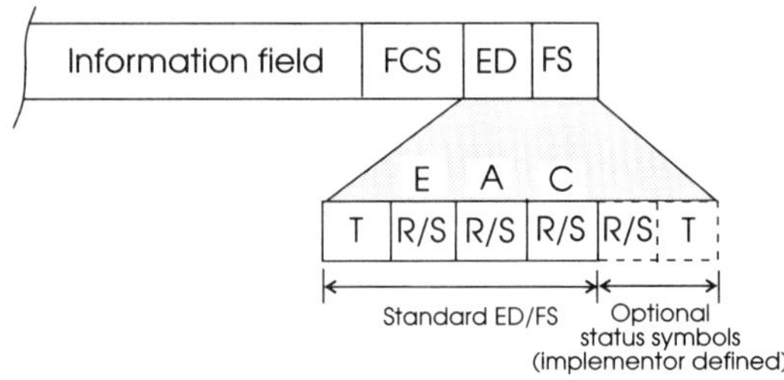

(a) Frame end delimeter and status

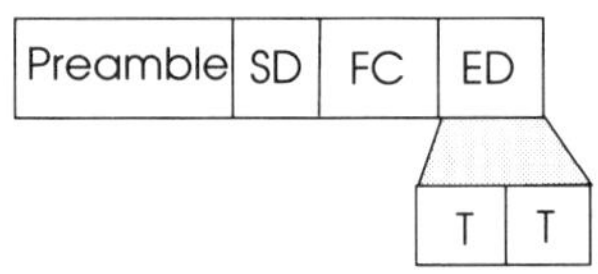

(b)Token end delimeter

Figure 4.5 *End delimiter and frame status fields*

stations in the network do not recognise these additional status symbols, they must still repeat them along with the frame. The total number of symbols in the ED and FS fields must always be an even number, hence a trailing terminate (T) symbol may be necessary to pad out the field.

A Basic Model for a Station

Now that we have looked at the structure of the FDDI protocol data units, and explained each of the fields within the frame, let us move on to look in more detail at how each station handles the token and frames as they enter and leave the station.

Figure 4.6 illustrates a simple representation of a single attachment station in FDDI. The model depicts the main functions of a station and its primary input and output paths, and is useful to explain the various operations that a station has to perform whilst in the ring. The serial bit stream entering a station (1) can either be copied into the input data buffer (2), thrown into a hypothetical data bin (3) and/or repeated on out of the station again (4). When a station wishes to transmit a serial bit stream onto the ring, it must first capture the token (5), before transmitting data out of its output buffer (6). When a station is idle, and not repeating an incoming bit stream, it sources idles (7).

When a station is idle, i.e. it has not captured the token and no frames or tokens are being received, then the station just continually sources idles on its output port, and throws anything that is not a valid PDU into the bin (Figure 4.7a). For a network that is totally quiet, only idles should be received. If a PDU is received, then the station does

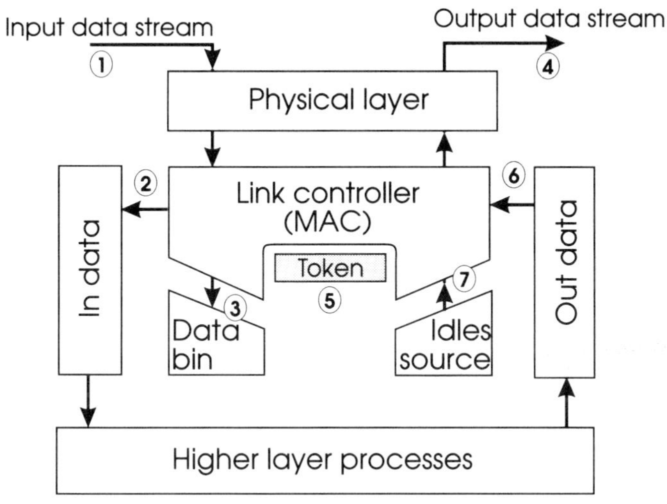

Figure 4.6 *Model representation for a single attachment station*

one of a number of things, covered in the following sections.

Transmission of a Frame

If the PDU received is a token, then the station either repeats it onto the next station or captures it, if it has data to be transmitted onto the network. A frame, or number of frames, may then be output until the station has completed its transmission, or it exceeds the allotted *token holding time*. Whilst the station is transmitting, anything that comes into its input port, such as a frame fragment created by the stripping process, is thrown into the data bin (Figure 4.7b).

Repeating and Receiving a Frame

When a station does not possess the token, if a *start delimiter* (SD) is detected, all the following symbols (provided they are valid) are repeated onto the next station in the ring regardless of whether they are for this station or not. When the destination address (DA) field has been completely read in, it is compared to the station's own address (MA – my address), and if the same, then the frame (minus SD and ED fields) is copied into the station's internal memory or receive buffer. If the frame is not individually addressed to this station, the frame may still be copied if it has either a broadcast address, or a recognised group address. If the address field does not match, then the frame is simply repeated onto the next station without being copied

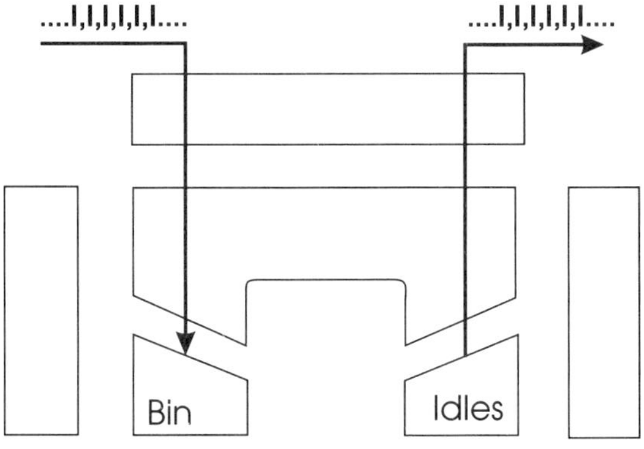

(a) Station inactive or idling

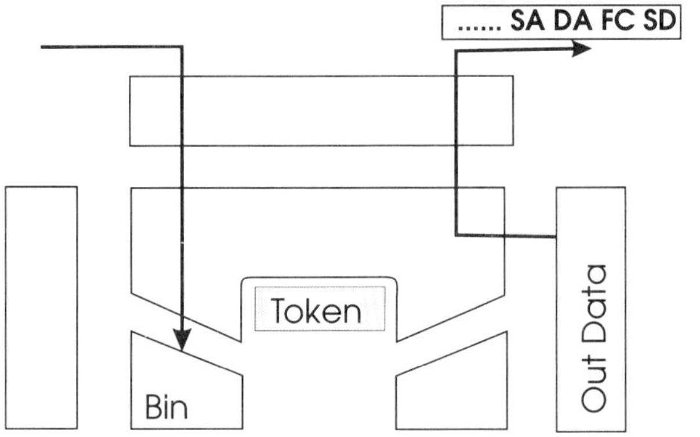

(b) Station captured token and transmitting a frame

Figure 4.7 *Station in quiet and transmit mode*

(Figure 4.8a). A match between the station's own address and the destination address field (indicating that the frame is for this station) causes the *address recognised* (A) field in the frame status to be set to S. This happens regardless of whether or not the frame is successfully copied, so that the originating station may see that the receiving station has at least seen the frame.

During frame reception (Figure 4.8b), once the frame has been completely copied into the receive buffer, the *copied* (C) symbol in the frame status field is changed from R to S. The C field is a useful indication to the sending station that the frame was successfully copied. It is possible for the receiving station to start receiving a frame, and then to abort copying the frame to its internal store due to a buffer overflow, for instance. In this case, the C field is left as an R, and appropriately detected by the

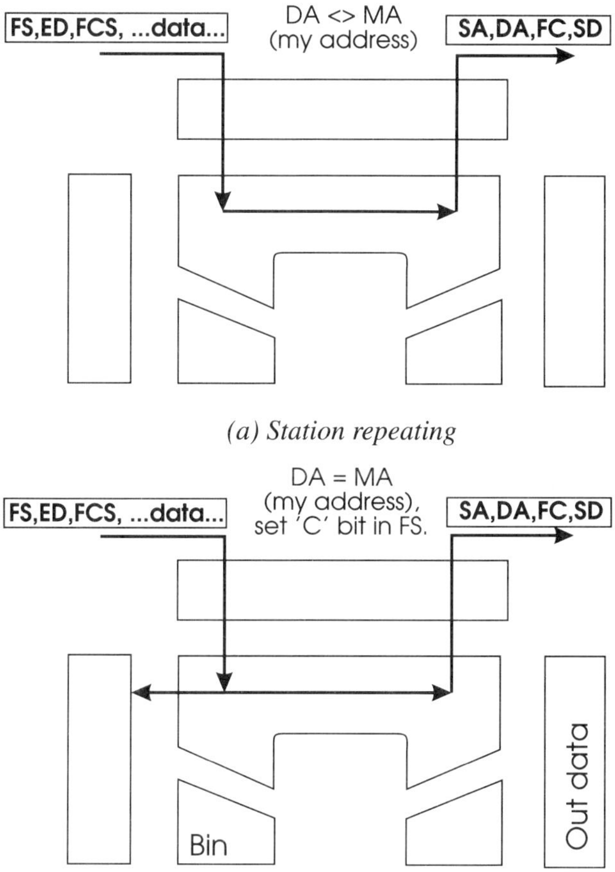

(a) Station repeating

(b) Station repeating and receiving a frame

Figure 4.8 *Station repeating and receiving a frame*

sending station.

The station also checks the frame checksum by recalculating it and comparing it with the value received. If these are different, indicating that the contents of the frame have been changed in some fashion, then the E or *errored* symbol field is changed to S. This errored condition is indicated to the station, which in normal operation, discards the contents of the section of receive buffer containing that frame. If the E field was already set by a previous station, then the same applies. Some stations, especially those performing network analysis or management, may wish to keep the received frame, even though it has an error, in order to analyse the problem.

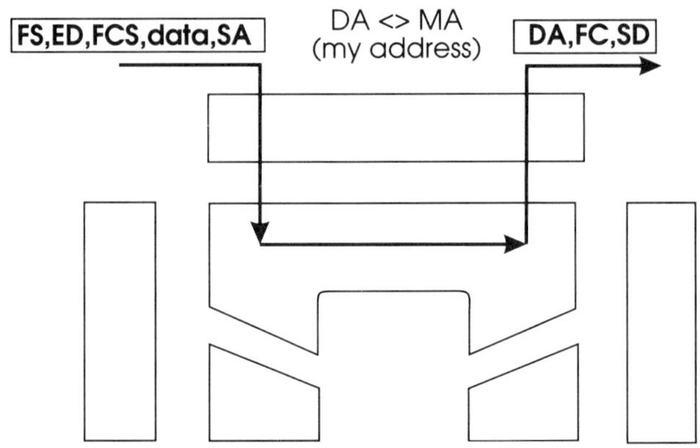

(a) Station starts repeating (DA<>MA)

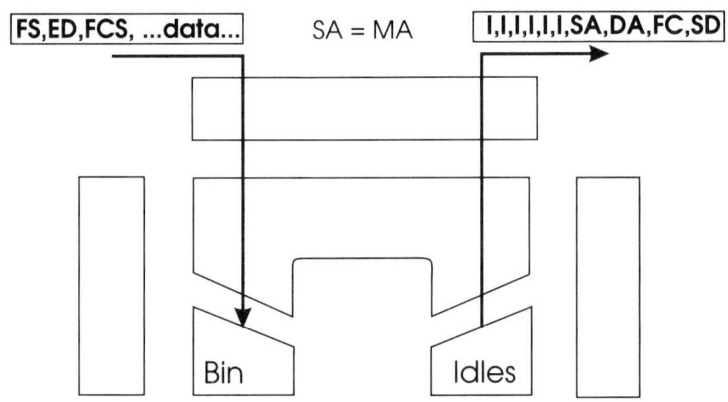

(b) As SA=MA (i.e., own frame), strips frame by sourcing idles instead of repeating

Figure 4.9 *Station stripping its own transmitted frame*

Frame Stripping

Once the frame has completely circulated the ring, and hopefully been copied by the receiving station, then it is the responsibility of the station who originated it in the first place to strip it from the ring. Figure 4.9 illustrates the process. The station starts by repeating the frame until it sees the frame's source address (SA) field, which in this case is equal to its own address. Once the SA field has been completely received and recognised, the station immediately begins throwing all further input symbols into the *data bin* and starts sourcing idles on the output port. This creates a *frame fragment* which continues to circulate around the ring.

At first sight, it may seem that after a while the network will become swamped by frame fragments. This is not the case. If we refer to the situation where a station has captured the token, then we see that all incoming symbols, regardless of whether or not they have a valid start sequence (i.e. a JK symbol pair), are all discarded (or thrown into our hypothetical bin). Hence these frame fragments are eventually removed when any station in the ring captures the token and starts transmitting, making the network self-regulating. If no station captures the token for a while, then fragments will not be removed, but as the network is not being used, this does not matter.

Example Ring Operation

Now that we have a better understanding of the various elements that make up a station, and how stations operate, let us take a look at an example of one station transmitting to another on the same ring structure (Figure 4.10).

For the purpose of this discussion, we will assume that the ring has been initialised and the token is already circulating around the ring. Another assumption we will make for such a small ring is that the delays between stations are over-exaggerated, such that a complete frame or token can exist between stations. In reality, it is most probable that on such a small network, a station will be receiving the front end of its own transmitted frame while it is still transmitting. The process is shown as is, to enable a clear picture of what is going on in the network. What typically happens in a real world transmission is examined later on in this chapter.

Figure 4.10 illustrates nine different stages in the FDDI transmission process between two stations, and also how the various 'leftovers' (fragments, etc.) are cleaned up automatically by the network. The ring starts off in an idle state, illustrated by the presence if idle symbols. Figure 4.10 also illustrates how *truncated tokens* are created each time a station captures a token, as the repeating process cannot identify a valid frame or token until the full FC field has been received, by which stage part of it has already been repeated. Even the truncated token is continually repeated around the ring until cleaned up by a transmitting station. Removing of frame and token fragments is carried out by a station that has captured the token, as illustrated in Figure 4.7(b).

Station A in this example starts by capturing the token and transmitting a frame destined for station C. The resulting truncated token and transmitted frame are repeated by B, and the frame copied by C. Copying the frame results in the *frame-copied* indicator being set as the frame is being repeated by C. Station D repeats the frame (and the leading truncated token), and A, seeing its own frame, strips it off the ring, creating a frame fragment in the process. Station D then captures the token in order to transmit, and whilst holding the token, throws the truncated token and frame fragments from A's activity into its data bin.

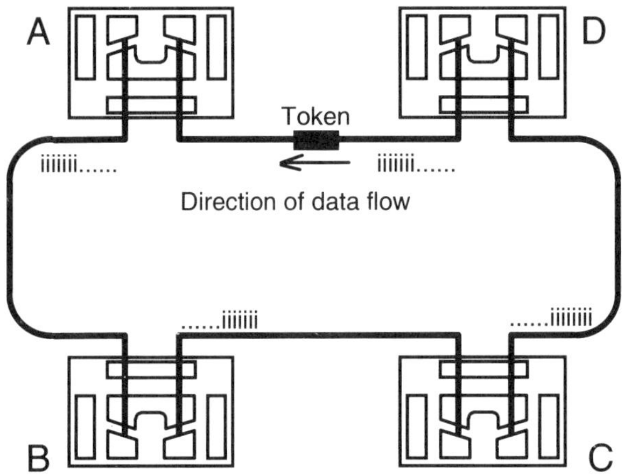

(a) The ring is quiet, with the token freely circulating around the network. All the Stations are transmitting idles on the output port, and throw anything other than a valid start of frame or token into the data bin. When a station sees the start of the token (SD), it starts repeating until it sees a valid end of frame terminator. As we shall see later, the ring does not contain purely idles if it has been operational before.

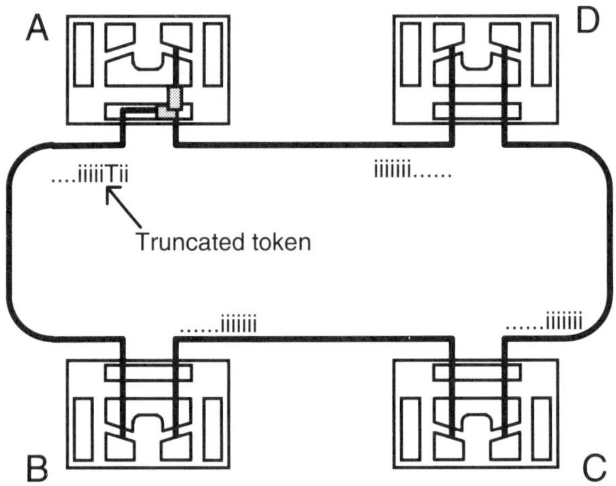

(b) Station A captures the token in order to transmit a frame. As it does not know that it is a token until it has seen the FC field, it repeats the SD portion, throwing the rest of the token away. Idles are transmitted immediately after the SD field, creating a truncated token (T).

Figure 4.10 *Example ring operation*

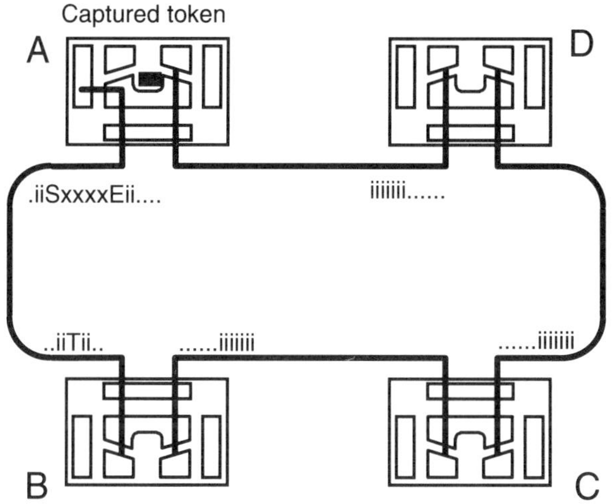

(c) Station A, now with a captured token, transmits a frame destined for station C. The frame starts to circulate the network towards B which is currently still in idle transmit mode (i.e. quiet mode), as are the other stations. When the truncated token arrives at B, it is simply regenerated at B's output as the SD is seen as a valid start of frame before the following idles are detected.

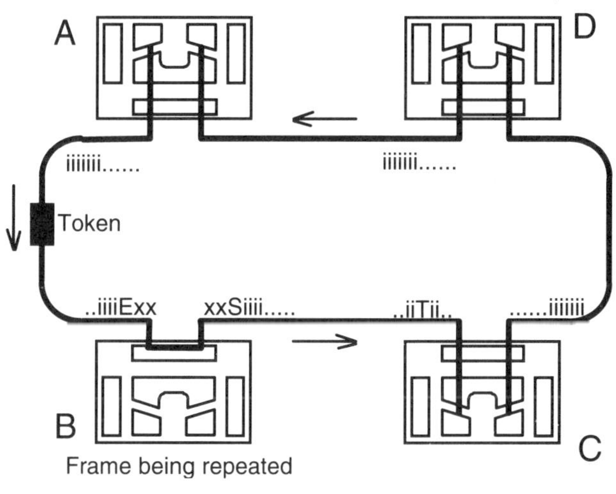

(d) Station B sees the frame header and starts repeating it. It also checks for DA=MA (B's frame?). Seeing it isn't, it continues to repeat the frame until is sees ED (E), checking for errors and updating FS field if necessary. After ED, B starts sourcing idles. A then releases the token as it has no other frames to send.

Figure 4.10 *Example ring operation (continued)*

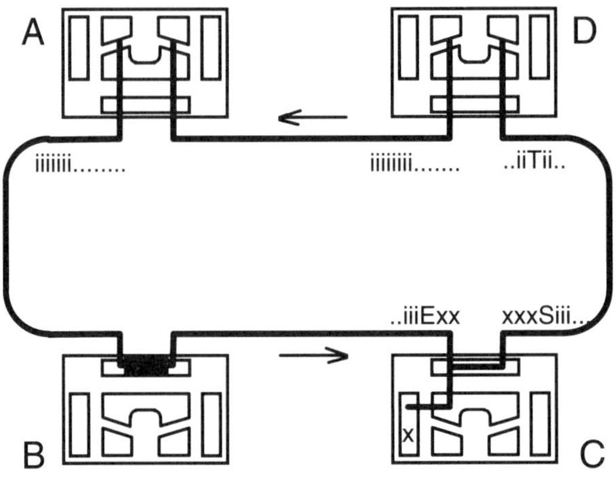

(e) Station C now sees the start of the frame, recognises the DA field as its own, and then starts copying the frame contents into its internal memory. Station C sets the address recognised (A) field in the frame status and also the copy field (C) if a successful copy occurred. Station B sees the token, and repeats it as it has no frames to transmit.

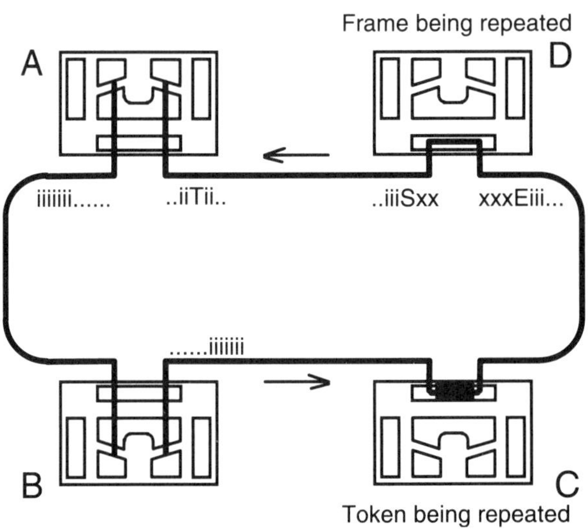

(f) The now received frame continues to circulate around to D, where it is repeated in the normal fashion. The token is repeated by C, again because C does not need to transmit anything yet.

Figure 4.10 *Example ring operation (continued)*

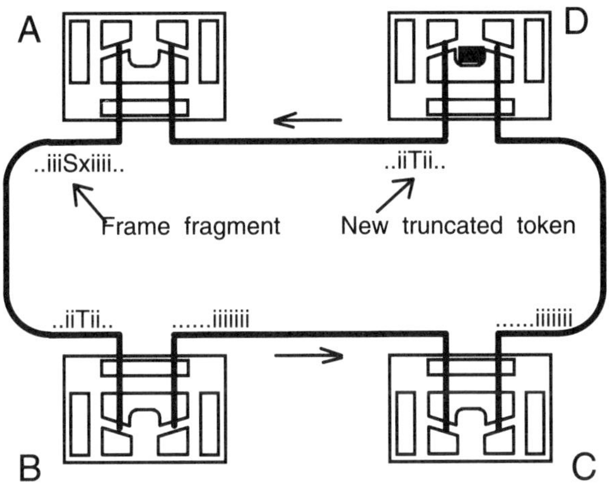

(g) We have now reached the point where A's original frame has come back. A does not know this until the SA field passes through, so it continues to repeat. Once it sees the SA, it starts stripping the frame by sourcing idles. Meanwhile, station D captures the token as it wishes to transmit data, creating a new truncated token in the process

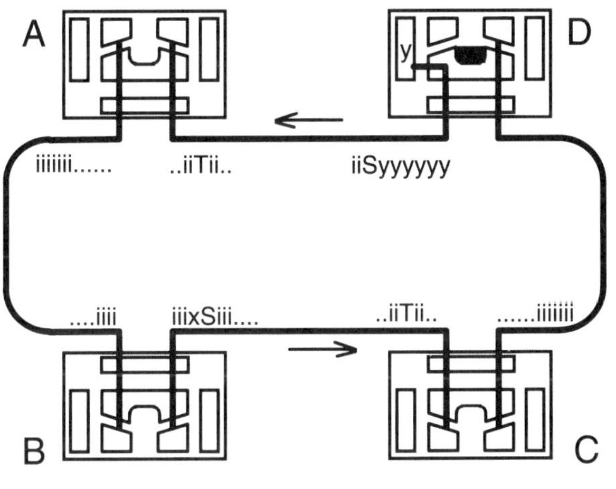

(h) Station D then starts transmitting a new frame onto the ring. The remaining fragments are still circulating the network, i.e. the fragmented frame from A and now two truncated tokens.

Figure 4.10 *Example ring operation (continued)*

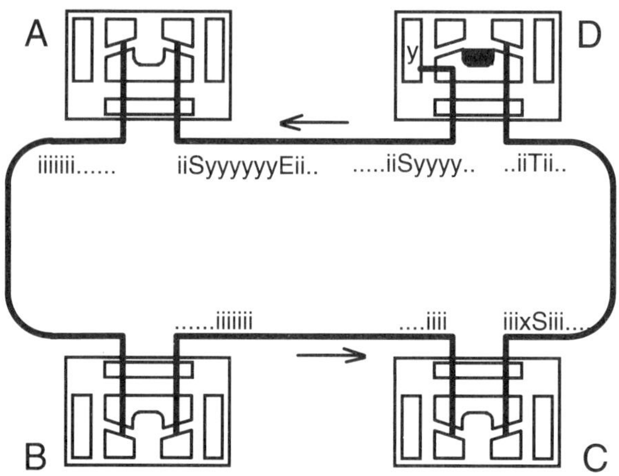

(i) D continues to transmit a second frame onto the network. Frame fragments are thrown away into D's data bin as D is the holder of the token. Thus, the first truncated token will be removed, the second will follow, and finally A's fragmented frame. The longer D holds onto the token, the more fragments will be removed from the ring.

Figure 4.10 *Example of ring operation (continued)*

Frame Transmission Services and Token Control

From the example operation shown in Figure 4.10, let us now move on to look in more detail at how frame transmissions are classified, and how FDDI implements the token access mechanism.

FDDI defines two classes of frame transmission service, namely *asynchronous* and *synchronous*. The latter provides a unique feature of FDDI networks, in that it allows data to be sent across the network in an almost deterministic and guaranteed fashion for many applications, a feature not found in other mainstream LAN technologies. By almost deterministic, we mean that data can be transmitted and guaranteed to reach its destination within a time limit related to the current token rotation time, as we shall see later. This means that a synchronous *channel* may be set up for transmission of time-critical data, such as real-time control information, and also multimedia traffic such as packet compressed video and voice, where compression has removed the strict requirement for a constant bit stream service. Asynchronous traffic is that sent after all critical frames (i.e. synchronous) have been transmitted, and there is still available bandwidth left. Asynchronous services are those normally used in most other LANs, such as Ethernet and Token Ring.

To allow such tight control to be maintained over the data frames and their transmission schedule times onto the network ring, FDDI uses what is referred to as a *timed token protocol.* A number of timers are utilised to ensure that each station handles the token correctly, and within an allotted time defined at network initialisation. Priority is given to any synchronous data frames the station may wish to transmit, and these are transmitted onto the network before any asynchronous frames are allowed to be transmitted. Priority levels may also be assigned to asynchronous frames queued in the station's output buffer, ensuring that certain predetermined asynchronous frames are transmitted before others.

The timed token protocol defines a process that decides if a station has enough time to transmit asynchronous frames onto the network, or whether it has to release the token it has captured and defer until next time round. The protocol operates such that fair access is given to every station on the network. This means that if a station misses out, or can only transmit a small number of frames because another station held onto the token for a maximum length of time, it will be able to get access later on. The whole mechanism has been carefully proven to ensure that the token is always guaranteed to rotate quickly enough to prevent the network falling over when heavily loaded (Johnson, 1987). A special *restricted token* mode is available for special cases where extended dialogue between two stations is absolutely necessary.

The following sections describe a number of important aspects of frame transmission, specifically how frames are queued within a station as they enter and leave, and the purpose and effect of the station's token timers, along with priorities in frame transmission. The example of Figure 4.10 is then analysed in terms of its timers.

Frame Queues

The concept of queuing is used frequently in LAN data frame transmission and reception. FDDI typically uses a number of these data queues for buffering frames for transmission or those received from the network. Figure 4.11 illustrates the basic concept of a transmission queue based on a cyclic buffer. Frames for transmission are placed into the queue by the host and removed by the FDDI LAN controller. Data pointers are used to keep track of the current frame positions, both for the host and the controller as they are always different when data is in the queue waiting for transmission. In a similar fashion, data is placed in a receive queue by the controller, and removed by the host. The size of the queues, and the number of data frames they may store depend on the data frames themselves, and the available memory allocated. For example, a total of 64 kbytes of memory may be available for a single queue, meaning that it may hold around fourteen maximum sized FDDI frames before its becomes full. As the queue is only a temporary storage location for data before it is either passed to the network or the host, the overall size is not so important as the ability of the host and controller to match each other's fill and empty rates. A queue is easily determined to be empty (i.e. nothing left to transmit or remove) when the 'write to' and 'read from' pointers point to the same storage location.

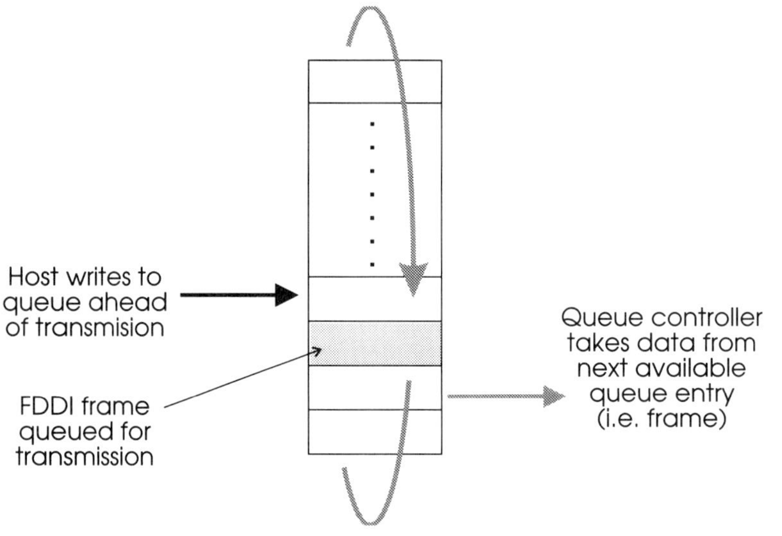

Figure 4.11 *Frame queuing principle*

FDDI stations use at least one queue or buffer for transmission, and one for reception. Normally, only a single receive queue is required, possibly two to separate out higher-layer (LLC) data traffic from SMT management frames, for example. For transmission, more than one queue may be employed, depending on the station's requirements. For instance, there may be a number of asynchronous queues for traffic of different priorities, and a synchronous queue if the station uses synchronous services (Figure 4.12). An additional queue is usually employed for storing special control frames (such as claim or beacon) that may be used when the station enters recovery mode.

The Timed Token Protocol

To implement the timed token protocol, each station in the network must have three mandatory timers. These are defined as follows:

- Token rotation timer (TRT)
- Token holding timer (THT)
- Valid transmission timer (TVX)

Each of these timers (Figure 4.13) is used to control the scheduling process of transmitting frames. Basically, they control the length of time a station may transmit a frame for, before the token is reissued. They also allow the total time taken for a token to travel completely around the ring to be monitored. A number of actions are possible

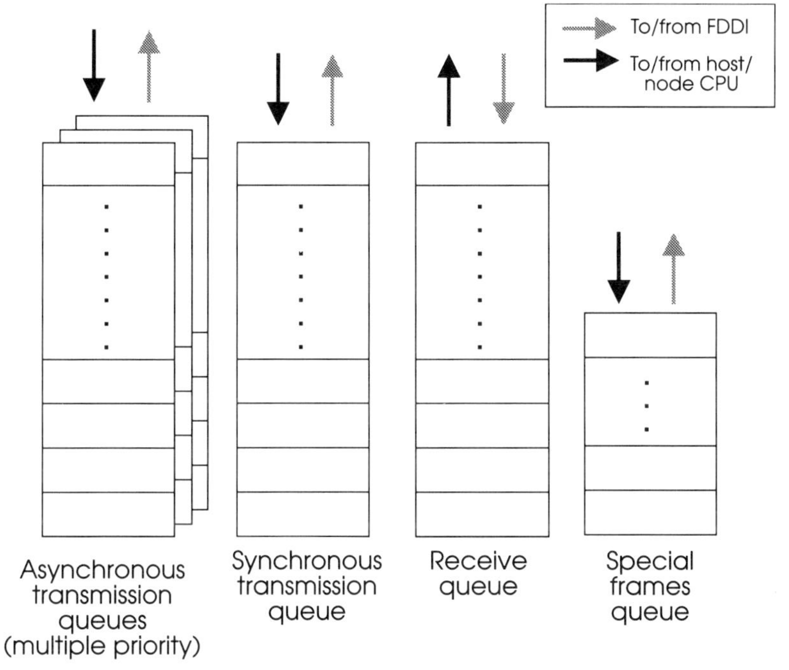

Figure 4.12 *Example frame queues for an FDDI station*

when a timer expires either normally or abnormally, and these will be discussed shortly.

In addition to the above three timers, a fourth synchronous timer may be employed if synchronous services are supported within the station. The timer itself is not specifically defined in the standards, but is often implemented as a hardware timer inside the MAC layer VLSI devices within a station. For the purpose of these discussions, the timer is referred to as the TMSYNC timer. This is preloaded with a value stored in a TSYNC register, defining the maximum length of time a station may transmit synchronous frames for.

The timers themselves are typically implemented as up counters (i.e. they increment with time), and hence for a timer to 'expire' i.e. reach the value zero, it is loaded with a binary 2's complement value of the parameter it is timing.

Token Rotation and Holding Timers

The purpose of the TRT is to monitor the time the token takes to traverse the ring completely and return back to a particular station. Every station in the network has a TRT, and hence monitors this parameter on an individual basis. During the network initialisation process, a *claim process* is used to establish what the average, or *target*

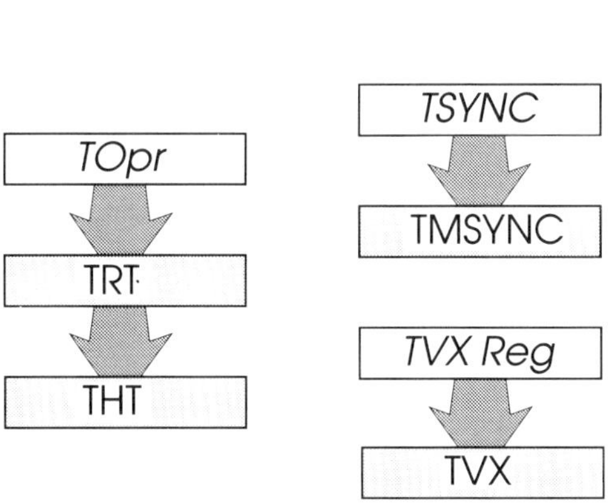

Figure 4.13 *Token related timers*

token rotation time (TTRT) should be. This is a process whereby each station bids a particular value and the station with the lowest time wins. The lowest bid wins because it is assumed that the station bidding the lowest value requires the token to circulate at this rate to meet its application communications requirements. Every station in the network stores in its TTRT register this lowest value, also referred to as the *operative target token rotation time*, or TOpr.

Whenever a token is received by a station, the value of TRT is effectively compared to the value of TOpr to see if the token has arrived before the operative rotation time, or after. If before, then the token is classed as an *early token* and may be captured for data transmission. This may be either synchronous and/or asynchronous data transmissions. If the value of TRT is greater than TOpr, the token is classed as a *late token* and only synchronous transmissions are possible. Once the token is captured, then the token holding timer (THT) is used to ensure that it is not held for too long. The processes involved are illustrated in Figure 4.14.

In any circumstances, the timers in a station ensure that the token is held for no more than TOpr, plus the time it takes to complete its frame transmission at the time of expiry (which could be just less than a full-sized frame). The net effect of all this is that the token should never take more than 2 × TOpr to completely circumvent the ring. If TRT should exceed this value, then the ring recovery process is initiated as it is assumed that the ring is no longer functioning correctly. This 2 × TOpr condition is detected by TRT expiring twice. The first time TRT expires, a 'Late_Ct' (late count) flag is set. If TRT expires while this flag is set, then ring goes into recovery mode, as illustrated.

THT is used only during asynchronous data transmission, and is disabled at other times, e.g. during synchronous data transmissions. It is loaded with the value of TRT following token capturc, provided the token is not late, otherwise it is set to expired to prevent any asynchronous transmission taking place. When THT is loaded with TRT, at the same time TRT is loaded with TOpr to start timing the next token rotation (even

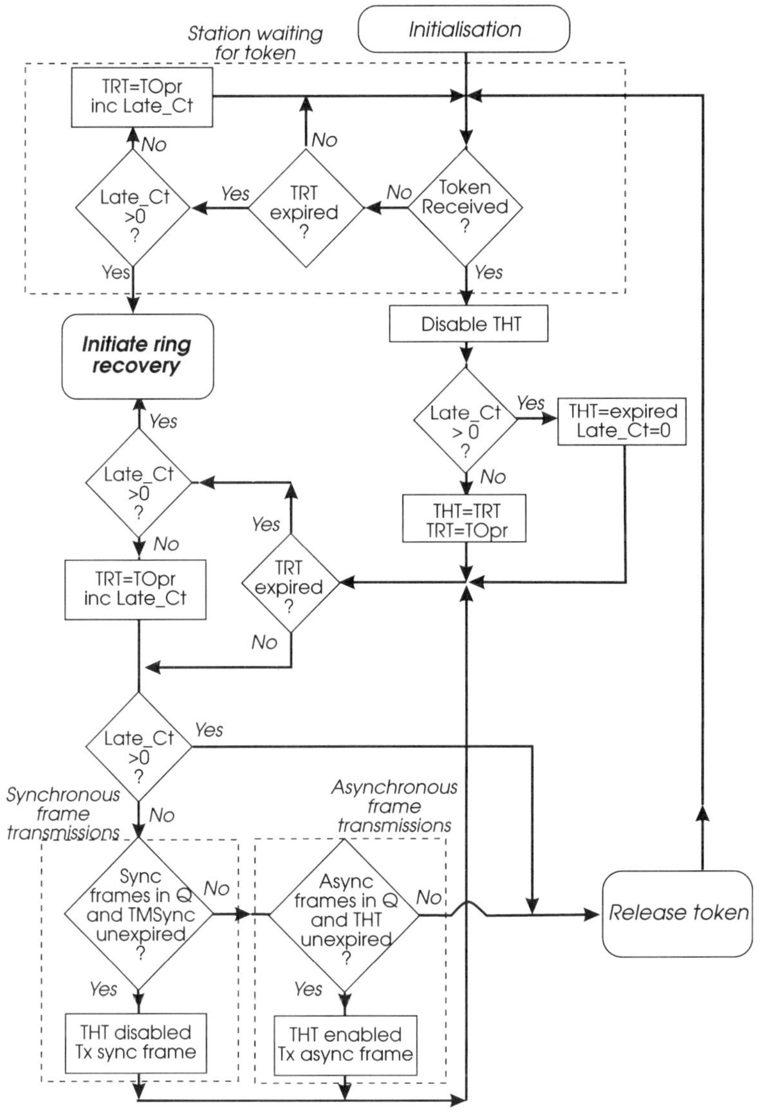

Figure 4.14 *High level timer operation*

though this station still has the token). Synchronous data frames are always given priority, and transmitted first. As the THT is disabled during this time, the other timer, TMSYNC, is used to control the period of synchronous frame transmission. Once completed, provided that TRT has not expired, THT is enabled, and asynchronous data transmitted whilst THT is unexpired. Once THT expires, the token must be released after the current asynchronous frame has been transmitted.

Synchronous Timers

As mentioned above, TMSYNC, is used for timing synchronous traffic. It is preloaded, as shown in Figure 4.14, with TSYNC before synchronous transmissions begin. Support of the TMSYNC timer is optional, and not required by stations that do not support synchronous transmissions. Also, note that TMSYNC and TSYNC are not defined explicitly by the standards, and are used here only for the purpose of explaining the restriction of synchronous traffic. They may well be referred to as something completely different in manufacturer's data, or other textbooks on FDDI.

The TMSYNC preload value, stored in the TSYNC register, is determined via a *synchronous bandwidth allocation* (SBA) process, which every station requesting synchronous bandwidth must go through before it can even use synchronous data transmissions. Hence, when a station first powers up, it will always have its synchronous value, TSYNC, usually set to its expired value, and any synchronous queues disabled. Chapter 7 discusses this process in more detail. A station requests a certain amount of synchronous bandwidth from a central SBA manager. The amount requested is based on a percentage of the overall network bandwidth (100 Mbps), and is also related to the token rotation time, TOpr. The total synchronous time that a station requests will be a percentage of the overall TOpr. For example, if an 8 msec TOpr is in operation, then it may allocate say, 1 msec for synchronous traffic. The actual requested values are based on allocations of 64 kbps units (125 μs time slot) from the telecommunication industry standard digital voice encoding scheme, pulse code modulation (PCM).

Once the TMSYNC timer has expired, the station then either starts its asynchronous transmissions as described above, or releases the token.

Frame Transmission Priorities

As we saw in earlier sections, the FC field allows an asynchronous frame to carry an appropriate priority indication. Up to a total of eight levels are defined, and these may be used to allow a station LAN controller to determine, in times of heavy network loading, which are the more important frames to transmit. On the receiving side, it may also detect the incoming priority of a frame, and place it into the appropriate queue to the host. To take a particular example, an application running on the host may wish to assign one traffic type, such as TCP/IP traffic (carrying mainly email), to a low priority level, Netware IPX to a medium level (client/server applications), and IBM SNA traffic to a high priority transmission queue (mainframe connection oriented connectivity). In FDDI, this would be carried out by setting up a number of queues for transmission (all asynchronous for this case) with appropriate TRT priority levels, referred to as TPri(*n*), where *n* is a value 0–7 corresponding to the eight levels of available priority. Hence, in our example above, the SNA frames would be assigned to TPri(0), IPX to TPri(1) and TCP/IP to TPri(2).

Figure 4.15 illustrates how each of the levels may be assigned to give the SNA traffic 60 per cent of the asynchronous bandwidth, and the IPX and TCP/IP traffic, 30 and 10 per cent respectively. The mechanism is such that when the token is captured, and asynchronous transmissions can commence, the controller will compare the current value of the THT timer against the values stored in the TPri(0–2) registers. If the value in THT on commencement was at point (a), then only high level and medium priority frames may be transmitted. At point (b), only high priority frames will be transmitted, and at (c), all types will be transmitted. [Note: (a), (b) and (c) correspond to the value that was transferred from the TRT timer on token capture (see Figure 4.14).] In some applications, the priority assignments are those of Token Ring, e.g. n=4 (#100b) is reserved for bridging applications frames.

At the time of writing, no equivalent priority levels have been assigned to the synchronous class, though bits are reserved for this purpose. Efforts are underway in ANSI to produce guidelines for setting of these fields.

Valid Transmission Timer

The TVX is used to detect transient ring errors, operating on a much finer timescale than errors detected by the token timer expiration method. It does this by monitoring the time between the reception of valid frames or tokens. If no frames meeting the validity criteria are received within the allotted time, the ring recovery procedure is initiated.

The TVX expiration time is calculated from a number of ring parameters defined in the standard, and must allow for the maximum length of the ring, the actual transmit length of the token itself, the maximum possible length of a frame and also for any allowable random noise on the ring. Its default value is defined as 62,500 symbol times

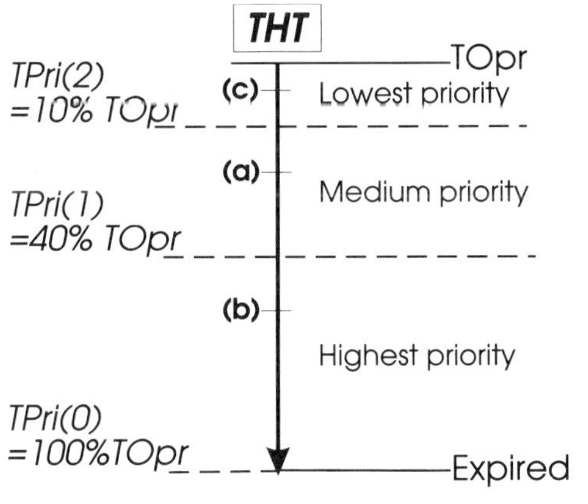

Figure 4.15 *Asynchronous frame priority levels*

or 2.50 msec, though for practical purposes, a value of 2.62144 msec derived from the hardware symbol clock is normally used. This value may be altered by the station if necessary by updating the TVX register which contains the TVX timer reset value. The receiver state machine resets TVX to this value if it sees a ED field of a valid token or frame.

The TVX timer allows a quick recovery mechanism to be initiated if nothing valid appears to be happening on the ring. Under normal circumstances, there should always be something passing by a station, i.e. the token or a valid frame. For example, if there is no activity on the ring, then a valid token is always circulating, and will be repeated (and TVX reset) well within the TVX default of 2.5 msec. If an upstream station captures the token, it should transmit frames immediately following the token capture, followed immediately by the token. However, if the upstream station captures the token, then does not transmit anything at all (or only transmits garbage) within the 2.5 msec, then this station will initiate a ring recovery as it will assume that there is a problem. A similar thing would happen if the upstream station held onto the token after its last frame (perhaps due to a crash), or was simply stuck transmitting garbage or a constant symbol stream. Of course, this would eventually be detected by a 2 × TOpr TRT timeout period as we discussed earlier. However, as a TOpr can be as large as 2 × TMax, i.e. 330 msec, then the TVX method is obviously a better approach. This also highlights the fact that a station should not capture a token unless it has frames already queued for transmission, otherwise it is likely to cause a ring reconfiguration.

Restricted Token

This is a special mode of operation where a number of stations on the network require full use of all available bandwidth on the network. This may be a high-speed memory device in the system somewhere, which receives emergency backup information from a central CPU controlling a device entering power failure, for example. Obviously, the use of a restricted token depends greatly on the application requirements, and is only used in very special cases.

What the restricted token allows is an extended dialogue between the participating stations, ensuring that they are not forced to give in to other stations as with the fair access protocol in non-restricted mode. The whole process is managed by the higher layers of software in the stations involved. One of the stations must first capture the token, and then transmit the necessary control or restricted mode dialogue frame to another station(s) on the network, before issuing a restricted token. This mode is then maintained until higher protocol layers (i.e. layers above the FDDI MAC layer) terminate the process, and return the network to normal operation. Both synchronous and asynchronous traffic is allowed on the network from the stations involved in the restricted mode. All other stations on the network that are not involved are only allowed to capture the token for synchronous transmissions. To ensure that gross unfairness does not result, part of SMT, the ring management or RMT process, monitors the total time that the restricted token mode has been active, and if greater than the value specified by the station management attribute, *T_RMode*, resets the MAC thus initiating ring recovery.

Example TRT and THT Timer Operation

In the example of Figure 4.10, two stations, A and D, transmitted frames onto the network. To illustrate the operation of the timers under such circumstances, consider the following situation.

A is a station that transmits only asynchronous class frames, whilst D transmits both synchronous and asynchronous. The ring has been fairly quiet up the point of transmission activity, hence the token is circulating the ring rapidly. Station A has two lots of asynchronous frame transmissions, the first shorter than the other. D, on the other hand, has a requirement to transmit synchronous frames with a period roughly 1.5–2 times TOpr, along with an asynchronous payload after the first synchronous transmission.

Figure 4.16 illustrates the two sets of timers for stations A and D. The TMSYNC timer has been left out of the picture to keep matters simple. Also, as the timers are effectively up counters, loaded with the 2's complement (i.e. negative equivalent) of the parameter being timed, they are shown as increasing to their 'expired' value of zero. The following stages are highlighted:

1. The ring is quiet, transmitting idles.
2. A captures the token as it has asynchronous frames now queued for transmission. THT is updated with the value in TRT, and enabled.
3. A releases the token before THT expires as it has emptied the asynchronous queue. THT has no relevance until the next token capture.
4. D captures the token on the same rotation as A released it, and starts transmitting synchronous frames for a period defined by TMSYNC, followed by asynchronous frames.
5. As D transmits, A's TRT expires, causing its Late_Ct flag to be set.
6. D is forced to release the token as its THT expires, even though it still has asynchronous frames queued.
7. A wishes to transmit more asynchronous frames, but cannot do so due to its Late_Ct being set. Hence it cannot capture the token when it arrives. On seeing the token, it resets Late_Ct (A) to zero.
8. The token arrives at D, and is recaptured to transmit the remaining asynchronous frames.
9. D releases the token just at the point before THT expires having completed its asynchronous transmissions.
10. A now captures the token, and completes its asynchronous transmissions, as its Late_Ct is zero.
11. A releases the token just before THT expires, with no more frames to transmit.

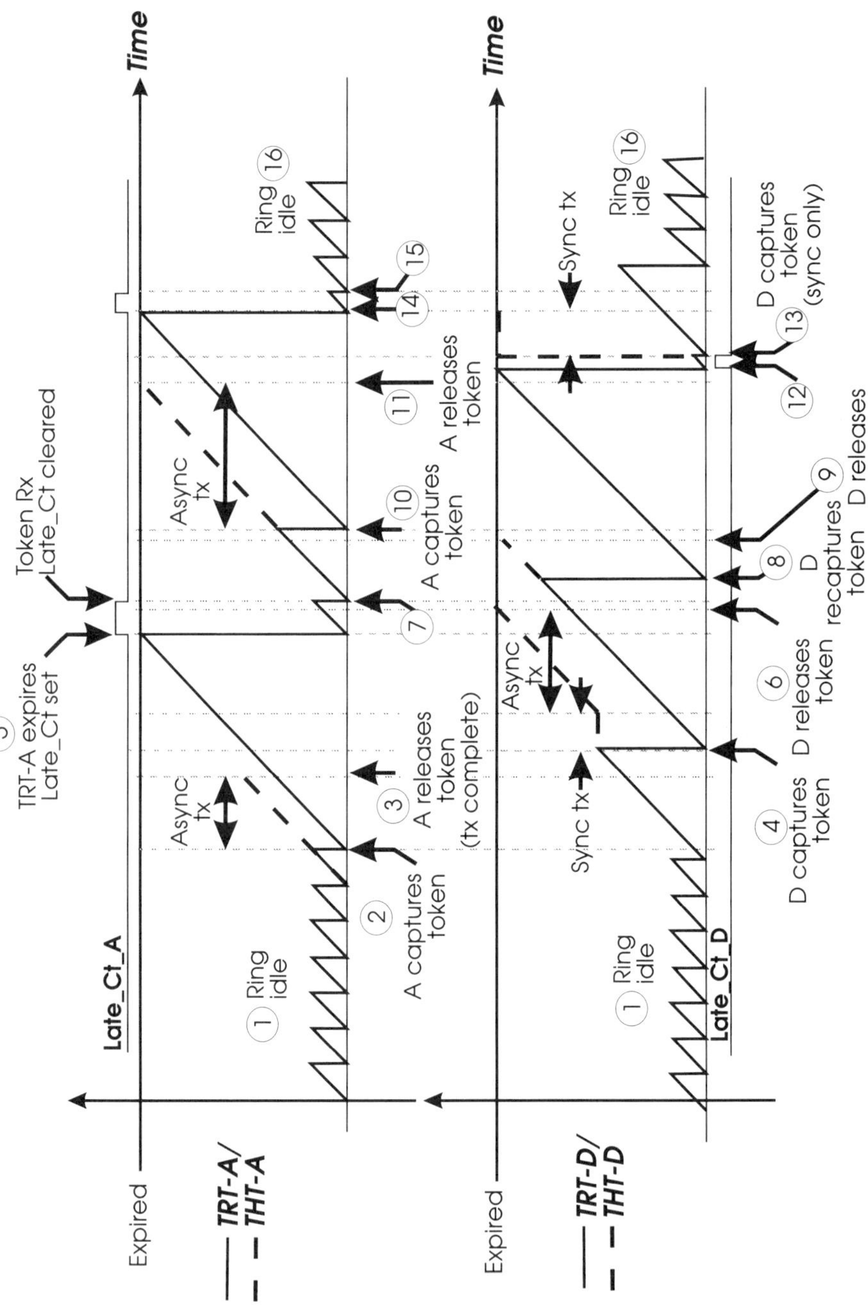

Figure 4.16 *TRT and THT operation for stations A and D (Figure 4.10)*

12. D's TRT expires before the token can arrive, resulting in D's Late_Ct being set.
13. Token arrives at D, and is captured as there are synchronous frames queued.
14. Station A's TRT expires, setting A's Late_Ct. A has no frames to transmit, so this does not affect it.
15. The next rotation of the token clears A's Late_Ct.
16. Ring returns to idle state.

Recall from Chapter 1 that Ethernet uses a CSMA/CD, or collision-based access mechanism, based on random backoff times to ensure that multiple stations do not continually collide. For FDDI, the balancing of the access to the available network bandwidth is much more predictable, and controlled. Notice from Figure 4.16 how station A is held off from transmitting any further frames at point (7). At first, this may seem unfair as it only transmitted a low number of asynchronous frames the first time round. D on the other hand used up its entire token opportunity, causing A to set its Late_Ct, yet it still captures the token the next time around. However, D's THT this time has less available time for transmission (even though D empties its asynchronous queue), hence D can only transmit for a fraction of the time it did before. Thus D is limited on its second time, allowing A (and other stations) to recapture some bandwidth due to D's shorter token holding time. From this, we see the dynamic loading capability of FDDI's timed token protocol a little clearer, ensuring that all stations get fair access to the network.

The Real World

Now that we have looked at the theoretical aspects of FDDI transmissions, based on exaggerated delays, let us take a little look at what actually happens in the real world.

Figure 4.17 illustrates a station that is transmitting single symbols as part of a frame. The symbol leaving the station is called symbol *n*, and the other, at some point on the network, *n+y*, where *y* represents the *y*th symbol ahead of the *n*th. The value t_{del} represent the typical delay encountered by symbols being repeated through a station, i.e. around 15 symbols (taken from the MAC standard for the sake of this discussion). If t_{sym} represents the time length for a single symbol, then as 8 nsec is the time for one bit in FDDI (1/125 Mbps), one symbol is 40 nsec. Thus the total delay through a station is around 600 nsec.

Taking a typical value for the speed of light travelling through optical fibre of 5.085 nsec/m (taken from MAC standard), then we see that a single symbol will take up roughly (40/5.085) m, i.e. approximately 7.87 m. Hence, a maximum sized 9000 symbol FDDI frame including preamble will occupy roughly 70 km. Hence you see that from our simple example in Figure 4.15, a single frame would more than fully occupy even a maximum length of single-mode fibre!

The above implies that a station, in a small to medium sized network, will more often than not be receiving the start of its own frame before it has even finished transmitting it. The maximum length of the frame that can exist on the ring at any one time is a function of the transmission line delay plus the delay through the station. Assuming the delay values above, then the number of symbols that can exist on a fibre ring at any one time is plotted in Figure 4.18 against the total stations and fibre length. This, of course, assumes uniform station delays, which in practice differ across different product types and vendors. For example, if two other stations were in a ring with 1000 m of cable, then after approximately 157 symbols (78.5 bytes) the station will start to see its own frame arrive whilst it is still transmitting. The graph shows the effect extrapolated out for greater ring sizes and stations.

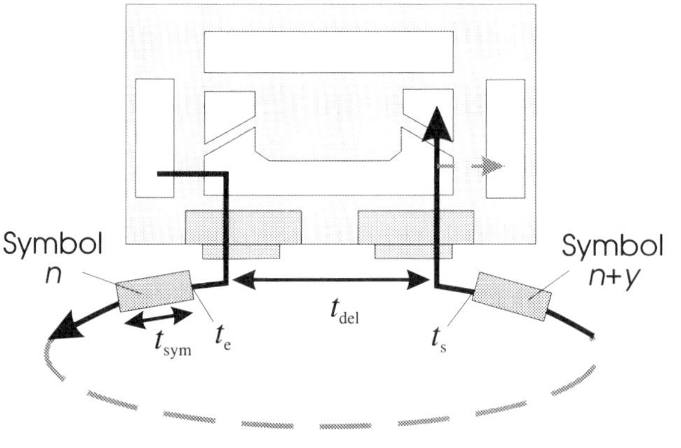

Figure 4.17 *Delays in the real world*

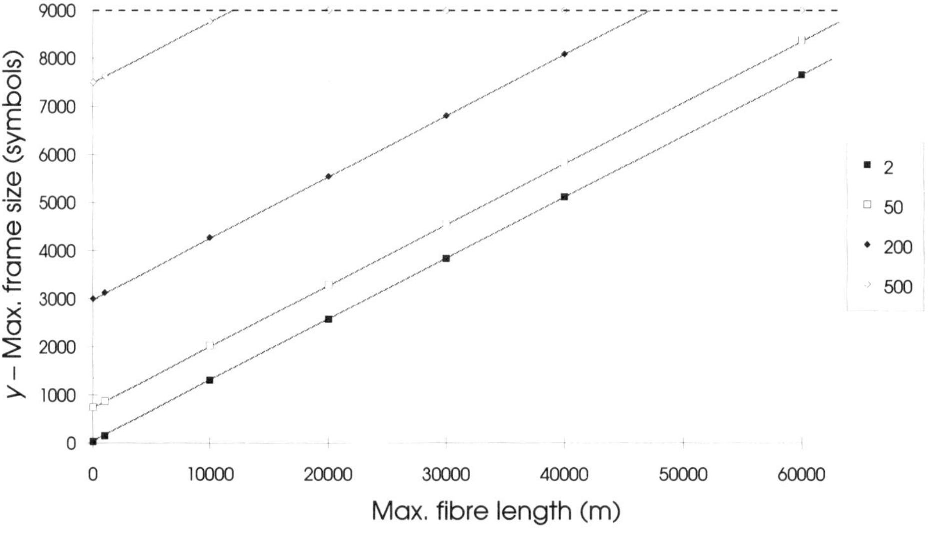

Figure 4.18 *Maximum symbols on ring vs. total fibre length and stations*

Higher-Layer Interfacing

Figure 4.4 illustrated some of the frame types encountered in FDDI, and their information field contents. The LLC frame carries higher-layer software and protocols. The MAC layer ensures the reliable delivery of each MAC-LLC frame, and also handles priorities (up to eight levels, as we saw earlier). What the MAC layer does not do is attempt to retransmit frames that were not successfully copied by the recipient, or that became corrupted *en route* to the destination. This is handled by the higher-layer protocols, based on the success/failure status provided by the MAC for each MAC frame transmission. The LLC layer provides a network transparent interface to the network layer and above, as we shall see in later chapters.

LLC Frame Format

Figure 4.19 illustrates the LLC frame format defined by the IEEE 802.2 standard. The LLC format uses an addressing scheme that defines a number of possible *service access point* (SAP) addresses in a peer-to-peer LLC communications process. These are referred to as the destination and source SAPs, or *DSAP* and *SSAP*. Unlike the MAC level addresses we have encountered earlier which address individual network MAC nodes, these addresses are applicable to different services or protocol stacks above the LLC sub-layer (Figure 4.20). For example, this may be a station running two separate applications in a multitasking environment, one utilising TCP/IP as its network protocol, and the other, say, Netware IPX. SAP addresses consist of two reserved bits to identify *global* or *local* addressing, and *group* or *individual* in much the same manner as for the 16/48 bit MAC addressing discussed earlier. Hence, a global SAP address will consist of all 1's (i.e. all SAPs, or broadcast SAP address). A SAP address of all 0's refers to the data link itself, and is thus not used for higher-layer protocol identification.

The control field of the LLC frame indicates the type of LLC frame (Chapter 1), along with specific control fields associated with the type. Three different LLC PDUs

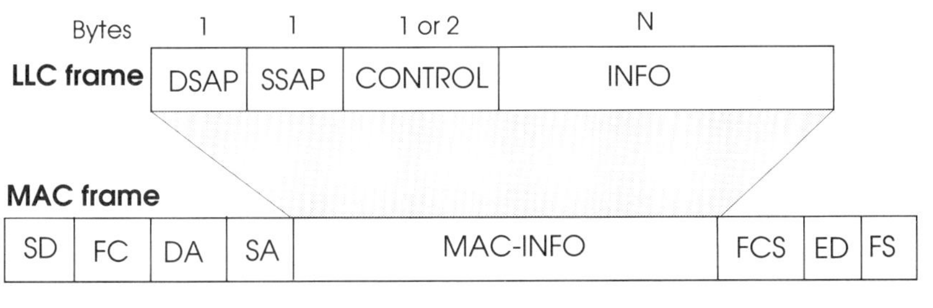

Figure 4.19 *Logical link control (LLC) frame format*

are defined, namely I-Format (I–information transfer), S-Format (S–supervisory) and U-Format (U–unnumbered). The one of particular interest in LANs is the LLC Type 1 unacknowledged connectionless datagram service, which uses U-Format PDUs between LLC end points without having to establish a logical link beforehand. For LLC U-Frames, the control field can indicate one of three categories, namely *UI* (unnumbered information), *XID* (exchange identification) and *TEST*. For the UI category, the service is true datagram, with no sequencing of frames (specific ordering of the frame stream) and no acknowledgements. The XID control frame allows interchange of identities and LLC type support between the peer-to-peer LLC entities on different stations. A XID *command* and *response* field is defined for the bidirectional transfer processes. The TEST control field, again command–response based, allows the LLC–LLC link to be tested with an echoed frame returned to the sender. In both XID and TEST control fields, a *poll/final* (P/F) bit indicates the command (P) versus response (F) types, these bits ensuring that each command issued by one LLC is acknowledged by the other. If a response with the F bit set is not received within an allotted time, the originating LLC initiates an error recovery procedure.

The remaining LLC types (2 and 3) include additional levels of control information to identify link set-up, sequence, acknowledgement, rejection, informational and disconnect frame categories.

As indicated in Figure 4.19, the LLC frame is placed by the MAC controller into the MAC informational field. For standard Type 1 LLC frames, this will incur an additional 3 byte overhead to account for the LLC header. From Table 4.1, we see that for 48 bit addressing mode, this allows up to 4475 bytes for LLC information (total overhead 22+3 bytes), which is itself typically carrying higher level protocol header plus information.

As LLC is used as the common interface to the networking layers and above, it is

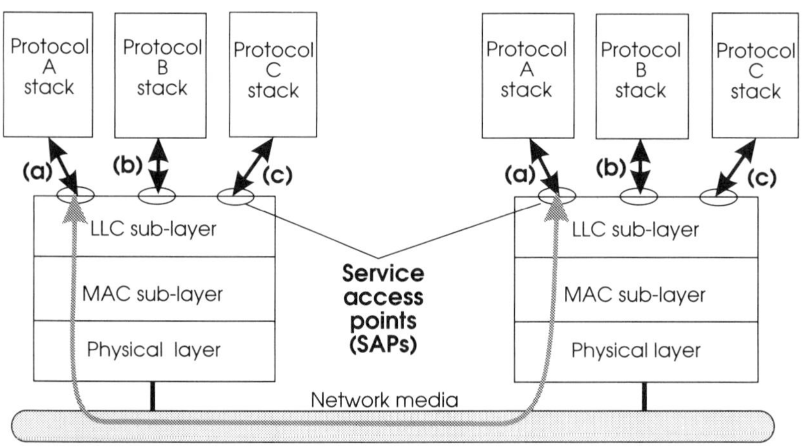

Figure 4.20 *Service access points in LLC (IEEE 802.2)*

very easy to see how a simple bridge to other LLC-compatible networks functions i.e. Token Ring (802.5) or IEEE 802.3.

MAC–LLC Interface

The passing of information between the MAC and LLC entities within a station is usually based on the queuing scheme outlined earlier, with the LLC placing the information into an appropriate transmit queue (asynchronous or synchronous), and the MAC placing receive frames into a receive queue. In both cases, status or control information is passed into and out of the queues alongside network information. A VLSI-based state machine provides a low-level LLC–MAC interface, controlling the queue accesses, and presenting the frames in the correct prioritised order.

The interface is driven largely by the availability of data for transmission and reception. The station CPU, for instance, wishing to transmit a block of data, will create a number of MAC frame blocks for carrying the data, and initiate the loading of the data from CPU memory into the local interface buffer memory, or FIFO, by a direct memory access (DMA) controller. The MAC state machine will detect the presence of the frames in its transmit queue and will capture the token at the next opportunity. The MAC will transmit the frames in the order they are passed by the station's DMA controller. Once all the frames have been transmitted, the MAC indicates back to the LLC process running on the CPU the status of the transmitted frames, indicating any frames that were not copied by the intended station. Additional information, such as the number of frames transmitted per token opportunity is made available by the MAC.

When frames are received by the MAC, and placed into a receive queue in the local buffer memory or FIFO, an indication is given to the LLC process of the frame status (EAC bits in the FS field) and any errors (FCS, wrong frame length, internal receive errors).

Summary

FDDI frame transmission and reception was explained using a simple model to represent an FDDI station. An example of a transmission between two stations was given based on the simple model, explaining how the ring automatically cleans up unwanted fragments and truncated protocol data units (PDUs). The operation of the token timers was explained in relation to the example given. Finally, the interface to higher-layer protocols, specifically LLC, was explained in relation to FDDI.

CHAPTER 5

Station and Network Initialisation

In the previous chapters we looked at some of the basics of FDDI, how data transmission and reception is handled, and how the data frames are constructed. In this chapter we look at how from first powering up an FDDI station, it goes through various stages before it can actually start communicating with the outside world. We will also look at the processes involved in the release of the very first token onto the ring, examining FDDI's claiming method in the process. The fault recovery and reconfiguration aspects of FDDI are discussed in Chapter 6.

Initialisation Processes

The main processes that a station goes through from initialisation depends on how the station entered its initialisation process (Figure 5.1). For example, from power on or hardware reset, a station usually goes through some or all of the following processes:

- Self-tests, including loopback testing of various internal network data paths inside the station.
- Port set-up, handled by part of the SMT process where the station determines a number of parameters, including the type of connection to a neighbouring station, whether it is allowed, how reliable the link is, and whether an optical switch employed or not.
- Internal PATH configuration, including connection of the PORT and MAC entities into the relevant paths (primary, secondary or local).
- Scrubbing of internal paths to remove any possibilities of errors caused by chopping and concatenation of frames.
- MAC configuration and initialisation of parameters.
- Claim process, where the stations in the network bid with their particular requirement for the target token rotation time (TTRT) which is related to how

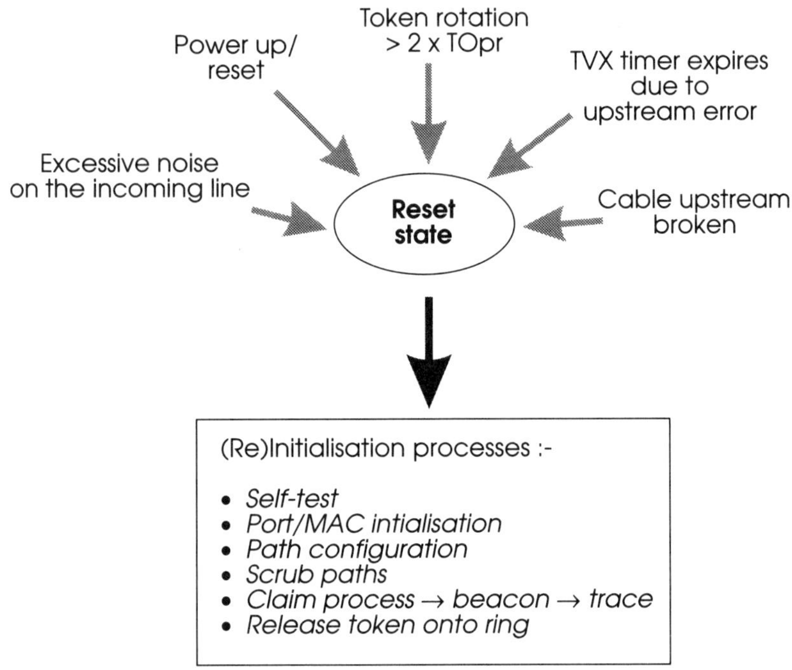

Figure 5.1 *(Re)Entering initialisation*

soon they need the token to return to support their particular applications. If this fails for any reason, then beacon and trace functions may be initiated.

- Initial token release (if winner of claim), or recognition of first token onto the ring.

A reinitialisation generally causes the station to start from the PORT/MAC initialisation phase, and depending on the reason for the restart, will either go straight through to the first token release phase, or divert off into a diagnostics, or fault-tracing process.

Overview of Station Management

Before proceeding with a detailed analysis of the processes involved in Figure 5.1, let us first take a look at the controlling entity within the station – the *Station Management* (SMT) process. SMT is responsible for managing the various hardware and software processes within the station. Figure 5.2 illustrates the main components of SMT as defined by the ANSI standard. Interfaces are defined to all FDDI layers, namely MAC, PHY and PMD. The components are as follows:

- *High-level SMT functions (frame-based services)* – see Chapter 7.
- *Ring management (RMT)* – responsible for the runtime management of the ring, and also MAC initialisation. One exists for every MAC in the station.
- *Connection management (CMT)* – responsible for the configuration of the station's ports and MACs into the various internal data paths. CMT is further subdivided into:
  (a) *Entity co-ordination (ECM)* – oversees CMT components, and also directly controls the optical bypass switch if present. Only one ECM process exists in the station.
  (b) *Physical connection management (PCM)* – controls the activity of its associated PORT and its connection to the remote PORT at the other end of the cable. One PCM process exists per PORT in the station.
  (c) *Configuration management (CFM)* – controls the state of its associated configuration control element (CCE). One exists per CCE in the station (one CCE exists for every MAC and PORT).

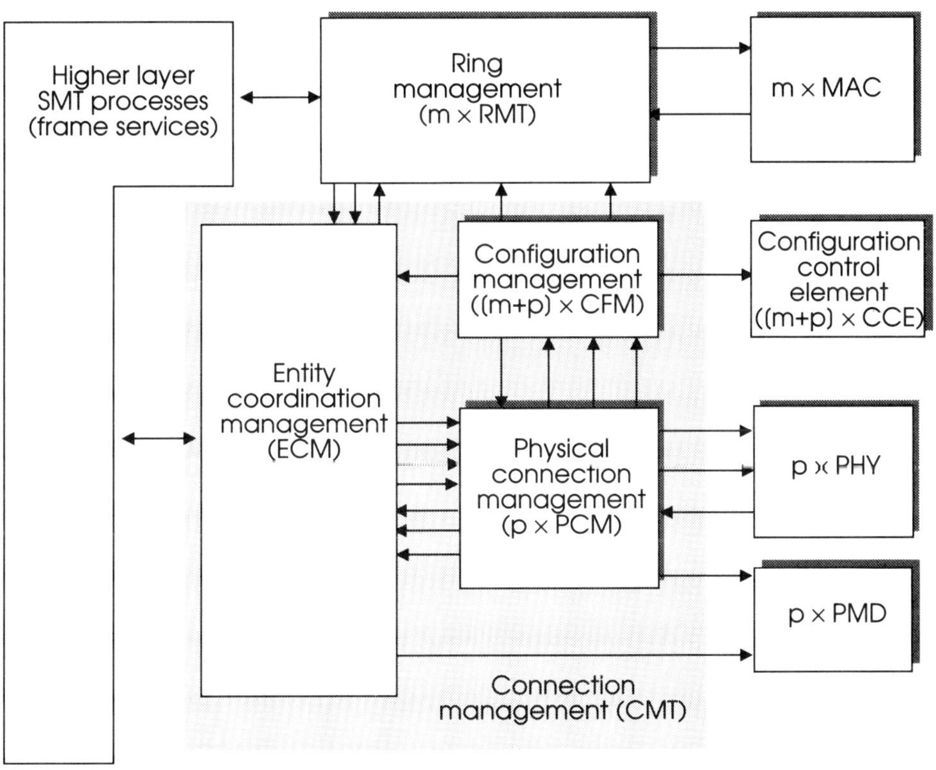

Figure 5.2 *Components of station management (SMT)*

All of these processes run within the station as pseudo-parallel processes, with one signalling to another a particular state, which the other acts upon.

SMT Timers

A number of timers are defined for use by the SMT processes:

- Timer, entity co-ordination (TEC)
- Timer, physical connection (TPC)
- Timer, idle detection (TID)
- Timer, noise event (TNE)
- Timer, ring management (TRM)

The main purpose of these timers is to ensure that all the various state transitions and events within the processes occur at proper rates, and to enable specific events to be accurately timed. For example, the TPC timer is used in the PCM process to monitor the respone time of a nearest neighbour. The usage of each of these timers will become more apparent as we look more closely at each of the SMT processes.

Station Self-Test

A number of tests are usually carried out by an FDDI station before inserting itself into the ring, or when a potential problem is detected in the ring. Firstly, these check out the various data paths that are present, the buffer memory integrity, and perform VLSI component verification (checking *built-in self-test*, BIST, signatures). Secondly, they allow the station initialisation processes to be entered from a known state. Tests usually involve the various components in the station being placed in *loopback* modes of operation. This way, either the MAC portion alone, or the MAC and PHY together, may be tested, allowing the station to isolate the problem to a specific point in the data path. The standard recommends the following tests as a minimum:

- Testing of all internal data paths, i.e. primary, secondary and local.
- Loopback testing as close to the PMD interface as possible, i.e. passing signals down as close to the transmission electronics as possible and back up to the higher-level hardware in order to determine the integrity of the data paths.
- Checking the operational parameters (token-related parameters, etc.) for the MAC entity.
- Testing of the MAC recovery process, including beacon and claim resolution processes.

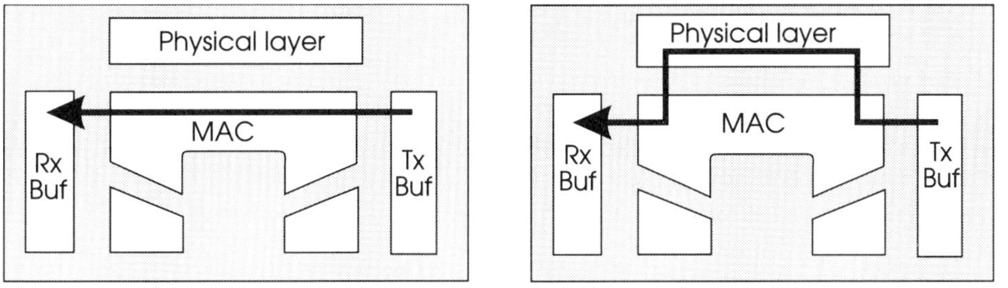

(a) MAC loopback test *(b) MAC and PHY loopback test*

Figure 5.3 *Loopback tests for MAC, PHY and data paths*

In particular, the path tests allow the ECM state machine to assume, before attempting to connect ports into the ring, that the data paths that flow through the various components (such as CCEs, MACs, PHYs) are working correctly. Once the self-tests have been carried out, the station management software can then proceed with getting the connections established with nearest neighbours in the network ring. In ECM, the variable *Path_Test* is used to record the current status of the test process, i.e. *none*, *testing*, *passed*, *failed*, *pending* or *exiting*. These results directly affect the operation of the ECM state machine.

Initialising the PORT Connections

The role of setting up and testing the various data paths and configurations that exist in a station or concentrator is carried out by CMT. Specifically, ECM controls or co-ordinates all the activities in this area, along with direct control of any optical bypass switches that may be in use. ECM starts any number of PCM processes, corresponding to the number of physical ports present in the station, following a signal from the higher levels of station management. A single ECM entity is always present in a station or concentrator, with one PCM process for a SAS configuration, two for a DAS, and *p* for a *p* port concentrator, where the number *p* includes all port types and is typically between six and twenty-four. Each PCM process manages the setting up of the physical connection between its associated port and the corresponding port on the station at the other end of the link.

An example of two connecting DASs is shown in Figure 5.4, with the individual PCM and CFM processes illustrated for each instance of a PORT or CCE, respectively. The PCM processes that are attached to each of the PORTs are responsible for interacting with a neighbouring PCM process in order to establish the connection between the two stations. As a MAC entity is not necessarily available at this point of the station's initialisation, there is no framing structure available to carry

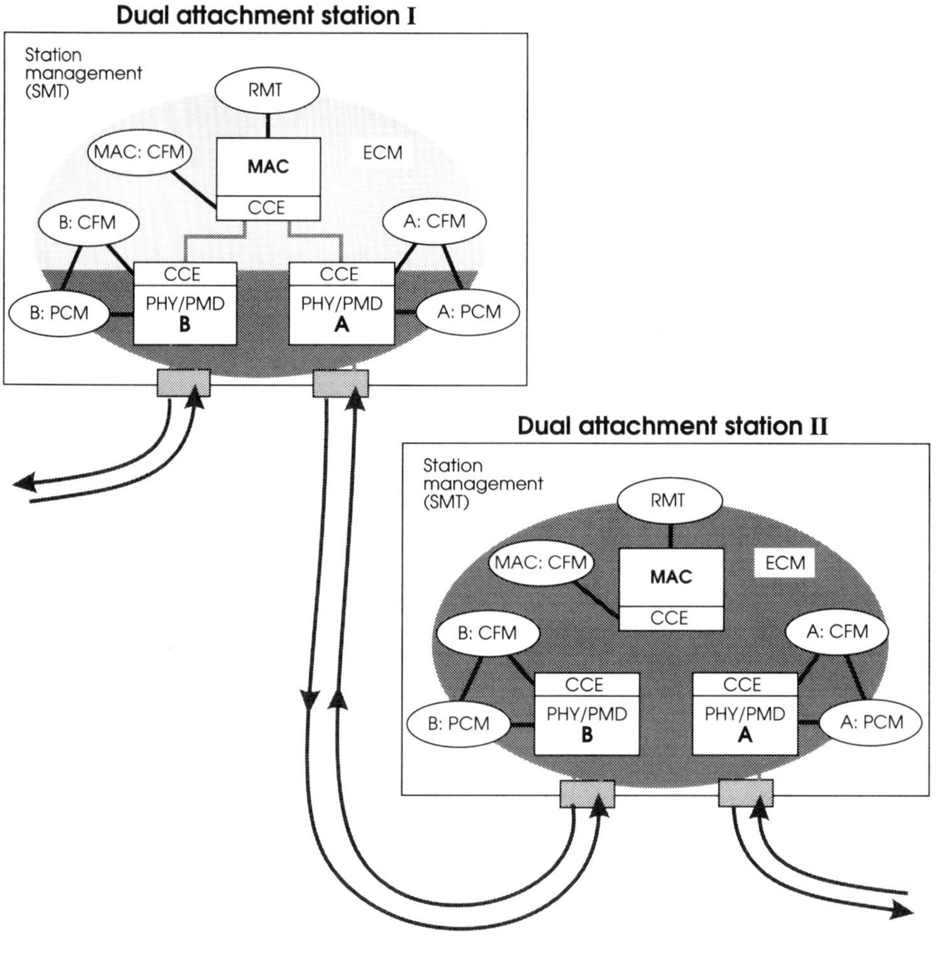

Figure 5.4 *Interconnecting processes during port connections*

management information between the ports. Instead, a physical layer signalling mechanism is required. The PCM process uses a low-level signalling technique, referred to as *pseudo-code* signalling, to verify that this connection is firstly allowed, and is also reliable. As the link is a bidirectional link, i.e. data can be passed in both directions over the primary out/in and secondary in/out, respectively.

The ECM process is shown in the background as a single entity that interacts with all the individual PCM, CFM and RMT processes, and the higher-level station management process. Thus, for the example shown in Figure 5.4 of two single MAC DAS stations (or SM-DASs), during the PCM phase, the DAS I station PCM-A process communicates with the DAS II PCM-B process over the link between the two stations. Likewise, the other PCM processes will communicate over the other PORTs to other neighbouring DAS stations. Once satisfied that the link may proceed, the PCM processes signal to their respective CFM processes to configure the MAC into the ring, and finally, the claim process and token initialisation may begin.

Entity Co-ordination Management

A more detailed examination of ECM reveals five main states that it may be in, reflecting the various stages of initialisation. Further states may be present if an optical bypass switch is employed in the station.

Figure 5.5 illustrates the main states for ECM and their interaction. For simplicity, the optical bypass states are shown combined. ECM is initiated with a *connect*

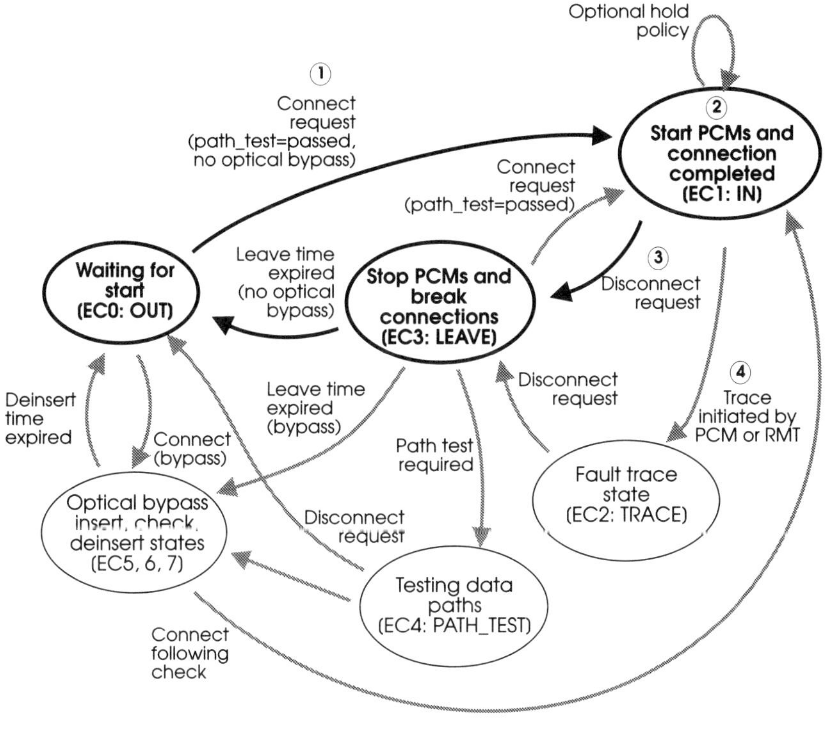

Figure 5.5 *Main ECM operational states*

request (1) from the higher-level station management process. Provided that a previous path test (performed either during self-test, or during a prior trace test) was successful, then the ECM state machine enters the normal operation mode (2), where each of the PCM state machines are started with a *PC_Start* signal. The main reasons for leaving this normal, or IN, state are when either a specific *disconnect request* (3) is received from upper management or a *trace propagation* (4) is signalled from PCM or RMT. The former takes the state machine through a timed disconnection state, which results in the quiet line state (QLS) being sent down the PORTs for a period of time measured by the TEC timer (default 5 msec) before entering either the initial state, or the data path test if the *path test* flag is set pending by a PCM process prior to disconnect.

Physical Connection Management

The PCM processes attached to each PORT in the station, as we discussed earlier, are responsible for establishing a reliable connection with a neighbouring station's PORT. The processes used to establish the connection include an element of testing, to ensure that the link is not suffering excessive errors. Once they complete, provided the connection is allowed, the link between the local and remote PORT is set up.

PCM is really the heart of the initialisation process within a station as it is also capable, with the help of CFM, of detecting unwanted connections, such as an A–A or M–M PORT connection between stations, and notifying the upper management process. Also, once it is established that a connection is valid, in conjunction with the other SMT processes, the reliability of the link may be tested at varying levels according to the level set by upper management. Hence, if the reliability of a link is in question, even at this level, it may be tested with valid MAC level frames for several tens of seconds, even minutes if necessary.

As mentioned above, the communication mechanism between the two PCM entities each situated in neighbouring stations is based on a special low-level code using various line states, referred to as the *PCM pseudo-code*. The capabilities of PCM are such that the remote PORT type can be determined, if the remote PORT accepts this PORT type as a valid connection. It can even establish if a break exists in a single fibre in the pair.

A high-level representation of the PCM state machine is shown in Figure 5.6. For simplicity, some of the lower level states are combined to make it easier to see what the main operational states are. The normal path through the state machine is highlighted with bolder lines. PCM starts in an inactive state, or OFF state (1), where it waits for the *PC_Start* signal from ECM. When received, it moves on to start establishing the connection with the neighbouring station's PCM process (2), which of course may or may not be ready or in the same state waiting to communicate. To ensure that the process at the other end recognises where this PCM is up to, QLS is transmitted, whilst in a BREAK state. This causes the PORT at the other end to enter its connection initialisation state, or BREAK state. This happens for a set length of time, enough to ensure this condition has been recognised. The PCM state machine at

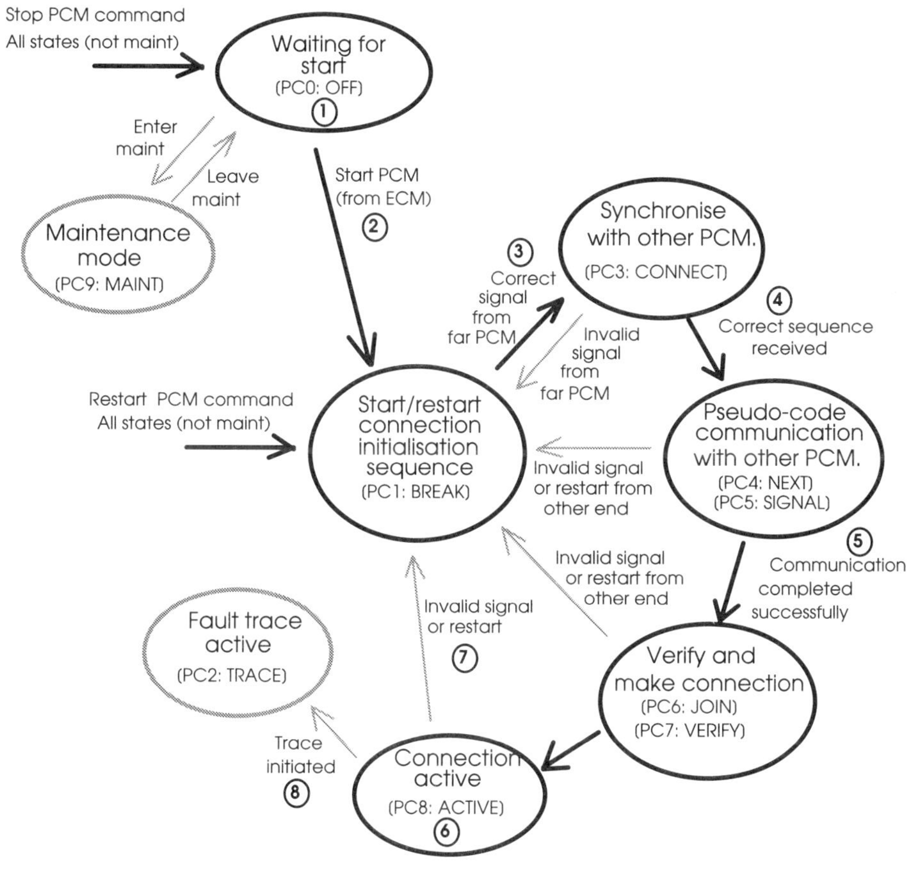

Figure 5.6 *PCM operational states and transitions*

the receiving end then proceeds to start the PORT connection process (3) by transmitting HLS (halt line state). This results in entry to the signalling state (4) where the two can start exchanging pseudo-code messages, and configuration information. A bit signalling counter is used to keep track of the number of symbols transmitted end to end, and this is reset on entry into the signalling state. Once signalling, and processing of the information has been successfully completed, the local and remote PCM processes go through a cycle to synchronise the point at which they both become active (5). This is accomplished with a HLS–MLS–ILS sequence in the join, verify and active state, respectively. Once in the active state (6), the PCM process may be reset to the initial state (7), or a trace function initiated for fault finding (8).

The active state is the point where the PORT is physically connected into the FDDI ring's token path, and a continuous stream of idle (I) symbols are transmitted. At this point a signal, *CF_Join*, to the CFM processes controlling the associated CCE for this PORT is generated in order to initiate the connection of the port into the relevant internal data path.

PCM Pseudo-code Signalling

The pseudo-code communication mechanism is based on a simple low-level line state signalling scheme. Specific line states are used to communicate PCM port types and to test the integrity of the local PCM to remote PCM link, including the MAC if necessary.

The line states and their usage during pseudo-code signalling are summarised in Table 5.1. Recall from Table 3.2 that these line states can be completely determined from the transmission of physical symbol patterns. Hence, the pseudo-code does not require an active MAC to operate. Thus the code signalling method can be used on all station types (including MAC-less concentrators).

Once the communicating PCM state machines are aligned, i.e. both are in the NEXT state (having received the HLS symbol), a simple bit stream consisting of HLS (1), MLS (0) and ILS (bit separator) is transmitted by each end, indicating their configuration preferences. The symbols are transmitted during the SIGNAL state, and the state machine alternates between the NEXT and SIGNAL states until the entire 10 bit sequence, plus a link confidence test (LCT), has been transmitted, and simultaneously received from the other end. The meaning of the bits, in the order of transmission, are detailed in Table 5.2, with an example in Figure 5.7.

Table 5.1 *Line state usage during pseudo signalling*

Line state	Meaning	Usage
QLS	Quiet line state	In BREAK state to force neighbouring PCM state machine into BREAK Also used to acknowledge end of TRACE
HLS	Halt line State	When received in BREAK, causes transition to CONNECT state, and counter set to 0 Represents a 1 or SET during signalling
MLS	Master line state	Represents a 0 or RESET during signalling
ILS	Idle line state	Used as pseudo bit (HLS/MLS) separator during signalling, minimum of 16 idles required by PCM Final transmit signal upon successful connection.

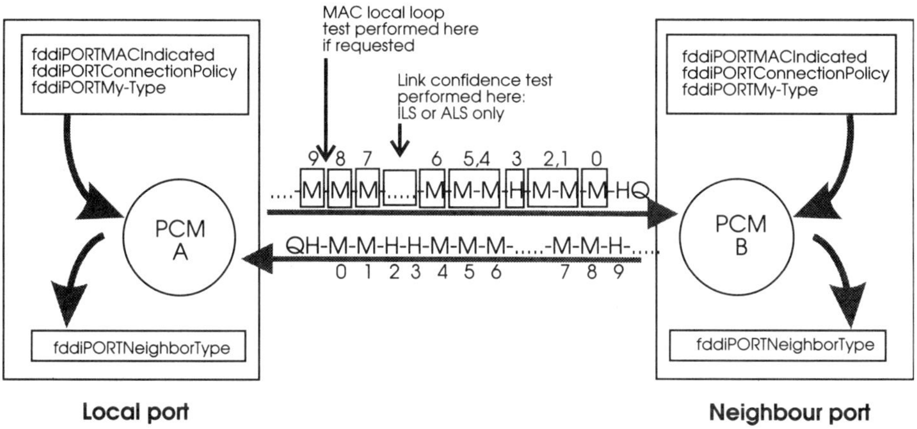

Figure 5.7 *PCM pseudo-code signalling (A–B port example)*

Table 5.2 *PCM signalling bits*

Bit number(s)	Name	Meaning
0	Escape bit	Always RESET (0) for SMT 7.3 - reserved for future use
1,2	PC_Type	Port type – 00 = A, 01 = B, 10 = S, 11 = M
3	Port compatibility	If the received BITS[1,2] indicate a valid connection, then bit 3 is SET to indicate OK. If the received BIT[3] is RESET, then the other PCM process is not accepting this connection (cf. connection policies)
4,5	LCT duration	Indicates the desired link confidence test duration. 00 = short (50 msec), 01 = long (500 msec), 10 = long (5 sec), 11 = extended (50 sec). Determined by higher managment based on PORT error history
6	MAC available for LCT	MAC will be in path during link confidence test, hence valid PDUs may be used
7	LCT failed	Indicates failed link test
8	MAC for local loop	Used to indicate MAC loop tests (only if both ends agree)
9	MAC on port output	MAC will be placed on output token path of port

Peer and Tree Port Mode

During the pseudo-code signalling phase, the two end-to-end ports of neighbouring stations exchange their port types. This is used by PCM as explained above, to ensure that the connection is a valid one.

The PCM internal variable *PC_Mode* is set to either *Peer* (P), *Tree* (T) or *None* (N) in order to indicate the connection type. 'Peer' indicates that the connection is a peer-to-peer connection, i.e. a dual ring A–B or B–A connection, where neither of the ends are of type M. 'Tree' indicates that either one of the connections (but not both) are of type M, i.e. a concentrator tree connection. A setting of 'None' indicates that the connection is either not valid, or not recognised. The remote PORT type (be it A, B, M, S or none) is stored in the PC_Neighbor variable for the local PORT. As we shall see in later chapters, this information is made available outside the station via the comprehensive frame-based management services as the *fddiPORTNeighborType*.

Connection Policies

The method a station uses to determine if a port to port connection is allowed or not is by way of a 16 bit value, referred to as the *fddiPORTConnectionPolicy* parameter, stored in the local station MIB. Each of the bits within the 16 bit parameter represent a particular rejection policy. For example, bit 0, if set, signifies that this station will reject an A–A connection attempt. The full list is illustrated in Figure 5.8. As there are only four port types in FDDI, then 16 bits covers every possible combination of port connections between neighbouring station ports.

Link Confidence Test and Link Error Monitor

Link confidence tests are carried out during the NEXT and SIGNAL states of PCM as part of the signalling process. This allows the physical link between the connecting ports of the two different stations or nodes to be thoroughly tested out before a connection is made. Once the connection is active, and running, the link error monitor

15	14	13	12	11	10	9	8	7	6	5	4	3	2	1	0
M-M	A-S	M-B	M-A	S-M	S-B	S-A	B-A	A-B	B-S	A-S	B-M	A-M	S-S	B-B	A-A

1 = disallow, 0 = allow

Figure 5.8 *ConnectionPolicy bit variable each bit set signifies a disallowed connection*

(LEM) portion of PCM takes over and ensures that excessive errors are not encountered during normal operation. As there is a PCM process for every PORT present in the station, then there is an LEM for every PORT also. Hence a dual attachment station will have two LEM processes, one for A and one for B. A concentrator will h ave one for each of its ports.

Various functional blocks are implemented for detecting link errors:

- *Link error event detector (LEER)* – This detects the number of symbol errors in the receive data symbol stream. In general, this is every time a Unknown Line State (ULS) indication is given by the PHY logic inside the station.

- *Link error event accumulator (LEEA)* – This keeps track of the total number of errors in an aggregate counter that is only ever reset on station reset.

- *Link error rate threshold test* – This monitors the current link errors detected, and compares this to a predefined alarm value. When the Link Error Rate (LER) exceeds a certain limit, an indication is given to the Link Error Monitor. This usually results in the link either being retested, or shut down.

- *Link error monitor estimator* – This provides a long-term indication of errors, and is usually used by external management processes to determine the longer-term errors associated with a particular port.

During the PCM signalling link confidence testing, there are four different levels of testing that may be utilised. In the example of Figure 5.7, this is set to *short* as it assumes this is a first attempt, or a link with no fault history. The test is repeated until it passes, or the PCM state machine returns to the BREAK state where initialisation is started again. The short test is the default, and is a stream of idles (resulting in ILS) or any symbols producing an active line state (ALS) issued by both end-to-end PCM state machines for a period of 50 msec minimum. All stations, as a minimum, should support this simple test, and under normal operation this is the only test performed. Errors are counted using the LEER process. The next level test involves transmission of actual frames or protocol data units, usually for a longer period of time. In this case, the MAC, where available, is usually employed to provide the frame formatting, etc. Again, the LEER process is used to count the number of symbol errors encountered during the test. The next level test again uses actual frames as the test transmission, but the error checking is done by counting the number of frame checksum errors in addition to the LEER process. Other forms of testing involve the loopback of symbols at the receiving (remote) end, and utilising the remote LEER process for a full round-trip test. The duration of the test is set using the fourth and fifth pseudo-code signalling bits as shown in Table 5.2, and varies from the default 50 msec (short) up to 50 sec (extended). Whichever station's value for the duration is the highest is the one used for the test. In general, the medium tests are requested when the short test fails, the long test whenever there are excessive link error rates, and the extended test whenever the link connection is to be withheld.

The LEM process is active when PCM has completed its tasks, and the network is operational. As explained above, the main purpose of the LEM is to provide an indication of the number of symbol errors encountered on the link by counting the invalid line symbols received, and also to automatically alert the higher-level SMT process to an excessive number of errors. Both short-term error tracking and aggregate are implemented inside the station, the latter helping to smooth out short-term or burst errors. As we shall see later, the TRACE function within PCM can help identify where possible errors lie. LEM is particularly important in dual-homed stations or idling secondary rings, where back-up paths and link elements are being continuously monitored. In this way, failures in back-up facilities can be detected and alerted to management before these facilities are called upon to operate in earnest!

The Timer Noise Element

An additional element of excessive line error detection is also employed in FDDI by way of the timer noise element (TNE). The purpose of this timer is to basically count the length of time since the last valid ILS, HLS, QLS or MLS line states were detected. active line state (ALS) i.e. JK symbol pairs and data symbols, do not affect the TNE counter, as these may readily occur in random noise sequences.

TNE is enabled when PCM is in the active state, and is started by a transition from ILS (idle line state) to ALS, NLS (noise line state) or ULS (unknown line state). It is loaded with a programmable value within the station, referred to as *NS_Max*. Valid ranges for NS_Max are from 0.7255 msec to 5.8 msec, with a default of 1.3 msec recommended by the standard. The values are chosen to allow two maximum frames worth of noise to occur (including preamble) before the TNE expires, hence allowing short breaks to be remade without causing the link to go down. If the timer expires before ILS is recognised again, the PCM state machine is forced into BREAK state (see earlier).

Configuration Management

CFM is responsible for the configuration of the various data paths between the MAC and PHY portions of the station. The data path is the path the network data (or token) takes through the station, i.e. the path of the logical ring. The level of CFM supported by a station will depend on the number of MACs and PORTs that exist. Hence, CFM has more components in a concentrator than a single attachment station, for example.

The individual PORT CFM processes are initiated by a *CF_Join* or *CF_Loop* signal from the associated PCM, indicating that the PORT is ready to be incorporated into either the primary/secondary path (CF_Join) or alternatively the local path or loop (CF_Loop). If PCM has indicated that a PORT has passed all link tests and that the connection is valid one, the CFM will switch the appropriate PHYs into the *requested* path, if available. Switching of the various PHY and MAC elements into the paths is carried out by the configuration control elements (CCEs). The MAC is inserted into a local path in a similar way by its CFM process. Which path the PORT or MAC entity is configured into is based on options specified by a *requested paths* and *available paths* variable within the station management process discussed in more detail later.

Configuration Control Elements

The CCE is the basic switching element that allows a PORT or MAC to be configured into the path of the token and data flow. It can allow the connection into a number of possible internal paths described below if supported by the station. Their implementation in the real world can range from a simple multiplexing facility built into the input/output interface of a MAC or PHY VLSI device, to a full-blown parallel data multiplexing device.

In their most general form, and that used to explain most of the following configuration aspects of FDDI, they support a primary, secondary, local path(s) and element interface paths. The element (PORT or MAC) may be switched into any of the paths shown, and also the primary in and out may be looped back onto the secondary paths as we shall see later. Figure 5.9 illustrates a general configuration for a concentrator.

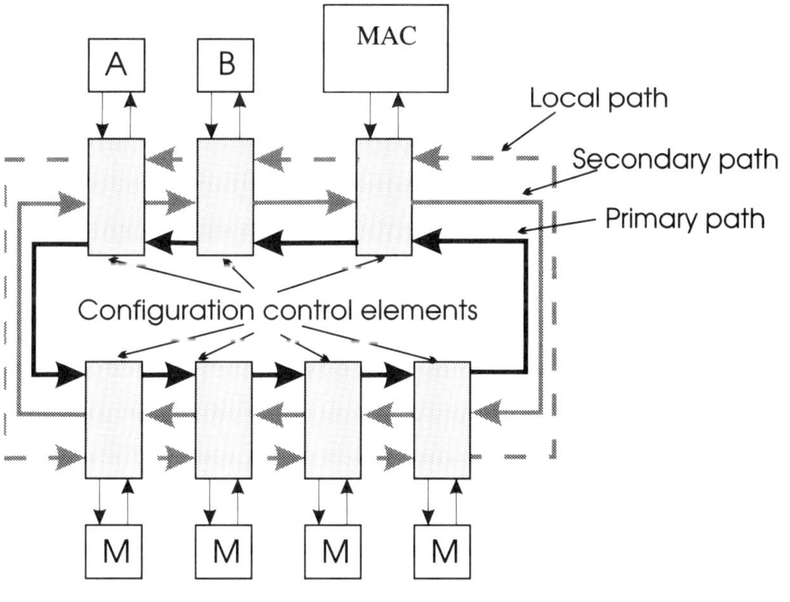

Figure 5.9 *Primary, secondary and local paths*

Primary, Secondary and Local Path Initialisation

A number of well-defined data paths can exist inside an FDDI station. As a minimum, a station must have at least a *primary* path to which the MAC and PHYs are attached, and for stations in the dual ring, a *secondary* path to provide a route for secondary ring data that may be passed back around a network break condition. Though the names used to identify the paths are similar to that of the rings, i.e. primary and secondary, it is not always the case that primary paths connect to the primary ring. This will become clearer as we unfold the purpose and configuration possibilities of the CCEs connecting to these paths.

Figure 5.9 illustrates the general internal path structure that may be implemented by a station or concentrator. Only a single local path is shown in this case, but there may be additional ones if necessary. The flexibility of a station or concentrator is dependent on the number of separate internal paths and the level of switching functionality in the CCEs.

Figure 5.10 illustrates how in the most flexible arrangement, each of the PHYs and MACs can be switched into any of the three paths shown. It is possible for multiple MAC stations or concentrators to have a MAC configured into every possible path, with separate FDDI network segment traffic passing through them (hence multiple tokens flowing through). This would allow a concentrator, for example, to connect to three (or more if local paths permit) totally separate FDDI LANs, and under management control, assign M PORTs to any one of the available networks connected to it. This is similar to the static port switching outlined in Chapter 1. In this case, the concentrator would have multiple MAC addresses. The *roving* MAC also follows this same principle, where an M PORT is configured along with the roving MAC, into its own local FDDI network on the local path for off-line (from the main network ring) diagnostic or preconfiguration purposes.

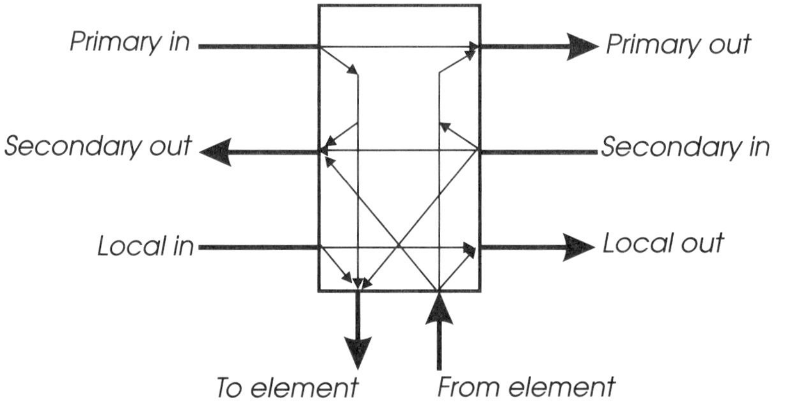

Figure 5.10 *Configuration control element (CCE)*

CCE Configuration States

CFM defines a number of states that a PORT or MAC configuration element process may be in. These are referred to as configuration element managers or CEMs in some cases (from earlier versions of the SMT standard). Four kinds of state machines are defined for PORTs, *A:CFM*, *B:CFM*, *S:CFM* and *Mn:CFM*, and one for a MAC, *Mac:CFM*. Each of these states machines, though very similar, have clearly defined and different state transitions.

In general, there are six CFM states, *local, isolated*, *primary*, *secondary*, *thru* and *concatenated* (abbreviated *LIPSTC* here) that individual PORT CCEs (A, B, M, S) or MAC CCEs may be configured into. These, along with the allowed transitions for each state implementation, are illustrated in Figure 5.11, the LIPSTC diagram. Each of the transitions shown are bidirectional, and the PORT or MAC entity that is able to follow a particular path in either direction is listed next to the transition path. We will be referring to the LIPSTC diagram to help to explain the particular states a station's ports and MACs may be in, within particular station types.

The *isolated* state indicates that the PORT or MAC is totally isolated from any of the internal paths within the station. This is the state the PORTs are in when a station is completely removed from the network. PORTs may be in this condition, for instance

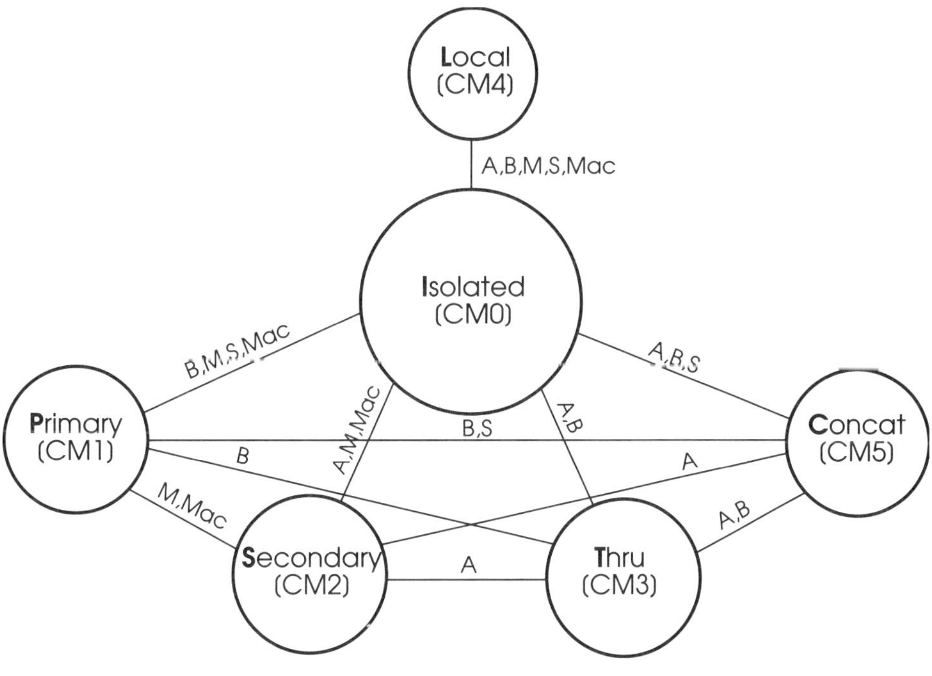

Figure 5.11 *CFM CCE state machine: A,B,S,M and Mac (LIPSTC diagram)*

due to either a network fault (wiring or illegal port-to-port connection attempt), or simply because the station has not yet been configured into the network. The *local*, *primary* and *secondary* states indicate that the PORT or MAC is configured to be only in the path indicated. For example, a simple SAS station will have its MAC and S PORT configured in the primary state, with the token path being along a single primary path inside the station.

The *thru* state applies to A or B PORTs only, and is the normal state during network operation for a dual attached node. As the name suggests, the primary and secondary paths are routed through the PORTs, the primary on one, and the secondary on the other. The 'loose' connections within the CCE on the primary or secondary are left unconnected (see Figure 5.12). Finally, the *concat* (concatenated) configuration for a CCE attached to an A, B or S PORT only, again connects the primary and secondary paths through the PORT, but this time the 'loose' connections within the CCE are connected to result in the concatenation of the primary and secondary paths. The reason for this kind of configuration will become clearer in the following section when the combined states of all PORTs within the station are considered. Figure 5.12 also illustrates the concatenated configuration for a PORT.

THRU, WRAP and C_WRAP Configurations

A number of terms similar to the individual CFM CCE states are applied to the combined configuration of the PORTs. For instance, the term *THRU* is applied to the state of a dual attached node when in normal operating mode, as both the A and B PORTs are in the *thru* mode. For the sake of clarity, when the term is applied in upper case as shown, it will imply a general condition of the station's PORTs and MAC CCEs, whereas lower case will signify an individual PORT or MAC CCE configuration state.

The term *WRAP* applied to the dual ring, as we saw in Chapter 2, refers to the condition where the station has reconfigured its PORT(s) due to a network fault or redundant link. Hence the station is no longer configured in its normal or THRU mode of operation. The effect as viewed from the outside of the station is to create a loopback condition on either incoming or outgoing data paths. Various wrap conditions are possible, namely *WRAP_A*, *WRAP_B* or *WRAP_AB*, depending on the state of the A or B PORTs. A straightforward wrap condition in general involves just a single path inside the station, such as the primary or secondary. If a PORT is configured into a concatenated wrap condition, referred to as either *C_WRAP_A* or *C_WRAP_B*, then the primary and secondary paths are joined internally. The concatenated conditions are implemented in concentrators as we shall see later. For a single attached node, the term *WRAP_S* is applied to the condition where the S port is inserted into the primary token path as normal. Hence for a SAS or SAC, a WRAP condition does not indicate a network fault, but normal operation.

Tables 5.3 and 5.4 summarise the possible states that either a dual or single attachment node may be in. The state conditions are stored in the station's internal management information base (MIB) as *fddiSMTCF-State* for access by external management devices.

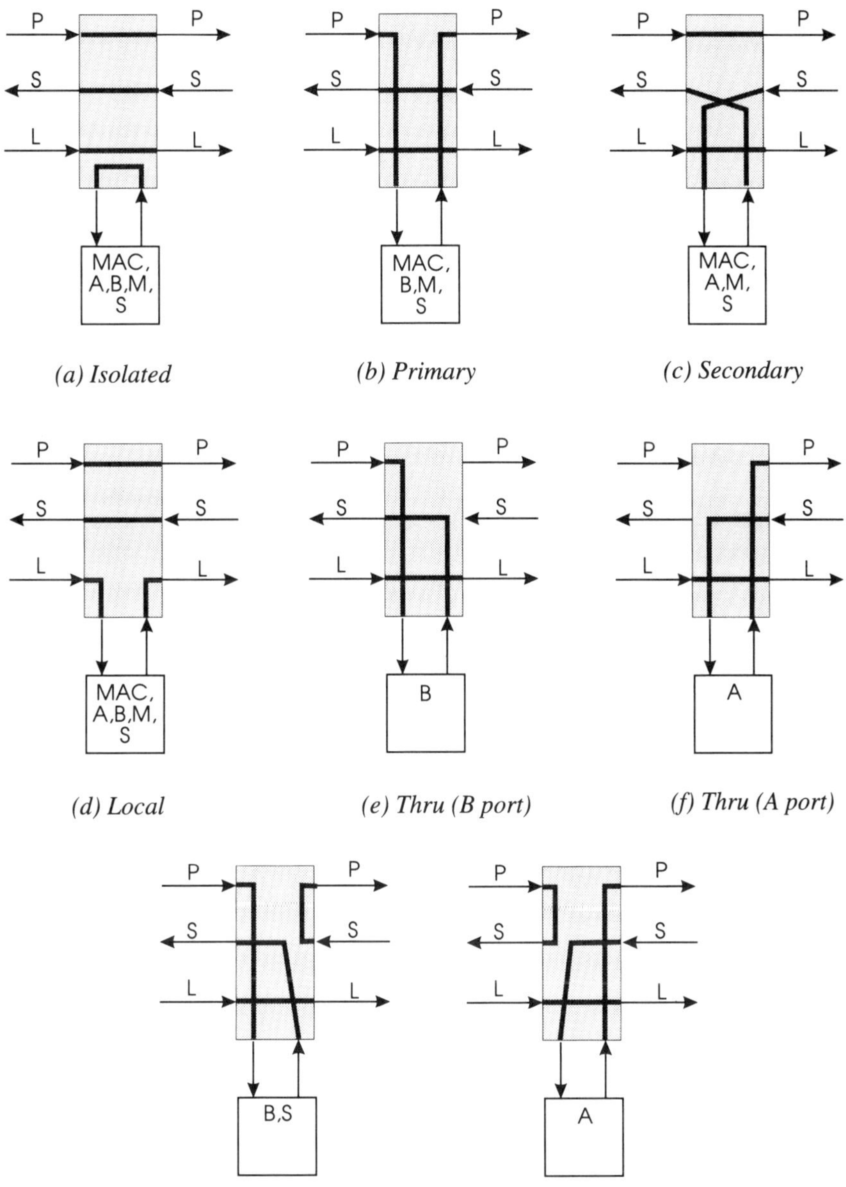

(a) Isolated *(b) Primary* *(c) Secondary*

(d) Local *(e) Thru (B port)* *(f) Thru (A port)*

(g) Concat (B/S port) *(h) Concat (A port)*

Figure 5.12 *CCE configurations vs. CFM state*

Table 5.3 *Dual attachment node state*

State	Description	A:CFM	B:CFM
ISOLATED	Not inserted into any path	I	I
LOCAL_A	A only is in local path	L	I
LOCAL_B	B only is in local path	I	L
LOCAL_AB	A and B are in local path	L	L
WRAP_A	Secondary path wrapped to A port	S	I or L
WRAP_B	Primary path wrapped to B port	I or L	P
C_WRAP_A	Primary and secondary paths joined and wrapped to A port	C	I or L
C_WRAP_B	Primary and secondary paths joined and wrapped to B port	I or L	C
WRAP_AB	Primary wrapped to B, and secondary wrapped to A	S	P

Table 5.4 *Single attachment node state*

State	Description	S:CFM
ISOLATED	Not inserted into any path	I
LOCAL_S	S is in local path	L
WRAP_S	Primary path wrapped to S port	P
C_WRAP_S	Primary and secondary paths joined and wrapped to S port	C

SAS and DAS Configurations

As mentioned earlier, the complexity of stations in FDDI can vary considerably, due to the high number of path and configuration possibilities allowed. The main purpose for additional flexibility is to allow the higher end stations, mainly concentrators, to be able to reconfigure themselves for extended diagnostics, segmentation, and so on. This is especially important for the hub-based FDDI products. For workstation adapters, the configuration is usually more straightforward, with only the primary and secondary paths implemented.

Figure 5.13 illustrates two main configuration states for a single attachment end station. The LIPSTC diagram is shown for the S PORT and MAC CCEs to show the valid states for the two entities. In the case of a SAS, as only a primary path is needed, the S PORT and MAC CCE configurations only implement a primary path connection or isolated state. In reality, for such a simple configuration, CCEs do not exist as discrete components within the station's hardware, but as a simple interface enable and

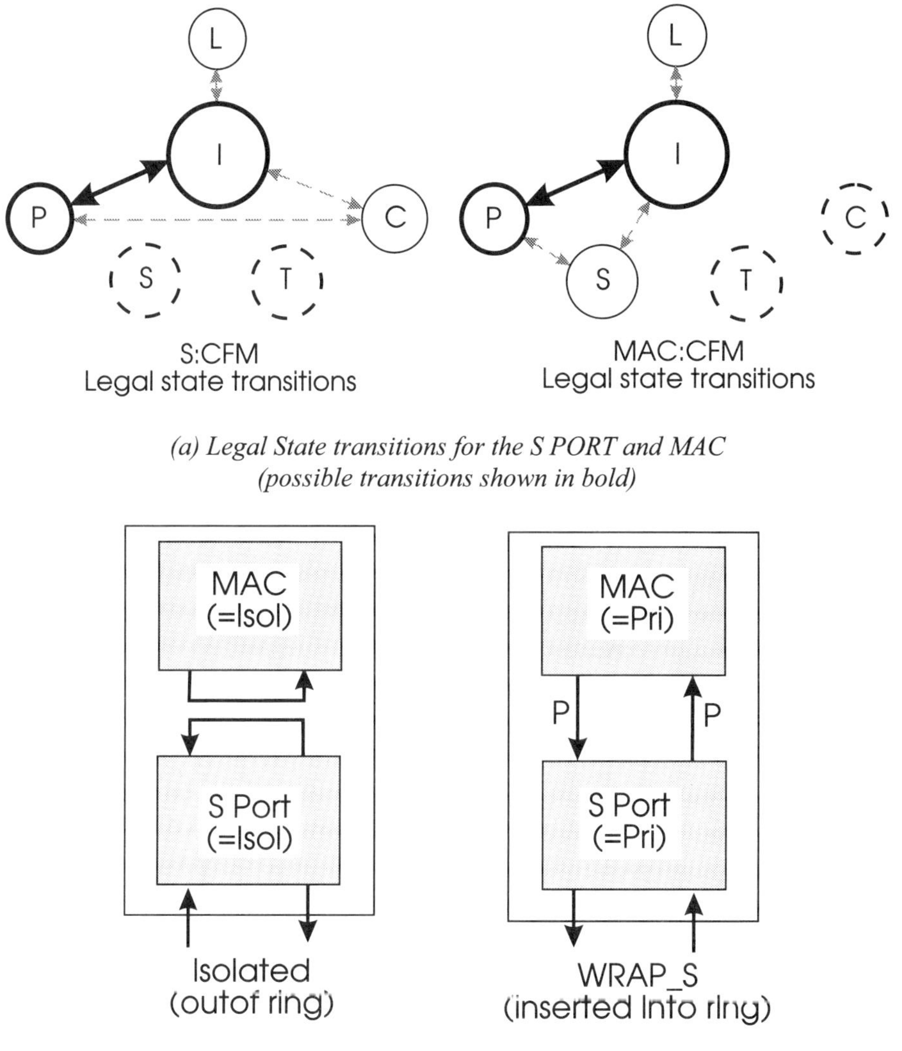

(a) Legal State transitions for the S PORT and MAC (possible transitions shown in bold)

(b) SAS configurations (simple end station adapter)

Figure 5.13 *SAS PORT configurations*

disable function within the VLSI components (MAC/PHY interface) themselves. The SAS *current path* state variable can only have two values: *ISOLATED* and *WRAP_S*.

In many of the adapter cards available for FDDI, a simple SAS card is often expandable to a DAS via an extension card. In this case, a secondary path for a SAS will be implemented which is redundant for standalone operation. When the extension card is attached via a dedicated cable, the card may be reconfigured to include the extender card with an additional PORT. Because of the architecture, typically the S PORT will then become the B PORT, and the extender card implements the A PORT.

A DAS can have a number of possible valid configurations. The main mode of operation for a DAS is the THRU mode, where both of the A and B PORTs are in the *thru* state. When a DAS is said to be in a wrapped state, i.e. WRAP_A or WRAP_B, one PORT is either connected into the primary or secondary path, whilst the other is either isolated or in a local path. Figure 5.14(a) illustrates the state transitions for a dual attached nodes with enough configurability to allow all the standard WRAP conditions to be realised. The C_WRAP state is used by concentrators.

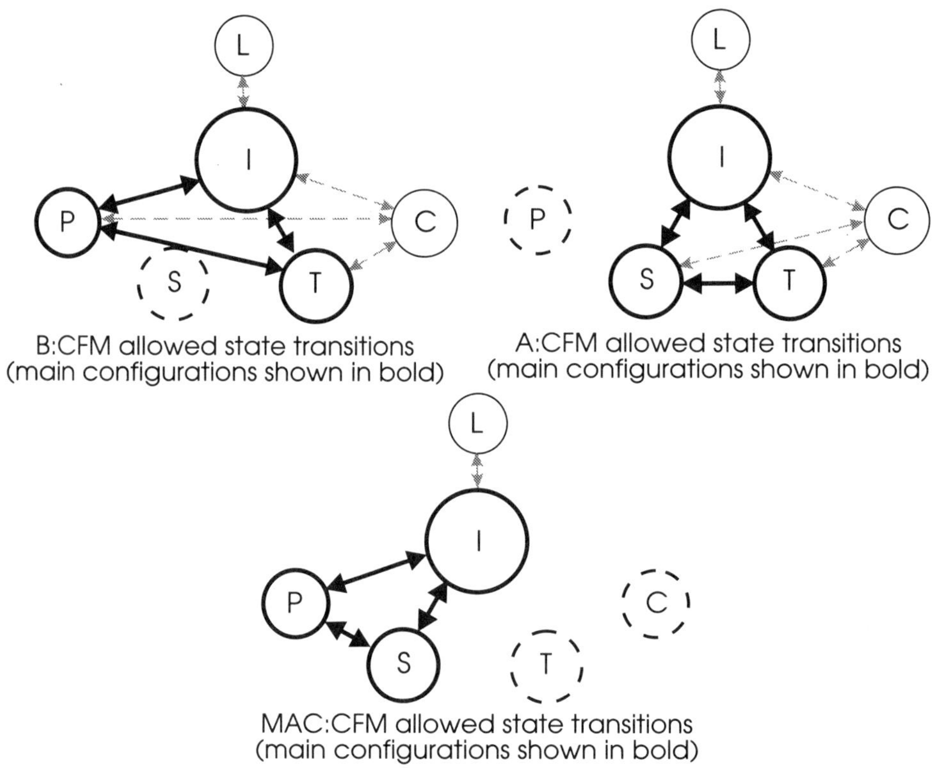

Figure 5.14(a) *DAS configuration states*

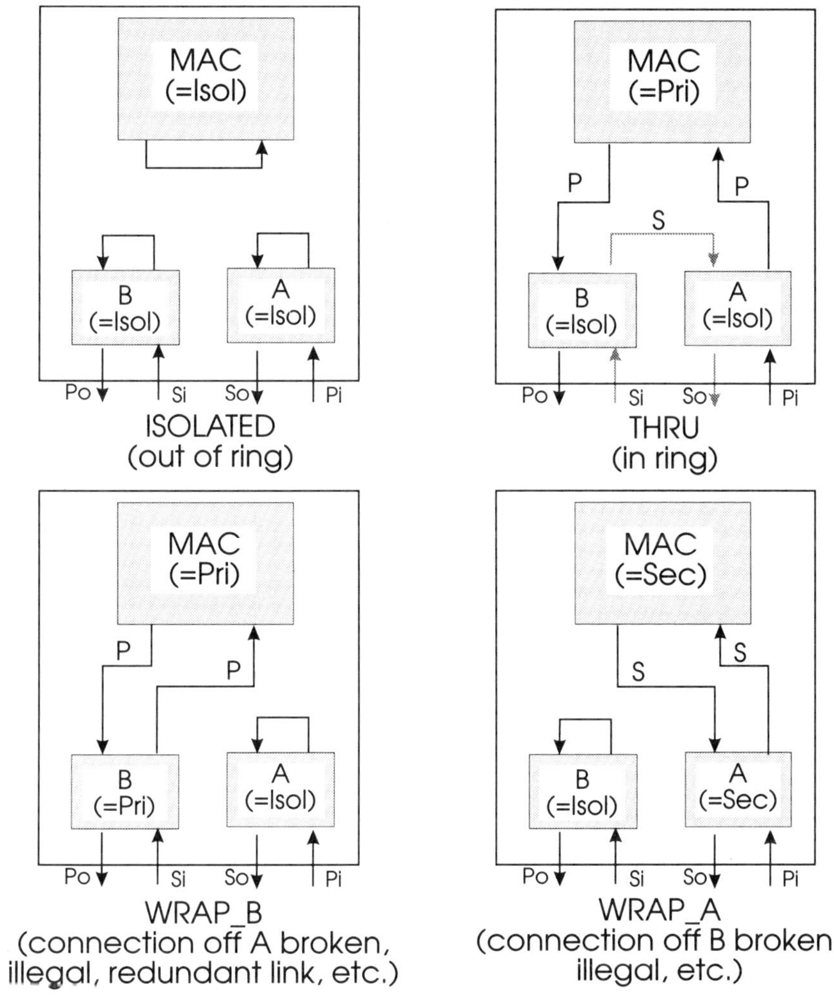

Figure 5.14(b) *DAS configuration states (continued)*

Concentrator Configuration States

The main distinguishing factor in concentrators is the presence of M (master) ports and more often than not, multiple paths and MAC devices.

In workgroup situations, there may be only one concentrator present, which can be a simple NAC (null attachment concentrator) or SAC (single attachment concentrator) as we saw in earlier chapters. In this environment, a single path concentrator is normally sufficient, with or without a MAC, depending on the required management capabilities. More likely, the concentrator is part of a chassis-based hub with much higher-level functionality, such as bridging or routing incorporated, along with other network types such as Ethernet or Token Ring. In this case, the configuration is likely to be far more flexible, with dual ring attachment or dual-homing facilities, and also the ability to support more than one active FDDI ring segment at a time. We will look at actual concentrator configurations and architectures in more detail in later chapters.

In Figure 5.9, a typical conceptual dual attachment concentrator was illustrated with four M ports for attachment to other slave (S port) devices. The possible CCE configurations for the M ports are illustrated in Figures 5.12 (a)–(d), i.e. *isolated* or inserted into *primary*, *secondary* or *local* paths. Note that the M port CCE cannot allow the concatenation of the primary and secondary paths as for ports A and B. The concentrator port states that are above and beyond a simple SAS or DAS configuration are LOCAL_S and C_WRAP_S for a SAC, and the LOCAL, C_WRAP_A or B and WRAP_AB states for a DAC. Figure 5.15 illustrates a DAC configured in its normal THRU mode, and then in a concatenated wrap mode with the ring wrapped on A. The WRAP_AB allows an active secondary ring to be extended to the M ports, and is used where both the primary and secondary are being used for data transmissions (i.e. 200 Mbps operation).

The fundamental difference for a DAC when it wraps the ring for any reason, is that the A or B port where the wrap occurs enters a C_WRAP state, i.e. the wrap port enters the *concat* state (Figure 5.12(g or h)), and the other port remains in the *isolated* state. This means that the A PORT in our example will be connected across the primary and secondary paths, with at the same time the CCE completing the loop by connecting the 'loose' ends of the secondary and primary paths together. For situations where the secondary ring had been extended into the tree by a WRAP_AB previous to a C_WRAP_A condition (see later), then this mode ensures that the secondary and primary data paths are collapsed into a single ring. Recall from Figure 5.14(b) that a standard dual attached node WRAP_A condition would result in PORT A reconfiguring to the secondary path only, which would effectively isolate the M ports currently connected into the primary path of the concentrator. Hence the need for a C_WRAP.

Dual-Homing Port Configurations

Dual attached concentrators connected in a dual-homing configuration normally wrap their B port, forming a C_WRAP_B configuration by default. If the B port connection for any reason is not possible, then as per the station connection policies, the DAC then (re)configures to a C_WRAP_A, effectively enabling the A port, and disabling the B port.

The SMT standard also allows for the situation where both the primary and the secondary rings may be extended down into the concentrator tree, used either for extending the fault reconfiguration of the network, or where both rings are being used for data transmissions. This is achieved through the WRAP_AB configuration, i.e. the

B port in the *primary* configuration and the A port in the *secondary* (Table 5.3). This results in two entirely separate paths, one attached to the primary ring, and the other to the secondary. A concentrator M port that is attached to another lower concentrator's A port in the tree may then be configured into the secondary path instead of the primary, further extending the secondary ring (Figure 5.16).

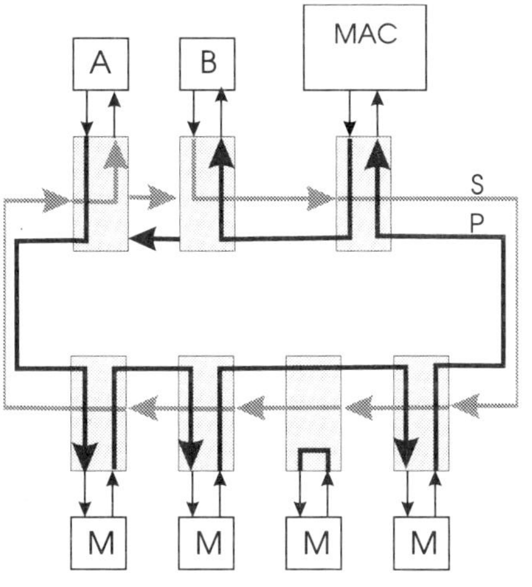

(a) THRU configuration

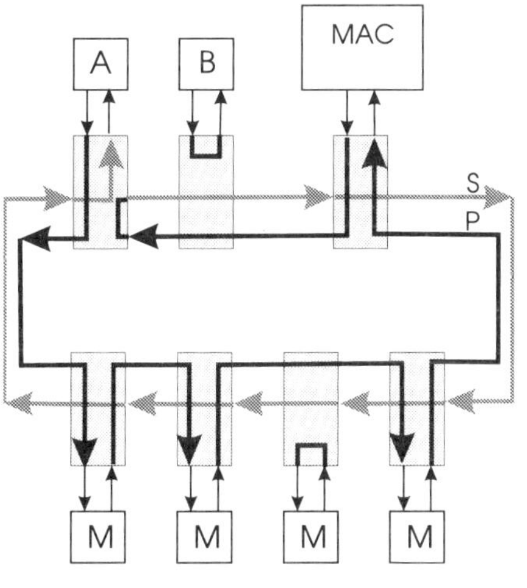

(b) C_WRAP_A configuration

Figure 5.15 *DAC configuration – dual path example*

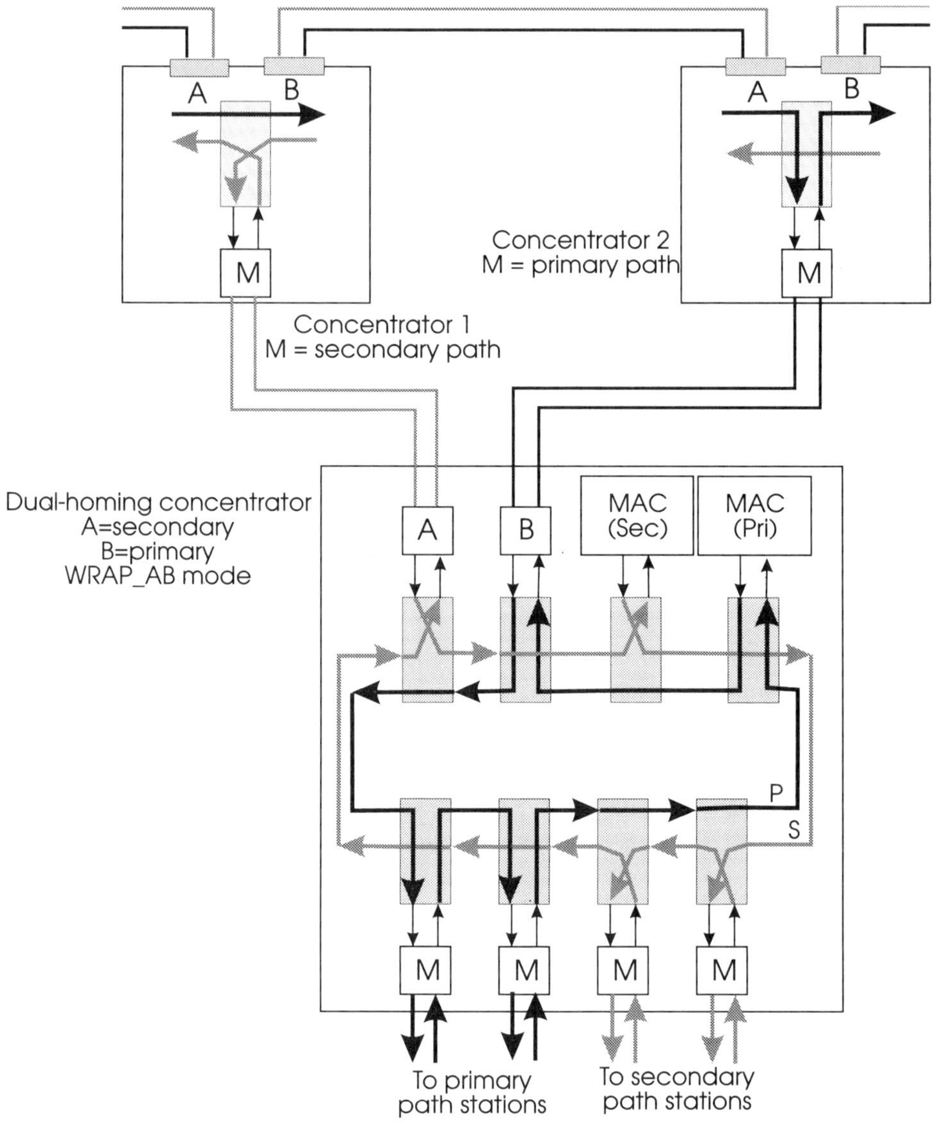

Figure 5.16 *Dual-homing stations and the WRAP_AB configuration*

MAC and PORT Placement Preferences

A MAC or PORT is placed into a path during the configuration management process according to the paths actually available, and those requested. The mechanism that

SMT uses to decide which path or configuration to place the MAC or PORT into is based on a number of selection criteria. A special MIB variable for each port and MAC is stored within the station, which specifies the preferences that associated CCE should adopt when configuring.

For example, an A and B port configuration in a dual attachment station will ultimately wish to configure into a THRU mode. If this is not available due to a cable error (forcing a wrap condition) then the alternative is for the wrapping port, for example A, to connect to its alternative path, in this case the secondary. If the station is a concentrator (DAC), then the alternative will be a concatenated wrap (C_WRAP_A) configuration, specifying a *concat* preference for A over a *secondary*. The format SMT stores this preferred, or *requested path* information, is in the form of an 8 bit variable for each PORT and MAC within the station. In the standard format, this is referred to as the *fddiPORTRequestedPaths* variable for a particular port, and *fddiMACRequestedPaths* for a particular MAC. Figure 5.17 illustrates for all ports, in any one of the three possible PC_Modes, i.e. None, Tree and Peer, the possible combination of bits that are possible within this requested paths variable. The bits are as follows:

Bit 7 Thru
Bit 6 Concatenated-preferred
Bit 5 Primary-preferred
Bit 4 Secondary-preferred
Bit 3 Concatenated-alternative
Bit 2 Primary-alternative
Bit 1 Secondary-alternative
Bit 0 Local

The allowed combinations for any particular ports will of course vary due to some PORTs being unable to enter specific paths or configurations due to lack of hardware support. As the names suggest, there are some paths that can be specified as *preferable* or as an *alternative*. These are evaluated from the Thru end of the variable (bit 7) until a possible path is found, i.e. primary, secondary or local indicated by the *fddiPORTPaths* and *fddiMACAvailablePaths* MIB attributes. Taking the example of a DAS , then we see that the A PORT in peer mode will start at bit 7 with Thru, taking this if available. If not, it then proceeds to the next alternative, which is typically the secondary-preferred bit. If the A port is within a DAC, then the alternative selection will be concatenated instead, for reasons we saw earlier. If no requested paths are available at all, then the port remains isolated.

The MAC is placed into a path using much the same selection criteria as for the PORTs, and is in fact similar to the M port in Tree mode in terms of its requested path options and defaults. For a MAC, requested paths can be local, secondary (alternative and preferred) and primary (alternative and preferred). The default settings for the *fddiMACRequestedPaths* is generally *local*, *secondary-alternative* and *primary-alternative* all set as illustrated in Figure 5.18.

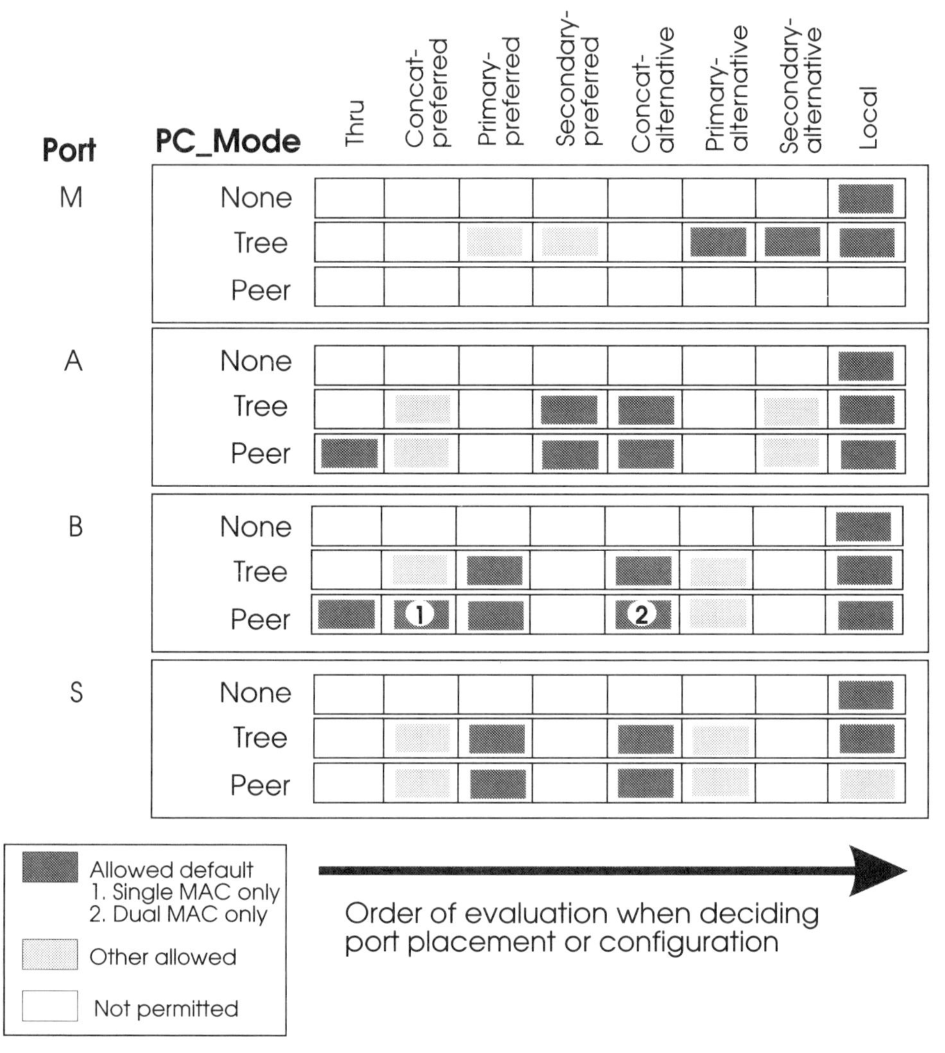

Figure 5.17 *fddiPORTRequestedPaths options and defaults*

Scrubbing and Frame Concatenation

There are a number of potential problems that can arise from CCE reconfiguration, and these have to be dealt with properly. The tracking of such problems is administered by the CFM portion of SMT. It applies in situations where a reconfiguration is occurring (e.g. due to a network fault, or a new station powering up into an active network) as

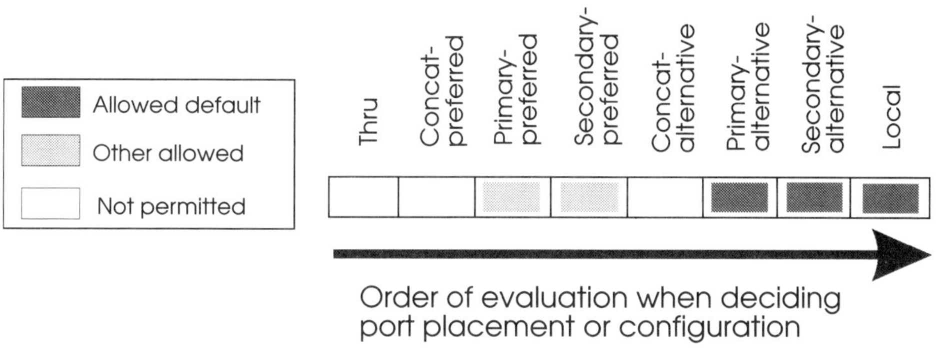

Figure 5.18 *fddiMACRequestedPaths options and defaults*

opposed to the network and all stations initialising for the first time. It is more than likely that when a station reconfigures, and attempts to connect into an active ring, that it will disrupt the data flow.

Scrubbing describes the process of removing all unwanted and *orphaned* frames by a port that potentially removes a MAC or MACs from the ring. Orphaned frames are those that no longer have their source MAC in the ring, hence cannot be removed by the normal frame-stripping process. For example, a SAS connected to an M PORT of a concentrator will cause it to perform a scrub of the token path (which includes the internal paths of the concentrator affected by the reconfiguration), as there may be frames sourced from that SAS still traversing the ring. There is no standards defined mechanism for removing such frames, though SMT recommends three possible mechanisms for handling such as situation:

- Transmit frames (e.g. claim or beacon frames) onto the ring for a period long enough to cause all current frames on the ring to be removed by the station at the input.
- Transmit idle symbols onto the ring for a period of time long enough to remove all current frames on the ring at its input.
- Station that is scrubbing also removes (i.e. strips) all its own source frames after changing CCE states.

If one of the first two methods are used, then the period of time that the frames or idles are transmitted for must be between the ring latency time (default 1.773 msec) and either four times the ring latency (default 7.092 msec), or twice the TVX time. Using the latter causes the expiration of the TVX timer in the MAC downstream, resulting in the initialisation of the entire ring.

There is also a danger when reconfiguring a CCE that any data frames that may be currently passing through it will be corrupted. These would be picked up by the next station in the chain as the data checksum at the tail end of the frame would be incorrect. However, there is a remote chance that during reconfiguration, where two previously separated paths are joined, that the front end of one frame will be added to the back end of another, and the checksum is valid. The chances of this are pretty remote, but have to be dealt with none the less. CFM deals with this situation by sourcing a minimum of 16 idles on all outputs of the CCE that have been changed. This ensures that frame fragments are generated, and eventually removed from the ring as outlined in Chapter 4.

Finally, a station when adding a new port or MAC to the token path must ensure that the logical ring has a consistent value for its negotiated token rotation time with respect to the rest of the stations in the network. The only true way to accomplish this is by initiating a claim process to re-establish the new target rotation time for the network. The technique of graceful insertion, where a MAC is inserted into an active ring without a global reconfiguration, is only normally carried out by multiple MAC higher end concentrators. For example, it is possible for a roving MAC to bring up a particular lobe of the network using a local internal path, then switch it into the main primary ring. There is no defined method for this, but a concentrator would probably have to capture the primary path token whilst holding the local path token, connect the paths, then release the token onto the combined network again.

MAC Initialisation

MAC initialisation is handled by internal state machines within the MAC layer devices themselves, and by the ring management (RMT) process within SMT. Ring management is also responsible for managing the MAC during its fully operational state. This includes recovery from faults, frame level error detection, duplicate address functions, monitoring of restricted token dialogues, and so on (Figure 6.8).

Before the final stages of the MAC initialisation, SMT will have set up the MAC parameters into their initial or default states, either with a reset, or a specific parameter initialisation command. Specifically, the MAC will be set up with the following parameters, some of which were discussed in Chapter 4:

- IEEE MAC address
- Any group MAC addresses
- Minimum and maximum supported TTRTs
- TVX timer values
- Requested TTRT value for claim purposes
- Token rotation time priority thresholds (asynchronous traffic)
- An option to receive either own transmitted SMT frames or all frames (including errored ones)

As with PCM processes, one instance of RMT is implemented for each MAC

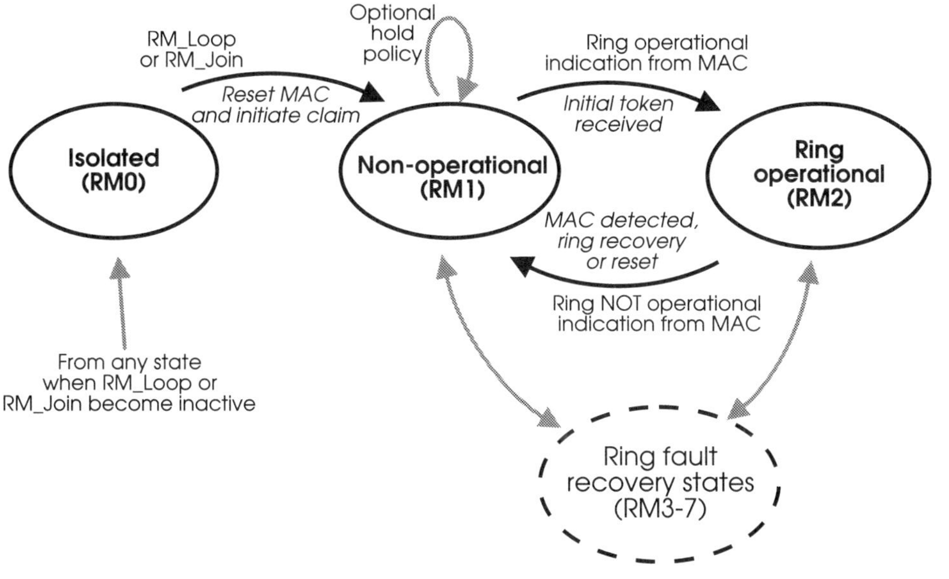

Figure 5.19 *Ring management (RMT) state machine*

present in the station. There is no real limit for the number of MACs, though the standard does place an upper limit of 1000. Typically one is sufficient for most configurations, with two or possibly three MACs only finding their way into high end dual attachment stations or concentrators. Any additional MACs must be initialised with unique addresses, either local or global as defined in Chapter 4.

Once the MAC:CFM process has completed the insertion of the MAC into a path within the station, it asserts a flag to the RMT process. When configured into the *primary* or *secondary* paths, the *RM_Join* flag is set, indicating a standard path configuration. If the MAC was inserted into the local path the *RM_Loop* flag is set instead. Once RMT sees one of these inputs going active, it transitions from its isolated state to a *non-operational* ring state. During the transition, RMT signals the MAC to reset its internal receiver and transmitter state machines to a known initial state. Whilst in this state, the MAC will proceed under normal circumstances onto the *claim* process, or if errors have been previously detected, the *beacon* recovery process. If the claim process (described below) completes successfully, then RMT enters its fully *operational* ring state as illustrated in Figure 5.19. Whilst in this state, the RMT process monitors various conditions, entering a number of fault recovery states if necessary.

The Claim Process

Once all the necessary physical connections have been made with neighbouring stations, the ports and MACs configured correctly, and inserted into the appropriate data paths within the ring, the station or concentrator may then start the claim bidding process.

What the claim process does is to establish across the entire network, what the eventual target token rotation time (TTRT) will be. This is carried out by a bidding process, whereby all the stations, on entering the claim process, start issuing claim frames. All stations whilst in this state continually issue a claim frame with their own particular requirements for TTRT, and analyse the incoming claim frames for either a lower requested value, or check to see if its own frame has returned. If its own frame has returned, then by the rules outlined below, it knows that it has won the claim, and is the designated station to issue the token onto the network. Hence, under normal circumstances, this is the last process in the network initialisation stage, prior to token release. The end TTRT value becomes the station's operative token rotation time, or TOpr (see Chapter 4).

The claim frame is a MAC supervisory frame, with fields as shown in Figure 5.20. The frame control field identifies it as a claim frame by a specific value as shown. Recall from Chapter 4 that the L identifies the length of the address field, L = 0 indicating 16 bit addresses, and L = 1, 48 bit addresses. The information field is 4 octets, or bytes, long (i.e. 32 bits), and contains the TTRT bid value requested by the particular station, identified by the contents of the source address field. In this case, the destination address field is not used in any real sense, and is commonly left as equal to the source address (i.e. DA = SA), i.e. a self-addressed frame.

A particular example of how the claim process works in a four station network is illustrated in Figure 5.21. The simplified representation identifies a number of cases where rules must be applied other than the simple 'pass it on if less than own' rule. For instance, if two stations are bidding for the same time, then there must be some form of arbitration to determine which frame is passed down the chain and ultimately who should be responsible for issuing the token. Otherwise, there would be multiple tokens issued onto the network, obviously an undesirable situation. Hence, for identical value TTRT bids, then the bid with the highest value of source address (SA) wins.

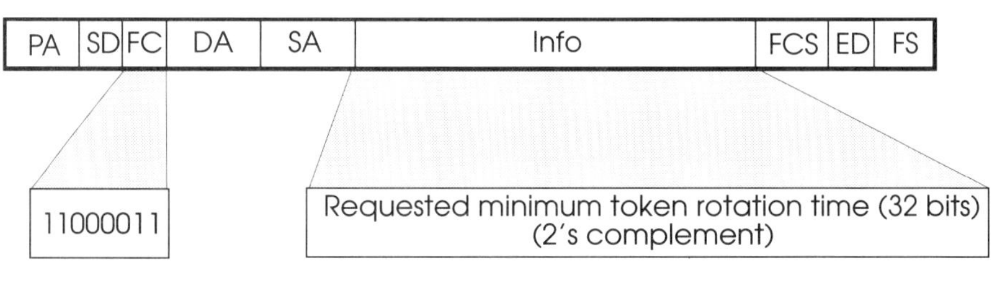

Figure 5.20 *MAC claim frame format*

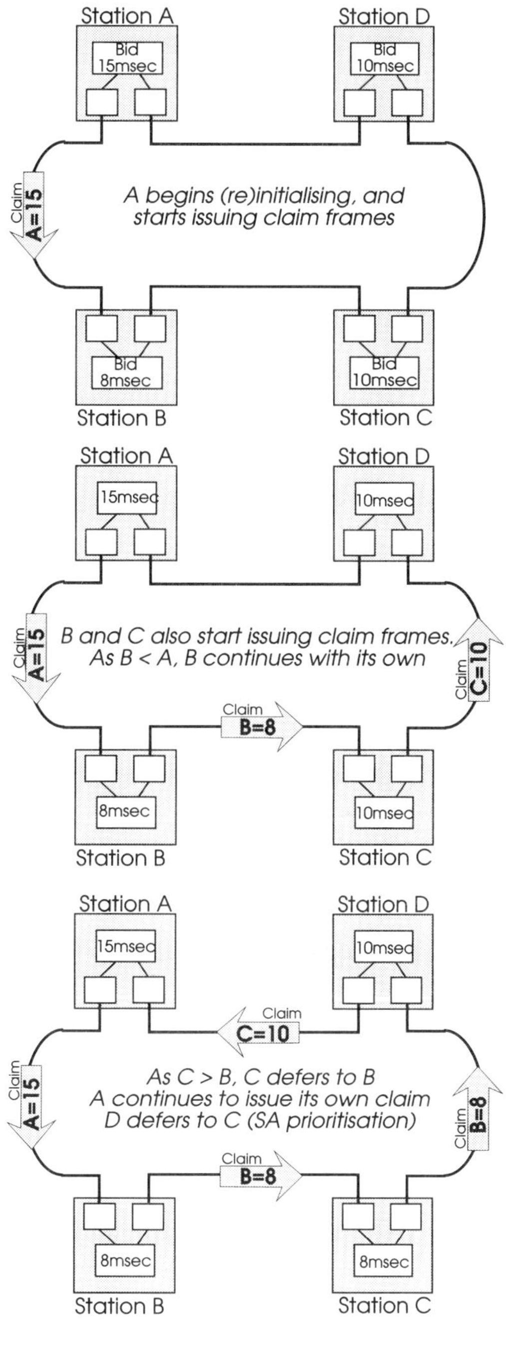

Figure 5.21 *Claim process*

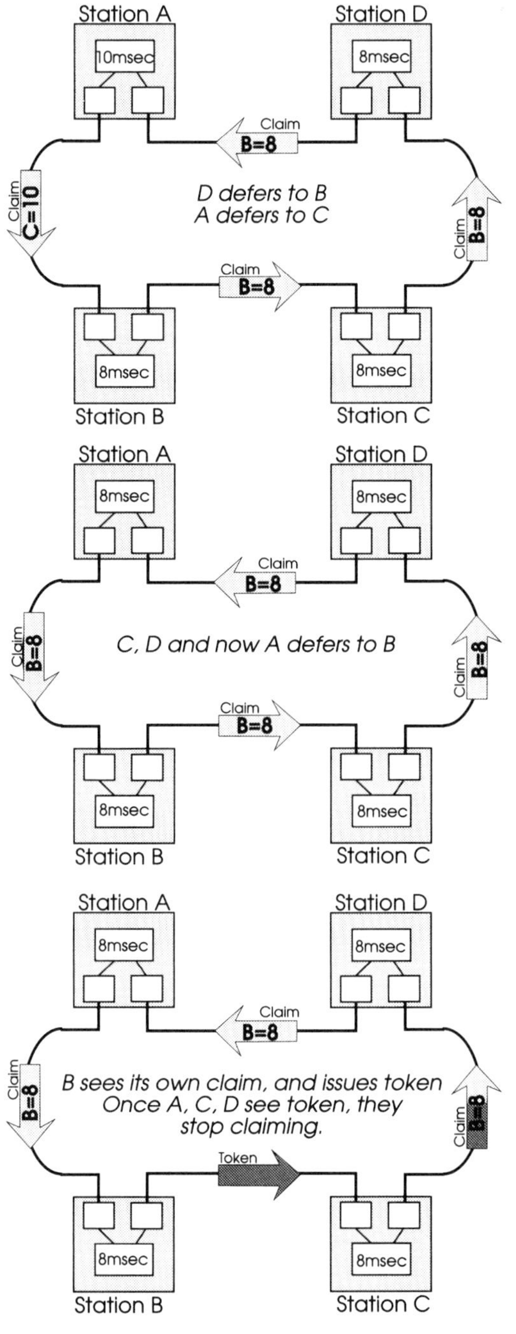

Figure 5.21 *Claim process (continued)*

In theory, the source addresses are never equal as they are individually assigned by the IEEE (see Chapter 4). Assuming this, the above process ensures that only one station ever wins in the claim process. In the case of our example, we see that stations D and C have equal bid values, but assuming that C has a higher 48 bit source address value, then it wins over D's own claim frame. In the event that two stations have the same addresses, then FDDI will detect this as we shall see in later chapters. Duplicate addresses are sometimes possible in network protocols where the MAC is reset to use an address setup by the network operating system and the new addresses have been incorrectly administered.

The above process ensures that eventually the only claim frames that exist on the network belong to one station. Once this one station (B in our example) sees its own claim frame on its input, it then proceeds onto the final stage of issuing a non-restricted token onto the network.

The Initial Token

Once the claim process has completed successfully, then the token may be issued onto the network and all the stations may initialise their timers and respective preload values (such as the TTRT) accordingly. The station that wins the claim process issues an initial non-restricted token onto the network, following initialisation of its token timers. This token circulates once around the network with no transmissions allowed, in order to align the TTRT values in all the stations and the associated timers. Each station once it has repeated the token for the first time stops claiming, and sets its timers to the last claim frame's TTRT parameter (i.e. TOpr) that was received. During this first rotation they also set their Late_Ct flag which allows only synchronous transmissions on the next rotation of the token. Asynchronous transmissions are only possible from the third rotation onwards. The Boolean variable *ring_operational* becomes active during this phase as an indication that the ring has exited the claim process successfully and the ring is now fully operational.

Summary

The operation of a station from the power-up, or reset state, has been discussed, leading to the eventual initialisation of the FDDI ring, and release of the initial token.

When an FDDI station initialises, it performs a self-test on its internal data paths before attempting to connect its ports to those of its neighbours. A pseudo-code signalling method is used at each port to communicate connection parameters, and to test the integrity of the point-to-point link. If there are path configuration devices present in the station or concentrator, these are initialised to ensure a correct token path exists through the station's port and MAC devices. Primary, secondary and local path types can exist, with the primary used as the main data-carrying path. CCE devices allow ports and MAC devices to connect to one of the available paths according to a station configuration policy.

Once all the individual elements within a station have been correctly initialised, the station may then proceed to connect into the ring using a claim process to establish its token timer parameters. Successful completion of the claim process leads to the initial token being released onto the ring.

CHAPTER 6

Reconfiguration and Fault Recovery

In Chapter 5 we looked at the way a station initialises the configuration of the ports and MACs within it, and then participates in ring initialisation by performing the claim process along with all the other stations in the ring. This assumes that all proceeds correctly, and that there are no breaks in the cable, interruptions, faulty stations, stations not responding correctly to the network protocols, etc. In the real world, however, many potential problems or what appear to be insignificant changes can arise that need to be adequately dealt with. Take the example of a user coming into work in the morning, switching on their workstation or personal computer, which in turn causes their station to insert into the network. A global reconfiguration of the ring occurs in just about every circumstance. On the dual-ring, reconfiguration is generally unavoidable (it is unlikely and inadvisable that a general user in a large network will ever be directly on a FDDI dual-ring backbone...). Some concentrator products claim to support *graceful insertion* (i.e. not resulting in a global network reconfiguration) on their M port links. There are many (non-standard) ways of doing this, one being to set up a local loop internal to the inserting station, with a roving MAC, check that its parameters are compatible with the existing network requirements, and then incorporate the station into the primary path at an appropriate point. In any case, as we can see, there are many factors involved just in this simple station power-up process.

For most cases, the reconfiguration of an FDDI network occurs very quickly, and so would only appear as a minor 'glitch' in any network traffic. It is still useful, however, to understand exactly what happens when, for example, a user inadvertantly unplugs a wrong cable, a cable breaks or a contact becomes unreliable, making and breaking, and so on. The first part of this chapter identifies some common principles, such as how a station automatically identifies a fault condition, and then follows on with a description of the mechanisms involved with recovering the network and re-establishing network operation. The second part will then identify how a fault-tolerant network topology may bc constructed, taking advantage of the various features within FDDI that allow for automatic recovery from network changes or faults.

Network Configuration Changes

The most common configuration change that results in a token path being broken is when an either a new network device is switched on/off or its cable connection (un)plugged from a concentrator port, interrupting the current operational token path. As we saw in Chapter 5, the SMT PCM and CFM state machines have well-defined mechanisms for dealing with such a situation. In addition, the physical layer device(s) within the neighbouring FDDI nodes will inform the CPU that a valid signal is no longer being received, and the connection will then be isolated by the PCM and CFM processes.

For instance, for a single attached node powering down, the M port that the station is attached to will change its state to *ISOLATED* (Table 5.4), scrubbing the paths affected within the concentrator (usually the primary path) as it does so. In most instances, after the paths are scrubbed by the CFM process, the ring enters the claim process in order to re-establish the new token operational conditions (i.e. TOpr). For a dual attached node leaving the network, the stations either side will go into *WRAP_A* and *WRAP_B* states accordingly, unless optical bypass devices are in use allowing the primary ring to be maintained (Figure 6.1). Again, the neighbouring stations will enter the claim processes following an internal path reconfiguration.

Categories of Faults

A number of reasons for a network reconfiguration due to a fault exist (as opposed to simply power cycling). These are broadly categorised as follows.

Physical Layer Fault or Cable Break

The most common example of FDDI network reconfiguration around a network fault is caused by a cable break occurring in a dual-ring configuration. As we saw in earlier chapters, the stations either side of the break, *wrap* their token paths back around onto the secondary ring, redirecting traffic onto the back-up link in the opposite direction. Depending on the capabilities of the CCEs within the network interface, all stations will still have access to the network including the stations directly attached to the broken cable section.

This kind of fault is detected and dealt with by the station management processes. The break in the cable results in quiet symbols (or QLS – quiet line state) being detected at the A port PCM process on the primary in connection of the station downstream of the fault. The PCM process enters the *BREAK* state where reconnection is attempted. If the break is intermittent, then at this stage the link should be re-established and the claim process initiated as necessary. If this happens too frequently (detected by the link error monitoring processes), then the link will eventually be shut

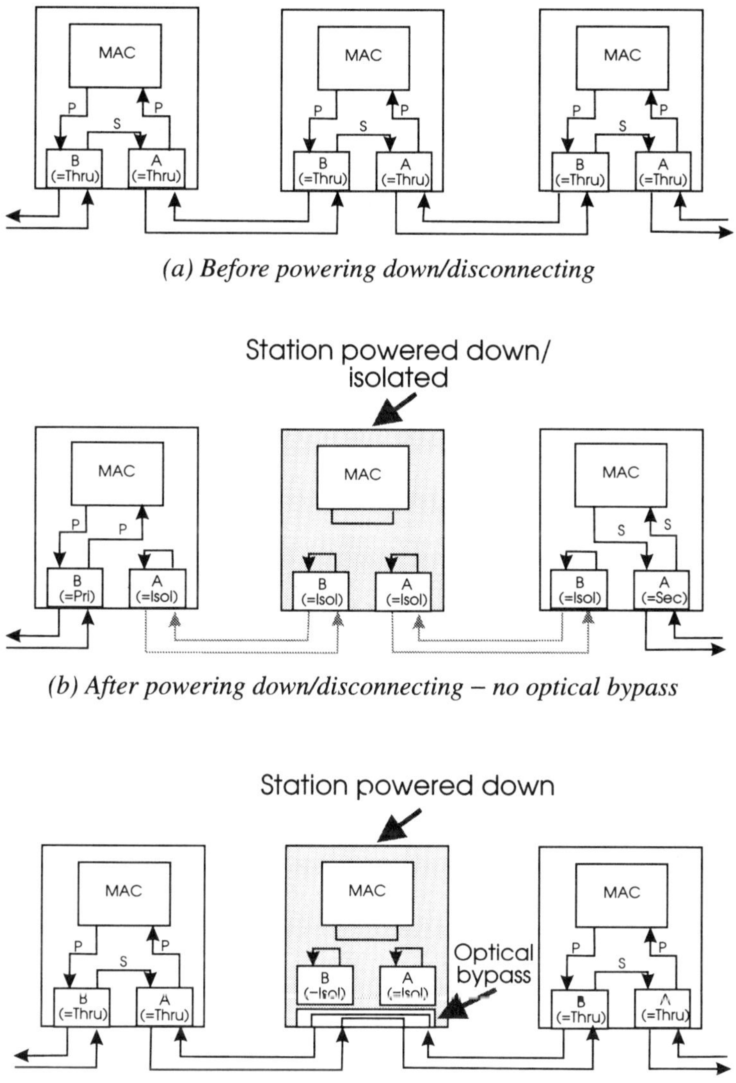

(a) Before powering down/disconnecting

(b) After powering down/disconnecting – no optical bypass

(c) After powering down/disconnecting – with optical bypass

Figure 6.1 *Effect of powering a station off – DAS example*

down. If a complete break has occurred, then the PCM and CFM processes will result in the offending link being isolated, with the downstream station entering *WRAP_B* mode, and the upstream station entering the *WRAP_A* mode (Figure 6.2).

Where the break is a SAS to concentrator link (M – S port link), then the link cannot be re-established, and both the concentrator M port and the station S port remain in the

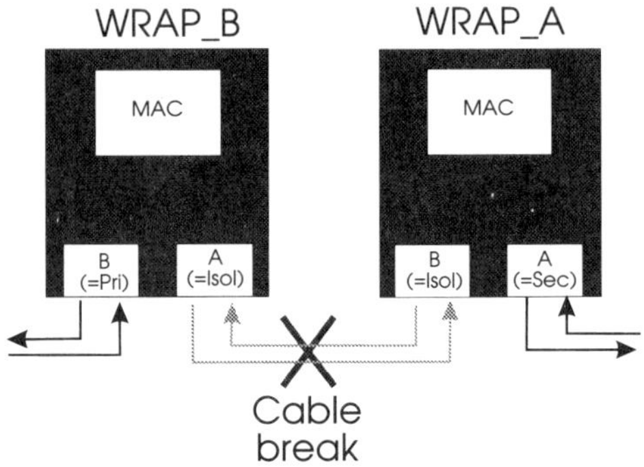

Figure 6.2 *Dual-ring fault reconfiguration*

isolated state (Figure 6.3), and the SAS is unable to communicate with the network until the cable fault is rectified.

Finally, where a dual-homing configuration is being used, the A port of the dual-homing station is normally isolated, with the B link acting as the primary token path link. If the B port connection is broken, then the B port is isolated and the A port becomes the active link, causing the attached M port to change from the *isolated* state to the *primary* or *secondary* (Figure 6.4). The dual-homed concentrator in the example shown (which can be any dual attachment device that supports dual-tree attachments) changes its configuration to a *C_WRAP_A* from a *C_WRAP_B* configuration.

Operational Fault

All the classic examples of FDDI network failure assume that faults only develop at the cable level, or at the physical interface level. The FDDI standard also caters for situations where the fault is less obvious, and falls within the domain of the station itself. Cable and physical layer faults are dealt with reasonably well by the SMT connection management processes.

However, there are instances where faults lie outside of their influence. These types of failure fall into two general sub-categories:

Internal Path Failure

There may be a case where the PCM processes can communicate outside the station to another similar process, and set-up the connection with no problems. At some future stage, however, a fault develops within the station itself such that the internal path is broken. How is this detected? Depending on the extent of the failure, this problem may not be instantly recognised, as data may be repeated correctly, for example, but when an attempt is made to transmit a frame, the MAC entity cannot transmit its data stored in buffer memory onto the current active token path even though it may think it has.

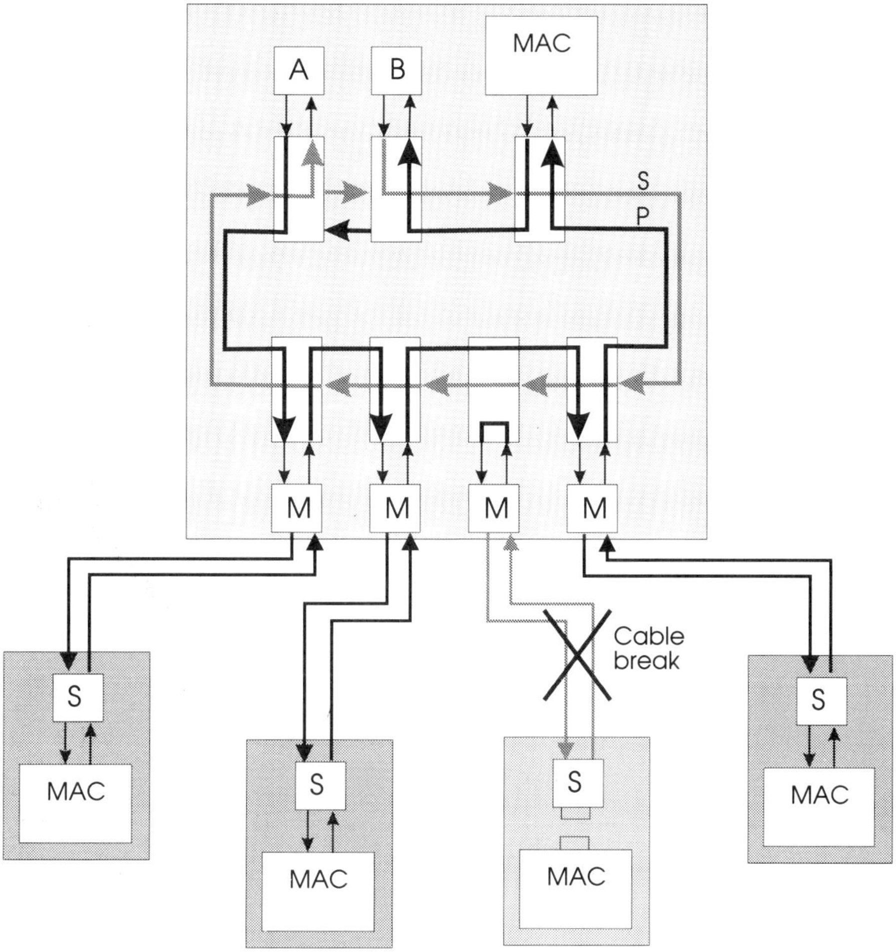

Figure 6.3 *Concentrator SAS bypass due to cable/line fault*

The only way this would be detected would be via a station self-test, or more specifically, a path test.

Failure due to MAC Fault

The MAC device itself may be reporting to the higher layers that it has transmitted its frames, but may have in fact entered a fault mode whereby it continues to transmit the same frame over and over again. Alternatively, the MAC may be stuck transmitting valid frames onto the network which are in fact old (i.e. repeated) or just garbage frames.

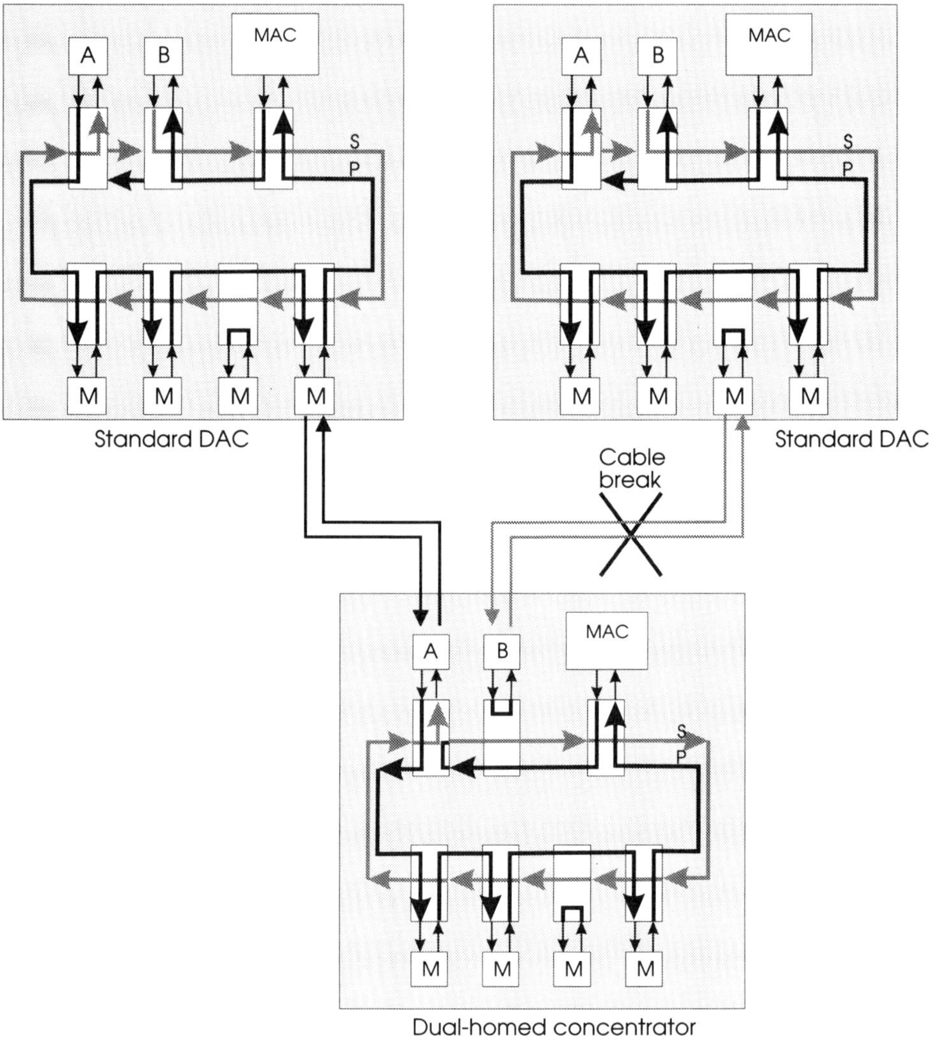

Figure 6.4 *Dual-homing fault reconfiguration*

Basic Principles of Fault Detection

The task of managing and co-ordinating fault recovery or reconfiguration is handled by a number of entities within SMT. As we saw in Chapter 5, there are a number of configurations that a station may adopt in the event of a particular path being unavailable that allow the network to operate as smoothly as possible. CFM handles the configuration elements within the station, following various policies that are internally set. ECM and PCM are responsible for configuring the link and monitoring the errors at the physical layer level within the station via the link error monitor (LEM) process. If excessive data symbol errors are encountered, then the management process within the station will be notified, and the link will be shut down if necessary. If applicable, off-line link confidence tests may be repeatedly run until the link becomes reliable again. RMT is another process running within station management that takes care of the MAC-level management at certain stages of the initialisation process, handling errors that cannot always be detected by the lower-level ECM/PCM.

In addition to all these lower-level 'safety nets' offered by FDDI, SMT also implements a higher-level process called the *neighbour notification* process, which allows each station quickly to determine its nearest neighbours, and also, for fault detection purposes, if a station with the same MAC address as this one exists on the network at runtime.

As we saw in Chapter 5, there are many possible causes of a ring configuration error, ranging from the low-level errors discussed already, and the higher-level errors due to misallocation of bandwidth resources, misuse of a restricted token mechanism by a number of stations on the network, and so on (Figure 6.5).

Low-Level Fault Recovery Mechanisms

Two main processes that are important in fault recovery are *beacon* and *trace*. The beacon and trace processes are initiated whenever the claim process fails, and are used as a means of detecting which particular segment of the FDDI token path (not just

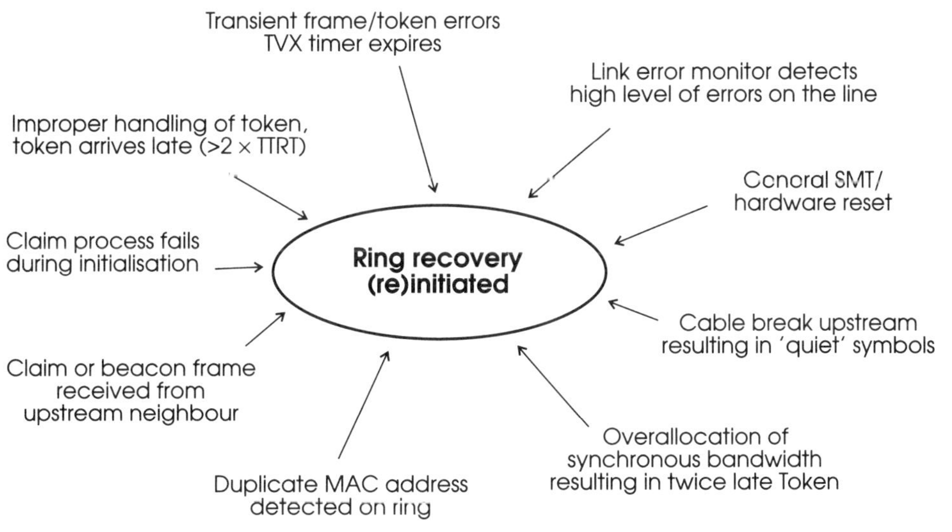

Figure 6.5 *Example events that (re)initiate the ring recovery process*

cable) has failed. When a station starts claiming or beaconing, this causes that station to deassert its *ring_operational* flag, i.e. the ring, according to that station, is no longer operational. In the previous chapter we examined the claim process, and how when successful, it allows the network to proceed with initialising the token timers, and ultimately release the first token onto the network. However, what happens when the claim process fails? How is the fact that the claim process has failed at all detected by the stations in the network? All these factors are handled by a combination of processes that lead to each station entering the beacon process. Finally, if the beacon process fails, the station can then enter the *trace* process in order to determine exactly why the previous processes have failed to complete successfully.

One of the essential conclusions of the whole beaconing and fault-tracing process is the *path test*. If a station or concentrator is within a network fault domain (i.e. an area of the network affected by a station or cabling fault) and undergoing a trace analysis, the path test will determine if there is a visible fault with any of its internal paths or hardware control elements, and then the station will readjust its internal path request control variable to reconfigure around the fault where possible. The station performs these tests off-line, so if a fatal fault is found such that the station cannot reattach to the network, then it will remain off-line until the problem is rectified.

The Beaconing Mechanism

The beaconing process is initiated either by a failed claim process, or by a request from the station's management process to directly enter the beacon mode. The beaconing stage is only ever reached if a significant break has occurred in the token path such that a single coherent ring cannot be re-established. Along with the follow-on trace process and subsequent path tests, it provides an automatic mechanism for detecting faults that are less obvious than a straightforward cable break.

A failed claim process is recognised by either the TRT value expiring due to the claim processing not being completed in time, a beacon frame being received from another station, or a reset being received from the physical layer. If a fault exists anywhere in the path (e.g. an intermittent cable break not detected by PCM, a station incorrectly configuring its CCEs), then the station(s) that is left with the lowest claim value will never see its own claim frame come back to it. This fault could also be due to the fact that another station has the same MAC address, and has incorrectly recognised the claim frame as its own. Hence the TRT will expire, causing the beacon process to be initiated.

In the case of the TRT expiring, recall from the claim process overview in Chapter 5 that the default TMax is used by the station as the TRT value during the claim process. This is usually set to the default value of 165 msec. Hence ample time is allowed for the station to see the initial token, or if it won the claim process, to release the initial token.

During beaconing, the station issues special MAC beacon frames (Figure 6.6) on its output port. For the situation where a claim process has been detected by this station to

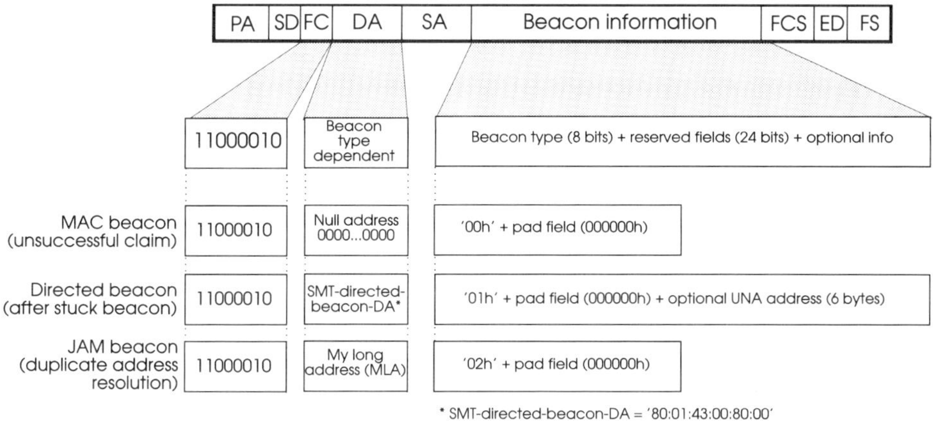

Figure 6.6 *MAC beacon frame format and types*

have failed, the beacon frame destination address is set to the null address (all zeros). The destination address in this case has no real use, as the source of the beacon frame can be identified by the source address field. The 32 bit information field indicates the beacon frame type, with the first 8 bits being used in this case, the remainder being reserved for future use by the FDDI standards body. The failed claim process sets this value to indicate unsuccessful claim (value 0).

A downstream station, when it receives a beacon frame, does one of two things. If it is in *ring_operational* mode (i.e. waiting for a token, or in repeat/idle mode), it enters *non-operational* mode and enters the idle or repeat mode, passing on the beacon frame of the upstream station. If it is already beaconing for some reason, with its own beacon frame, it again enters the idle or repeat mode, and repeats the beacon frame of the upstream station. This situation continues until all stations are beaconing as illustrated in Figure 6.7. If for some reason the ring had suddenly rectified the fault that caused the claim process to fail, and was a complete path again, the very first station that started beaconing would eventually see its own beacon frame. If this happens, then the station usually re-enters the claim process again, unless prevented from doing so by the station management process.

If the case is that a genuine break in the token path exists, then once the whole ring is beaconing, it is said to be *stuck beaconing*. The method of recovering from this condition is handled by the ring management process within the station that never sees a beacon frame on its input (A in our case).

Recovery from Stuck Beacon Conditions

In Chapter 5 we looked very quickly at the way ring management (RMT) within station management performs the MAC initialisation and management functions. Most of the functions described above, i.e. the claim and beaconing processes, are controlled within the MAC layer itself. What RMT does is to monitor the ring recovery mechanisms that the MAC instigates, and address the situation where the MAC itself cannot recover the ring fault condition.

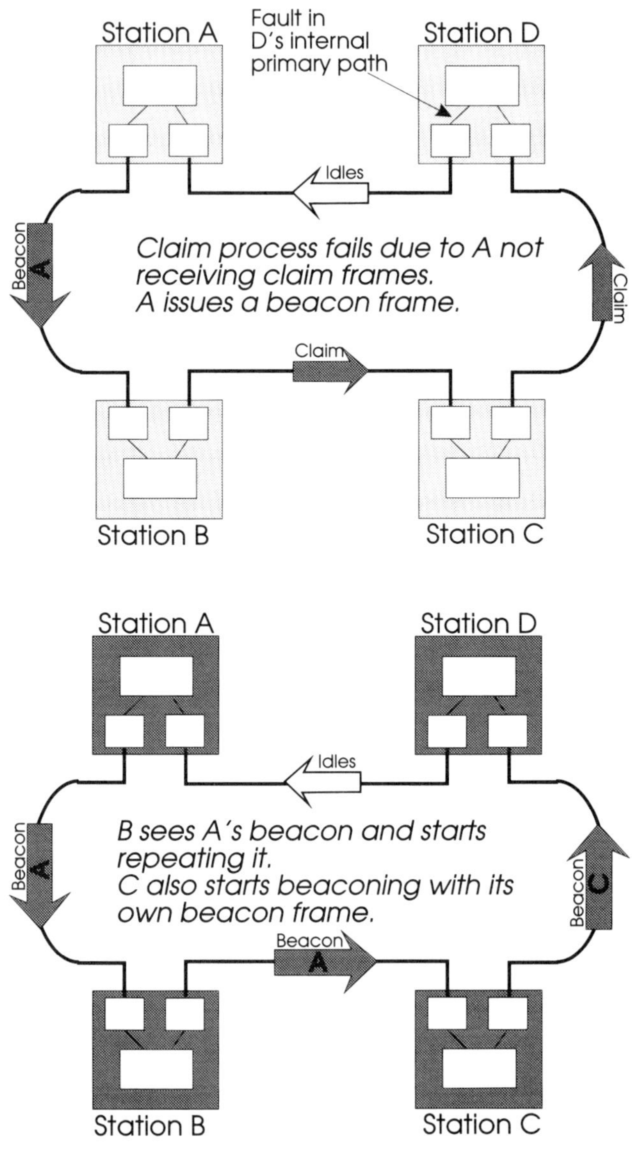

Figure 6.7(a) *Beaconing*

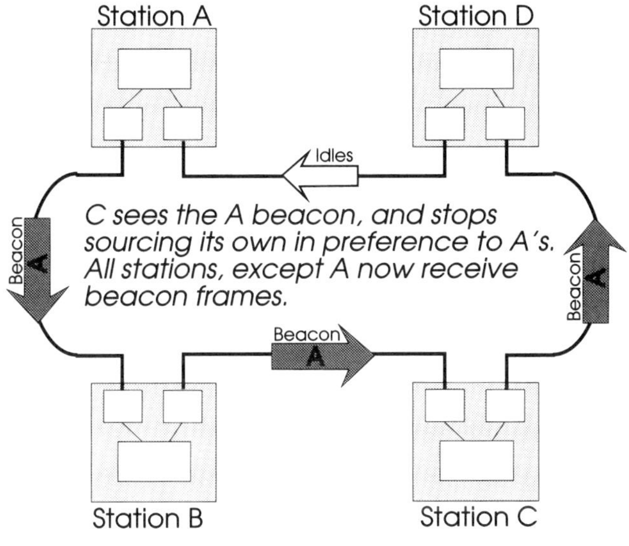

Figure 6.7(b) *Beaconing (continued)*

Figure 6.8 illustrates the RMT state transitions that occur during the recovery process. Once the ring enters the non-operational state (*ring_operational* flag reset), RMT goes through its *non-operational* state to the *detect* state, where it monitors the claim and beacon processes. A TRM (timer ring management) timer is used to time the various stages that the MAC goes through. For example, the transition shown from the non-operational state to the detect state is due to the TRM timer exceeding a *T_Non_Op* value. This is normally defaulted to around 1 sec. Once in the detect state, the TRM timer is reset and set to count the period of time that the MAC spends attempting to recover the ring beaconing. The value *T_Stuck* is used in this case, which is defaulted to around 8 sec. Also in this state, the possibility of a duplicate MAC address is checked. Once the TRM expires, the MAC is reset, and configured to send *directed beacons* for a fixed length of time (*T_Direct*) long enough to ensure that the directed beacons traverse the entire ring (default 370 msec). Directed beacons are of beacon type '01', and may also optionally include in their information field the *upstream neighbour address* (UNA) if known. RMT then initiates the *trace* process, which is used to determine the location of the fault on the network path.

The TRACE Function

The *TRACE* function provides a mechanism for getting out of the stuck beaconing condition, and identifying fault domains that are outside the scope of the simple PCM-to-PCM link. The goal of the trace process is to locate the fault between any two

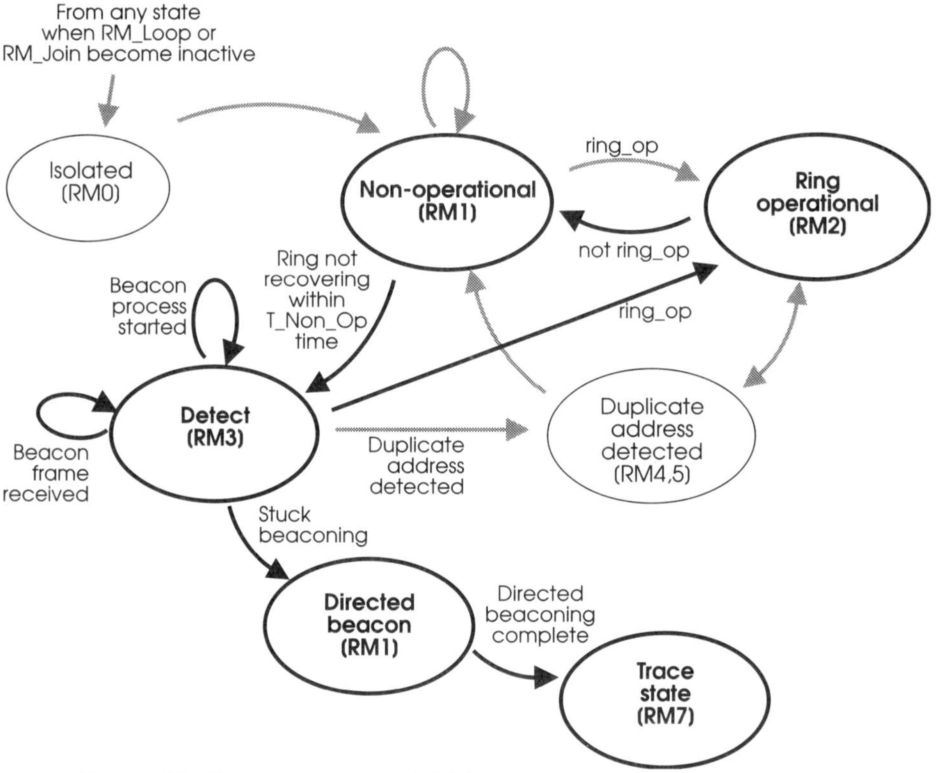

Figure 6.8 *Ring management (RMT) state changes during ring recovery*

MAC entities within the network.

With the connection to the outside world still made, a number of the lower-level SMT management processes namely RMT, PCM and ECM, enter the trace state. The RMT *stuck beaconing* process initiates the trace function after a timeout period, *T_Stuck*. From Figure 6.7 for example, station A will never see a beacon frame at its port A primary input due to a probable internal path fault in D not identified by the D–A PCM-to-PCM pseudo-code process. Station A will in this case be a *trace initiator*. As the next available *upstream* MAC is connected to the B port of station D, then the trace will be *terminated* at D. There are in fact several states of the trace process that the port entities along a trace path may be in:

- *Trace initiation* – the port attached upstream from the MAC stuck beaconing.
- *Trace propagation* – a port that receives a trace signal but is not attached to the output of a MAC.
- *Trace termination* – a port that receives a trace signal, and is attached to a MAC output.
- *Trace acknowledgement* – the return signalling that the terminating port has been reached, and is now leaving the network and performing a path test.

Let us now look at a simple example of a trace process between two neighbouring DAS devices, based on the two stations A and D from Figure 6.7. What the trace process involves is propagating a signal using special non-data line states against the normal token flow, backwards towards its upstream neighbour. In our example, station A will initiate a trace process within its PCM state machine that controls the A port. Alternating halt (H) and quiet (Q) symbols are transmitted on the secondary out link to the next upstream physical entity, creating a MLS, or master line state condition. This is recognised by the B port of station D as shown in Figure 6.9, by the PCM-B process, which terminates the trace and sets an internal flag to say that an internal path test should be initiated. On receipt of MLS, the ECM state machine within station D verifies that port B is attached to the output of a MAC (i.e. the end of the MAC-to-MAC trace has been reached), and issues a *PC_Stop* to port B, thus removing its connection. ECM then proceeds to a path test where the integrity of all the internal paths may be tested, and faults bypassed if possible by rerouting the token path (e.g. on a secondary path). The path test will determine ultimately if the station can enter the ring or not in any configuration. As the PCM-B state machine has been stopped by ECM, QLS is propagated back along in the direction of station A, which serves as a trace acknowledgement. On receipt of QLS, station A's port A will set its internal path test flag, indicating that a test is to be performed, and finally exit to perform a path test.

Figure 6.10 illustrates the trace processes that occur for two SAS stations performing a fault trace through a concentrator. Again, in this example, station D has a fault on the primary token path between its MAC and S port. Station A achieves the stuck beaconing stage, and starts a trace (step 1). MLS is transmitted back to the concentrator port M3 in this case, which detects the incoming trace signal and notifies the ECM process in the DAC (step 2). The ECM then determines the next port upstream, which in this case is M1 as M2 is in the isolated state (i.e. has no active connection off its port), and propagates the trace (step 3) as there is no MAC

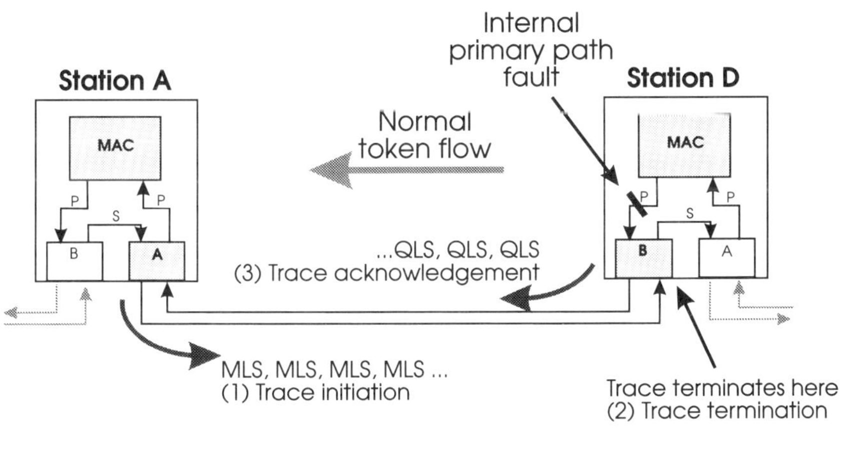

Figure 6.9 *Trace process between two DAS stations*

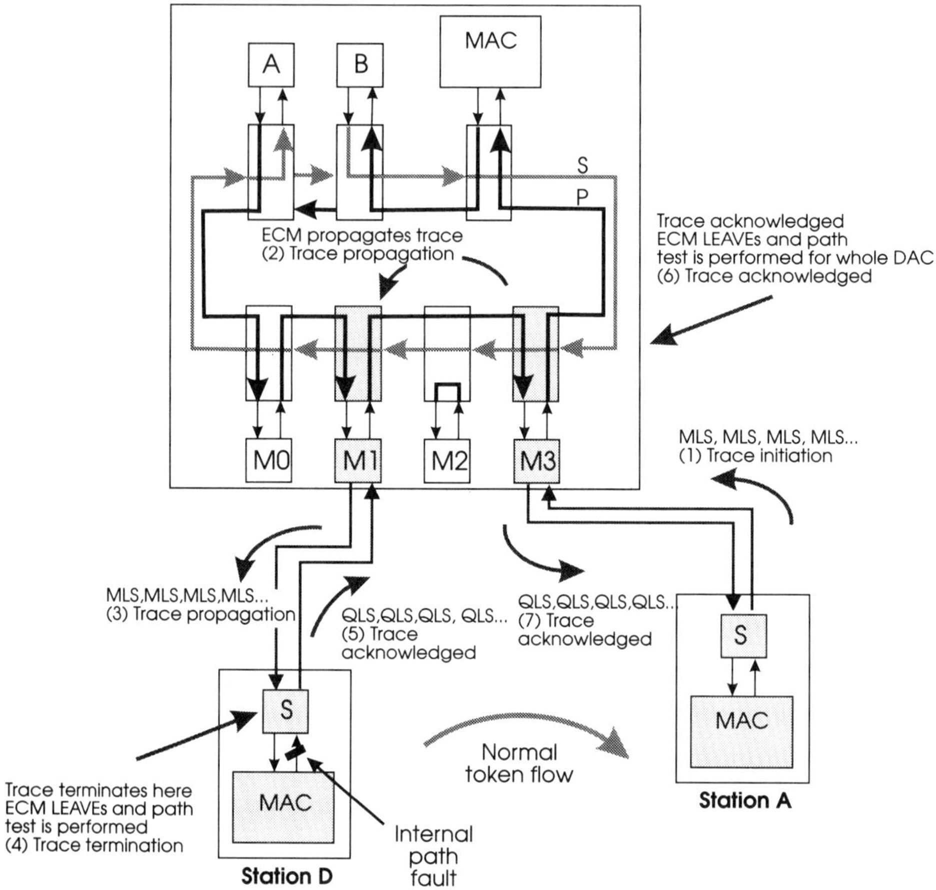

Figure 6.10 *Trace process between two SAS stations*

connected to port M1's input. Port M1 starts transmitting MLS (QH) which is detected by the S port of station D. Station D's ECM process determines that a MAC is connected to the S port input, and terminates the trace at that point (step 4). ECM then removes the port connection, causing QLS to be propagated back to the M1 port (step 5). Station D then performs its path test off-line (step 6).

As the M1 port is now seeing QLS on its line input, the DAC's ECM process takes the whole DAC off-line in order to perform a path test on the path the trace was propagated along. This in turn causes QLS to be transmitted out on all affected ports, including that connected to station A (step 7). For ports that were not in the trace state (e.g. port M0 and the corresponding external station), this results simply in the connection being broken, sending the PCM at the other end of the M0 port back to its

BREAK state. For port M3, QLS indicates that the trace has been acknowledged, and station A now removes itself from the ring and performs a path test. Hence, each of the stations within the trace fault domain remove themselves one at a time and perform paths tests until the original station that initiated the trace is reached.

A timer is employed in each of the station ports in the trace domain to ensure that the affected part of the network does not end up being stuck in the trace state. The default maximum length of time allowed for stations to complete the trace process is set at 7 sec, which is derived from the maximum possible network latency and the length of time that each station in a maximum sized network would take to propagate the trace signal. In addition, a time of 12 msec default is allowed for each of the stations to react to a received trace signal, i.e. the time from receiving the trace to either propagating it to the next port, or terminating if a MAC is encountered.

The final outcome of the trace process, of course, is that station D, if it cannot rectify its internal path problem, will leave itself removed from the ring (i.e. withhold its connection) hence allowing the whole ring to complete successfully the initialisation/claim process, and become fully operational.

Detecting and Recovering from Duplicate MAC Addresses

There is always the possibility that two or more stations can erroneously have the same MAC address. This can cause a number of problems, such as during normal network operation the wrong station(s) receiving packets, missing packets, packets arriving out of sequence, and so on. During initialisation, where it is more likely that the condition will have its first effect, problems can occur with the claim and beaconing processes, causing the incorrect release time for the initial token for example.

The ring management (RMT) process is responsible for the off-line (i.e. non-operational) monitoring of duplicate address conditions, and for taking the necessary action to remedy the situation. The condition in most cases can be easily recognised by the stations that have duplicate addresses themselves. For instance, during the claim process, if the station detects a claim frame with its source address equal to its own after having already yielded in the claim process to another claim frame of a lower bid value, then it knows that the incoming frame must have originated from a station with the same address. This is because it had stopped transmitting own claim frames earlier. A similar case exists during beaconing (if it gets that far).

The RMT process can take one of three corrective actions outlined in the SMT standard:

- Completely remove its own MAC from the ring, reporting the error on the user console, for example.
- Modify its own MAC address (MA – my address) to something unique.
- Perform a *jamming* process to ensure that the other stations also know that a duplicate address exists and take the necessary action.

In the case of jamming, the MAC is configured in such a way as to lose the claim process (i.e. set a large or maximum sized bid value). It then transmits a jamming frame onto the ring, which is a special beacon frame (see Figure 6.6). Whilst in this state, the MAC is prevented from interfacing to the higher LLC protocol requests to prevent it from sourcing any frames onto the ring. Though not covered here in any detail, there are two jamming techniques. The first involves simply transmitting a beacon frame onto the ring with the DA field equal to its own address in order to notify the other station with the same address of the condition. The second involves sending a second beacon frame after the first (termed *double beacon jam*) in order to ensure that the other station does not miss or discard the first due to a claim timeout, for example.

During network operation, if the duplicated address condition still exists (i.e. because it was missed by the non-operational process, or because an address was modified after initialisation), then SMT's neighbour notification process (see Chapter 7) will monitor and detect this condition. An option allows a station to issue a self-addressed SMT frame with its source and destination addresses equal to its own, thus detecting if it correctly circulates the ring without being copied by another station. For such an option to work, the station must be capable of operating its interface in a full duplex mode in order to receive an incoming frame at the same time as transmitting. Some of the earlier station adapters could not support this feature, meaning that they could not perform a full station loopback test.

Implementing Fault Tolerance

From what we have encountered so far, we see that there are basically two cabling options that give a form of fault tolerance. The first is the standard *dual-ring* set up, with each network device implemented as a class A, or dual attached device. Each of the critical components are then wired in a dual-ring configuration using primary and secondary fibre optic cabling. The second is the *dual-homed* set-up, a situation where backup links are created through the use of redundant links in a dual attachment tree configuration.

Which form of redundancy is chosen depends heavily on the end application and physical wiring topology of the network. However, there are a number of common approaches that may be used.

Dual-Ring and Concentrator Tree Approach

If we take a classic multi-storey building which has a requirement for a high-speed backbone network such as FDDI, and also for guaranteed services to two servers, then as illustrated in Figure 6.11, there are a number of ways to configure the FDDI backbone network in the vertical riser section of the cabling.

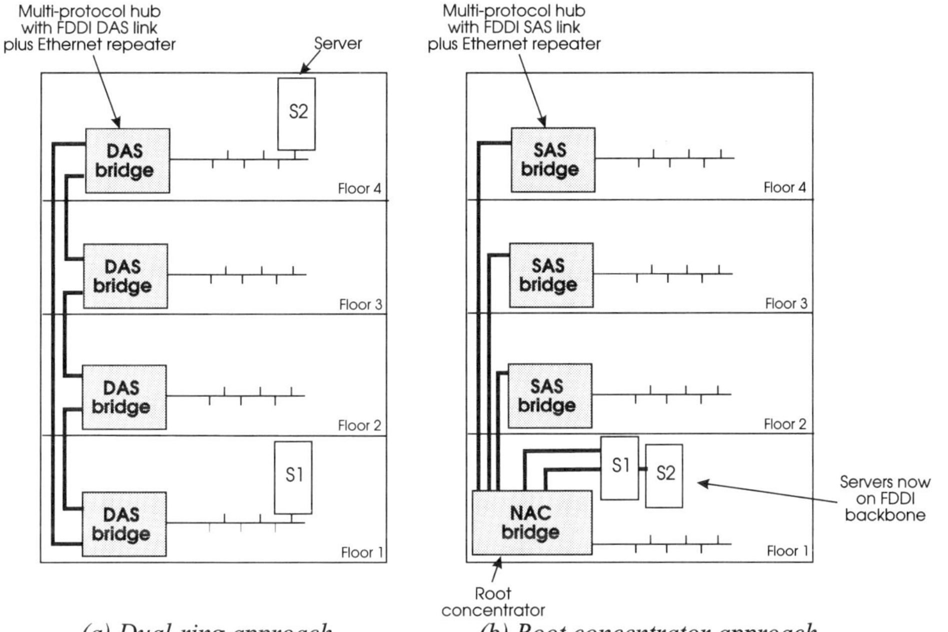

(a) Dual-ring approach *(b) Root concentrator approach*

Figure 6.11 *Standard methods for wiring multi-storey buildings*

Method (a) uses the traditional distributed or dual-ring of stations approach, which relies on the secondary ring as its backup. In such a system, a single FDDI link failure at any point will still allow all the stations to communicate with both servers on the network. The servers remain on the horizontal network running at the slower non-FDDI network speed of 10 Mbps in this instance, but may also have full FDDI 100 Mbps links to increase bandwidth. If two link failures occur using method (a), then the backbone will fragment into two separate networks, and depending on where the link-break occurs, will result in stations on the various horizontal segments being unable to talk to one or both of the servers (Figure 2.13). This is usually acceptable as when the first link failure occurs, it will hopefully be rectified before a second one develops.

Method (b) wires the network in a different way, using only single attachment connections at the interface to the horizontal network segments. All connections are brought back to a common root concentrator, which can be configured as a null attachment concentrator (NAC). As a single link failure can effectively shut off a whole segment, the servers are both placed directly onto the backbone for added performance and security.

The latter approach is being used in more and more cases, as it allows for greater flexibility in the way fault tolerance is added, and also provides an upgrade path to future switched backbone structures using networks such as ATM. Additional fault-tolerant links can easily be added using the root concentrator approach combined with the dual-homing feature. This is useful, for example, if the second server has to remain on the top floor, but still requires a recovery from single link failures.

Dual-Homing Approach

Figure 6.12 illustrates a campus-based configuration that utilises a dual-homed configuration to achieve fault tolerance in the backbone FDDI network due to the predominant star wiring from the central campus building. Again, two distributed servers exist, with a link to a central mainframe in building I. The various FDDI stations and connections employed are as follows:

A NAC or root concentrator (part of an intelligent hub)
B Single attached concentrator (m port attached to backup link)
C Dual-homed station or concentrator
D and E Single attached stations or concentrators

What the dual-homing approach shows is that it is much easier to add in fault-redundant links, such as that shown between stations C and B, at a later stage. If the fault redundant link was not initially installed with the rest of the backbone,

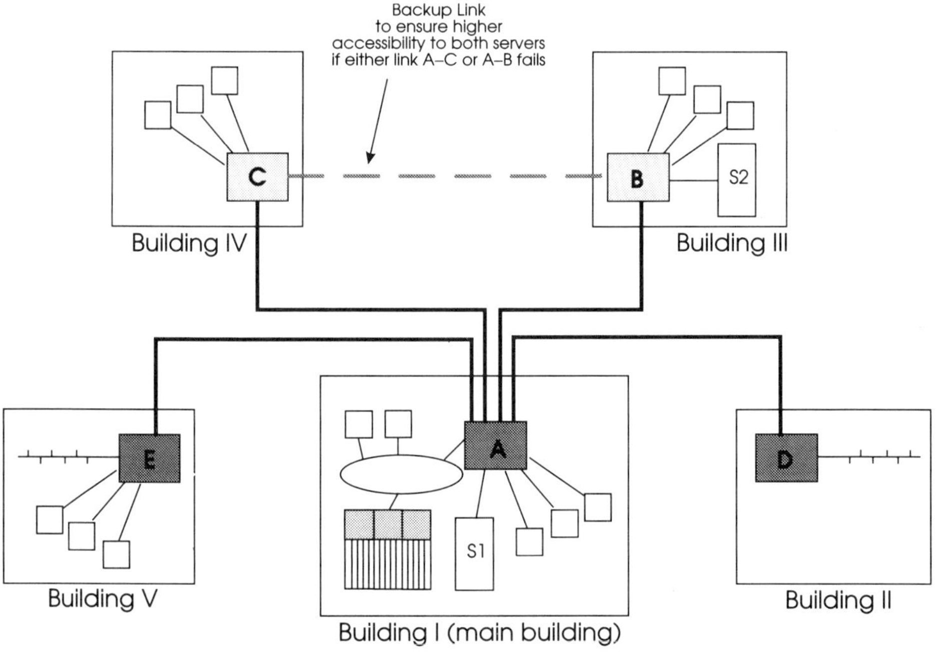

Figure 6.12 *Campus backbone, with dual-homing links for fault tolerance*

stations B and C would have been simple single attach stations or concentrators. To add the additional fault tolerant link, the following steps would be employed:

1. Install the additional fibre optic link between buildings III and IV.
2. Upgrade the C station from a SAS to a dual-homed-DAS.
3. Upgrade the B station SAS interface to be a SAC, adding an M port to link to the C station A port.

Faults Due to Cabling Errors

A number of undesired, but sometimes operational, topologies can arise from incorrect wiring of cabling between stations. Specific cases of these are twisted rings, and the illegal tree of rings topology created by an M–M port connection.

Twisted Rings

It is possible, due to improper wiring, for a station to have its A port connected to the A port of another station, and/or its B port to another B port. If the mechanical keying is wrong, say, then the A and B cable connectors could accidentally get swapped. This results, as illustrated in Figure 6.13, in a twisted ring.

What happens in a twisted ring is that the primary and the secondary rings become interlinked. In our example, only a single station is affected. The net result of this is that the station at the crossover point, which has its MAC device (the means of accessing the network) connected as normal to the internal primary input and output paths, never sees a token or data frame as is not on the main path. In fact if you trace the paths through each of the stations, then you will see that there are two separate paths, one with three station MACs, and one with a single station MAC (where the changeover is). Hence, if a station was unaware of this, it would assume it was the only station on the network. However, the low level initialisation process discussed earlier ensures that this is detected, and the station that is isolated will probably get an error message on its user console indicating the problem. In addition, the neighbouring stations in this case will also detect this situation, and set a status variable which a central management station will pick up as part of the management process.

Tree of Rings

If the M port of one concentrator is connected to another M port this would create what amounts to a tree of rings topology. Figure 6.14 illustrates the effect created if the M–M connection were to proceed. Two separate rings would be created within the tree structure, highlighted in this example by the black and grey lines. As we saw in

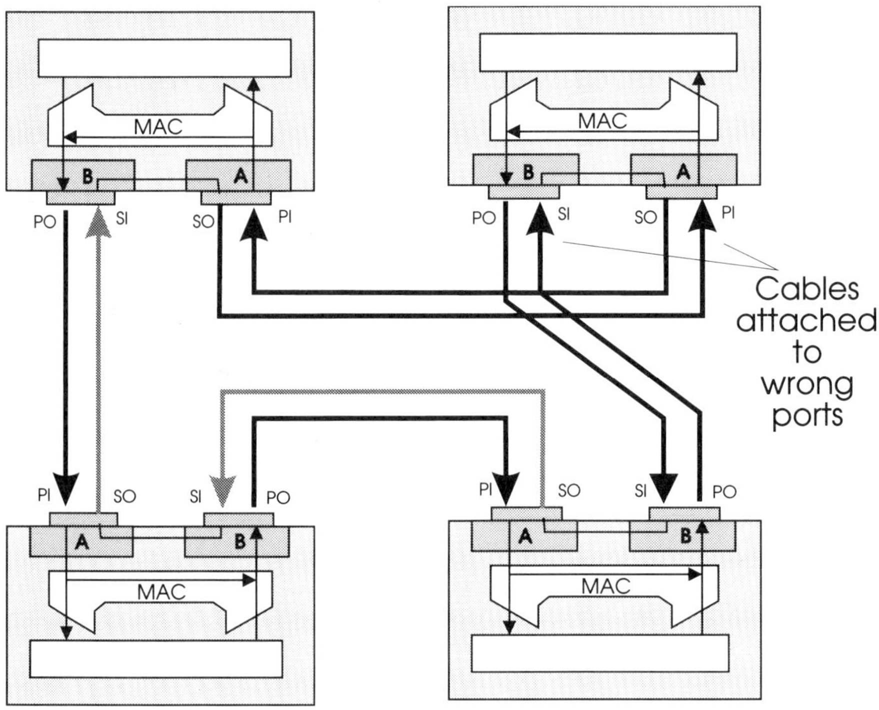

Figure 6.13 *Twisted ring due to swapped A and B connections*

Chapter 5, this connection would be withheld due to the station connection rules, as it is illegal.

Other Undesirable Configurations

Other connections that can be made, but again split the ring into a number of segments in a non-obvious fashion, are master (M) port connection back-up the tree to an S or A/B port from which the M port path was originally derived. These are quite easily done, as they are valid connections in FDDI. However, as they effectively loop back up the tree as opposed to 'growing' downwards, they create a split path where stations will be placed on totally separate sections of the network. This may or may not be the desired effect, and can lead to much confusion over which station is connected to what ring, and should be avoided where possible.

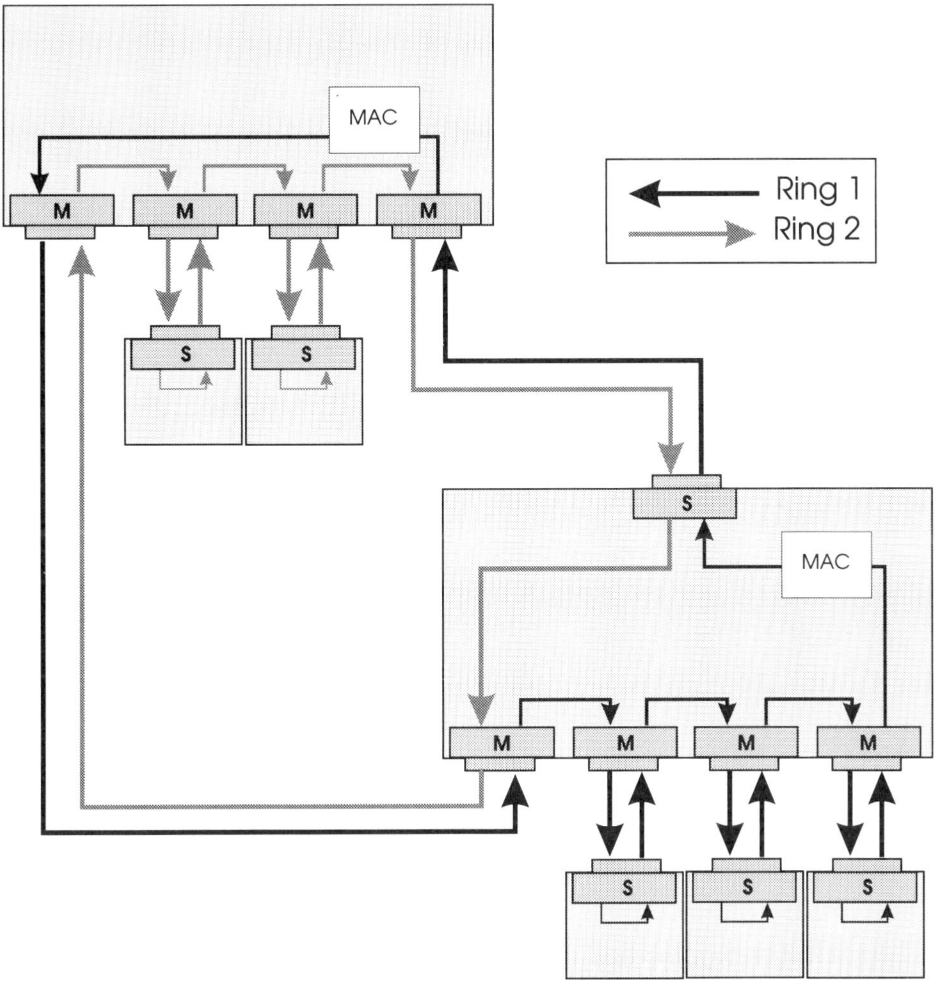

Figure 6.14 *Tree of rings (effect of illegal M–M connection)*

Summary

FDDI has an automatic recovery mechanism built into every station, allowing it to recover from a variety of errors involving breaks in both cables, and internal connections within a station. A beaconing mechanism is used to determine where a break in the token path exists, preventing a station from successfully completing the claim process outlined in Chapter 4. Depending on the severity of the break, a trace process may be used to establish at which point a fault exists between neighbouring MACs. Once the problem has been identified, the station can reconfigure around it (if it is capable) and notify management processes.

By planning the cabling of the FDDI network carefully, the fault recovery mechanism provides a robust network topology. There are two basic methods for connecting stations in a fault-tolerant configuration: dual-ring and dual-homing.

CHAPTER 7

Management of FDDI Nodes

So far, we have looked at the mechanisms involved in initialising and recovering an FDDI network. The next underlying task is to establish the management structure and mechanism used by FDDI across a single segment, and beyond into multiple segment and media networks. FDDI has a built-in mechanism that ensures a standard level of management across all stations, defined by SMT's frame-based services. Special SMT MAC frames allow information between stations to be exchanged, and a set of management objects to be regularly updated and kept within the station's *management information base* (or MIB). All this occurs automatically within a single FDDI segment (as it is a mandatory part of the FDDI standard) in the background to the normal data transmissions.

An everyday user of an FDDI station would never see what is going on in the background as far as management traffic is concerned, nor the effects these management frames have. This is visible to the designated network management station or network analyser. It is even more likely that the management station is not located on the same logical ring as the end user if the network is of a reasonable size. Such a management station may access information about a particular station via other industry standard management protocols, such as Internet's SNMP (Simple Network Management Protocol), or ISO's CMIP (Common Management Interface Protocol).

Basic Management Principles

There are many excellent texts covering the ongoing efforts of the standards committees to produce standards that address the management aspects independent of network types and topologies. For this reason, only the basic principles will be covered in order to clarify the framework with which the management of FDDI networks are presented. Readers are referred to other books such as Stallings (1993) and Rose (1991) for a greater insight into the standards aimed toward coherent and common management of networks.

Incorporating management into any of today's networks is extremely important as both the demands on, and the sizes of the networks grow. Management is important to both the network management personnel, as well as the end users. A network manager in a central information services department wishes to monitor, and more importantly, remotely control the operation of the network. This applies to both local sites, and remote branch office locations. Various marketing reports indicate that anywhere from 75 to 90 per cent of all intelligent hub ports are managed (all technologies), so there is no doubt that management is a very important aspect of a network. The growth in managed networks is also related to the growth in the size of LAN installations and users, and in many cases, the networking administration budget does not grow proportionally. In fact, in many cases, the administration budgets are actually being cut, even though there is substantial growth, again making intelligent managed networks all the more necessary.

In general, the facilities a network manager wishes to have access to are the following:

- *Fault management* – fault alerting and control functions.
- *Accounting* – usage charting, and if necessary, costing usage by user or department.
- *Network configuration* – controlling segmentation and topology where possible.
- *Performance monitoring* – gaining statistics about network utilisation.
- *Network security* – restricting network access by user, port, segment, address, and so on.

Other considerations at systems level are also important, such as software loading, which is not discussed here.

Network Management Programs

There are many flavours and types of network management programs, each with their strengths and usual slants towards a particular manufacturer's equipment and capabilities. Most run on dedicated workstations in the larger corporate networks, and also on general user workstations for smaller branch office networks where a local PC may be used to check on the status of the network.

There are a number of common capabilities across all management programs. For example, such programs support the ability to extract network configuration information and bandwidth on an individual user basis. The interface to the network manager is usually a graphics-based program, which can represent in a combined chart or graph format a particular aspect of the network characteristic. Figure 7.1 illustrates a simplified picture of such an example output for the total number of good frames (i.e. those without CRC errors, and not rejected for some reason) a station receives, and

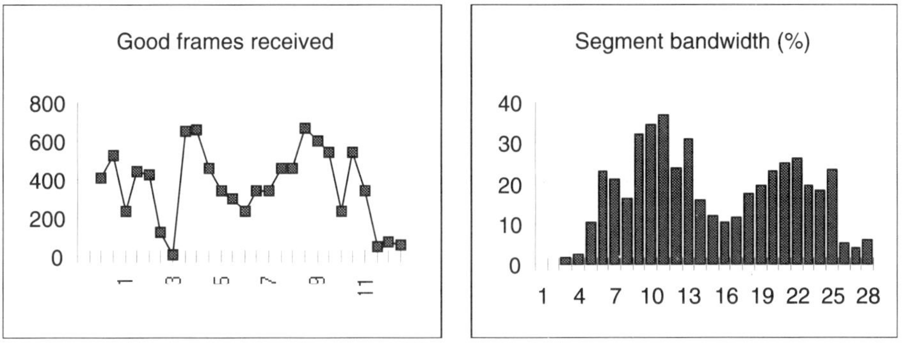

Figure 7.1 *Example output from a management package*

also the overall network segment utilisation. Such information can be represented in many ways, and is heavily dependent on the particular program being used.

A more important consideration is the ability to control the configuration of a station or node. For instance, the network monitoring program may highlight that a particular node has been receiving an abnormal number of bad frames, or may be randomly transmitting bad or garbage frames, and overloading the network. Using the management control panel for the intelligent hub that the station is connected to, for example, the manager can shut down the link to that station, effectively isolating it from the network until corrective action is taken. If it is still possible to communicate with the stations, the network manager may decide to instruct the station to go off-line and perform a self-test, sending the results back to the management station when back on line again. The amount of flexibility and control will depend greatly on the capabilities of the program being used, and the equipment that is being controlled.

Lastly, a common capability that fits in nicely with FDDI's capabilities is the ability to construct network topology maps. This is generally a network technology independent process that uses something like SNMP to extract the information, and build a global or segment-by-segment map of the network. In most cases, the map is built and updated automatically by the management program without the need for manual intervention.

Revision of Management Principles and Standards

Figure 7.2 illustrates the standard set of processes that exist within a managed network, with the emphasis here on FDDI. If the management station is on a network segment of different technology, standards-based network management protocols such as SNMP have to be also implemented on the individual stations. Alternatively, a single

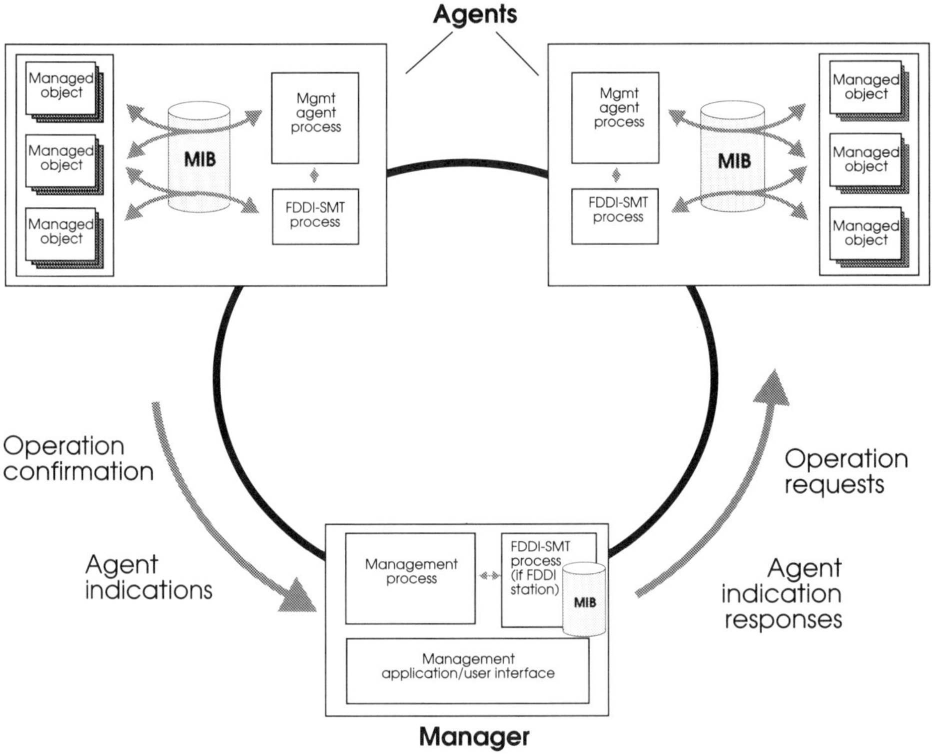

Figure 7.2 *Components of management*

station may be designated a *proxy* agent that effectively converts the alien protocol into SMT-based requests (see later). Otherwise, within a single FDDI segment, standard SMT protocols may be used.

There are basically two main processes: the main *manager* process, running on the management station, and the *agent* processes running on the target nodes. The method of communication in most management systems is based on the manager originating an *operation request* packet and the agent responding by taking the necessary action, reporting back to the manager with an *operation confirmation* packet if required. In addition, the agent process can be configured to automatically transmit agent *notification* or *indication* packets to the manager to signify a significant change in status, or a potential problem report. The manager may, or may not depending on the severity, respond back with an *indication response* packet.

As outlined earlier, the fundamental component behind the management capability of a network is the MIB. All operations on the end node are carried out by writing to and reading from the various MIB *variables* or *attributes*, or specific *action*-oriented data objects within the station. Some result in a direct action being taken by the node (such as a *perform self-test* action variable), and others specify various operational preferences, such as acceptable link errors before a notification is given. The manager may either read or write to the various MIB locations inside the station. This is accomplished in the wider networking context via management protocols, such as the Internet SNMP using the *get* and *set* operations. The ISO CMIP-based protocols have a number of additional operational commands that allow the easier creation and deletion of MIB attributes and managed objects. For notification in SNMP, a *trap* may be set within an agent to allow a particular event to be captured and communicated to the manager via the notification processes. Similar processes exist in the ISO standards. In the local (FDDI only) context, then SMT protocols, described later, may be used.

Another area of considerable importance is the emerging trend towards a more distributed management technique. This involves delegating some of the management sub-tasks out to a particular management agent. A good example here is the remote monitoring (RMON) addition to the SNMP set of standards. An RMON-capable station or node can collect management information for the sub-network that it has responsibility for. For example, it may keep track of the total number of errors for that segment which it is part of. In addition, it may keep track of host-to-host communications traffic, sampling packets where necessary. It is in effect a remote network analyser as well. The benefit of such an approach is that it takes the load off the main central manager, and cuts down on the amount of time spent overall in passing management information over the various router and bridge boundaries. Only summary information (ready processed for that segment) need be passed across, as opposed to every station's parameters, making it a useful feature of remote LAN segments.

In the mainstream industry standard protocols, standard MIBs are defined, such as MIB-I and MIB-II for SNMP. In general, these define standard or common attributes across several network types, and are thus higher-level by nature, consisting of network-specific sub-groups where the information becomes more technology specific (e.g. *total collisions* apply to CSMA/CD and not ring-based networks). The structures of these higher-level MIBs is not covered here, and the reader is referred to Stallings (1993). The important thing to note is that there exist lower-level MIBs, such as the FDDI SNMP/SMT MIB and IEEE802.3/Ethernet MIB, that are defined to cover the network technology specific areas.

Industry Standard Management vs. FDDI SMT

It is perfectly reasonable to ask why the higher-levels of management portions of FDDI's SMT exist if there is already a very capable mechanism such as the ISO CMIP or Internet's SNMP. SMT's management protocols have, as we shall see, a number of features that could be classed as overlapping considerably with those of a standards-based protocol. However, it must be remembered that most of the standards-based systems today have not been around as long as FDDI, and are geared up to be more network independent. Hence, there is a need for an FDDI internal protocol that will make much of the standards-based protocols life a great deal easier, and transparent to the internal workings of FDDI.

SMT also covers a broader range of issues, such as the initialisation of the station, runtime monitoring, and interchange of neighbour information to ensure a much more reliable network than, say, the current Ethernet implementations. Hence, it is an entity that goes a long way to implementing a lot of the functions that support SNMP or CMIP protocols, allowing a high-level of monitoring and control to be achieved using a fully standardised mechanism as outlined in the FDDI standard. Further, as it is part of the SMT standards documents, a guaranteed minimum level of support is available for all FDDI products.

For situations where a number of stations in an FDDI network only support SMT, and no standards-based management protocols, then a *proxy agent* may be employed. This is used in IBM's 8240 FDDI concentrator, for example. As the name suggests, the proxy agent acts on behalf of the non-supporting stations, taking the standard management protocol, and converting this to SMT, and vice versa. For SNMP, a single device therefore acts as the proxy on the ring, and alleviates the need for dedicated SNMP agents on all nodes in the network. This is useful for networks that were installed before protocols such as SNMP were widely available, and are still subject to changes.

SMT's Managed Objects

In Figure 5.2, we saw the basic high-level structure of SMT in terms of its various components, *connection management* (ECM, PCM and CFM), *ring management* (RMT) and *frame-based services*. SMT frame services control the transmission and reception of SMT frames carrying the station management control and status information.

Figure 7.3 illustrates the SMT management model, and the interaction between the station's managed objects and agent process. The management objects that are shown refer to actual attributes that may be either monitored or changed. An example is the configuration state of the CCE elements that allow ports or MACs to be configured into a token path as we saw in Chapter 5. This would be represented as a variable, representing the LIPSTC states that are possible for that CCE, e.g. *fddiPORTCurrentPath = isolated.* The CMT portion of SMT, in particular the specific CFM state machine, is responsible for maintaining the *fddiPORTCurrentPath* variable for that particular port. As we shall see later, the state of this variable is accessible to an outside management station using an SMT PMF *get* frame. Alternatively, an SNMP *get.request* frame addressed to an SNMP management agent would also allow access to the equivalent MIB variable, *fddimibPORTCurrentPath.*

The managed objects in this case are divided into four main types: SMT objects, MAC objects, PATH objects and PORT objects. There is only ever one instance of the SMT object, but there can be multiple instances of the others depending on the number

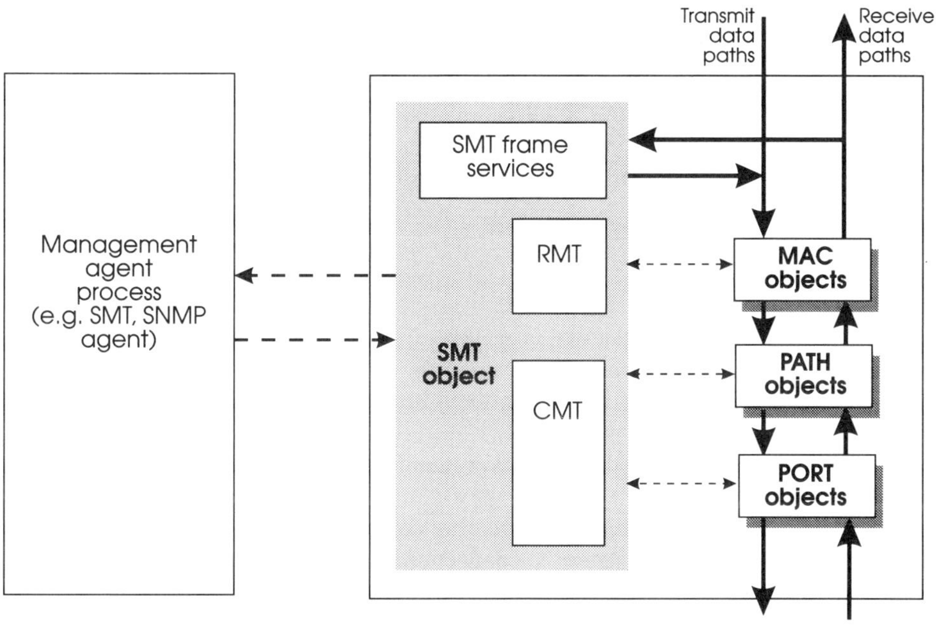

Figure 7.3 *SMT management model (source: ANSI SMT standard)*

of physical entities present (Figure 5.2). In the case of the latter, there always exists an indexing method to access the correct object instance. For example, in a standard DAS node, there will probably exist a single SMT object, two PORT objects (A and B), two PATH objects (a primary and a secondary), and a single MAC object.

The FDDI MIB divides its attributes, actions and notifications into these four main components or *classes*. Figure 7.4 illustrates the contents of each of the classes at group level. Within each of the classes exists a number of attributes, actions or notifications that affect various aspects of the managed object they are part of. The diagram is formatted in such a way as to show the naming convention used by the SMT standard to name the various groups. For example, *fddiSMTStationConfigGrp* refers to the StationConfig group shown under the SMT branch. As the full list of MIB contents within each of the object classes is quite extensive, the reader is referred to the SMT standard for more detail if required. A complete list of the SMT-MIB is contained in the Appendix.

Within each of the various classes, there exist a number of mandatory and optional MIB items that are supported. Optional ones tend to be those dependent on the level of complexity offered by a particular station or concentrator type. For instance, the optional MIB variables associated with a bridging (e.g. FDDI to Ethernet) station need not be supported by all of the stations, only those that have the bridging capability.

Mandatory ones are those that a node should implement as a minimum to claim conformance to a particular SMT version.

Attributes can either have a *get* only access status if purely a status variable, or a *get-replace* status if the variable can be remotely updated by an external manager. Actions are initiated using the SMT parameter management protocol. Notifications generate the appropriate action from either the management agent, or via the SMT status report protocol. Each of these protocols will be examined later.

SMT Object Class

The SMT MIB section provides the necessary support for managing the node at the highest level. Within this group are defined the various station-level preferences or control variables – the configuration policy, station insertion and removal control, general station status, and so on.

Within the *StationIdGrp* there exists a number of variables for identifying the station and the manufacturer. The version of the MIB can also be identified from this group. The *StationConfigGrp* is where the configuration of the station may be determined, or where the station's connection policy may be remotely set. For example, from this group we can remotely determine how many paths, MACs and PORTs are available, if there is a optical bypass capability, and what the current connection policy is (Figure 5.8). The StatusGrp allows the current state of the station to be determined, e.g. CFM state (*ISOLATED*, *WRAP_A*, etc.), SMT-ECM process state, if the station is in a peer wrapped state, and so on.

MAC Object Class

This object class contains all the MIB variables for controlling and monitoring the configuration and status of all the MAC devices within the node. These include all the parameters for checking that frames and tokens are being transmitted and received correctly, and that the node has the correct timer parameters for the timed token protocol. In addition, the various priority thresholds may be set up and verified for asynchronous frame transfers. Excessive frame errors may be checked for using the MAC object class, and the appropriate notification given when errors at the MAC level (i.e. too many CRC errors) become excessive.

PATH Object Class

This object contains all the MIB variables for controlling and checking the status of all paths contained within the node, i.e. the primary, secondary and local paths. Synchronous bandwidth management acts on attributes in this class (see later).

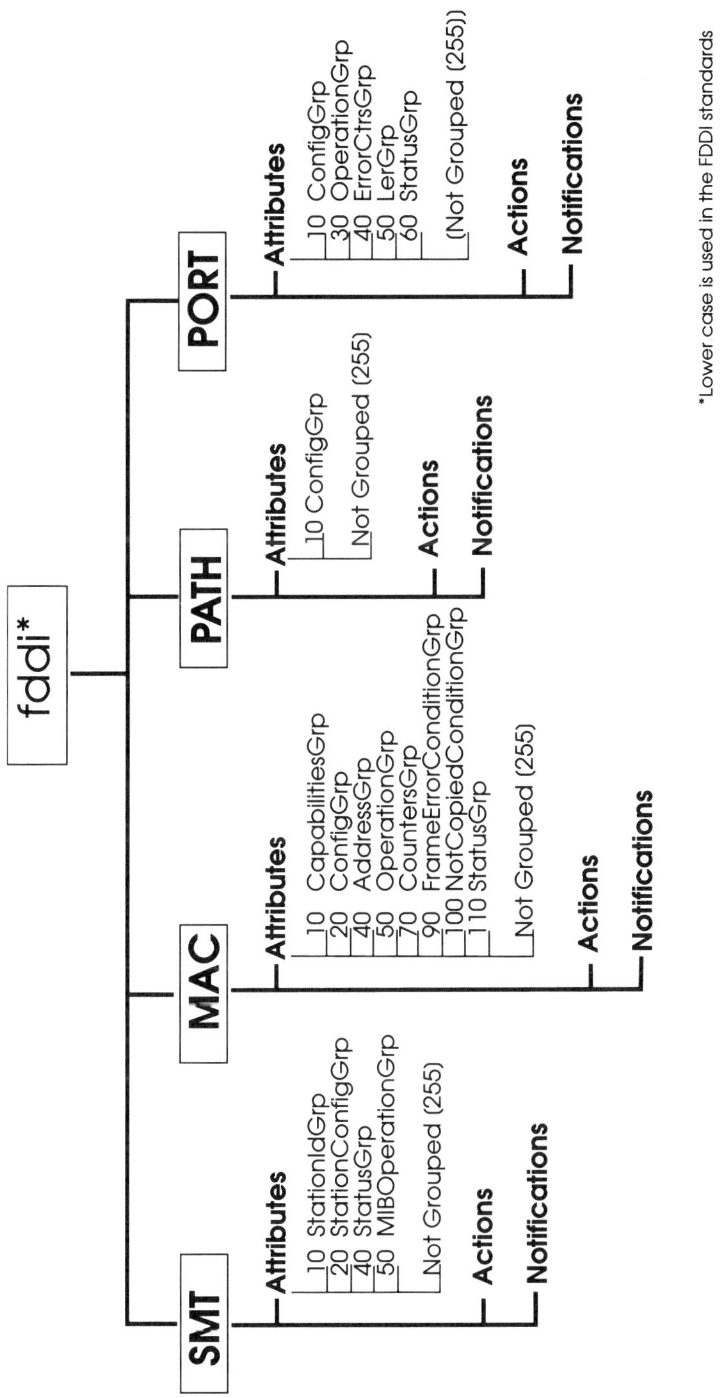

Figure 7.4 *FDDI MIB structure*

PORT Object Class

The PORT object class allows the control and monitoring of all PORTs within a station. In particular, link error monitor counters for each PORT may be accessed, whether a PORT has withheld a connection for any reason, which PATH the port is configured into, and so on. Of particular importance to the network manager is the ability to set link error thresholds and alarms, causing a notification to be given via the status report protocol when the errors on link exceed a preset threshold.

SMT's Frame-Based Management Protocols

Having identified what there is to manage within an FDDI node in terms of MIB groups and managed objects, let us now look at how the built-in SMT process handles the access and control of this information.

The following protocols are defined:

- Neighbour notification protocol
- Status report protocol
- Parameter management protocol
- Station status polling protocol
- Echo protocol
- Synchronous bandwidth allocation protocol
- Extended service protocol

A special MAC SMT frame (Figure 7.5), carries a number of management frames as listed in Table 7.1. An SMT frame is simply a standard PDU frame with a special FC field to indicate the SMT functionality, and with the SMT-specific data contained within the information field. The FC either indicates a SMT-Info (01000001b), or a next station addressing (01001111b) frame. The SMT protocol data unit is further split into two sections: the header and information field. The overall length varies depending on the purpose of the frame. Table 7.1 also indicates where each of the frames are used, and the three possible types that an SMT frame can have, i.e. announcement, request or response. The 'o' and 'm' fields of the table indicate whether support is optional or mandatory.

Each of the parameters fields (type, length, resource-id, parameter value) shown are divided into to basic types: those carrying MAC, PATH and PORT objects, and those carrying SMT objects. For the SMT object classes, the resource-id field is omitted altogether.

The basic purpose of each of the protocols are as follows:

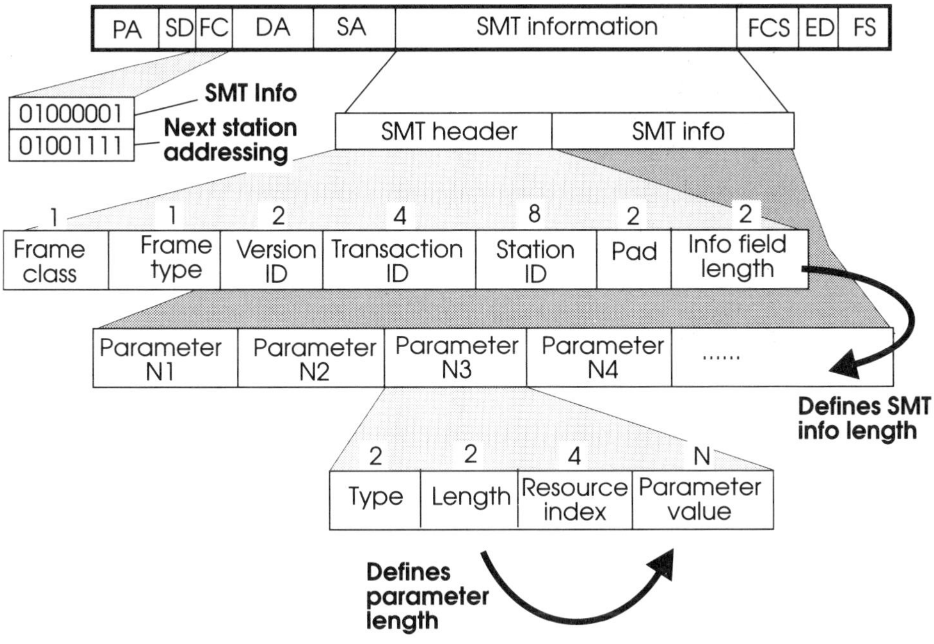

Figure 7.5 *SMT frame format*

Neighbour Notification Protocol

The neighbour notification protocol allows the station to determine its logical upstream and downstream neighbour addresses, and is ultimately responsible for keeping the *fddiMACUpstreamNbr*, *fddiMACDownstreamNbr*, *fddiMACOldUpstreamNbr* and *fddiMACOldDownstreamNbr* MIB attributes up to date within the fddiMAC MIB class. This protocol has the secondary function of identifying any duplicate SMT addresses by monitoring the SMT frames received. NIF frames are used to carry the protocol. NIF request frames are issued to the downstream neighbour and resulting NIF response frame dealt with by an *NNTransmitter* process within the station. In a similar way, an *NNReceiver* process deals with the upstream communications. Hence in every FDDI node in the network, there will be two co-operating NNTransmitter and NNReceiver processes between neighbouring stations on the logical ring. The transmission of NIF requests occurs anywhere between 2 and 30 sec depending on the setting of the *fddiSMTT_Notify* MIB attribute parameter within the node. The default is normally 30 sec. If a management node wishes to construct a logical map of the whole FDDI segment, then it may do so by using the MIB variables above, accessing them via the PMF protocol.

Table 7.1 *SMT frame classes and types usage*

Frame class		Code	Frame type	Usage	
Neighbour information	**NIF**	#01	[01]Announcement [02]Request [03]Response	o m m	Neighbour notification protocol
Status information	**SIF** configuration	#02	[02]Request [03]Response	o m	Station status polling
	SIF operation	#03	[02]Request [03]Response	o m	
Echo	**ECF**	#04	[02]Request [03]Response	o m	Echo protocol
Resource allocation	**RAF**	#05	[01]Announcement [02]Request (SBA) [03]Response (SBA)	o o o	Synchronous bandwidth allocation (SBA) protocol
Request denied	**RDF**	#06	[03]Response	m	For notifying when any request frame is not supported in some way
Status report	**SRF**	#07	[01]Announcement	m	Status report protocol
Parameter management	**PMF *get***	#08	[02]Request [03]Response	o m	Parameter management protocol
	PMF *set*	#09	[02]Request [03]Response	o o	
Extended service	**ESF**	#FF	[01]Announcement [02]Request [03]Response	o o o	Extended service protocol

Status Reporting Protocol

This protocol is used to periodically announce specific node conditions by sending a SRF frame out to a designated multicast address (SMT-SRF-DA '80:01:43:00:80:08' – MSB representation). Whenever a condition changes or an event occurs that warrants an external manager knowing about the status change, an SRF frame is constructed and continuously send out (if the *fddiSMTStatRptPolicy* is set true). This occurs initially every 2 sec, and at a decreasing rate (time interval is multiplied by 2) until the interval gets to 32 sec. If the condition or event is no longer valid, then the SRF frame transmissions are discontinued after the last frame is transmitted with the inactive conditions/event indications present. If whilst the status frames are being transmitted a new condition or event becomes true, then the SRF frames are transmitted at the 2 sec rate and the time interval increased after every transmission as before. The kind of conditions that are reported via this protocol are things like frame or link error conditions exceeding thresholds, duplicate address detected, a station wrap condition present, and so on. Events that get reported include MAC and PORT current path changes, MAC address neighbour changes and undesirable connection occurrences. Vendor-specific conditions or events may also be included.

Parameter Management Protocol

This protocol allows a remote management process to access all the MIB attributes either individually, or by groups, and also to instigate various actions by setting the appropriate MIB action variables. The protocol uses two basic operations, indicated by using either a PMF-Get frame or a PMF-Set frame. The manager requests the contents of a MIB attribute or attribute group using a PMF-Get request frame with the appropriate details of which area of the MIB it wishes to interrogate. A PMF-Set request is used if the manager wishes to change a MIB variable. The target station responds to the PMF request frames with a corresponding PMF-Get or PMF-Set response frame. The response frames indicate if the request was completed successfully, otherwise the appropriate error condition is reported. For example, the response may indicate an unsupported MIB attribute was requested, the parameter was out of range or the operation was illegal.

Station Status Polling Protocol

By using SIF request frames, any station can enquire about the general status of any other. Using the parameter management protocol allows the network management station to collect information by individually addressing the relevant MIB attributes or groups. However, this can be very time consuming. Hence the SIF frames and associated protocol provide a condensed view of the station status and configuration. This method provides a mechanism for building physical ring maps, establishing the configuration and connection capabilities of a station, and is also useful for obtaining statistics such as total frames received per MAC within the station, how many link errors have been detected, and so on.

Echo Protocol

This is used as a simple mechanism for checking that the path between two SMT processes within a network are operating correctly. The ECF request frame contains vendor-specific data, and is simply sent to another SMT entity within the network, which responds with an ECF response frame containing the same data that was sent within the SMT info field of the ECF request. This protocol is useful for a network manager verifying the connection to a target end station. The end station has to support the ECF response frame, but only optionally needs to generate ECF requests.

Synchronous Bandwidth Allocation Protocol

This optional protocol is used by those stations in the network that require the use of the FDDI synchronous data services (see Chapter 4). RAF request and response frames are utilised by a central allocation manager (which can be a management station, or any other designated synchronous management station) and participating stations to allocate a slice of available synchronous transmission time. The purpose of the protocol is not to manage the overall synchronous transmission across the network (e.g. setting up end-to-end communication channels), but solely to allow the allocation and monitoring of the available synchronous bandwidth to ensure that no ring instabilities due to overuse or misuse of allocation occurs. A station wishing to obtain an allocation of synchronous bandwidth must send a RAF request frame to the predefined SBA manager's SMT address (SMT-SBA-DA '80:01:43:00:80:09'). The central allocator will respond to the request with a RAF response frame indicating if the station may or may not receive an allocation of synchronous bandwidth. The protocol also allows for the case where a station may request allocation on behalf of a number of other stations, and in turn sub-allocate this to the group of stations once it has successfully obtained it. The central allocator has responsibility for ensuring that the correct allocation is made, is in accordance with the rest of the network parameters (such as TTRT, etc.) and in the case of over-allocation, recovery of the ring.

The allocation of synchronous bandwidth is also possible using the parameter management protocol discussed earlier, as each of the MIB parameters associated with synchronous bandwidth (*fddiPATHSbaPayload*, *fddiPATHSbaOverhead* and *fddiPATHSbaAvailable*) are externally accessible and may be changed remotely this way. A specific example of the usage and meaning of these variables is covered later.

Extended Service Protocol

This protocol allows for extensions to the SMT protocols not already allocated or covered. If a station does not support this protocol, it simply ignores the request.

Management Process Examples

Having identified the various protocols that are employed by SMT management, let us now look a few examples of how they may be utilised by a network management station. The first examples will look at how station configurations and status may be determined, how a ring map may be built up and how simple diagnostics may be carried out. The final example will look at setting up and monitoring synchronous bandwidth allocation.

Determining Station Type and Status

One of the simplest methods for determining the type of stations that exist on the network, whether a station or concentrator, the number of ports and the current status, is simply to monitor the NIF request frames periodically sent out by every station (with a MAC) as part of the neighbour notification protocol. Figure 7.6 illustrates the format of the NIF request frame. As we saw from Figure 7.5, the MAC address of the station that produced the NIF request can be obtained from the SA – the source address field.

The two important parameters in the NIF request frame are the *station descriptor* and the *state* parameters. From the descriptor field, we can tell the type of node:

- Node Class – '00h' indicates a station (no M ports)
  – '01h' indicates a concentrator ($n \times$ M ports)
- MAC_Ct – indicates the number MACs at that node
- NonMaster_Ct – number of A, B and S ports
- Master_Ct – number of M ports

From the status field, the current topology of the station is indicated, allowing us to determine the current port configurations, if the station is configured to issue a status report frame (SRF), and also if the station is currently using the synchronous class of data transmission (Figure 7.7). Note that this status field is available through other SMT protocols, such as the SIF protocol. From this status field, we can determine if any of the stations have cabling problems. For example, the twisted ring depicted in Figure 6.13 can be easily detected by examining the second and third bits. We could also determine if a concentrator is at the top of a concentrator tree as the root (bit 4), or if it has no active connection higher up the tree (i.e. A, B or S port inactive – bit 1).

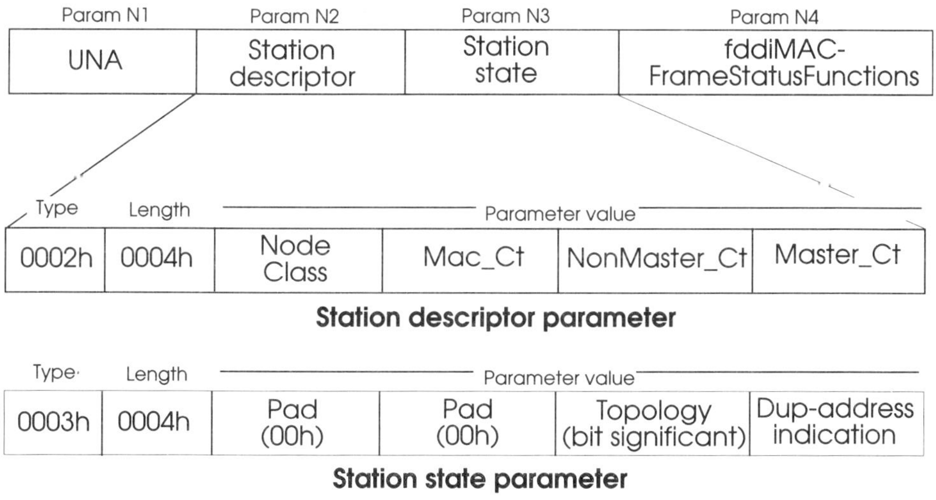

Figure 7.6 *NIF request frame parameters*

Building a Ring Map and Monitoring Changes

From the various protocols that are available, it is easy to see how by interrogating each station in the ring, or by monitoring NIF frames, a map of the network may be obtained. This allows each of the station types and configurations to be mapped out graphically on the management console. Figure 7.8 represents such an output (a simplified picture), in this case only the address information is displayed. Additional information, such as manufacturer information, may also be displayed, along with the configuration capabilities of each of the stations, status, current activity and so on. Typically, additional information is available by simply clicking the mouse button whilst pointing to the station in question.

In situations where a management station actively wants to determine the current topology and status of the ring, it may use the following technique for obtaining the information.

Step 1 Management station issues an initial broadcast SIF configuration request frame.

Step 2 Each station responds with a SIF configuration response frame, which amongst other things, includes the following information:

(a) present state – a variable indicating: peer wrap condition, unattached concentrator or rooted station, twisted ring, status reporting enabled, synchronous bandwidth utilised conditions (Figure 7.7);
(b) present duplicate address conditions;
(c) station policies (which connections it will accept or reject);
(d) MAC neighbours – the current UNA and DNA values per MAC;
(e) PATH descriptor per MAC and PORT – type of PORT (A, B, S or M), connect state, remote/connected PORT type and if MAC at other end and MAC address.

Step 3 Display selected information.

Step 4 Either periodically send out a SIF configuration request, or in order to keep network management traffic to a minimum, simply monitor the NIF frames to check for changes in neighbour addresses. Also, the station reporting protocol may be employed to update any configuration changes.

7	6	5	4	3	2	1	0
Not used	Sync service	SRF enable	Rooted station	Twist ring B–B	Twist ring A–A	Unattached conc.	Peer wrap

Bit set ('1') to indicate condition active

Figure 7.7 *Station status parameter*

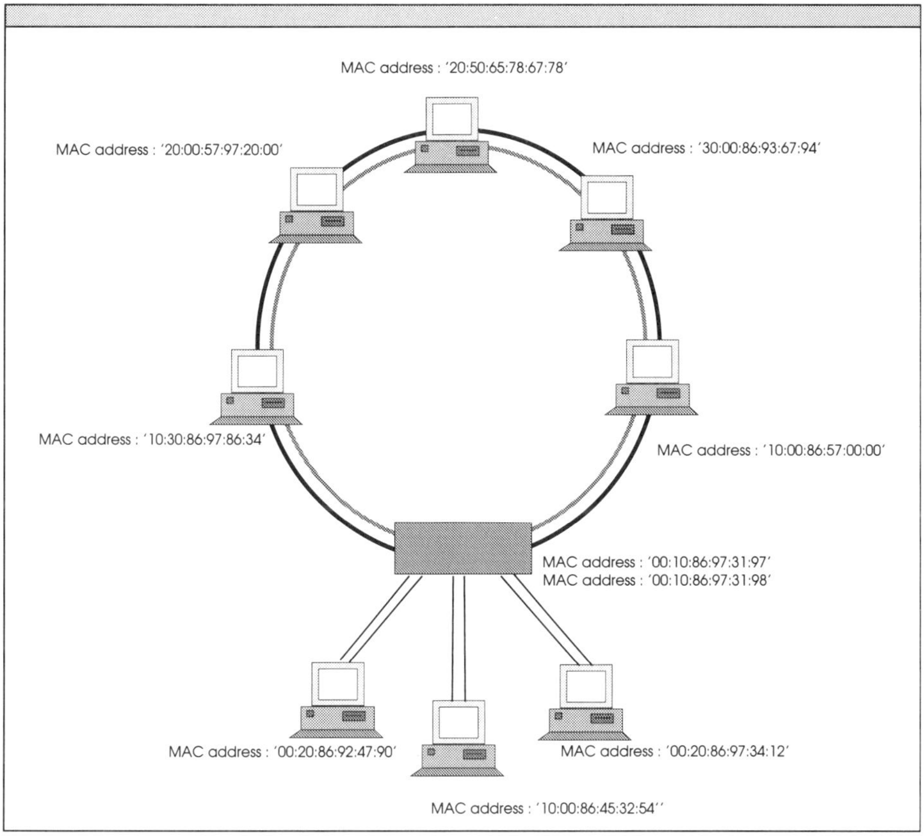

Figure 7.8 *Example of management console ring map display*

The benefit of the above SIF approach is that the results are collected faster than using the NIF approach, as there would be no wait of up to 30 sec for the NIF frames to be transmitted.

Performing Station Diagnostics

A quick examination of the MIB variables in the Appendix, and their get-replace status, reveals the potential for setting up error/status monitoring and performing station configuration set-ups.

A simple example would be to configure a station to report any excessive errors that result in data corruption. The network administrator may decide that a particular station is receiving more than its fair share of bad frames, or is experiencing a large number of corrupted data symbols, and decides to configure a station to attempt to report such errors. This is carried out by firstly using the PMF *set* facility to set up the various MIB threshold or alarm variables, e.g. *fddiMACFrameErrorThreshold*, or *fddiPORTLer-Cutoff and fddiPORTLer-Alarm*. The network management program must then write to the *fddiSMTStatRptPolicy* MIB variable to enable SRF transmission following a MAC frame or PORT link error attaining their predefined threshold.

For multiple path and MAC concentrators, using the vendor's management tools to assist, it will also be possible to take various stations off-line from the main ring, and configure a local test loop in order to localise a network fault to a particular station or lobe of the ring.

Allocation of Synchronous Bandwidth

As outlined earlier, the *synchronous bandwidth allocation*, or SBA protocol, is used to manage the allocation/deallocation and monitoring of synchronous data traffic on the FDDI network. The protocol does not, however, define the processes that may be employed to set up the usage of synchronous bandwidth as this is implementation specific. There are on-going efforts, however, to standardise on the way synchronous services are used in order to create an interoperable specification for vendors to adhere to. Ultimately, these will be defined to operate over multiple network types and media.

The fundamental MIB components used during the SBA process for end stations utilising the synchronous service are *fddiPATHSbaPayload* and *fddiPATHSbaOverhead*, and for the SBA manager, *fddiPATHSbaAvailable*. If a station implements both the SBA manager function as well as utilising synchronous bandwidth itself, then it supports all three.

To illustrate the process, consider a simplistic set-up consisting of five stations on the logical ring, two requesting a live bidirectional video conference link (stations A and C), and two others (stations B and D) a unidirectional playback video link to a video server (E) as illustrated in Figure 7.9. The video conference links require a 384 kbps link or session in both directions, i.e. from A to C and C to A. The playback video sessions require 2 Mbps from the video server, E, to the end stations, B and D. There are two possible mechanisms for allocating the synchronous bandwidth – either *statically* (e.g. at power up/initialisation), which assumes that the allocations never change whilst the network is active, or *dynamically*, which uses a runtime allocator to set-up and remove allocations on an 'as required' basis. In this example, the dynamic approach is preferred as the video conference sessions will not be running constantly, and will only be set-up when needed. A similar case exists for the video server, running full motion compressed video over the 2 Mbps sessions.

End Station Synchronous Considerations

Taking the end station requirements first, as a dynamic allocation process is being

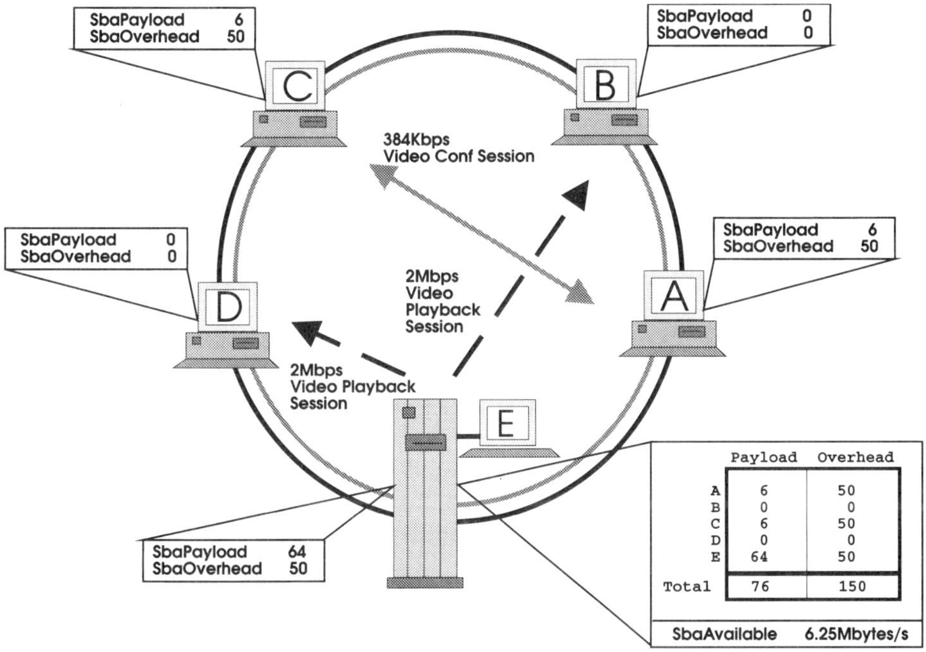

Figure 7.9 *Synchronous bandwidth allocation example*

used, the two stations A and C must first communicate using standard asynchronous protocols (implementation specific or using industry standard call set-up and tear-down protocols). Following this, they each request a slice of synchronous bandwidth as both need to source synchronous traffic. This is carried out by the requesting stations issuing RAF request frames with the following SBA request parameters:

- PATH type – usually the primary path.
- SBA payload and overhead requested incremental values – see below.
- Current payload and overhead values.
- Allocation address – source address (SA) of the requesting station (= MA if not sub-allocator requesting).
- Category of allocation – static or otherwise (e.g. dynamic).
- Max TNeg – maximum token rotation time acceptable for this request.
- Minimum segment size – smallest sized data packet utilised for the requested payload.

The SBA payload parameter is defined in the standard as the number of 125 μsec data units (rounded to an integer) required to service the synchronous data stream for this station:

SBA payload = (Required bit rate / 8) × 125 μsec

In our example, a 384 kbps rate results in a payload

SBA $payload_{384k}$ = (384k / 8) × 125 μsec = 6

Hence, A and C will each request an *incremental* value that will result in their overall allocated bandwidth being 6. If the existing is zero, then this will be 6 of course. For stations B and D, note that as they are only receiving the synchronous data, they do not request a payload. Station E requests two lots of 2 Mbps bandwidth in order to service the two stations. Using the equation above, this results in a rounded payload value of 64 (2 × 32), for station E.

The 125 μsec units are derived from the standard pulse code modulation (PCM) techniques for digitising voice data. It is sometimes more useful to think of the payload variable in terms of units of 64 kbps, as this fits more nicely with telecommunications standards such as ISDN (a single B-channel) and ITU's H.261 or the Px64 (where the P is the equivalent to the FDDI SBA payload parameter), which breaks down such traffic into 64 kbps segments. This gives the following:

SBA payload = Required bit rate / 64k

Hence, using ratios of kbit per second values, to the next nearest integer value, for stations A and C in Figure 7.9:

SBA $payload_{384k}$ = 384 / 64 = 6

For the video server (station E in Figure 7.9):

SBA $payload_{4M}$ = (2000 / 64) + (2000 / 64) = 64

The SBA overhead is a less complex figure, and is basically the total overhead in terms of bytes required to capture the token, the first part of the data frame PDU (preamble, frame control and address fields) and any additional bytes in the information field used for higher-level synchronous traffic protocols. Typically, this is around 50 bytes, and is usually a constant across all stations, being a fixed size in order to cut down on the amount of processing needed to calculate the total maximum overhead for a single token rotation.

Finally, the end station, in its request to the SBA manager, provides some indication of the minimum sized packet it will use for synchronous transmissions in order to determine the worst-case overhead situation. The end station also indicates what the maximum token rotation time that the synchronous payload can handle. The minimum segment size is related to the current negotiated token rotation time (TNeg), and the requested payload. In general, the minimum segment size needed to support a particular payload in terms of bytes is given by the following:

MinSegmentSize = (payload / 125 μsec) × TNeg

Hence, for the 384 kbps and 2 Mbps sessions, and assuming a typical TNeg of 8 msec, then the segment sizes come out as follows:

$MinSegmentSize_{384k}$ = (6 / 125 μsec) × 8 msec = 384 bytes

$MinSegmentSize_{2M}$ = (32 / 125 μsec) × 8 msec = 2048 bytes

What this tells us is that in the worst case, an end station may support the required 384 kbps rate by sending one 384 byte payload packet (overhead bytes will increase this to slightly more) per token rotation. If less than 384 bytes are used, then the required rate will not be achieved. This does not mean that the station will only ever send 384 byte payload packets. If we take a typical 4k data packet produced for a low end video conference session, then it may be far more practical to send it in a single packet, once every ten token rotations or so. All will depend on the nature of the synchronous data payload itself, its origin, data generation rate and so on.

The maximum TNeg indicator lets the SBA manager know what the maximum token rotation time can be for this allocation. For example, a video conference application may generate a 4k frame every 1/12th of a second, i.e. one frame every 83 msec. For this example, 8 msec should be more than enough, depending again on how the station fragments the payload across successive token rotations. If, due to a reconfiguration, the TNeg changes, then the SBA manager must determine if the new TNeg will have any impact on the current allocations and take the necessary action to correct the situation. The exact process will depend on the current set-up, and may result in the SBA manager keeping the TNeg value to the old one (forced during a claim process) if the end stations cannot tolerate the new value, or deallocating bandwidth across a number of stations in the network and so on.

The Synchronous Bandwidth Manager

For the SBA manager process, resident in the video server in this example, the SBA available variable is the main factor in calculations of how much bandwidth is available for the FDDI segment. This is usually set by a network administrator in accordance with the current network applications and usage, and also the current token rotation time for the network. In our example, the available bandwidth is set to 50 per cent of the overall network capacity, i.e. 50 Mbps. The *fddiPATHSbaAvailable* MIB variable is defined in terms of bytes per second, hence the maximum value (100 Mbps) would be 12.5 Mbytes/sec, and for 50 Mbps, this would be 6.25 Mbytes/sec.

Internally, the SBA manager would also maintain a table of all the current allocations, individual payloads, overheads, etc., in order to control the overall bandwidth allocation, and monitor the changes and network conditions to ensure smooth operation. When an end station requests an allocation, the SBA manager receives a RAF request, with the contents as detailed above. The global table is consulted to ensure that by adding the requesting station to the allocation, the overall bandwidth constraints are met. If successful, a RAF response frame is sent back to the station with the appropriate indication of success, to grant the allocation request. A successful grant of allocation results in the requested payload and overhead parameters being sent back to the end station as they were received by the SBA manager. If there was not enough bandwidth available, then an unsuccessful response frame would be issued, with an indication of what bandwidth is left so that the station can determine if it wishes to reapply with a lower allocation request.

For the example we have been using, the total allocation that the manager uses to compare against the SBA available is worked out from the sum of the individual station payloads plus an overhead factor. For total current allocations that are nowhere near the maximum available, then in most cases the overhead factor may be ignored, especially as in some cases an overhead been incurred by rounding up the payload value. For our example, the total payload value is 76 × 64 kbps, or 4.864 Mbps, and nowhere near the 50 Mbps limit, hence the overhead factor may be safely discounted. If the number of sessions increase to nearer 40 Mbps+, then the overhead factor might start being considered by the manager.

The SBA management process is not defined by the FDDI standards, so implementations are usually vendor specific. An FDDI Synchronous Forum was set up to standardise the way SBA allocation and management processes were implemented, so that vendors could all conform to the same specification. An example implementation of a SBA management state machine is illustrated in Figure 7.10. Four main states could be used to implement the management function, with two main states handling the routine functions. For instance, the main *active* state responds to allocation requests from requesting stations, and also monitors the NIF protocol frames in order to detect stations that are using synchronous bandwidth (see Figures 7.6 and 7.7), but have not requested it via this manager (1). A timer is normally implemented for every station registered with the manager as having a synchronous bandwidth allocation in order to prompt the manager to poll the synchronous stations (using RAF requests) to check the allocation status (2–3). Other states would be needed to handle *recovery evaluation* and *change allocation*. These would be needed to respond to changes in T_Neg (the negotiated token rotation time) which could cause over allocation of synchronous bandwidth, and to also deal with RAF response frames.

Management of Bridges

There are a number of MIB attributes that allow a station's bridge functionality to be determined. Using the PMF protocol, a management station may interrogate the state of a *fddiMACBridgeFunctions* attribute, which is *get* variable only. The value of this attribute, from the present SMT standard, may be set to the following:

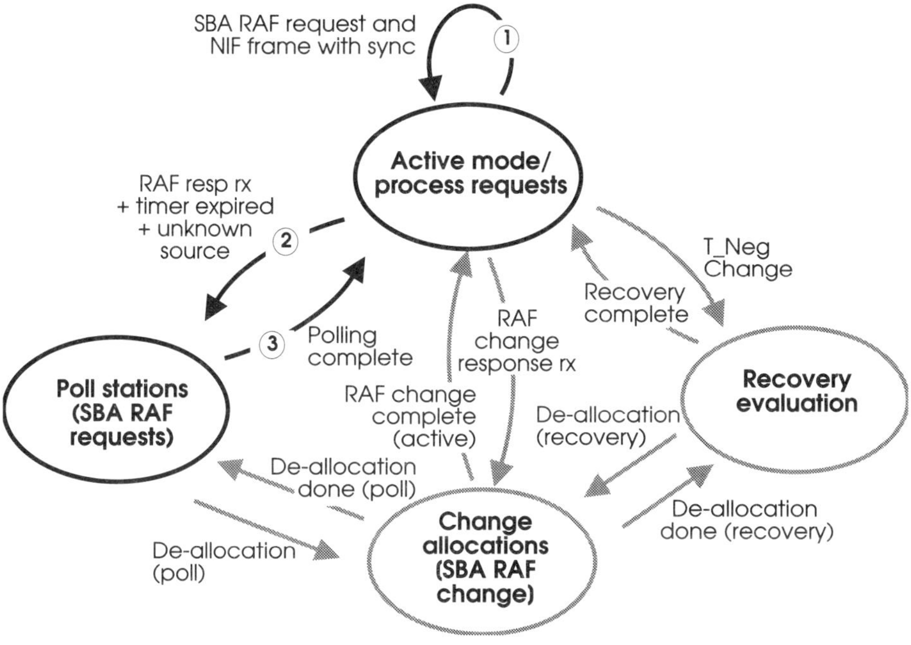

Figure 7.10 *Example SBA management state machine (based on FDDI synchronous forum example)*

0 transparent bridging active
1 source routing active
2 source routing transparent active

If a station is not a bridge, then as the above attribute is optional, it will return a parameter response frame with 'unsupported attribute'. Some additional aspects of FDDI bridges and their functionality will be explored in more detail in Chapter 8.

On a much broader scope, management of FDDI bridges within the OSI Management Framework is defined by the IEEE 802.1D and 802.1I standards. IEEE802.1I is a supplement to the main 802.1D standard, defining the specifics for FDDI. For example, the *PortType* encoding value is expanded to have a value 87 for FDDI. For the Internet SNMP management standards, an additional Bridge MIB is defined by RFC 1286 which has some overlap with the IEEE802.1D definitions (see Bibliography).

Management within an SNMP Environment

FDDI is, more often than not, used within a TCP/IP protocol environment. This means that the network management station will use SNMP for accessing information about the network nodes and traffic. SNMP has evolved over the years from a number of other earlier protocols, and has become the most widely implemented management protocol standard. SNMP is based on the following protocol processes:

- *Get*. This enables the management process resident on a remote station to access MIB objects or variables, in much the same manner as the PMF *get* we saw earlier.
- *Set*. This enables the management process to set a particular variable or object within the station.
- *Trap*. A notification from the end station agent process that some significant event has occurred.

These basic processes form the basis of SNMP. SNMPv2 added features such as security to the basic SNMP. Standard MIBs are defined for supporting stations, with extensions provided (as Internet RFC documents) for specific implementations, e.g. an Ethernet, Token Ring or FDDI MIB. Many of the issues relating to SNMP are beyond the scope of this book, and readers are referred to books such as that by Stallings (1993) or the RFC documents provided over the Internet.

SNMP and FDDI

As all stations in FDDI implement SMT management, then it is relatively easy to support additional MIB objects needed for SNMP. In fact most of the SNMP FDDI managed objects overlap considerably with those defined for the SMT MIB. Hence, most products, especially concentrators, support the SNMP MIBs (MIB I and MIB II) and the FDDI MIB extensions (see later). However, for a station to support SNMP, it must also implement the UDP and IP protocol stack (Figure 1.16), which if the station is already supporting TCP/IP, should not be a problem.

In cases where the end workstations do not support SNMP, then a concentrator or bridge/router product can act as a *proxy* agent on behalf of the stations. The proxy agent takes in requests (SNMP *get/set*) from the management station, and using the FDDI-SMT protocol, accesses the appropriate object. It then passes the result back to the management station using the standard SNMP response. In a similar fashion, if a notification is issued by an FDDI SMT agent (e.g. SRF frame), then this will be translated into the appropriate SNMP *trap*.

SNMP FDDI-MIBs

The main MIBs defined for SNMP management are the MIB I (RFC 1156) and MIB II (RFC 1213), the latter being a superset of the first.

MIB II defines the following groups, also described more fully in Stallings and

RFC 1213:

- *system* – high-level information group
- *interfaces* – information on the more general aspects of the physical interface (common to most network types)
- *address translation* – mapping of network (e.g. IP) to physical addresses (e.g. MAC)
- *ip, icmp, tcp, udp, egp* – protocol information groups
- *transmission* – transmission scheme and access protocol information
- *snmp* – information about the SNMP implementation on the node

Within the interfaces group, a number of MIB objects are defined, indicating the type of physical and link protocol employed. If there are a number of interfaces, as found in a bridge, then an index points to the relevant port. For an FDDI interface, the *ifType* under the MIB II interfaces table (*ifTable*) entry is 15, i.e. *ifType* = fddi (15). Also within the same area, an *ifSpecific* variable is defined, indicating the specific MIB reference for the *ifType*. As there have been a number of draft pre-standard implementations of the FDDI SMT, there currently exist two different SNMP MIB definitions. These are the RFC 1512 'FDDI Management Information for the most recent SMT 7.3 and final published ANSI SMT standard, and the earlier RFC 1285 'FDDI Management Information Base' for SMT v6.2 (see Bibliography). Products today can sometimes support both the new and older standards. The reason for the two different standards is because the SMT 7.3 was significantly different from the earlier SMT 6.2. To signify this, two different *ifSpecific* values are provided, namely 73 for the RFC 1512 definition, and 15 for the earlier RFC 1285 version. The two versions, as sited in RFC 1512, cannot be classed as compatible.

Other entries in the MIB II interfaces of interest are the *ifMtu*, indicating the largest PDU in octets that can be transmitted over the LAN interface, and also *ifSpeed*, indicating the data rate capacity of the line. For FDDI, these are usually 4500 and 100E6 respectively. For Ethernet and Token Ring these will correspond to their relevant values, hence it is possible to build up a reasonable picture of what the capabilities of the interface are before even knowing the specific type.

The detail of the SNMP FDDI MIB itself is defined within the MIB II transmissions group for the RFC 1285, and for the newer RFC 1512, within its own entirely new branch of the MIB tree, identified by the object id, *fddimib*. For the earlier RFC 1285, the following groups are defined:

- SMT group (*snmpFddiSMT*) – corresponding to much of the mandatory options within the FDDI fddiSMT group
- MAC group (*snmpFddiMAC*) – corresponding to much of the mandatory options within the FDDI fddiMAC group
- PATH group (*snmpFddiPATH*) – corresponding to much of the mandatory options within the FDDI fddiPATH group
- PORT group (*snmpFddiPORT*) – corresponding to much of the mandatory

options within the FDDI fddiPORT group

- ATTACHMENT group (*snmpFddiATTACHMENT*) – representing a PORT or pair of PORTs, including optical bypass, that are managed as a functional unit. ATTACHMENT objects are closely related to the snmpFddiPORT objects.
- Chipset group (*snmpFddiChipSets*) – undefined in RFC 1285.

The newer RFC 1512 SMT 7.3 MIB does away with a specific *Chipsets* group, but defines an optional MIB *Counters* group. Each of the groups, as they are a totally separate MIB branch definition (fddimib), start with an *fddimib* prefix, as opposed to *snmpFddi*, e.g. fddimibSMT. Hence the groups are:

- *fddimibSMT* group
- *fddiMIBMAC* group
- *fddimibMACCounters* group, includes counters such as TokenCts, TvxExpiredCts, RingOpCts, etc.
- *fddimibPATH* group
- *fddimibPORT*

Summary

FDDI's station management (SMT) provides a comprehensive means of controlling and monitoring end stations. Its standards-based MIB ensures that all stations support a minimum level of management for all the main components of a station or concentrator, specifically the SMT, MAC, PATH and PORT objects. SMT's frame-based management protocols provide a standard method of accessing information about the ring operation, supporting neighbour notification of MAC addresses, status reporting, and synchronous bandwidth allocation.

Management within an SNMP-based network environment is provided by Internet RFC-defined MIBs.

CHAPTER 8

Implementations and Products

In this chapter, we take a look at how FDDI-compatible stations are constructed, and what options are available to the end user in terms of 'off-the-shelf' networking components. The make up of the hardware is illustrated from the semiconductor chip level up to a fully modular intelligent hub supporting FDDI. As hardware and software change so rapidly, no attempt is made to highlight a specific vendor's product in detail. Enough understanding is given in order for the end user to identify the sort of features that should be looked for when building up an FDDI network.

VLSI Components

Very large scale integrated (VLSI) circuits have been available since 1987 to support FDDI. In general, most of the MAC, PHY and PMD functions we have looked at in previous chapters are all implemented in VLSI components. Today there are several vendors making such devices at varying integration levels; Advanced Micro Devices (AMD) offered the first ever available chipset, SUPERNET1, followed later by National Semiconductor and Motorola. In all cases, the device functional blocks are more or less separated into the same areas as the standard itself is divided, i.e. a MAC layer device, a PHY layer controller and clock recovery device, and a PMD layer transceiver device. It is possible that many of these functions will be integrated into a single device in the future, as semiconductor technology develops. Figure 8.1 illustrates one such chipset, called SUPERNET2 from AMD, for a SM-DAS FDDI MAC/PHY layer implementation (i.e. single MAC, dual PHY). The chipset consists of a single FORMAC+ device implementing all the MAC layer protocol handling plus the local buffering of incoming and outgoing data packets, and three smaller devices implementing the physical layer (excluding PMD), namely the physical layer controller, physical data receiver and transmitter devices. Higher levels of integration are possible in the future.

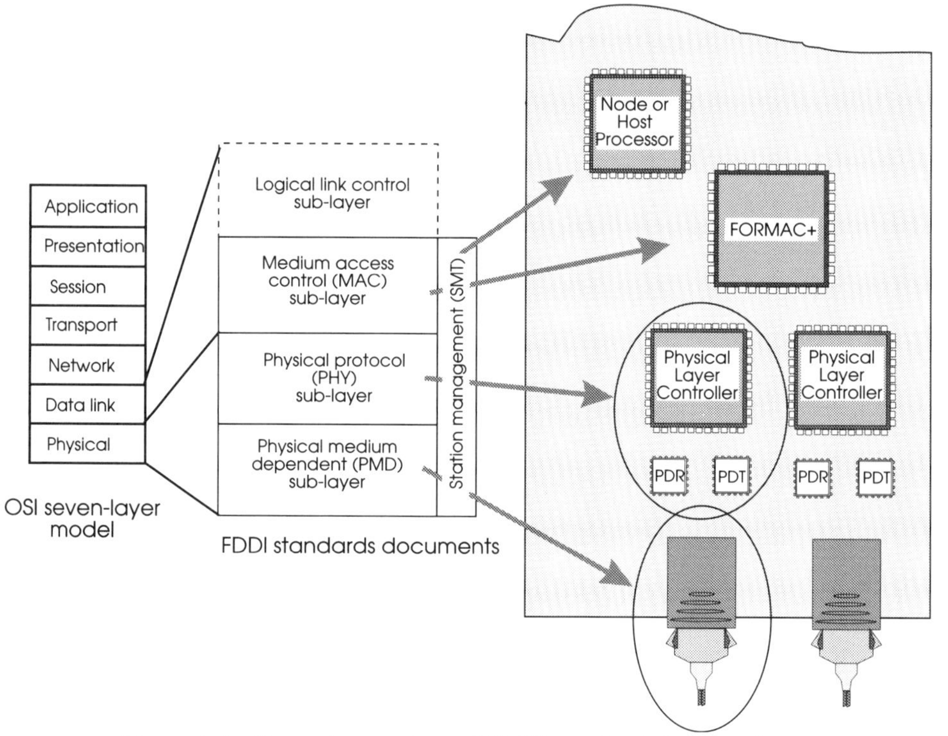

Figure 8.1 *Example mapping of FDDI standards into hardware*

MAC layer devices implement all the functions associated with the media access control layer as described in Chapter 4, i.e. the timed token protocol (all the timers, etc.), token capture and release, transmission and reception of valid frames, frame validity checking, repeating and stripping of frames, and so on. Additional functions beyond the standard usually include support for a node or host processor for controlling the interface and accessing the data frame buffers or fifos, and frame type sorting.

Physical layer devices perform all the necessary conversion of the raw symbol stream created by the MAC devices into the 4B5B encoding required by the PHY layer standard. Clock recovery (on the receive side), symbol error checking, implementation of the elasticity buffer are typical functions of this device or devices. In addition, link error monitoring and PCM signalling functions are typically integrated into the devices due to the accuracy and fine timing resolution required by these functions. As advances in VLSI technology are made, it is likely that the PHY layer devices and the MAC layer device, plus any systems interface logic, will all be combined into a single chip for a SAS implementation. More recent PHY controller devices also implement the TP-PMD stream cipher scrambler function so that a common controller may be used for both fibre and copper versions of equipment.

The physical medium dependent portion is implemented using purpose-made transceiver devices or modules, which also house the appropriate connectors, i.e. the MIC connector in the case of optical fibre, and the D-type or RJ45 connector for copper, and so on. Within these transceivers are usually all the electronics needed to detect an adequate light or signal level reception from the remote port connection, and also the various signal conditioning electronics (waveform shaping, etc.).

SMT contains functions that operate at all levels of the FDDI standard, hence is usually spread across a mixture of hardware and software. For example, large portions of PCM and CFM are easily integrated into a VLSI device as they are fairly well defined and are similar to a simple state machine. They also reduce considerably the loading on any node processor that may be employed during pseudo code signalling, and symbol error monitoring functions The frame-based management services however, depend on the level of SMT support required by the node, hence they are usually implemented in software on a dedicated node processor, or as part of the host CPU's activities. Many adapter cards, for instance, offer the ability to upgrade the firmware on board the card itself, hence making revisions and feature upgrades very easy for the end user. Even though the SMT standards are now relatively stable, some aspects such as synchronous bandwidth allocation, are still being worked on, hence upgradeability or programmability of FDDI equipment can be extremely important.

Adapter Cards

Adapter cards are available for FDDI and its copper derivatives for almost every popular workstation and personal computing expansion bus available today, e.g. S-BUS (Sun Workstation), EISA, MCA and PCI (IBM PC compatibles and workstations), and NU-BUS (Macintosh). In general, the complexity and cost of the card is related to its performance, amount of built-in intelligence (node processor, etc.), and availability of software support for the various network operating systems (NOS). The higher-performance cards generally have a dedicated custom gate array or ASIC device to act as the *systems interface*. The reason many cards employ a custom device is to ensure the maximum possible performance and features out of their card. This ASIC may also provide the data to the host in a format that allows the higher networking layer software to interpret the data in a timely fashion, e.g. in Unix environments. This is particularly true of some of the workstation adapter cards, such as HP's FDDI/9000 board. Other features, such as software configuration of interrupts and DMA channels (*'jumperless'*) are often built into many of the PC-based adapters.

Figure 8.2 illustrates a general SAS FDDI card, plus DAS extender, with a dedicated node processor for handling the general control and initialisation aspects of the card, and also to process and support all the SMT frames that come into the card. The benefit of a dedicated node processor, as opposed to using the actual host CPU to perform the SMT frame processing, is that the host does not have to think about maintaining the FDDI-MIB, neighbour notification protocols, parameter management

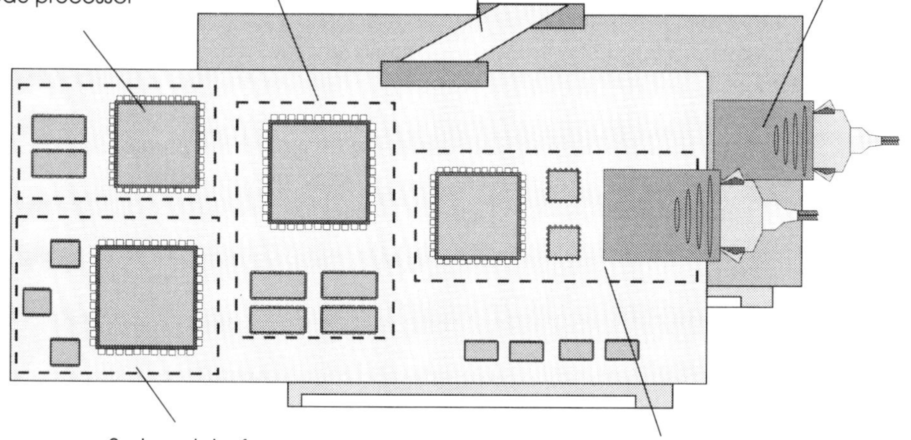

Figure 8.2 *SAS FDDI adapter card with separate DAS extender option*

requests, status reporting, and so on. Though the code for this is implemented on the card itself, field upgrades are made possible by the use of *flash* memory (reprogrammable ROM) or host-loadable RAM for the node processor. It is quite common for a SAS card to have the upgrade option to convert it via an extender or daughter card to a DAS, though the lowest cost will be SAS capable only, probably with a simpler system interface. Combined DAS cards are also available.

As far as physical media cabling options are concerned, as the transceiver part of the card is usually based around a standard footprint, a common adapter board can be configured to take most PMD types at the manufacturing stage. Hence, a single form factor can handle single-mode or multimode fibre, and also copper TP-PMD modules, amongst the other pre-standard copper implementations such as IBM's SDDI. Extremely low-cost boards are usually copper PMD based only, in order to support low-cost connectivity to an FDDI-based network.

Finally, in some higher end adapter and intelligent hub module implementations, a hardware-implemented address lookup table mechanism may be employed. This scheme is designed to expand the on-board individual and group address capability of the MAC devices. Special VLSI devices, called CAMs (contents addressable memories) are available that may be interfaced to the FDDI chipset to allow a set of addresses (loaded up by the controlling CPU) to be compared against the incoming destination address field on the fly, and without CPU (node or host) intervention. This extended address recognition scheme is sometimes referred to as *perfect address filtering*. Some of the more recent FDDI devices may incorporate such a scheme directly on the device itself.

Performance Trade-offs in Adapter Cards

A significant difference in the performance of an adapter card in terms of Mbytes throughput exists according to the architecture of the card. If connectivity to FDDI and low cost is the main driver, then this will not be so important, and the architecture is less important than the cost of the card itself.

All cards available support the maximum line rate of 100 Mbps, as per the standard. However, taking the overall system constraints into consideration, such as available bandwidth on the host CPU system bus and the amount of local buffering, a big variance in the achievable performance is possible. The ability of the card to buffer incoming frames, and just as importantly, transmit the maximum number of frames within a token capture opportunity will determine the throughput possible. Roberts (1992) in his paper on the effects of local buffer memory size on the overall FDDI throughput shows that the system bus latency and bandwidth is an important factor in determining how much the adapter card needs to buffer both outgoing and incoming data packets. Roberts takes a typical token rotation time (TTRT) of 8 msec, and system based around the popular EISA bus, the latter capable of 33 MBytes/sec burst rate across the bus at 8 MHz clock rates. He assumes that other devices, such as SCSI bus masters or Ethernet bus masters are present with a particular loading, and normal CPU to memory transactions and memory refresh cycles are also taking place. The basic conclusions are that when the FDDI ring becomes heavily loaded, too small a buffer memory size can cause performance problems, not only for the adapter, but also for the ring as a whole. Roberts shows that an adapter buffer memory size of 64 kbytes can lead to an optimum performance, and guarantees a reasonable performance across all network loading and TTRT conditions.

Examples of adapters that are carefully designed to exploit the best of the system bus that they are attached to can lead to performances close to 10 Mbytes/sec or 80 Mbps throughput, before higher-level protocols are taken into consideration. For the IBM PC compatibles, over a 32 bit EISA bus, 7.5–8.5 Mbytes/sec (60 Mbps) have been shown to be achievable within a Novell and LAN Manager networking environment when running standard LAN benchmarks (independent tests carried out by LANQuest Labs, San Jose, CA – Figure 8.3).

Synchronous Service Support

Not all adapters support synchronous services, in either hardware or their software drivers. The advantages of synchronous services is that data that is time sensitive, i.e. has to be regularly transmitted within a known time interval, can use this service to ensure timely delivery of the data. Server to server links, industrial control applications and multimedia services are a few examples of its use. Synchronous transmissions take priority over the normal asynchronous, hence can be used as a means of prioritisation of important data transfers.

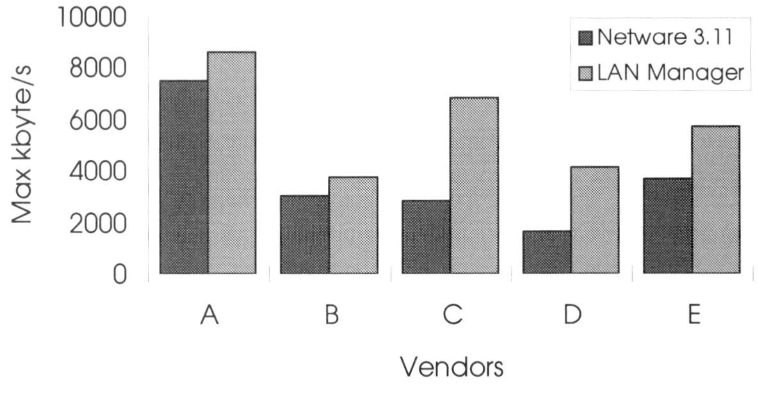

Figure 8.3 *EISA 32 bit adapter card performance comparisons for a two-node network using 486/66 Pcs (source: LANQuest Labs, 1993)*

An adapter card handles synchronous services by supporting in hardware and software the ability to place the synchronous data into a dedicated synchronous queue (Figure 4.12). The hardware must also support the necessary timers (Figures 4.13 and 4.14). The adapter's MAC then takes the data from the queue, and transmits it using the synchronous protocol. The end station software drivers (e.g. NDIS or ODI drivers) must also allow the data to be handled correctly. A management station assigned to handle the SBA protocols, and manage the allocations across the network, has to also implement an SBA manager as detailed in Chapter 7.

Concentrator Architectures

The main features of concentrators relate to the number of internal data paths and MAC devices, along with the level of management software integrated into the product. Taking the latter, for instance, a concentrator in the tree portion of the network does not even need to have a MAC device at all, making it unmanaged. Alternatively, a number of MAC devices may be employed, with a higher-performance processor performing higher-level SNMP management protocols, and even RMON-like functions, involving statistics gathering. In general, concentrators have MAC devices, and hence are an addressable node on the network. Multiple path concentrators, as we saw in Chapter 5, allow a corresponding number of MACs to be employed for managing multiple rings, graceful insertion of single attach stations or lobes, or extended diagnostics and testing.

Low-Cost Concentrators

Starting at the lower end of the scale, the lowest-cost concentrators, such as workgroup or compact level, employ a single path only, extended down to the M ports. A secondary path is only needed when configured as a DAS or DHS, providing the minimal necessary support for wrapping onto the secondary ring or redundant link respectively. Such a configuration is shown in Figure 8.4.

A single medium-performance CPU is capable of handling many PHY devices as most of the PCM pseudo-code signalling state machine, scrub functions and link error monitoring are handled directly by the individual devices, leaving the higher-level, less time intensive tasks to the CPU. The primary path for most implementations is an 11 bit parallel bus, carrying 10 bits of decoded symbol pair information plus a parity check line. The CPU bus is typically a 16 bit address data bus, as is the CPU itself. If the concentrator is implemented on a modular basis, then both the CPU bus and the primary data path bus will be carried across the backplane as either the raw signals, or converted to a vendor-specific bus specification. Otherwise, the whole of the electronics for a low-cost concentrator may be implemented on a single monolithic motherboard, with a field upgradeable daughter card to allow full-blown DAS

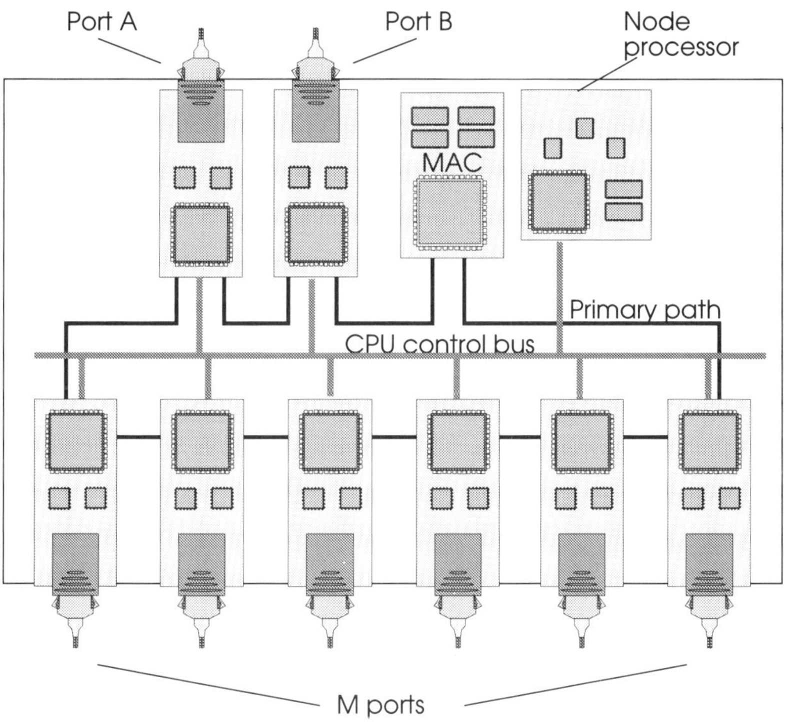

Figure 8.4 *Single path six port DAC example implementation*

operation when installed. Different footprint compatible PMD modules (or custom versions), as for the adapters, are installed at the manufacturing stage to configure as a fibre- or copper-based unit.

Mid- to High-End Concentrators

The next level of concentrator usually employs greater flexibility, and is based on a more modular approach, being capable of co-existing with other networking technologies and internetworking components. Multiple paths are employed, to enable extension of the secondary ring, and enable the roving MAC features.

Figure 8.5 illustrates the additional level of electronics required to support the multiple paths, in this case for a primary and secondary (two path). The switching element can be a standalone custom device, implementing a discrete CCE function for the A, B, S and M ports, or integrated into the PHY level device itself as found in some cases. If it is a standalone device, then to support two 11 bit paths (or 10 bit if no parity error checking employed), then approximately seventy pins would be required, increasing to around ninety for three paths. It is possible to implement a higher-speed narrower bus, but then the complexity inside the switching device rises due to the funnelling process required. Hence, it is easy to see why multi-path concentrators start to increase the overall cost of the device. The switching type device would also be needed for every MAC, to enable it to be configured into the appropriate path.

A standard ASIC (application specific integrated circuit), called the MASIC (Management And Security Integrated Circuit; see Bibliography), is available from a vendor called XLNT Designs Inc., based on work carried out by an industry

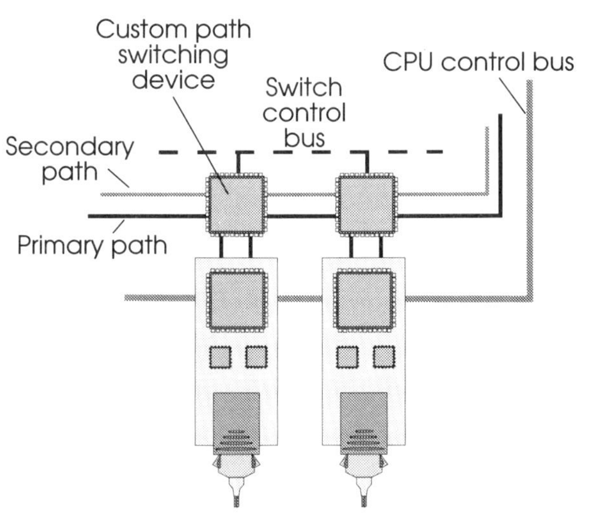

Figure 8.5 *Custom switch elements for CCEs – two path*

consortium, CALM (Consortium for Advanced LAN Management). The chip is basically a custom path-switching device, supporting a local path in addition to the primary and secondary paths shown in Figure 8.5. It also contains additional features to support further port monitoring and statistics collection functions beyond that provided by standard FDDI. It provides hardware support for security encryption and decryption of data, and graceful insertion and removal of stations from the ring.

FDDI in Intelligent Multiple Media Hubs

The use of intelligent hubs has grown rapidly in recent years. An intelligent hub provides many advantages over earlier fixed-architecture, fixed-technology hubs, such as an Ethernet only or Token Ring only hub. Some of the many advantages include the ability to mix different networking technologies, support terminal servers, different cabling options, comprehensive cross technology management, integrated routing and bridge support, hot swappable modules, and so on. All this is achieved with the use of a chassis-based system that has a backplane running between many multi-purpose expansion slots as illustrated in Figure 8.6, making it extremely easy for an end user to

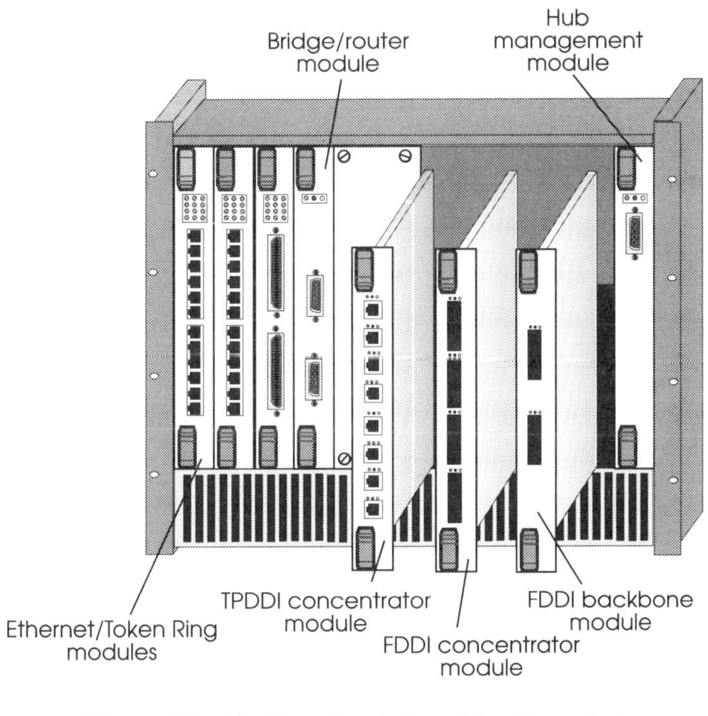

Figure 8.6 *Modular chassis based intelligent hub*

build a system to meet their exact needs.

Hubs are also an enabling technology for the newer switching architectures that are now growing in popularity, and also the reason for the term *collapsed backbone,* where what used to be a physical network in its own right has now literally become the backplane within a hub. A typical intelligent hub may have several Ethernet, Token Ring and FDDI backplanes that allow many network segments to be created within the hub itself, combined into a heterogeneous network with the use of bridge or router modules.

FDDI itself is supported within these hubs with specific modules, such as a two-port, single/dual MAC multimode fibre card for connecting the hub to an FDDI dual ring backbone. Optical bypass switches are also usually supported as an option. A dual MAC option allows the testing of any FDDI-SAS nodes that may be connected to the hub whilst isolated from the main ring. Concentrator modules allow a number of M ports to be added, usually in multiples of 4 (fibre MIC) or 4/8 (copper DB9 or RJ45), depending on the size of the enclosure and architecture of the hub itself. Many applications will only require the use of the DAS module plus an FDDI bridging module in order to connect their lower-speed networks onto an FDDI backbone. Such a system is illustrated in Figure 8.7 where two departments independently combine several LANs and dumb terminals into a single chassis hub, and connect them together to the mainframe via a dual FDDI ring or dual-homing set-up. This probably forms the largest single application for FDDI to date.

Dedicated Workgroup Hubs

In addition to the higher-end intelligent hubs, a number of vendors provide dedicated FDDI hubs, typically referred to as a *workgroup hub*. These units are standalone or 19 in. rack mountable, and either have a fixed number of ports, or like the intelligent hub scheme have a backplane plus module scheme. The advantage of the latter is that it enables a far greater flexibility as to the choice of physical media. The advantage of the fixed port types is that they are built on a single motherboard, and are thus cheaper and more compact.

The number of ports that a workgroup hub provides can sometimes be larger than an intelligent hub, as the latter may have a limited number of slots available for expanding the number of concentrator M ports. Typically, workgroup hubs support between twelve and twenty-four ports, at a cost per port roughly ten times that of 10Base-T Ethernet technology. Most of these units are also SNMP network manageable in addition to supporting standard SMT frame management. Optical bypass switch support is also an option for the main A and B ports in a DAC configuration. For the modular-based workgroup hubs, bridge/router modules may also be available, providing a neat integral backbone connection module for a number of high-performance workstations.

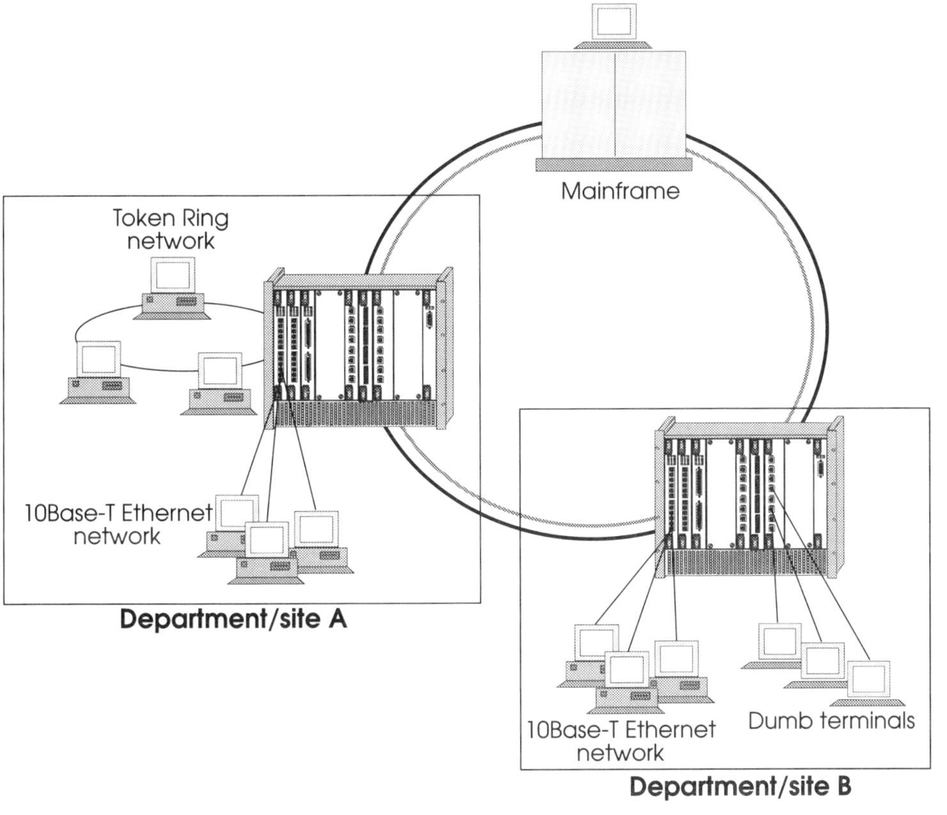

Figure 8.7 *Example hub configuration: Connecting an ethernet network into an FDDI backbone*

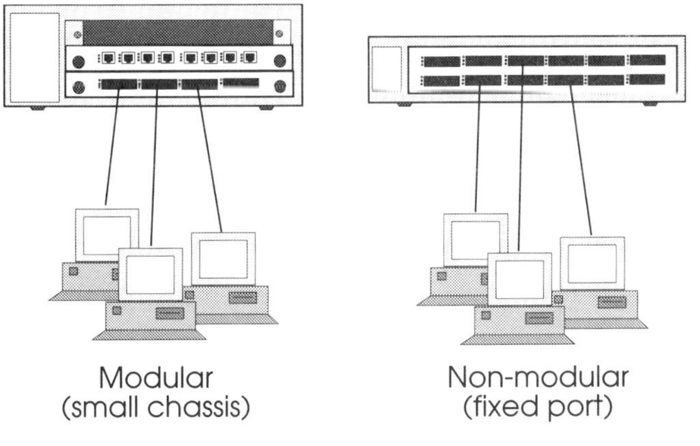

Figure 8.8 *FDDI workgroup hubs*

Switched Hubs

LAN technology is constantly evolving, with the never-ending goal of both reducing cost whilst enhancing performance and reliability. One of the biggest factors is the preservation of existing investments in end station adapter cards. For instance, there are literally millions of networking devices that use an Ethernet interface as their primary means of communication to the outside world. Hence, when new technologies such as FDDI or ATM come along that promise greater performance and features, but at the expense of ripping out your old Ethernet or Token Ring interfaces (if this is possible at all – e.g. motherboard-mounted interfaces), it is not surprising that network implementors are not always ready to jump on the bandwagon. This is one of the primary reasons that *switched* hubs have become popular, in particular for Ethernet, as they preserve the end adapter interface for the time being, whilst significantly increasing aggregate bandwidth.

What switching hubs provide are dedicated LAN segments to each user. That is, each user has a dedicated maximum bandwidth link that no other station uses at the same time. Another name commonly given to such as scheme is *dedicated* networking.

Switched Ethernet and FDDI

To give an example of the benefits of switching, consider an Ethernet implementation of Figure 8.9, where four stations attach to a sixteen port switched 10Base-T hub. Because each of the stations can effectively talk on independent links to another station, it is possible in this case to achieve 20 Mbps bandwidth through the hub, as opposed to a single segmented Ethernet, where one transmission would be held off until the network became free again. If two more stations were introduced to the network, the capacity would increase to 30 Mbps, and so on. All sixteen ports in this example would in theory allow up to 80 Mbps bandwidth capability for multiple point-to-point communications only.

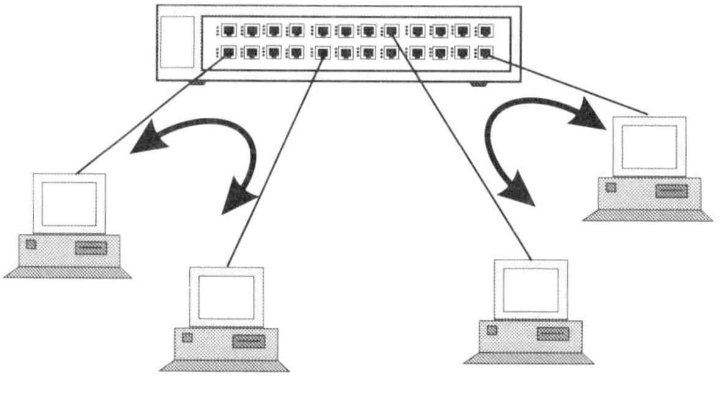

Figure 8.9 *Switched, or dedicated networking*

This kind of scheme, though nice in concept, does not always lead to such performance increases. In fact, if the network protocols being used employ many multicast frames, then the system starts to degrade as more and more multicast or broadcast frames are used, to the ultimate point where you arrive back to a standard shared media Ethernet performance again. Also, what benefit is this kind of system if the stations all want to talk to the same end station, i.e. the server(s)? As the latter is the most common situation, then switched Ethernet only becomes a benefit when the data has somewhere to go to, i.e. it is not being blocked by a congested link to the server. It is for this reason that switching is targeted firstly at the router market where vast performance improvements can be made connecting multiple network segments with a switch, and secondly, where faster network links or *pipes* to the server are required.

One of the prime uses of FDDI is as a high-speed link to a server for these lower-speed networking technologies, thus removing the bottleneck of traffic to the server (Figure 8.10). Utilisation of a higher-speed link to a server in this manner is sometimes referred to as implementing a *fat pipe*, as it enables more traffic to be accommodated than the slower links. One FDDI link is in theory able to carry the payload of ten switched 10 Mbps Ethernet links or segments (a segment carrying more than one station's payload like conventional Ethernet). Of course, the actual performance figure will depend greatly on the speed of the Ethernet-to-FDDI bridge

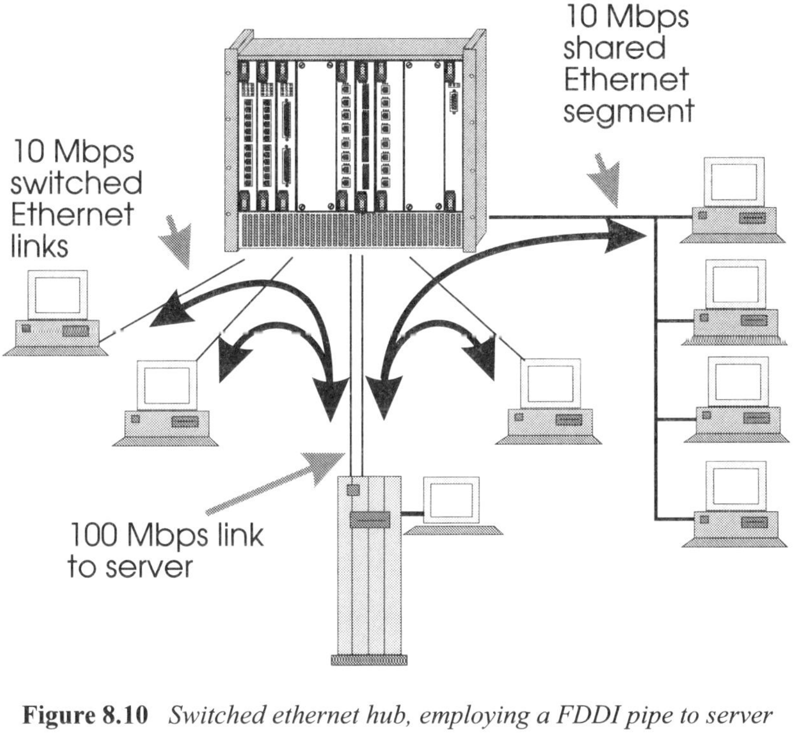

Figure 8.10 *Switched ethernet hub, employing a FDDI pipe to server*

translation, and vice versa. If the same switching technique of forwarding a frame as soon as the destination address field has been received (cut-through bridging), then this should be reasonably close to the full 100 Mbps.

Lastly, if both the primary and secondary rings are capable of carrying data simultaneously (i.e. dual attach, dual MAC architectures are employed at each station), then 200 Mbps total bandwidth to the server is available.

Switched FDDI

So far, the discussion has been centred around FDDI as a backbone link to the server in switched hub architectures. Provided the hub can support it, there is absolutely no reason why FDDI frames cannot themselves be switched. This is implemented inside DEC's GIGAswitch, for example. This entails creating a number of FDDI segments, each with their own circulating token, that are effectively bridged by the central switching fabric of the hub. Hub vendors implement switching backplanes capable of carrying many gigabits per second (10^9) of bandwidth, enabling the hub to cope with the traffic from several FDDI network lobes or segments simultaneously. An FDDI switch is capable of providing higher forwarding rates than a conventional bridge, using techniques such as cut-through bridging, and hardware-assisted switching techniques. Switched FDDI implementations are discussed in more detail in the following sections on bridging and routing.

FDDI Bridges

One of the primary applications for FDDI is as a high-speed backbone network, where several bridges allow the connection of a number of different LAN technologies into a common heterogeneous network. At the point where FDDI meets these other LANs is always a bridge or router device (or combination). For a more in-depth discussion on the functionality of bridges and routers in general, readers are referred to Perlman (1992).

Types of Bridge

As the need for bridges evolved, a number of proprietary methods were used to bridge LANs such as Ethernet and Token Ring over FDDI. These were before any standards were put into place that would allow different vendors' products to interoperate. Early FDDI bridges were generally based on encapsulation techniques (and referred to as an *encapsulating* bridge), where the non-FDDI MAC frame(s) was placed within the information field of an FDDI frame, with proprietary headers and protocols to enable the correct destination LAN segment to be reached. Once standards were available, these bridge products converted over to the vendor-interoperable bridging standards defined by the IEEE.

The IEEE 802.1D standard defines methods for bridging 802-compatible LANs (FDDI included), based on translational techniques, i.e. the frames are converted to the format of the destination LAN at each bridging stage. This is carried out in such a way that the two (or more) communicating stations on the different LAN segments are unaware of the bridges' presence. For this reason, such bridges are referred to as *transparent* bridges. For 802-compatible networks, this is generally not a problem, as all are based on the same MAC–LLC interface, and have very similar MAC frame formats. Hence, MAC addresses are identical (though need some attention during translation as we shall see), and the higher sub-layer LLC information carried by the incoming frame simply transferred into the information field of the destination frame format. Transparent bridges also implement a protocol for exchanging information with other similar bridges in larger networks. The use of many bridges can lead to multiple destination paths being available between two communicating stations, thus these protocols allow a single active path to be set up between the bridges. The specific name given to this process is the *spanning tree* protocol.

Another type of bridge commonly encountered is the *source-routing* bridge, originating out of Token Ring development efforts. Transparent bridges enable the end stations to remain totally unaware of any intermediate bridges that may be between them. This relies on a reasonable amount of intelligence in the bridge itself. Source-routing, on the other hand, assumes that the end stations themselves know where to send the packet through the various bridge stages. This simplifies the bridge design, but means that a specific protocol needs to be implemented across all the end stations to allow them to determine, or discover, specific paths to end stations. This occurs using a *route-discovery* protocol. When an end station transmits a source-routed frame, it uses a redundant bit within the source address (SA) field of the MAC. Recall from Figure 4.3 that 48 bit IEEE MAC addresses allocate the top bit to indicate individual or group addressing (I/G bit). In source addresses, this is not required as the frame will always originate from a single station. Hence, a '0' in this field indicates a normal MAC frame, whereas a '1' indicates a source-routed frame, which contains an additional routing information (RI) field within the first part of the MAC information field. Specific sub-fields within the RI field govern how the frame should be handled by the source-routing bridge, and whether the frame is part of a normal end-to-end transmission, or a route-discovery frame.

Standard FDDI bridge products must support transparent bridging as per the 802.1D specification. Source-routing is an optional addition, and where supported, results in a *source-routing transparent* (SRT) FDDI bridge. At the time of writing, standards for source-routing support in FDDI are still being thrashed out to ensure compatibility between vendors. Practical limitations force FDDI networks always to ensure the use of only transparent or SRT bridges, as mixing the two kinds of pure bridges (source-routing and transparent, with special source-routing to transparent conversion bridges) proved unworkable (see Perlman, 1992). In addition, as more features are being added to bridges that start approaching network layer functionality, the dividing line between a pure bridge and router becomes less clear. Hence, many of today's bridges are in fact more correctly described as bridge-routers, or *brouters*.

Operation of a Transparent Bridge

As discussed above, bridging in local area networking is largely based on the IEEE MAC layer bridge specification defined by the IEEE 802.1D document. Extensions to this have been added for FDDI, and documented in the IEEE 802.1I supplement. A MAC bridge, as defined by the IEEE, consists of three high-level functions; interfaces to a number of IEEE LANs (MAC/PHY level interfaces), a MAC relay function or entity, and a bridge controller or bridge protocol engine (Figure 8.11).

The main functions of a simple multi-port transparent MAC bridge illustrated in Figure 8.11 are as follows:

1. It attaches to two or more LANs, listening and receiving every packet (i.e. listens promiscuously) from every LAN, letting only traffic addressed to stations of a different LAN to cross over (i.e. forwarded). Each of the LANs may be of a different type, e.g. FDDI, Ethernet or Token Ring, but generally all compatible at the LLC–MAC interface level.

2. Based on a learning process, or specific routing algorithms, it uses an *address look up table* (ALUT) or filtering database to determine which station MAC addresses reside off which port. This is refreshed over time to ensure that the ALUTs are kept up to date. The filtering function is performed by the MAC relay entity within the bridge, and may be a centrally shared address table, or distributed across the LAN interface modules. Contents addressible memories (CAMs) are commonly used to implement this function in hardware.

3. When user data packets arrive at the ports, the MAC relay function usually buffers the entire frame, and then performs the following:

   (a) Discards the frame if the destination station is known to be on the same LAN as it came from, thus preventing the packet from appearing on the other LAN connections unnecessarily (i.e. filters). The frame is also thrown away if an error is detected (e.g. FCS error).

   (b) Forwards the frame to the individual port off which the destination station resides (or is accessible from if many bridges have to be crossed) based on information in its ALUTs (Figure 8.11b). The IEEE destination and source address field remain unchanged, and the frame format translated as necessary. For like LANs, FCS information is not usually recalculated. Where a translation has occurred, a new FCS has to be generated. Most simple bridges only forward asynchronous user-level frames, hence FDDI synchronous frames, unless specifically catered for, will not be forwarded.

The frame priority field, if present, is forwarded unaffected, or set to a level specified by a programmable management variable.

(c) Forwards the frame to all ports (except the source LAN) if the destination address is not in any ALUT (i.e. the bridge has not yet learned where the destination station resides), translating where necessary. In this case, the source address field of the frame is associated with the particular LAN port the frame was received at, and recorded in the filtering data base or ALUT.

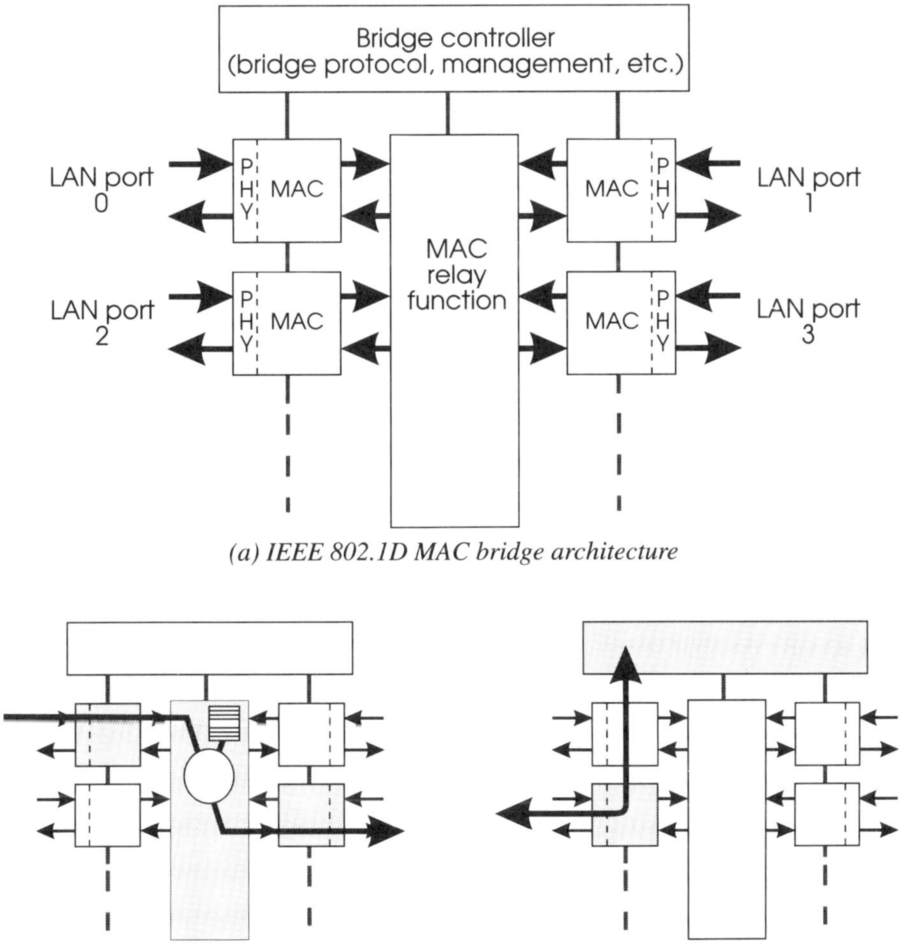

(a) IEEE 802.1D MAC bridge architecture

(b) Filtering database and frame forwarder directs frame to correct port

(c) Bridge protocol data units (BPDUs) and management frames (e.g. SNMP) directed to bridge controller

Figure 8.11 *MAC layer bridges - forwarding and control/management*

4. Specific frames that are addressed to the bridge unit itself are internally routed to the bridge control module (Figure 8.11c). Bridge protocol data units (BPDUs), for example, are specific frames that a number of bridges in a large network use to communicate with one another, specifically during the setup of the Spanning Tree active topology. For such protocols to work, bridges generally respond to a universal group address, this being in the case of IEEE 802.1D bridges, 01-80-C2-00-00-00. Individual bridge identifiers and port identifiers are also needed. Other types of frames may carry SNMP or IEEE 802.1B (CMIP) protocol information for access to the internal bridge MIB. In the case of FDDI bridges, SMT frames, will be dealt with by the bridge controller function, or a sub-controller process resident on the LAN port interface module itself.

There are a number of important issues that need to be considered when translating frames into the FDDI frame format. During the MAC bridging process in IEEE 802-compatible LANs, the original station's 48 bit source address and final 48 bit destination address are maintained across all the LANs, irrespective of the fact that FDDI's MAC protocol relies on the sourcing station being resident on the same token path. This leads to FDDI bridges having slightly different modes of operation to that of a standard FDDI station in terms of copying and stripping frames.

Copying and Removing Bridged Frames

When a data packet arrives, say from an Ethernet network, it is converted to an FDDI frame format and transmitted over the FDDI LAN with the original Ethernet MAC source address and destination address. If the destination address is on another Ethernet network segment, another FDDI–Ethernet bridge will receive the frame, and transmit it onto the second Ethernet LAN (Figure 2.9).

The rules governing the translation and forwarding of the frame from one LAN to another mean that the FDDI frame that the second bridge received from the transmitting (Ethernet–FDDI) bridge only has the 'C' field set in the end of frame delimiter (Figure 4.5), indicating that the frame was successfully copied off the FDDI LAN. The 'A' field is left unaffected, as the destination address does not apply to the bridge MAC address, but to an address it recognises as being on the attached bridged Ethernet LAN. This is contrary to the standard FDDI MAC sub-layer rules, where both the 'A' and 'C' indicators are usually set. Note that where a bridge is unable to copy the frame, due to buffer limitations for example, the 'C' field does not get set, allowing the sourcing bridge to recognise that the frame was not successfully copied. In practice, however, higher-layer protocols are responsible for recognising undelivered frames.

Furthermore, the source address field in the FDDI frame does not match that of the FDDI station that originated it, but matches that of the original sending station on the first Ethernet LAN. This means that a frame now exists on the FDDI LAN that will not be stripped off in the manner described in Chapter 4 (Figures 4.9 and 4.10), as the original Ethernet station that transmitted the frame is not resident on the FDDI LAN. Thus the bridge that sourced the frame must have some way of removing it to ensure that the FDDI LAN does not fill up with 'sourceless' or *orphaned* frames, which may cause multiple retransmissions to the destination LAN if left unattended.

There are a number of methods that may be used to address this issue. The FDDI bridge that sources a bridged frame can account for the total number it has transmitted, and keep a record of the source addresses, stripping frames that match the list of current active frames the bridge has transmitted. This can be difficult to implement, so an additional technique is often used, called *void frame stripping*. This feature is usually supported directly by the VLSI components within the station, enabling it to run automatically in bridge configurations. Void frames are special FDDI MAC frames identified by the control field (see Figure 4.2) that in this case have the destination address field equal to the source address. The addresses are that of the FDDI bridge itself, not those of the bridged frames, hence have relevance on the FDDI LAN. The basic mechanism is illustrated in Figure 8.12.

The process works as follows. Immediately following the last forwarded frame, typically two void frames are transmitted, followed by the token. A special stripping mode is then entered such that any frames (including those originally sourced by bridge A) with addresses that do not match that of bridge A are stripped regardless, until the void frames are received and stripped. At this point, bridge A knows that all frames on the ring have been stripped, and it immediately stops the indiscriminate stripping mode, and operates as per normal, i.e. only stripping frames with the source address (SA) field equal to its own address (my address – MA). A frame counter is also employed in some cases to keep track of the number of frames that are stripped from the network. This counter is preloaded with the number of bridging frames that were originated from any of the station's queues, and decremented during the special stripping mode until zero, hence ensuring that the correct number are stripped.

Frame Translation Issues

Translation of Ethernet- and 802-compatible LAN frames into FDDI frame format, and back again, depends very much on the source frame type and even the protocol type carried by the MAC frame. Bit ordering in the MAC address fields, frame types (Ethernet or 802.3) and the length of the frame are also important factors. The performance of a bridge is affected by the speed with which it can make translation decisions, and not just by the speed of address lookup and internal forwarding functions.

Bit Ordering Differences

A bridge must ensure that when an Ethernet or 802.3 frame is translated, the bit ordering in the address fields is reversed. Both Ethernet and 802.3 transmit on a least-significant bit first basis, with the first bit of the address field transmitted being

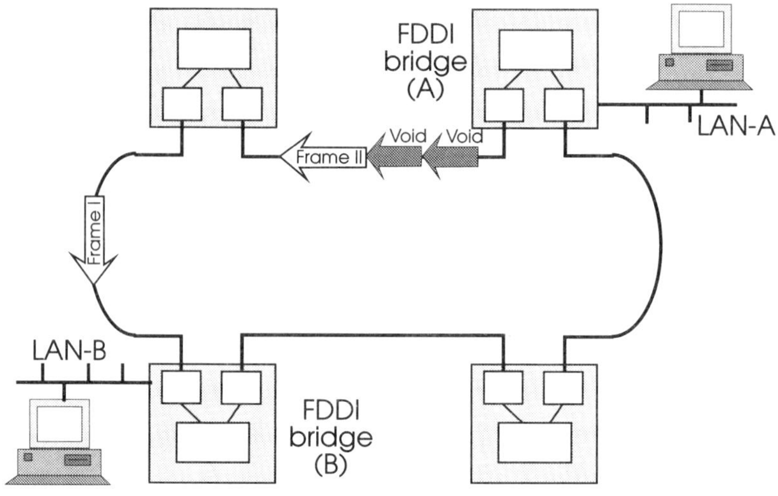

Bridge A receives frames from a station on LAN-A addressed to a station on LAN-B and transmits them onto the FDDI LAN (following token capture), followed by two void frames. The token is then released.

Figure 8.12(a) *Void frame stripping method in FDDI bridges*

the individual/group (I/G) bit (Figure 4.3). FDDI, on the other hand, uses a most-significant bit transmission order scheme. This is a common point of confusion when considering translation of one frame format to another, which a bridge has to deal with. Fortunately, this is normally transparent to an end user.

Translating Frames to FDDI Format

The easiest task for an FDDI bridge is 802-compatible frame translation, as the frames are already in a format that can be carried by FDDI directly, with only small modifications. For example, in the case of the 802.3 CSMA/CD LAN, the MAC header consists of IEEE destination and source address fields in the same format used by FDDI, plus a 2 byte LLC length, indicating the length of the LLC information content within the MAC field. The destination and source addresses are simply placed into the corresponding FDDI frame after bit reversal, the length field stripped off as FDDI does not require their use (IEEE 802.3 requires a minimum size of 64 bytes, so the length field is required to ensure correct interpretation of the LCC field within the MAC frame, especially when less than 64 bytes of LLC frame are present, the rest being pad bytes), the frame check sum (FCS) recalculated, and finally the rebuilt frame transmitted onto FDDI (Figure 8.14a). IEEE 802.5 translation is again, relatively straightforward. As FDDI has frame sizes greater than 802.3, frame size is not a problem in the Ethernet–FDDI direction. For the reverse direction, frames originating

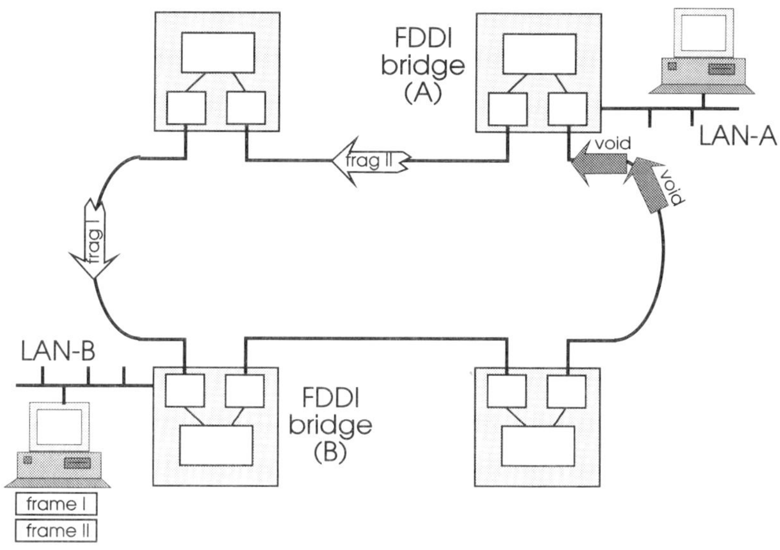

Bridge B copies the frames off the FDDI LAN and transmits them onto LAN-B to the destination station. Bridge A strips all FDDI frames (not just with those SA = MA) until the void frames are received, also using a special counter loaded with the total forwarded frames.

Figure 8.12(b) *Void frame stripping method in FDDI bridges (continued)*

from an FDDI station must ensure that they are not too large for Ethernet. In pure bridges, there is no standard method for dealing with frames that cannot be forwarded if they are too large, so they are usually dropped.

Problems arise when additional protocol types are in use on the LAN, such as Ethernet. Ethernet frames differ from their 802.3 cousins by the use of the LLC length field as a 2 byte 'EtherType' protocol identifier (identifying IP, ARP, Novell IPX, Appletalk content, etc.). In 802.3, protocol identification is embedded within the LLC header (described later). As translational bridges are based around LLC, the general convention is to convert Ethernet frames into an LLC-compatible format so that it is easily dealt with on the basis described above. As Ethernet has been a common LAN technology for TCP/IP-based networks for some time, the convention adopted was that described by the Internet document, RFC 1042, which defines the transmission of IP datagrams over 802 networks. The RFC 1042 frame, as it is referred to, uses an LLC-SNAP (Sub-Network Access Protocol) format to carry the Ethernet payload. Recall from Chapter 4 (Figure 4.19) that LLC frames, carried within the information field of the MAC frame, consist of DSAP, SSAP and a control field header. These are set to predefined values of 'AA' hex (170 decimal) for the DSAP and SSAP, and '03' for the control field, indicating un-numbered (UI) category of service (i.e. datagram, connectionless) for the SNAP format. The reason for this is that the single byte DSAP and SSAP values for identification of protocols (service access points) were soon found to be a constraint, due to the large number of protocols in existence, including vendor proprietary versions. Hence, the Internet community defined a SNAP header following the LLC header, consisting of 5 bytes as illustrated in Figure 8.13. The SNAP header consists of an organisationally unique identifier (OUI) field of 3 bytes (24 bits), as used by the IEEE 48 bit universal addressing scheme (see Chapter 4, Frame destination and source addressing), and a 2 byte protocol identification field, the same as that used by Ethernet in its type field (i.e. the EtherType field). For a SNAP header, the OUI field is reset to all zeros (00-00-00).

Thus, when an Ethernet MAC frame (not 802.3) enters a translational FDDI bridge, its destination and source addresses are used (after bit reversal) directly as before, but an LLC-SNAP header is added to the front of the MAC information field, with the OUI = 00-00-00, and the MAC protocol type field transferred into the SNAP protocol type field, before the frame is transmitted onto FDDI (Figure 8.14b). At the point where the frame is translated back from FDDI to Ethernet, the fact that it was an Ethernet frame originally, and not an 802.3 frame, is recognised by the SNAP header with OUI = 00-00-00, i.e. as an RFC 1042 frame. If the OUI is any other value, the frame is converted to an 802.3 frame.

The RFC 1042 frame translation works in just about all cases, except for AppleTalk networks, where AppleTalk I uses Ethernet, and AppleTalk II uses 802.3 frames. Unfortunately, Appletalk II uses an LLC-SNAP format the same as for an RFC 1042 frame. Hence, a problem arises when an Appletalk II frame is bridged via FDDI to another CSMA/CD LAN, in that according to the above rules for Ethernet translation, it will be converted to an Ethernet frame and not an 802.3 frame on the outgoing bridge port.

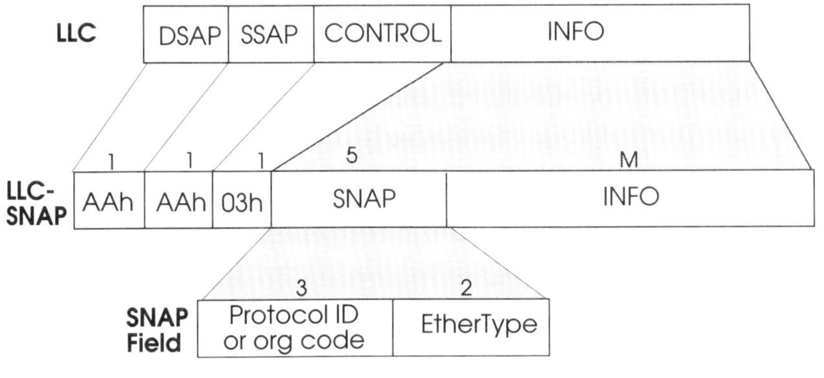

Figure 8.13 *Sub-network access protocol (SNAP) field in LLC frame*

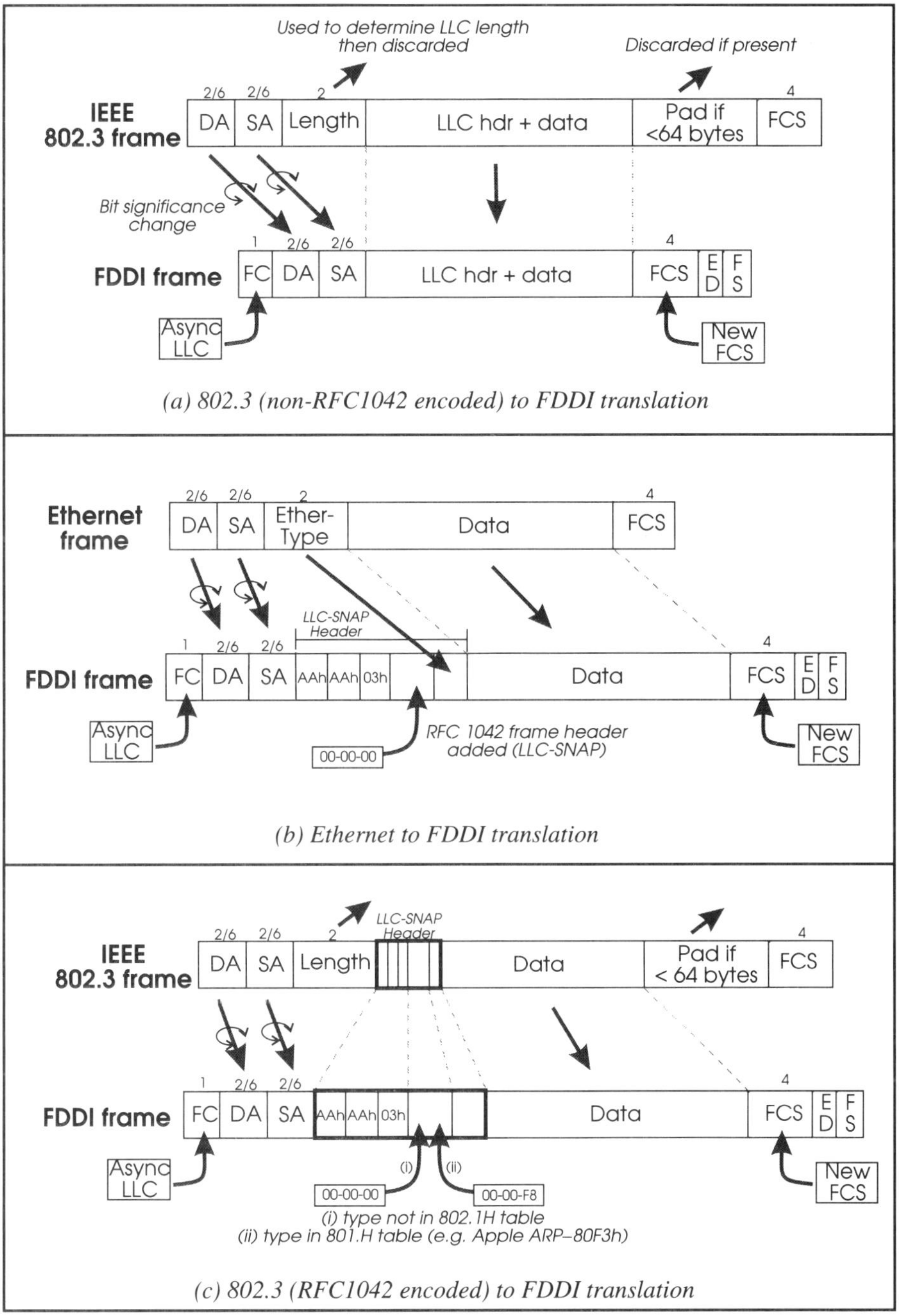

Figure 8.14 *Common frames translations to FDDI format*

To handle this, the IEEE has drafted a recommendation to deal with such a situation, documented in its IEEE 802.1H standard. IEEE 802.1H details a *bridge tunnel service*, which still uses an LLC-SNAP header, but with a value of 00-00-F8, rather than 00-00-00, assigned to the OUI field to distinguish it from a RFC 1042 frame (Figure 8.14c). In order to preserve the RFC 1042 service still supported by other bridges and protocols in the network, a *selective translation table* is defined by 802.1H, which contains a list of 2 byte protocol types (EtherType) that will be converted to the bridge tunnel format. If the protocol is not listed in the table, it is then translated and forwarded in the RFC 1042 format as before. At present, the only protocol id listed in the table is that of AppleTalk Address Resolution Protocol (value '80F3' hex) to handle the above problem. In general, most protocols should be designed to avoid this problem, and the table generally contains exceptions to the rule. Figure 8.14 summarises the FDDI frame conversions discussed.

Cut-Through Bridge and Switch Operation

Cut-through bridging and switching capable hubs or nodes allow the fast forwarding of incoming frames to their destination bridge port, before the entire frame has been received. *Store-and-forward* bridges (i.e. standard IEEE 802.1D translation or source-routing bridges) are usually designed to receive an entire frame (i.e. store the entire received frame) at the input bridge port, and before forwarding, check the frame for errors and validity. Cut-through bridges and switches, on the other hand, start forwarding the frame as soon as it has checked for its validity (i.e. correct type) based on the fact that all information for forwarding is available in the frame header. Frames are forwarded, irrespective of FCS errors, which is deemed acceptable by the fact that significant performance improvements can be made using this fast forwarding technique. In fact, some high-performance switches can start to forward frames as soon as the MAC address information has been received.

Figure 8.15 illustrates the differences between a store-and-forward bridge and a cut-through bridge or switch in terms of input–output frame latencies. In theory, if a switch is able to forward a frame based on the destination address field only, then the frame gets forwarded after the preamble and start of frame, control field (if present) and destination address fields have been received. In practice, some time is taken looking up the destination address field, and setting up the forwarding connection. Taking FDDI as an example, for a 64 byte frame (including preamble), this means that the frame is capable of being forwarded after only 10 bytes (see Table 4.1) plus some forwarding connection setup time, as opposed to after 64 bytes. On the basis that it would take at least a few microseconds (if not tens of microseconds) to perform a lookup and connection setup, it is unlikely that in FDDI's case any savings can be made for minimum sized frames. However, if we take a maximum sized 4500 byte frame, then as it takes around 360 μsec to receive the complete frame, if the frame can be forwarded after say 40–60 μsec, then the latency has been reduced by around

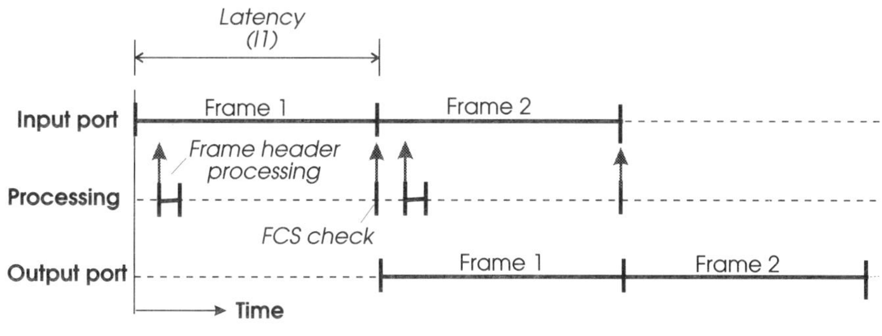

(a) Store and forward frame latency

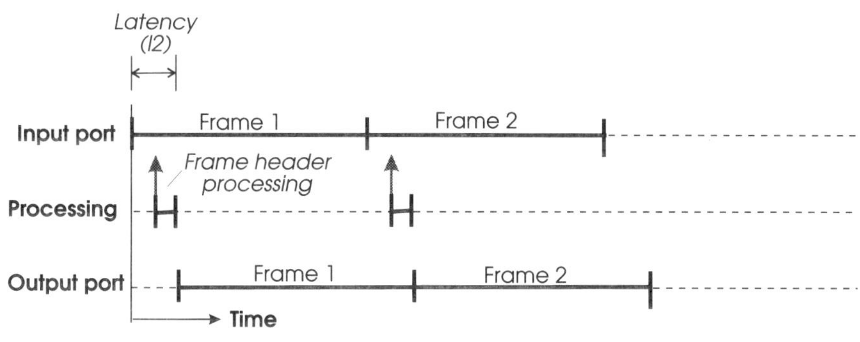

(b) Cut-through/switching frame latency

Figure 8.15 *Frame latency reduction using cut-through or switching techniques*

300 μsec. Where higher-layer protocols use many acknowledgement packets, this can significantly increase (typically by a factor of 2 in some tests) the overall communications rate.

The differences between a cut-through bridge and switch are very small in terms of functionality, and hence the terms are often used interchangeably. Architecturally, they can be quite different. In these discussions, it is assumed that a cut-through bridge is more like a standard store-and-forward bridge that has been upgraded to forward frames without having to wait for the entire frame to be received. Hence, from an architectural point of view, they look very similar to a standard bridge, with LAN interface modules interconnected by a common internal bus or highway (Figure 8.16a). A switch, on the other hand, generally employs a dedicated switch fabric (Figure 8.16b), a separate hardware and software entity, with hardware-based routing or switching engines to forward frames to the correct port(s). For both types of fast forwarding bridges, an option is usually available to operate in store-and-forward mode, i.e. full buffering of frames and error checking before forwarding. Full buffering is nearly always a requirement, even in switches, as they have to cater for the destination LAN port not always being ready to accept an incoming frame, or the internal switch fabric being congested.

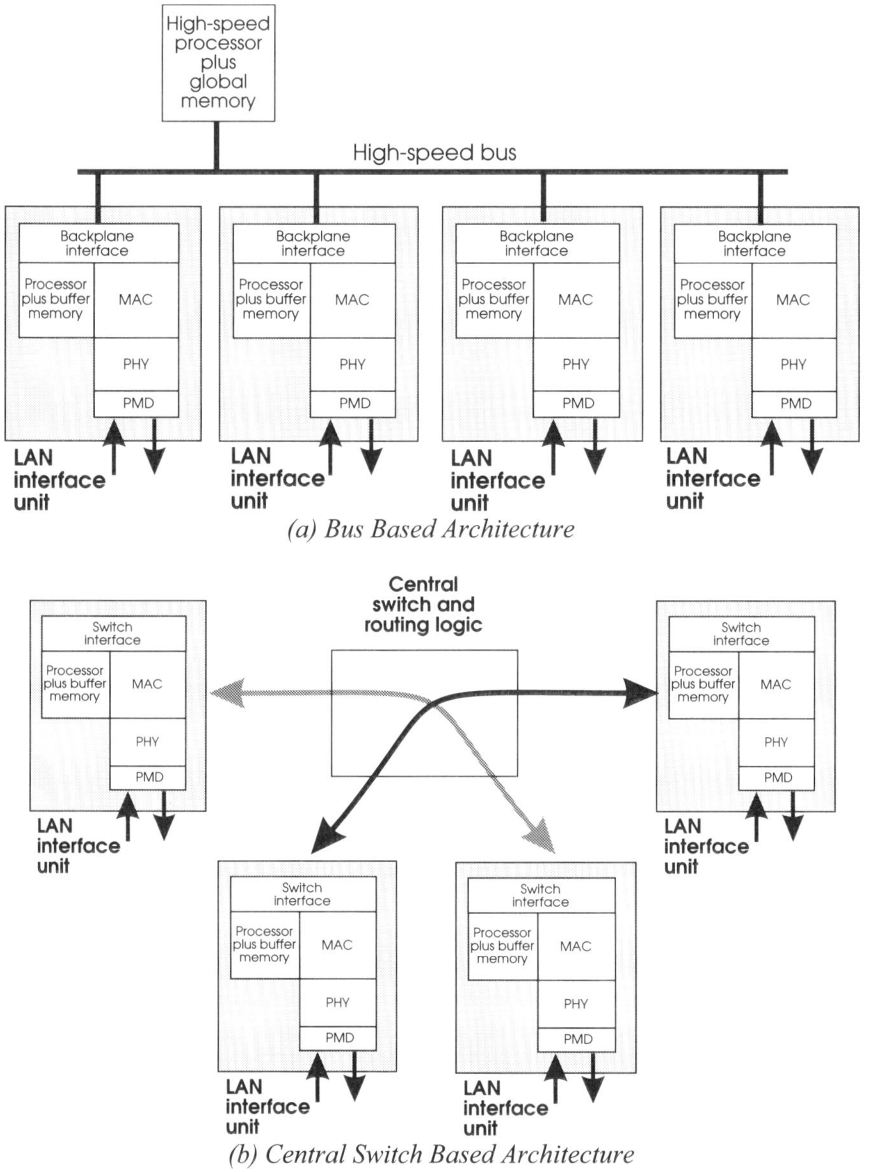

Figure 8.16 *Fast forwarding bridge architectures*

In general, the higher-performance switches employ a dedicated switching entity, allowing very fast forwarding rates to be achieved compared to the bandwidth limited bus arrangement shown in Figure 8.16(a).

Principles of Switching

Frame forwarding, as with bridging in general, involves the extraction of the destination address of an incoming MAC frame, in order to determine which port to send the frame on to. Fast forwarding speeds this operation up, and as previously mentioned, starts forwarding the frames onto its destination port as soon as possible. Figure 8.17 illustrates the general process, in this case for a central hardware switch based architecture. Switching schemes based on a common backplane generally employ DMA techniques to transfer the data from port to port, buffering frames within each LAN interface unit, or alternatively in a global buffer memory.

In Figure 8.17, frames arriving at the source LAN port have their frame header information (frame control, destination address, source address plus any routing

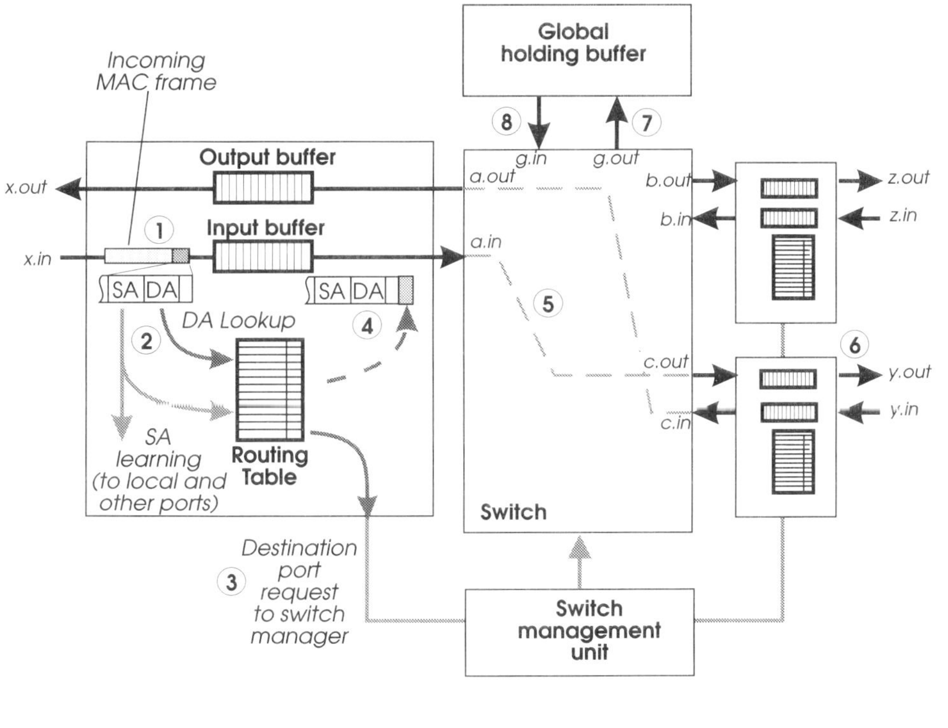

Figure 8.17 *Frame switching processes*

information in the information field) examined as they arrive (1). Source address information is used to detect any new station addresses that have not transmitted before in the bridge-learning process as described earlier. This is updated in each of the lookup tables at every port. Destination addresses are compared in a local lookup table to determine which port it should forward the frame to (2). If a central switch controller or arbiter is used, a request is sent via a dedicated bus to open up a point-to-point connection to the destination LAN port (3). Alternatively, if a self-routing switch is employed, additional header information is added to the frame (or replaces the received frame header altogether) to allow it to find its way through the switch to the destination port (4). Once the request has been granted (or a connection is made available to the destination port), the frame is transferred across the switch (5). This can be as soon as the destination address has been detected and mapped to a destination port within the switch, or anytime up to the point where the complete frame has been received (and stored) in the input buffer memory. At the destination port, the frame is usually buffered for the length of time it takes for the port to gain access to the network (6). If the original frame-addressing information had been replaced with shorter local switch port addresses (saving the length of time it takes to transmit the 48 bit addressing fields), the original frame is reconstructed before being transmitted onto the destination LAN. If the LAN type is different, then the frame translation may also take place here, or alternatively, at a central controller.

In the case of multicast, broadcast, management (e.g. SNMP), bridging control or bridge translational frames, these are generally dealt with by a central switch controller responsible for the global buffer memory. A multicast frame, for example, will be sent to the global memory (7), where the central controller will determine which ports, if not all, the frame is destined for. It will then make sure that the frame is sent to each of the destination ports, either all together, in groups, or one at a time (8). This also has the advantage of the central controller being able to regulate the amount of multicast traffic, combined with protocol information if necessary, to decrease the chances of overloading LAN segments with too many multicast or broadcast frames, controlling flooding, and so on.

In some switched hubs, a data-link layer independent switching fabric may be used to allow the mixing of many different LAN types. ATM cell switching is a common way of achieving this, with the LAN port interfaces translating all the incoming LAN frames into ATM cells before entering the switch. The cells are then converted to the destination LAN frame type before transmission. This has the added benefit of transparently bridging dissimilar LANs.

Figure 8.18 illustrates two basic types of switch fabrics: (a) a crossbar where every input port can be connected to one or more output ports, and (b) self-routing switches that use a simple header to route the data packet as it traverses the switch via small routing elements. Crossbars generally provide the most flexible switching, as it is possible to connect any input to any output, regardless of any other point-to-point connections made in the switch. This, of course, applies where there are point-to-point connections only, and is referred to in this context as a *non-blocking* switch. If, as shown, there are one-to-many (i.e. multicasting) connections, then some outputs will

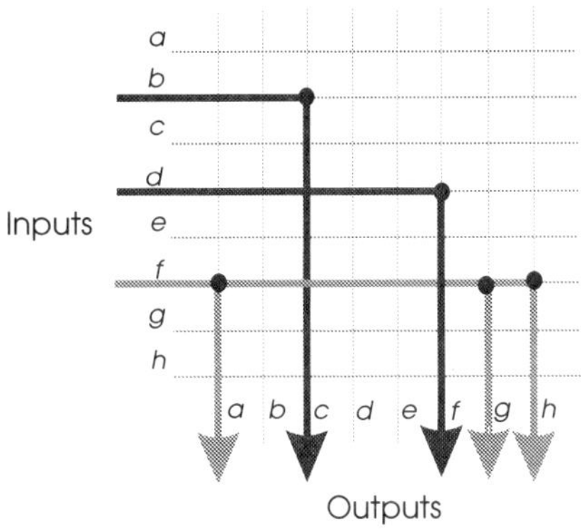

(a) 8 × 8 crossbar switch

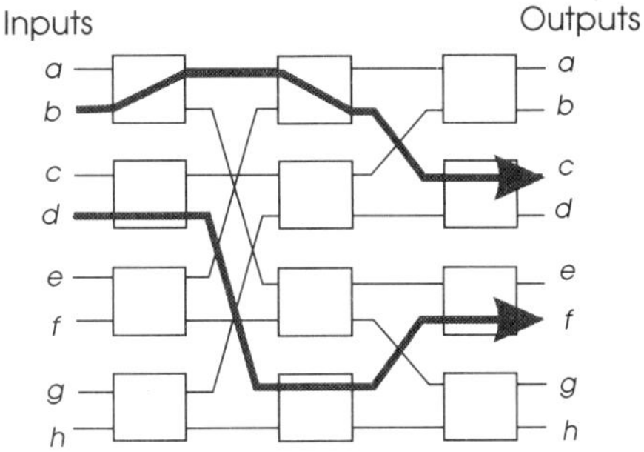

(b) 8 × 8 self-routing switch (Banyan or Omega switch)

Figure 8.18 *Switching fabrics*

be blocked, as they are already in use. In the multicast case, the frame is generally held in the input port queue until it can be successfully transferred to all the destination ports, or it is stored in a global buffer or queue, and handled by a separate processing engine.

Self-routing switches are cheaper to construct as they contain less switching elements, but suffer from blocking even in point-to-point cases. For example, in Figure 8.18(b), if input *e* wished to connect to output *a*, it would be prevented from doing so as the *b–c* connection at the middle stage prevents input *e*'s traffic from getting through. Such switches are generally referred to as *blocking*. Though this is a problem, some architectures overcome this limitation using clever queuing techniques. The additional header that is added to the frame is usually a simple binary bit sequence that guides the frame through the small two way binary switching elements. For the 8 × 8 example shown, three routing bits would be required, one for each stage of the switch. (A good summary of various switch types, including this one, is contained in De Prycker, 1993, Chapter 4.)

FDDI in Ethernet Switches

As we saw earlier, switched hubs utilising FDDI technology can be single LAN technology based (i.e. FDDI only), or mixed LAN technology, combining translational bridging techniques to provide a bridge to FDDI. For a switched Ethernet hub, with a FDDI port providing a high-speed backbone or server connection, frames can be switched very quickly between Ethernet ports (carrying Ethernet- or 802.3-compatible frames) without any translation involved. As soon as a frame is destined for the FDDI port, the frame must be translated accordingly, to meet the bridging translation rules discussed earlier. This may still be performed without full buffering of the frame before transmission, but needs a little more decision making based on LLC-SNAP header information before the frame can be correctly translated and transmitted onto FDDI, and similarly, when translating from FDDI to Ethernet (Figure 8.14).

Hence, as a minimum, an FDDI interface within an Ethernet switch must be capable of handling Ethernet, IEEE 802.3, RFC1042 and bridge tunnelling frames (to handle AppleTalk II), in addition to the mandatory SMT processes. If the FDDI link is only employed as a fast pipe to a server, then this level of bridging functionality should be sufficient. In larger networks, where multiple bridges are present, and the LAN segment attached to the switch may itself contain a bridge, the switch must be able to support the appropriate bridge and management protocols (for example the spanning tree protocol). A management interface is usually provided to enable some of the full bridging features to be turned off in order to optimise the switch for a particular network installation.

FDDI Switches

Due to the higher data rates involved, switches that support fast forwarding of FDDI MAC frames generally employ a 100 Mbps or higher rate switching element. DEC's GIGAswitch, for example, uses a 36 × 36, 6 bit wide crossbar switching fabric to connect ports together (Souza *et al*, 1994). In DEC's case, a proprietary arbitration scheme, called 'take-a-ticket', is employed to control the port arbitration process. Connections can be point-to-point, or one port to many, depending on the destination address being uni- or multi-cast. Connections are capable of bidirectional communication, enabling support of full duplex FDDI operation (see below). A central buffer and controller handles multicast or broadcast frames, along with management or bridge protocol specific frames addressed to the switch as a node in its own right.

Full Duplex FDDI

One of the benefits of switched FDDI is the ability to operate in full duplex mode. This allows an FDDI node to transmit and receive at the same time, giving an effective combined I/O rate of 200 Mbps. This is only possible in a tree or mesh architecture using M–S or M–A/B type port connections, as full duplex can only operate on a point-to-point basis. The performance advantage seen by using full duplex links is through the ability of the nodes to overlap any acknowledges with incoming data traffic. If the link is a bridge-to-bridge connection, two different communications could potentially be passing along the cable at the same time (in opposite directions).

At the time of writing, there are no standards in place for full duplex FDDI, and thus most offerings currently available are vendor proprietory. Efforts are underway to establish full duplex negotiation protocols (or low-level signalling) allowing different vendors' full duplex capabilities to be compatible.

Routers

Routers are devices that make decisions based on information higher up the communications stack (network layer) than a bridge, typically based on the type of higher-layer protocol. For instance, routers make forwarding decisions based on whether the packet is an IPX (Novell Netware) or IP (Unix), only allowing specific protocol types through to a particular segment. Most routers nowadays can handle many different protocols (i.e. are multi-protocol routers). Typical examples include IP, IPX, DECnet, OSI, Appletalk, Vines and XNS protocol support. Network managers are able to configure which protocol is supported on a port-by-port basis, effectively filtering certain protocol traffic types by LAN segment. Hence, where a bridge would forward any packet with a destination address that matches that connected to one of its ports, a router would only forward the packet if the appropriate protocol is allowed through for that particular port.

Routers provide firewall protection from LAN broadcast storms, which pure bridges cannot prevent. As routers deal with networking layer issues, they also know more about the packet's destination, how many MAC frames are used to carry the networking layer information, the number of router hops the packets will have to go through, and so on. They also route packets using a networking layer address (e.g. IP address) as opposed to MAC addresses, and can make routing decisions based on the best path available to them (where several exist, that is). Routers exchange path information, etc. using routing protocols such as RIP (Routing Information Protocol) and OSPF (Open Shortest Path First). Another capability of a router is to handle the different frame sizes by performing fragmentation and reassembly of packets, where a pure MAC bridge would normally drop them.

Routers are designed to be independent of the LAN over which they transport information to and from, hence, to an ideal router, knowledge of the underlying LAN technology is not important. In practice, a router has to be aware of certain limitations and constraints imposed by a particular LAN type. From the perspective of FDDI, perhaps the most important networking layer protocol that is used is IP, due mainly to the large installed base of TCP/IP backbone networks. The benefit of TCP/IP is that it can run across numerous communications channels, including the wide area, making it a good networking technology independent communications protocol for corporate networks. Other important, emerging protocols, are those based on OSI.

Internet Protocol (IP)

The Internet Transport Control Protocol (TCP) and Internet Protocol (IP) play an important role in many corporate networks as the main internetworking protocols above the data-link layers. IP is the network layer protocol used by TCP and UDP, as we saw in Chapter 1. TCP is an applications based transport protocol running on top of IP. IP also supports other transport level protocols such as User Datagram Protocol

(UDP) that is used as the main transport protocol in SNMP management applications.

The IP protocol, and its associated Address Resolution Protocol (ARP), is encapsulated into LLC frames using the LLC-SNAP format defined by RFC 1042 as we saw earlier (Figure 8.13). RFC 1188 further expands the transport of IP in RFC 1042 for single MAC FDDI stations (dual or single attachment). Within the SNAP field, the protocol type is identified by a 2 byte field, being set in this case to 0800h for IP, and 0806h for ARP. Table 8.1 details examples of other possible values. Note that as these are the same as in the Ethernet protocol identification field (EtherType), some values are not allowed as they would conflict with an 802.3 length field. As it stands, all EtherType values are above the maximum LLC length field, allowing Ethernet and 802.3 frames to be distinguished by the value within the EtherType/LLC Length field position.

Netware's IPX

Novell's Netware is one of the most popular PC-based network operating systems, and though it supports TCP/IP protocols, it more commonly uses its own specific SPX/IPX (Sequenced Packet Exchange/Internetwork Packet Exchange) transport and network protocols. SPX/IPX were derived from the Xerox Network Systems (XNS) protocols.

Netware's IPX is transported across FDDI (and 802 LANs in general) using the standard LLC frame format. Though IPX packets are limited to 576 bytes in size, it is quite common for network drivers to use the full capabilities of the FDDI MAC frame size to transport more than one IPX packet at a time to increase throughput. The LLC DSAP and SSAP fields (Figure 4.19) for Netware are defined to be EOh. An IPX header is placed in the first part of the following LLC information field.

Table 8.1 *Protocol types used by Ethernet and LLC-SNAP*

Protocol id (EtherType)	Value (hex)
Reserved for LLC Length Field	0000–05DC
DoD IP	0800
X.75 Internet	0801
X.25 Level 3	0805
ARP	0806
Banyan Systems	0BAD
3-COM Corp	6010–6014
DEC LAN Bridge	8038
Appletalk	809B
Appletalk ARP	80F3

Performance Issues in Bridges, Switches and Routers

Most internetworking products base their performance figures on the number of packets, frames or millions of bits, that they are capable of forwarding per second. This figure is dependent on a number of factors related to the amount of buffering used to store frames or partial frames within the bridge, the power of the processor or protocol engine used, the internal frame routing hardware, and so on.

As the loading on a bridge protocol engine can be fairly significant for a number of LAN ports, a RISC processor is quite often used to ensure maximum speed of operation for software-based decisions. The RISC processor may also be used to move the frames or frame fragments around the inside of the switch from port to port(s) along a common bus or busses. Such architectures, especially modular ones, sometimes allow for additional processors to be added to share the load of many LAN bridge ports. The fastest, but more hardware-complex option involves the use of dedicated hardware routing engines (e.g. high-performance DMA engines) or switch fabrics as shown earlier. The latter are, of course, found in the newer cut-through bridge and switch products supporting fast forwarding of MAC frames.

Figure 8.19 illustrates some typical throughput figures in Mbps for a standard transparent bridge (a), and router (b), taken from vendor test lab results. (The gaps in the chart are due to no test results being produced for that frame size.) The test equipment used a single FDDI ring bridged or routed onto either ten Ethernet segments or seven Token Ring segments (16 Mbps). The rationale behind this was that, in theory, FDDI's 100 Mbps rate should be capable of being bridged to 10 × 10 Mbps (= 100 Mbps) Ethernet segments, or close to 7 × 16 Mbps (= 112 Mbps) Token Ring segments, when directing frames to each segment equally. Frames, from a frame generator on the FDDI ring, were transmitted to stations attached to each of the target segments. Frames were addressed to stations on each LAN segment in a round-robin (or 'Gatling gun') fashion. Typical bridge throughput (without switching or cut-through bridging) varied according to frame size, and for Ethernet was shown to be around 4.49 Mbps for 64 byte frames, rising to 9.86 Mbps for 1518 byte frames per segment (for the best product tested in that category). The reason the smaller frames have worse throughput than the larger ones is due to the larger portion of the packet being taken up by the MAC header, and the faster arrival rate, resulting in a greater number of decisions or lookups per second required by the bridge or router, per port. These results vary considerably across different vendors' products, though bear in mind that these are a snap-shot representation of products available at the time the tests were carried out. Products are likely to improve as newer models are introduced, and different vendors enter the market.

What exemplifies the earlier statement about dependence of the forwarding rate on architecture are the figures for Token Ring: 0.08 Mbps at 64 byte, and 12.24 at 1460 byte frames. Whilst the higher frame size (the greatest supported in this test) was respectible, the 64 byte frames in pure bridging mode were not, an affect of the underlying architecture. The use of back-to-back 64 byte frames in performance testing

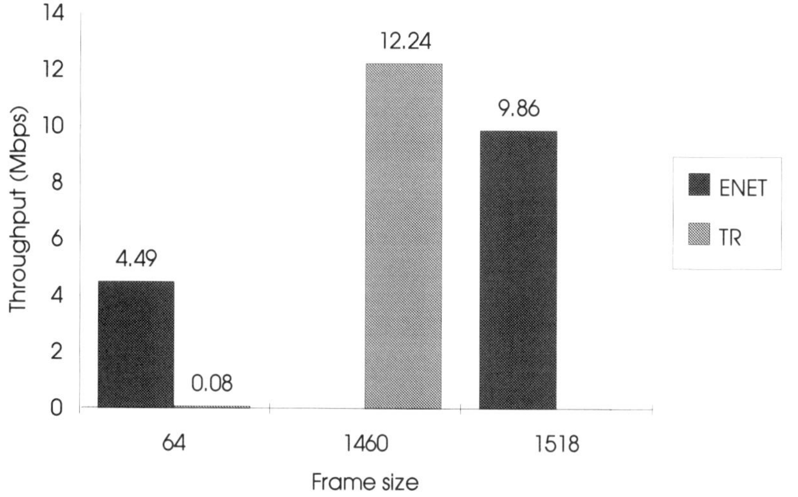

Transparent bridging from FDDI to Ethernet/Token Ring

Figure 8.19(a) *Throughput examples for standard bridges and routers (IP) vs. frame size. (Source: Datacommunications, August 1993, 'FDDI Bridges and Routers'.)*

of any kind of bridge is a useful indication of how fast the device is capable of performing all the necessary lookups and translations before the next 64 byte frame arrives. If the buffering used at the input port is too little, then it would soon overflow if the forwarding of frames took longer than the arrival interval of 64 byte frames. In Ethernet, 64 bytes can arrive at just over 50 µsec intervals (hence in theory a bridge should be capable of forwarding before the next one arrives). For Token Ring, the interval decreases to around 32 µsec. For FDDI, this reduces drastically to just over 5 µsec. Thus, the demand placed on all bridge types when fed with back-to-back short frames is high, especially as the data rates increase. The other important factor to consider is the length of time it takes to gain access to the destination LAN. In token-based networks, this is the length of time to capture the token. For Ethernet, this is the time it takes for the media to become available, including potential collisions, if already in use.

In the case of routing (Figure 8.19b), it was found that the throughput numbers actually improved in some vendors cases when routing 64 byte IP frames versus 64 byte MAC frames, illustrating again how the internal decision-making process implementations can affect the throughput from vendor to vendor.

Cut-through bridging techniques and switching provide a mechanism to speed up the bridging process as shown earlier (Figure 8.15), and also to provide higher

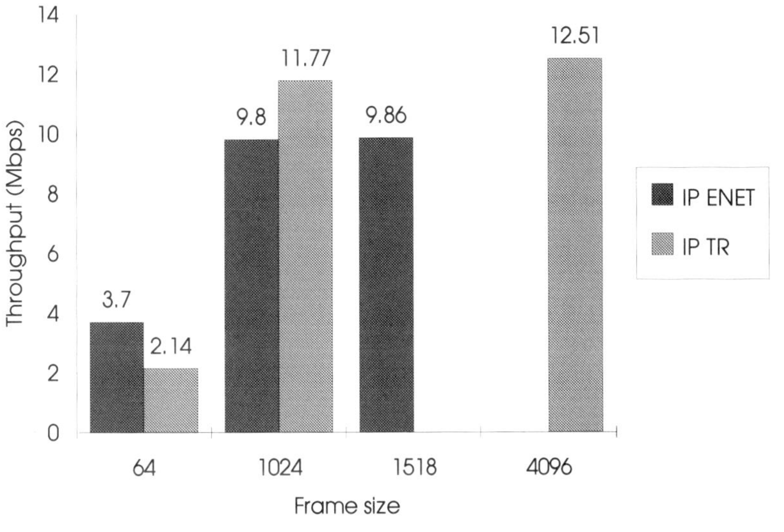

Routing IP frames from FDDI to Ethernet/Token Ring

Figure 8.19(b) *Throughput examples for standard bridges and routers (IP) vs. frame size. (Source: Datacommunications, August 1993, 'FDDI Bridges and Routers'.)*

aggregate communications bandwidth to each segment. A switch may be able to forward frames at a fast rate (e.g. 40 μsec latency for Ethernet switches), but if the switch cannot handle high levels of traffic for the reasons discussed above, then it starts to drop packets depending also on the type of switching employed. Some switch or cut-through bridge architectures employ a throttling technique at the source ports instead of dropping packets, to prevent too many frames from arriving once the switch/bridge has reached full capacity.

In the case of pure FDDI frame switching, the worst case typical short frame arrival rate is of the order of 440k per second, per port. In the DEC GIGAswitch for example, this means that 1.3 million lookups (880k of which are 48 bit values) have to be performed, per second, per port (see Souza *et al*, 1994). To meet this requirement, DEC use an address hashing technique to allow fast lookup of destination addresses. In addition, frame buffering is used at the input port before entering the 36 × 36 crossbar switch, and also at the output port to ensure that frames can be buffered for the length of time it takes to acquire the token. The switch itself is capable of 6.25 million connections per second. These, and other features, allow DEC to achieve forwarding rates of greater than 200k frames per second, per port. Two-port FDDI modules allow a total of twenty-two ports to be switched, with expansion possible to the full 36 with four-port FDDI modules.

FDDI Products

FDDI products, as we saw in Chapter 2, fall into a number of categories, namely adapters, hub modules, standalone concentrators, internetworking and LAN analysers. It is not practical to detail all the available products available in the market place, as these change over time. However, to get a clearer picture of what is available, the following sections detail which of the major systems and networking vendors support FDDI.

DEC Products

Digital Equipment Corporation (DEC) have long supported FDDI, having produced their own VLSI devices (later licensing the technology to semiconductor vendors AMD and Motorola) to support FDDI MAC and PHY layers. DEC produce a small booklet (see Bibliography) outlining their earlier product support, and covering some of the basic concepts of FDDI. Their product support consists of the following:

- DECconcentrator 500 – chassis based design consisting of a number of plug in modules. Either backbone connected, or a standalone workgroup concentrator. As a NAC, can support up to twelve SAS, and as a DAC/SAC, up to eight SAS. Dual homing is supported. Additional PMD offerings include DEC's ThinWire Coaxial and Shielded Twisted Pair. SMF provides up to 40 km distance support.

- DECbridge 500 – an Ethernet/802.3 to FDDI intelligent bridge, performing translation from FDDI to Ethernet frames and vice versa. Connects to a DECconcentrator 500 as a SAS, allowing multiple bridges to be connected to FDDI non-disruptively.

- DEC FDDIcontroller 700/700-C – a DEC TURBOchannel-based workstation/server SAS adapter card for DEC's RISC based servers.

- DECcontroller 400 – SAS adapter card, enabling connection of VAX 6000/9000 computers directly onto the FDDI ring through the DECconcentrator 500.

- DECconcentrator 900MX – a standalone or hub based configurable eight port unit, with four ports being software configurable as A, B or M ports. With SNMP-compatible agent built-in, it is remotely manageable by any SNMP network management package. The 900MX also installs into the DEChub 900 MultiSwitch, a segment switching hub (total aggregate bandwidth of 3 Gbps) supporting multiple FDDI, Ethernet, Token Ring and ATM. Combined with the integral bridging capabilities of the DEChub 900, a single intelligent hub can combine all the main networking technologies in one unit.

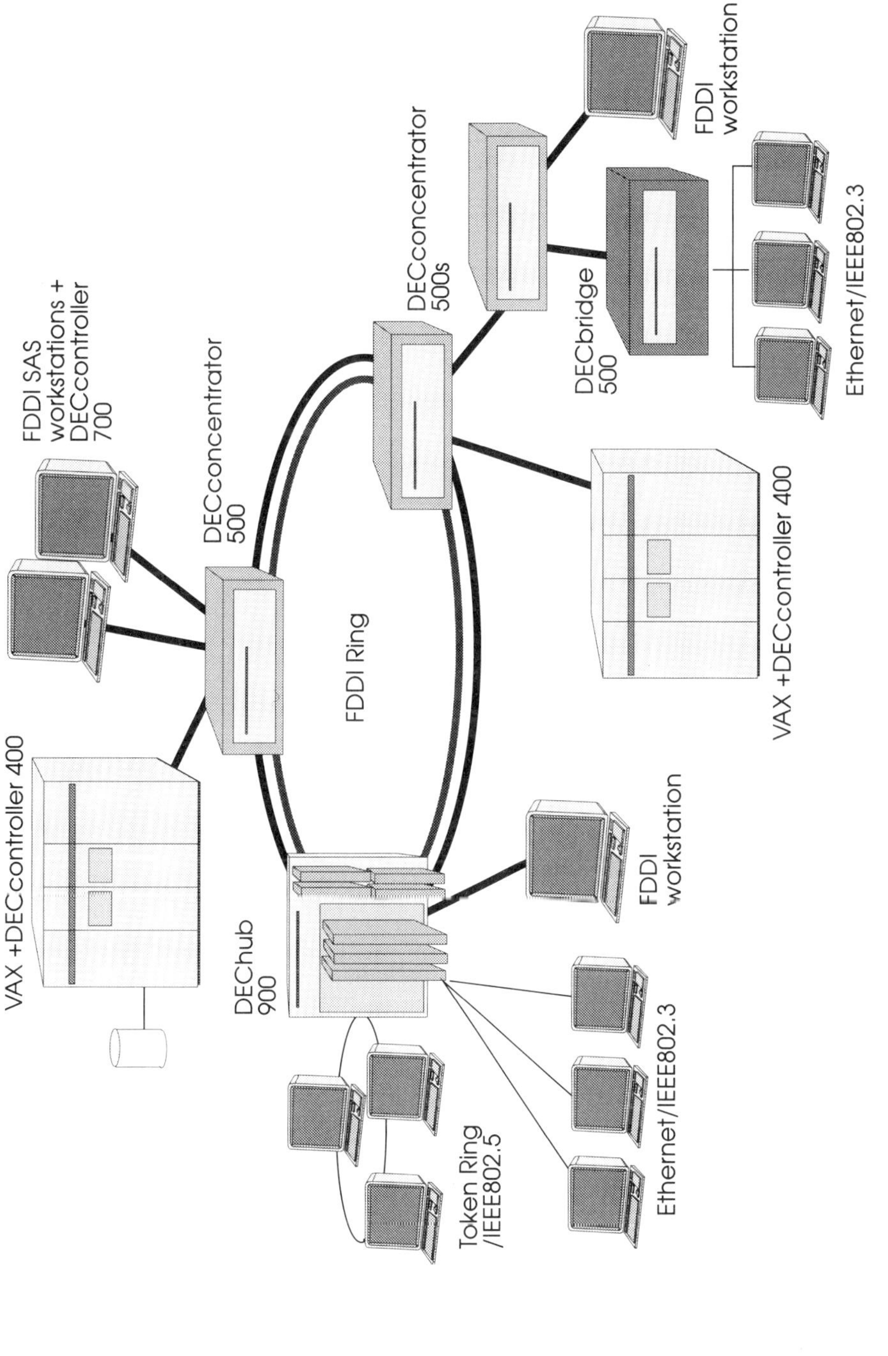

Figure 8.20 *DEC FDDI products*

- DEC GIGAswitch – an intelligent high-speed switching FDDI bridge. Throughput of 3.6 Gbps, with a forwarding rate of more than 227k packets/sec (minimum frame size), per port. Filters up to 440k packets/sec. Full duplex FDDI operation is supported. Up to fourteen slots are available, three taken up by system control units and the crossbar switch, leaving eleven for four- or two-port FDDI line cards. The unit is SNMP managed, and will also support ATM connectivity.

IBM Products

International Business Machines (IBM) have a number of FDDI products, including end station adapter cards and interfaces to their mainframe equipment. Support for the System/370 and System/390 mainframe environment is provided by a 3172 Interconnect Controller module, which acts as a gateway between the FDDI LAN and IBM's high-speed channel based ESCON back-end network. They also have a twenty-four port (maximum) concentrator, the 8240, and provide support for FDDI in their 8250 intelligent multi-protocol hubs. End station adapter cards are available for the IBM PS/2 and RISC System/6000 workstations. Adapter cards are also provided for non-IBM EISA bus based machines. All IBM's FDDI products support copper interfaces (SDDI), including the more recent TPDDI standard, and may be configured in many cases on a port (or group of four ports) basis. Specific products include the following:

- IBM's 3172 Interconnect Controller – provides a gateway into the IBM host (VTAM/SNA, TCP/IP, AIX, OSI) environment via IBM's high-speed ESCON serial channel network or serial VTAM/CTC channel. FDDI support is provided in version 2.1. The 3172 is a multi-protocol device, also supporting Token Ring, Ethernet/802.3 and Token Bus 802.4 (MAP 3.0 and SNA).

- 8250 Intelligent Multi-protocol Hubs (17- and 6-slot versions) – supports FDDI/SDDI/TPDDI, Token Ring/IEEE 802.5, Ethernet/IEEE 802.3 and will support switching (static and dynamic), with an eventual upgrade path to ATM. IBM have a technology exchange and distribution agreement with CHIPCOM.

- 8240 FDDI Concentrator – a modular design, able to take a ring interface card (dual attachment module), four-port optical fibre attachment modules, and four-port copper (SDDI) attachment modules. A total of twenty-four ports (type M) are provided (i.e. six expansion modules). The 8240 also has a built-in SNMP proxy agent, which is useful for supporting the SAS stations that do not directly support SNMP themselves. AIX NetView/6000 or any SNMP based management program may be used to manage the 8240. A remote program update (RPU) allows simple upgrading of the 8240's internal software, for revision changes, etc.

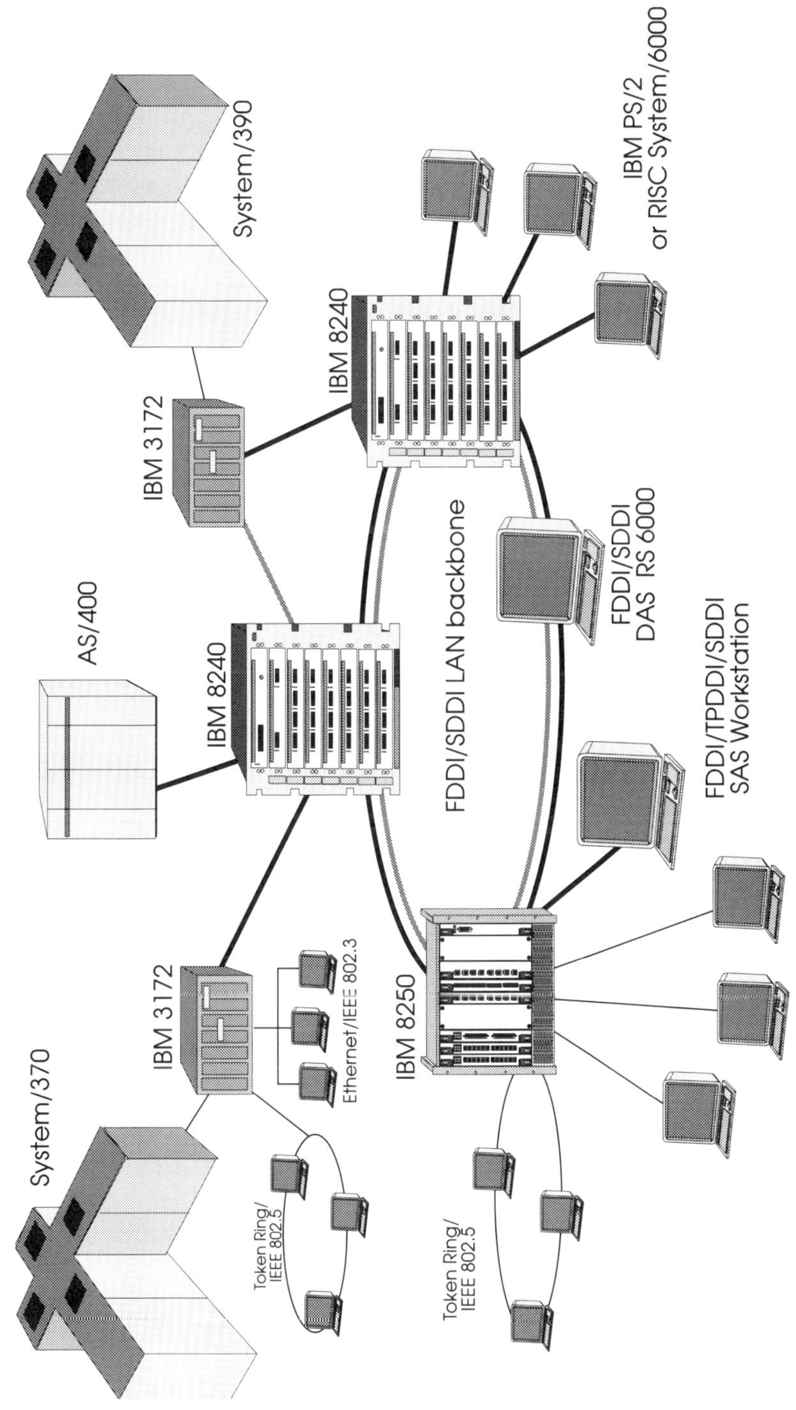

Figure 8.21 : *IBM FDDI/SDDI products*

- AS/400 Adapter – support is available for both FDDI and SDDI (8664/8664), and provides both dual attachment, single attachment and dual-homing connectivity to FDDI for the AS/400.

- IBM PS/2 and RISC System/6000 adapter cards – adapter cards are provided for all IBM PS/2, PS/Value Point and Industrial computers that support MCA and AT (ISA) bus specifications (including non-IBM computers). In addition, EISA bus standard cards are provided for non-IBM computers (such as Compaq, Dell, AST, etc.). A dual or single attachment fibre based board is available for the RS/6000. In all cases, the dual attachment capability is provided by a second expander board (taking up an additional slot in the workstation) which bridges across to a single attach baseboard. In the case of the PS/2 adapters, most cabling types are supported (i.e. FDDI, SDDI and TPDDI). IBM's adapters and drivers also support the synchronous data transfer mode of FDDI for applications such as interactive video conferencing, multimedia playback from a video server, and other similar applications.

Other Hub/Concentrator Vendors and Products

There are a number of intelligent hub and workgroup hub vendors that provide support for FDDI. Support is generally provided by plug-in modules that can be inserted into both the high-end chassis-based hubs (more than ten slots) and the smaller workgroup hubs (around six or less slots). Such vendors include Cabletron, Chipcom, Fibronics, Synoptics, U & B, 3-COM, to name but a few. All offer similar features as far as FDDI is concerned, mainly centred around a modular approach. A number of other vendors, such as Schneider & Koch/SysKonnect, Compu-Shack and Cisco/Crescendo, offer workgroup level FDDI concentrators to complement their adapters, providing a complete workgroup solution. Plates 8.1 and 8.2 illustrate some typical products available at the time of writing.

Workstation and PC Adapter Card Vendors and Products

The most common platform found today for FDDI adapters is IBM PC compatibles, i.e. EISA, MCA and ISA based adapters (Plate 8.3). Vendors such as Compu-Shack, Cisco/Crescendo, Madge, Schneider & Koch/SysKonnect, NPI and 3-COM are some of the vendors providing such cards. The performance of these cards can vary, for reasons discussed earlier. For the Macintosh platform, NU-Bus adapters are also available from some of these and other vendors.

In the workstation arena, vendors such as DEC, HP, IBM and Sun provide adapters for their own particular workstation ranges. DEC and IBM we looked at earlier. HP provide an FDDI/9000 board for their series 800 business servers, and a lower-performance derivative, called the Installed Integrated FDDI/9000 card, for their 700

Plate 8.1 *Synoptics System 5000 intelligent hub (courtesy Synoptics)*

series workstations. HP's design achieves close to 80 Mbps performance through the use of a system ASIC and dedicated node processor, which also performs protocol acceleration. Sun also provide a card for their workstations, along with one or two third-party vendors.

Internetworking Vendors and Products

Vendors supplying bridge/router products include 3-COM (Netbuilder II and Linkbuilder 3GH), Cisco (routers), DEC (DECnis600), Fibronics (FX8210B and FX8610), Proteon (CNX 500), Schneider & Koch/SysKonnect (SK-FDDI Router), Synoptics and Wellfleet Communications Inc. (Backbone Concentrator Node – BCN). Other vendors, such as Madge also provide a modular approach based on a PC platform. Switched Ethernet hubs with FDDI connectivity are also provided by a number of vendors, e.g. the Alantec Powerhub, Artel Communications' Galactica, Cabletron's ESX-820, 3-COM LinkSwitch, Cisco/Crescendo Catalyst and Networth PowerPipes products, with others promising similar products in time.

Plate 8.2 *Cisco's Catalyst switched hub (courtesy Cisco.)*

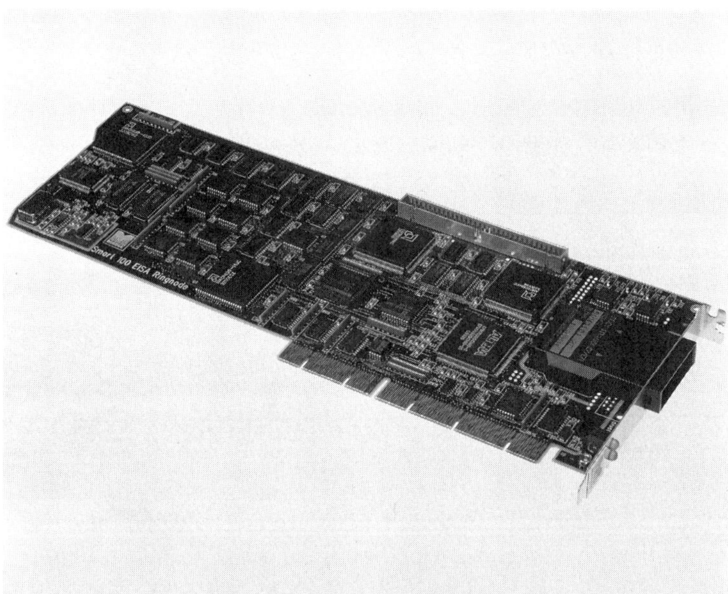

Plate 8.3 *MADGE Smart 100 EISA Ringnode FDDI adpater (courtesy MADGE)*

In addition to the standard products, some vendors, such as Fibronics with their MAVIX, provide direct coupling of video services into an FDDI ring. MAVIX (Multimedia Audio Visual Information eXchange) in particular provides a unit (the FER2100C) for compressing PAL or NTSC analogue video signals into a ITU H.261 (Px64) stream that is output on an Ethernet port. This is then linked to the FX8610 Workstation Server, which is effectively a switched Ethernet box with an FDDI connection option. Hence, live video can be compressed using such a scheme for transportation over an FDDI backbone network.

Fibronics also provide an FDDI repeater unit (FX84xx), for converting to and from multimode and single-mode fibre. Figure 8.22 illustrates how two multimode FDDI ring sections may be linked together, the distance between the two repeater units being up 40 km (category II SMF) or 20 km (category I SMF). The FX8400 series are available either as single or dual links. Optical bypass switches are also employed to enable the links to be isolated if necessary. Signal processing techniques are employed to keep the integrity of the transmitted signals over such long distances.

Test Equipment

FDDI LAN analysers and frame generators come from various vendors, and include differing features and capabilities. Vendors include Hewlett Packard (HP Network

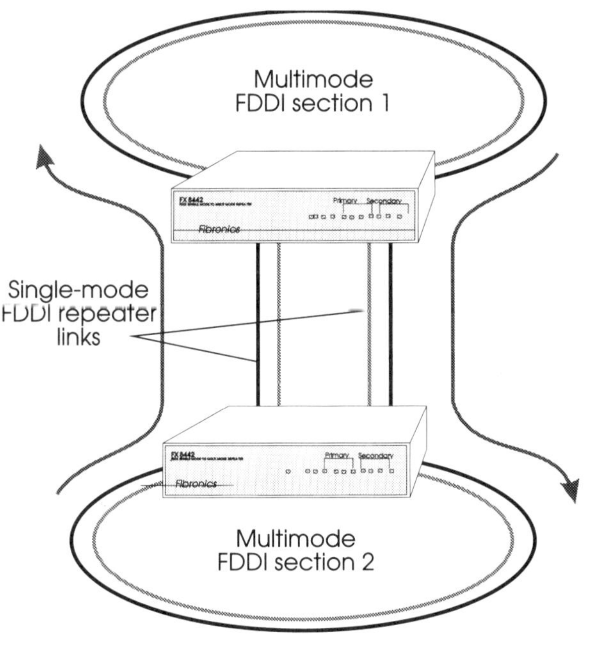

Figure 8.22 *Fibronics' FDDI repeaters*

Advisor), IBM (Dataglance), Tekelec (Chameleon), Wandel & Goltermann Technologies (DA-30), Siemens Industrial Automation (Protocol Tester K1100), Network General (Expert Sniffer) and Lanquest Labs (Framethrower) (see Bibliography – Data Communications International, 'How accurate is your logic analyzer'). Most of these products have either the capability to generate and/or capture FDDI frames at the maximum possible rate, and are part of a general product supporting other network types such as Ethernet or Token Ring. For example, the higher range analysers can monitor FDDI frames at up to 166,650 64 byte IP frames/sec, where the theoretical limit is about 171,000 fps.

For the developers of FDDI equipment, many other forms of optical test equipment are also used for testing fibre installations and connections, such as optical waveform receivers, digital spectrum analysers, fibre optic test sources and power meters. Much of this equipment is available at the FDDI interoperability test houses.

FDDI Product Conformance Testing

A final important product issue is conformance testing. Testing FDDI stations for conformance to the most recent ANSI/ISO standards has become an important area, driven by the need for products from different vendors to interoperate. To this end, a number of establishments have set themselves up as test houses for FDDI products, the best examples being the Advanced Networking Test Centre (ANTC) in Sunnyvale, California, and the EANTC at the Technical University of Berlin. Facilities such as these provide a vital link in the growth and acceptance of FDDI.

Testing of FDDI equipment usually involves exercising of the SMT, MAC, PHY and PMD entities using a specific test for each case. Some of the tests are more hardware oriented, and hence require a lot of optical or transmission line measurement equipment. Others are more software intensive, and require testing the end station as a 'black box' by sending a number of test frames and sequences into the FDDI interface to ensure that it processes the information correctly. One-on-one tests are usually carried out in the first instance to ensure that the basic optical light levels or line voltages are within specified limits. The station may then be tested at the higher-levels (i.e. MAC and SMT) again on a one-on-one basis using another reference station. Finally, testing in a fully configured FDDI network with a number of other reference stations is then carried out to see how the station performs under normal and heavy load circumstances (Figure 8.23).

Summary

VLSI devices implement a large portion of the FDDI protocols, with the higher-level management aspects of SMT usually carried out by a dedicated CPU. The partitioning of the MAC and PHY layers into separate devices allows a common VLSI chipset to

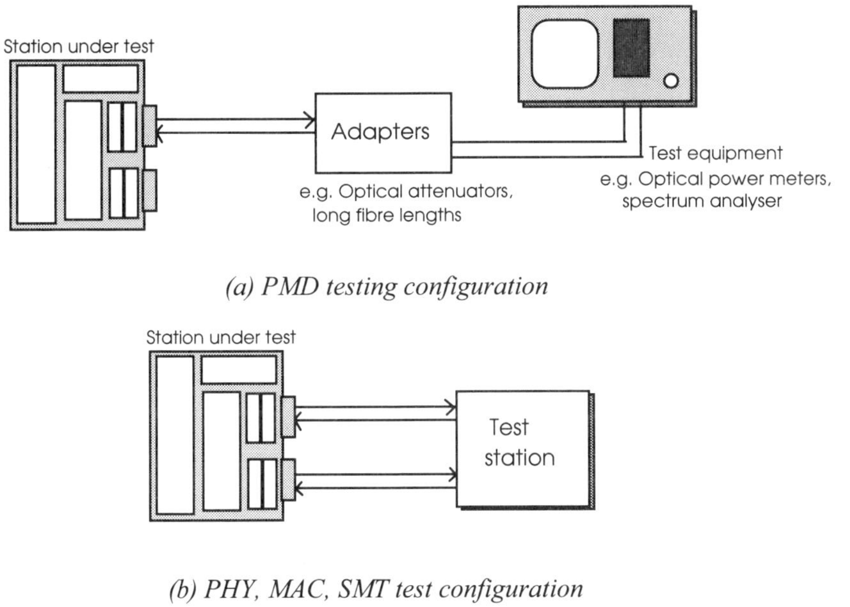

Figure 8.23 *One-to-one configurations for testing FDDI equipment*

be used for both adapters and concentrators. Additional complexity is found in concentrators due to the multiplexing of ports and MACs into multiple paths. Different levels of concentrators thus exist, ranging from single-path, single MAC concentrators, to multiple-path, multiple MAC. Concentrator functions can be incorporated into intelligent hubs, or implemented as standalone, dedicated workgroup hubs. Switching hubs also utilise FDDI as a high-speed pipe to a server(s), with switched FDDI providing a fast multiport bridging architecture for bridging multiple FDDI networks.

Large computer vendors, such as DEC and IBM, provide many FDDI products for both their own proprietary equipment and workstations, and industry standard workstations and PCs. Many other smaller vendors provide server cluster and workgroup level products. All FDDI products are tested for conformance to the FDDI standard, and for interoperability with each other at dedicated test houses, such as the ANTC.

CHAPTER 9

Applications

FDDI has become a well-established backbone technology for linking many lower-speed LANs together. In particular, because of its use of fibre optic cabling, it is perfectly capable of linking many buildings up to 40 km apart, and further if necessary. Its high degree of built-in fault tolerance compared to other conventional networks such as Ethernet or Token Ring has helped it establish this position of leadership too. However, as cost of implementation comes down further, and especially with the introduction of copper cabling options for FDDI (TPDDI), it has become increasingly feasible to utilise it right to the desktop for those applications that need it. Other developments, such as client/server computing, downsizing, peer-to-peer networking, have also led to increased interest in higher-speed networks, FDDI being a popular choice for today.

The next chapter presents typical and possible applications for FDDI/TPDDI. The areas covered are broken into backbone and high-speed networking, followed by a discussion on desktop multimedia applications. Where possible, real examples are used to illustrate how FDDI has been applied. Firstly, it is worth considering just when, and if you actually need FDDI at all.

When is FDDI Required?

The main question that needs answering about FDDI from any applications viewpoint is when and why do you need to install it. In many applications there is still no need for the bandwidth offered by FDDI; Ethernet or Token Ring are perfectly adequate. So how do you know at what point you need to start thinking about switching over? Of course, a lot depends on your particular circumstances and application. With ATM and other technologies looming on the horizon, it is easy to wait for these new technologies to arrive, putting off the upgrade to your network. With good planning, there is no reason why FDDI networks cannot be installed today, and also be easily upgraded to handle newer technologies as they come along. All the other technologies such as ATM need to go through a significant proving ground before they can be accepted as a general interoperable standard. Until then, FDDI will be installed as it is the most mature, widespread standard for high-speed internetwork and desktop communication, backed up by widely available products.

As we touched on in Chapter 1, the typical reasons anyone would ever consider the need for FDDI are as follows:

- The number of users on the current Ethernet or Token Ring only networks has grown to the point where performance, network access times, and downtimes due to crashes are no longer acceptable.
- Different departments already heavily using their own LANs now need to access other LANs, which are typically of different technologies. Lower speed bridging technology does not meet the performance or robustness requirements.
- The company is moving towards client-server computing, or new network based applications thus placing a larger load on the network.
- There is a great need for fault tolerance, reducing the downtime of a network, in turn saving lost revenues.
- New applications are appearing on the LAN, such as desktop video conferencing or live video playback facilities for company education programs and workgroup intensive applications.

In many cases, the life of a network can be extended by employing bridging and routing techniques to segment out the networks in order to spread the load amongst several LANs of the same type. This method is commonly and successfully employed. However, in times where the loading on networks is growing very fast, and also as the amount of traffic and nodes increases, it is unwise to plan for anything less than five years ahead to ensure that money is spent wisely. In just about all cases, decisions to implement a new technology can be very daunting, and the costs look prohibitive up front, so it is even more important to consider every option before launching the company and its money into new technologies, such as FDDI.

Network downtime is an important consideration in any network. The cost of not being able to access important data when needed, or a real-time control system being held up, can seriously affect cashflows. One network manager recently calculated the cost of his network downtime as roughly £3000 a minute; another arrived at a figure of £10,000 an hour. Obviously, neither of these are trivial, and greatly overshadow the cost of any networking hardware. The application in this case was controlling a car manufacturing production line, in which any stoppage would cause a great deal of disruption to the production flow, holding numerous stages up until the problem was fixed. Similar requirements can exist in the publishing and printing world as we shall see later. Hence, the cost of the network itself, in terms of implementation, is often very insignificant to the impact it may have on the companies bottom line, a point well worth considering.

Running out of Steam

Most network managers have a good idea exactly how, and how often their network is being utilised. Many figures are quoted by various manufacturers about when the point to change over from an existing backbone technology to FDDI. These range from an average 30 per cent utilisation of existing Ethernet or Token Ring backbones, upwards. Of course, it is not always as straightforward as this, as economies of scale come into effect. If the network usage is fairly stable, i.e. the number of users is constant and the applications are unlikely to change over the next few years, then so long as all the current performance and reliability criteria are being met, there is no reason to change over. If, however, the numbers of stations and LANs connected to the current network are growing significantly, then this is an indication that the network utilisation is going to exceed the current bounds.

As well as node growth factors, a quick analysis of the types of application are needed to establish loading factors from the existing installed base. New operating systems have been introduced over the last few years that include networking functionality. This includes the standard PC compatible and Apple Macintosh operating systems, traditionally the domain of the high-end workstation arena. This in turn has resulted in a sudden increase in the traffic on the network, as the operating system starts to run background operations and tasks behind the main applications running on the computer. A good example of this is Microsoft's Windows and Windows NT products, and in the Apple world, System 7 and upwards.

Other new applications, such as *multimedia*, require a significant increase in the amount of bandwidth and level of access time predictability. Example applications include video conferencing, or utilising CD-ROM based video servers for educational purposes to play back video sequences over the network simultaneously to many stations. These are just too much for a shared bandwidth Ethernet or Token Ring network, as a single video stream can occupy as much as 2, possibly 4 Mbps, i.e. 20–40 per cent of the peak capability of Ethernet, and 12.5–25 per cent of Token Ring.

The amount of internetworking traffic is also a key consideration. In the larger corporations today, it is quite common for software development teams, for example, to be working in different buildings. The software team's server may be located in an entirely different building, hence a large amount of traffic may be thrashing back and forth across the backbone. This was in fact the case at Microsoft, where an FDDI backbone was installed to increase the performance across the campus backbone and improve access to the distributed servers.

FDDI Backbones

The largest application for FDDI is as a high-speed backbone campus network, usually linking multiple Ethernet or Token Ring networks into a single heterogeneous network. A single FDDI network can link together as few as two, and as many as several hundred, smaller departmental LANs, depending on loading and applications. These can create a network with many thousands of nodes that can communicate over a single seamless network.

Below, a few real-world examples of FDDI networks are illustrated. Hub vendors are usually more than happy to provide you with examples of where their hubs have been used, and with testimonies or customer profiles from particular installations.

CASE STUDY I: Antarctic Scientific Research Program

(National Science Foundation, USA – courtesy Synoptics Communications Corp.)

This network, based in research centres at the Antarctic (Figure 9.1), utilises an FDDI backbone that is connected in a highly fault tolerant configuration across three main sites. The majority of the connections within the FDDI network segment are made using dual-homing techniques, with only two root FDDI DAS concentrators on a dual ring. Three routers are attached in a dual-homing configuration to the root DACs so that if any connections go down on the active links, they can automatically re-configure to use the backup links into the second concentrator. The high fault tolerance in this case is due to the climactic conditions (temperatures average –56°F), hence even the optical fibres used in this network had to be tested to ensure their operation when embedded in ice! Also, the network downtime had to be minimised as the research centres can be cut off for up to six months at a time from their supply line. The hubs at the bottom of the tree attach to multiple segmented 10Base-T networks, with the routers handling the multi-protocol traffic requirements of the network (Novell Netware, Appletalk, TCP/IP and so on). Satellite links allow the network to be connected to the global Internet network. Total end stations exceeded 300 (as at August 1993).

CASE STUDY II: Union Tribune Publishing Company, San Diego

(Courtesy 3-COM Corp.)

Union Tribune are a newspaper publishing company in the United States, and have a main headquarters with a number of remote sites. A Tandon host computer runs a customised editorial application, and fault-tolerant networking is essential to ensure that the publishing deadlines are met. The FDDI backbone in this case connects nine of 3-COM's NetBuilder II multi-protocol bridge/router products. Fault redundancy in this case is implemented with redundant NetBuilder IIs to ensure that in the case of failure of one of the nodes on the ring, access is still possible. Up to 320 users are catered for, with enough expansion for the additional 500 users that were planned following the installation of the network as shown in Figure 9.2. This particular example uses many smaller units, such as stackable hubs as well as the bridge/router products, as opposed to the larger chassis-based hubs, allowing the cost objectives of the installation to be met.

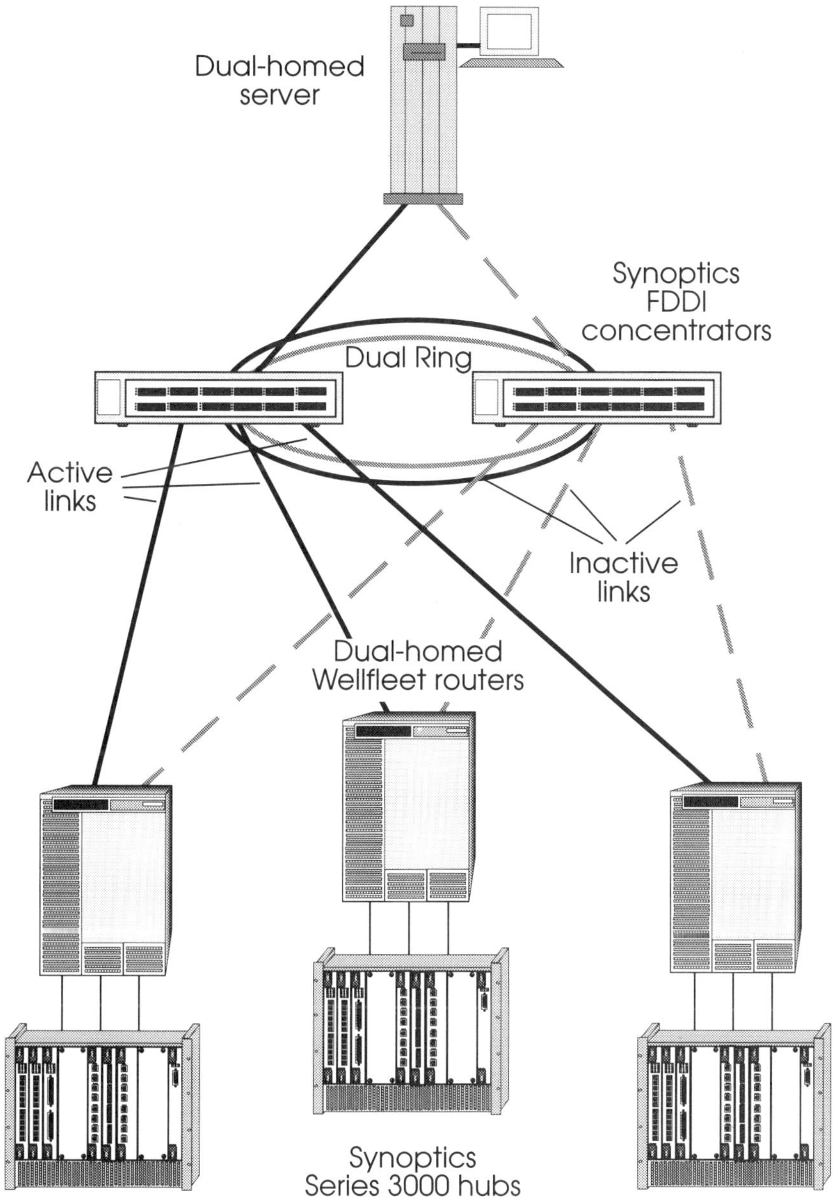

Figure 9.1 *Antarctic Support Associates (ASA) MCMnet – highly fault tolerant FDDI backbone. (Courtesy Synoptics Communications Corp.)*

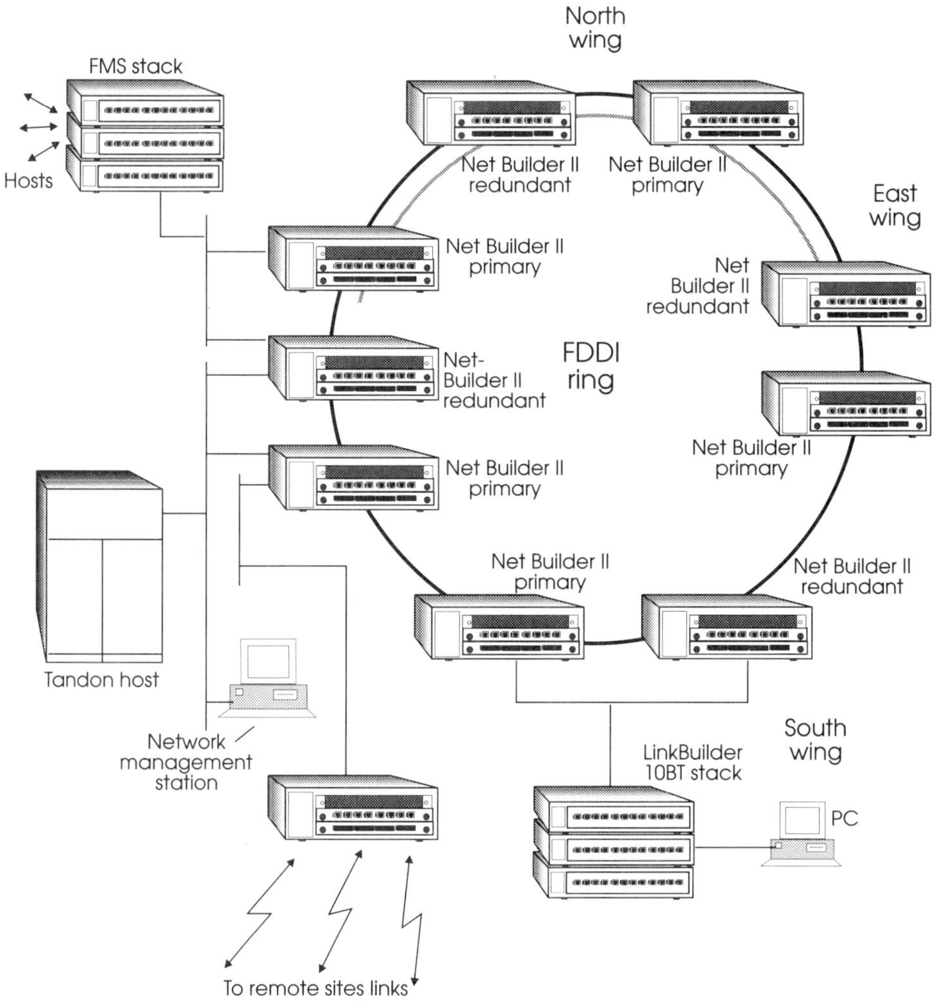

Figure 9.2 *Union Tribune Publishing Company FDDI backbone. (Courtesy 3-COM Corp.)*

Improving Server Access Performance and Security

There are a number of ways of using FDDI to increase server access and performance without impacting too much on the networking administration budget. It is also possible to increase network reliability and security at the same time.

Server Clustering

In this type of application, all the servers in a network are clustered together on the same FDDI network segment, be it a dual ring backbone, or simply all connected as SAS links into the same concentrator (Figure 9.3). Performance is further enhanced if the hub is switching based, giving each of the servers its own dedicated 100 Mbps link to each of the lower-speed LAN segments as we discussed in Chapter 8. The benefit of clustering is that the load balancing involved with individual bridges is removed.

Depending on the current installation, it is possible as a minimum to upgrade the server adapter cards to FDDI, and install an FDDI translational bridge and concentrator module(s) into the hub. This gives the servers 100 Mbps access to one another, and capability to carry the payload of several Ethernet or Token Ring segments. For situations that do not employ a chassis-based hub, a standalone FDDI

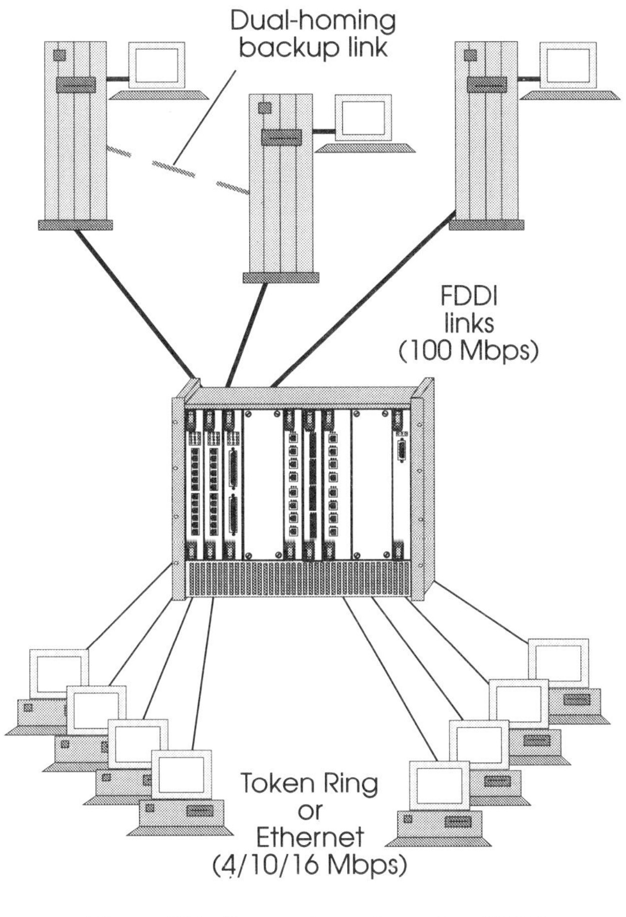

Figure 9.3 *Server clustering using FDDI*

bridge and concentrator may also be used. If, as hinted in Figure 9.3, the servers were previously on individual segments along with the end station, the situation has improved greatly, as each of the servers is now 'equi-distant' from the end stations, with much better load balancing. The bridge ensures that no excessive traffic crosses onto the FDDI server LAN, only that destined for the servers, important where peer to peer network operating systems, such as Microsoft's Workgroup for Windows, are in use on end stations.

CASE STUDY III: CLR Tax Automation Firm, Carrollton Texas

(Courtesy SysKonnect.)

CLR (Computer Language Research) Inc. are a tax automation firm who solved their 16 Mbps Token Ring backbone bandwidth problems by migrating the network-intensive applications over to FDDI.

CLR's applications typically included computation-intensive information processing, built around the Lotus Notes workgroup platform. Lotus Notes allows users to manage their information, and is implemented around a distributed database, where a number of servers contain information that is very closely coupled together (regularly updated and kept in sync). Notes implements a client/server computer information system. In CLR's case, the tax-processing software created a large volume of traffic, and combined with the Lotus Notes platform, easily saturated their Token Ring backbone. Typical tax files were around 300–400 kbyte in size. Large amounts of data had to be archived on thirteen 13 Gbyte dedicated servers. Data also had to be moved to a 2 page/sec laser printer (Xerox 9790), with an estimated 1.9 million lines printed per day. In addition, the company was moving away from its large-scale mainframe, to two smaller RISC machines running a SYBASE application. All this initially was connected by Token Ring.

The solution was to move the archive servers (with tape backup systems) and SYBASE RISC servers onto FDDI, freeing up more bandwidth for the Lotus Notes servers (which were left on Token Ring). Each of the servers were connected, via SysKonnect adapters, into a 3-COM LinkBuilder 3GH routing hub, which handled the Token Ring to FDDI bridging and routing. CLR's internal testing showed a 70 per cent increase in throughput using FDDI adapters over 16 Mbps Token Ring equivalents. Over time, CLR plan to move the Notes servers over onto FDDI as well.

Utilising Both Primary and Secondary Rings/Paths

In some applications it is possible to utilise simultaneously both the primary and the secondary rings for data transmissions (Figure 9.4). Possible applications are performance doubling, and the other is security.

A simple method of effectively doubling the bandwidth to 200 Mbps is to configure the dual ring as two independent FDDI rings, or create two separate rings within a tree

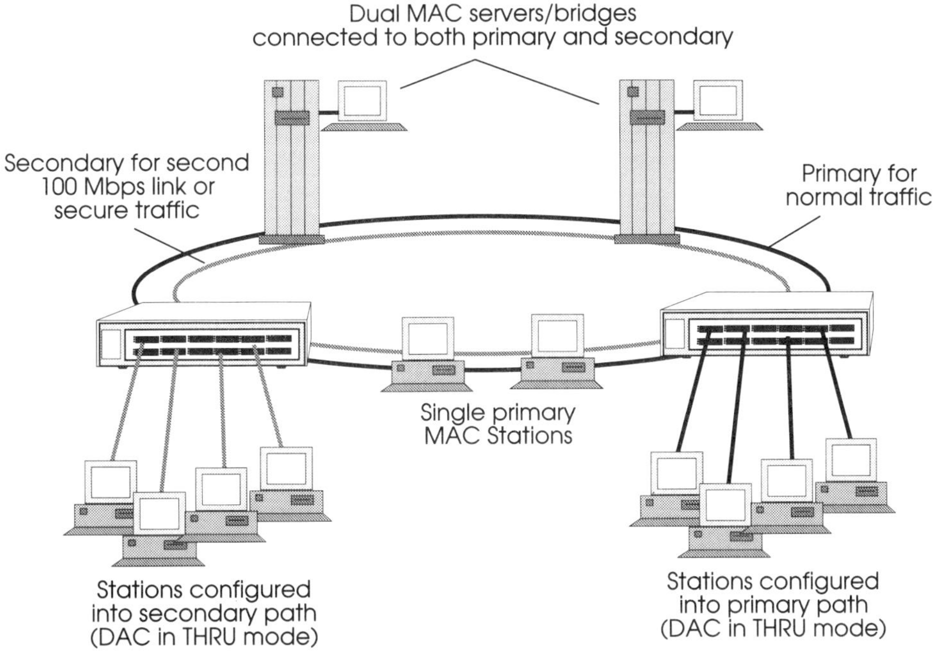

Figure 9.4 *Utilising both rings for 200 Mbps operation or security*

topology as we have seen in previous chapters. This means that two tokens exist in two independent paths. For class A stations (dual ring attach) to take advantage of this, they must have two MAC devices, one attached to one path or ring, and the other to the second path or ring. The fault tolerance is still maintained in the case of the dual ring, as the ring reverts back to being a single 100 Mbps FDDI ring whenever either of the paths are broken. Great care must be taken to ensure that all stations operate correctly under such circumstances, especially when faults develop causing some stations in the ring to wrap. As such, there is no general approach for handling such a set-up, though the standard does define an optional hold policy for stations wishing to implement such a scheme that prevents the station entering wrap until all transmissions from this station on the secondary ring or path have ceased.

Concentrators that have the capability can be remotely configured to connect their SAS stations into either the primary or the secondary, or a mixture of both. Under such circumstances, the control of which ring the end user is on is totally handled by the network manager via a suitable SMT or SNMP management program.

Servers may use this alternative path for inter-server applications, file mirroring, etc., without disturbing the main ring traffic flow. Utilising the dual rings in such a way also has an advantage in that network secure data may be passed over the secondary link, preventing only single primary ring MAC stations being able to configure into, and eavesdrop on the sensitive data. This is becoming especially important in this day and age, as more and more sensitive, corporate data, personal files, company confidential information, etc. resides in a LAN somewhere. This scheme allows only stations that are configured in hardware (hence cannot be reconfigured via software) to access this information, and also easily detects when an intruder attempts to get access.

Server Mirroring

Novell's Netware SFT III product introduced the concept of mirroring servers in order to improve fault tolerance by having two servers each mirror one another's actions and storage capabilities. Though only one will ever be active, a primary and secondary server (IBM PC compatible) synchronise their memories and operations in such a way that if the primary becomes non-functional, the secondary will be automatically enabled. All the network will see is a small glitch where a packet or two is lost. Anyone attending Novell's product demonstrations will remember the anvil crashing down onto one server, illustrating how quickly the secondary enabled and carried on where the primary left off.

Though Novell use a specific interface, an MSL board, which is a high-speed bidirectional point-to-point link, there is nothing to stop the usage of a standard LAN solution. In fact some vendors, such as Schneider & Koch, have written drivers to hook the SFT III system into a standard LAN interface, such as FDDI. This is where a dual-homing backup link could be used, or the secondary ring, hence providing little, if any, impact on the normal traffic flow. Combined with FDDI's fault tolerance, this makes a very secure server environment that starts to approach the levels currently found in the larger mainframe systems. In today's downsizing trends, where smaller distributed networked computers are being employed, schemes such as server mirroring and FDDI provide a neat open standards approach to fault tolerance.

FDDI Desktop Applications

Applications that demand the performance of that offered by FDDI or TPDDI to the desktop are starting to become more commonplace. It is highly unlikely that FDDI networks will ever replace or reach the installed base of Ethernet or Token Ring, but will rather be used in applications that demand high degrees of performance and network access times. Some example applications that fall under this category include high-performance workstations running high-resolution graphics applications, multimedia (video playback) and video conferencing. In just about all cases, the application involves graphics or large file transfers across a LAN.

TPDDI has now put FDDI networking technology within reach of most networking budgets for desktop applications, in some cases allowing the cost of the connection for FDDI to be reduced by over a half. This is changing all the time, however, and there is no doubt that we will see some reasonable installations of TPDDI as it is backed up by

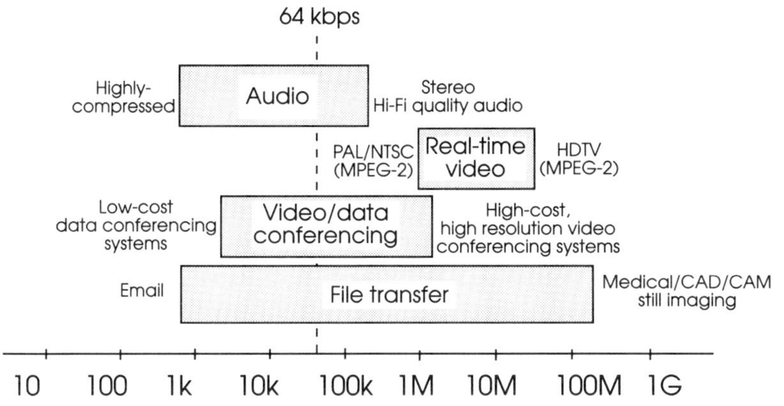

Figure 9.5 *Bandwidth requirements by application*

a well-defined and tested, approved open standards networking technology, a status not yet enjoyed by many of the other competing technologies such as 100 Mbps Ethernet or 155 Mbps ATM.

What is increasingly apparent is that many more applications that were previously confined to either telecommunications or proprietary systems are now making their way into the standard LAN world. IBM, for instance, offer their Person to Person system for video and data conferencing over the LAN. The drive to get these applications to run over existing LANs is because of the widespread deployment of installations across the world. If a vendor can create a product that will utilise any of the existing technology out there, without having to replace any communications infrastructures significantly, then they are obviously onto a winner. There are problems posed by LANs however, that can make it difficult to achieve many of the applications. Bandwidth is one of them. Figure 9.5 illustrates typical bandwidth requirements for many of today's applications that are being used across the LAN.

High Performance Workgroups

Applications such as CAD/CAM, graphics modelling or simulation, and medical imaging all require bandwidths ranging from anywhere in the low kbps right up to 1–2 Mbps on average. Peak rates can be much greater than this. As the graphical user interfaces and client/server applications that are emerging in these fields grow, so does the continuous loading on the network. LANs are typically very suited to bursty traffic offered by these kinds of applications, where very large bit-mapped files are transported across the network. Centralised computing resources accentuate this. Take, for example, a still graphical image from a 2048 × 2048, 24 bit pixel colour display. When stored as a pure bit-map, as is the case in some medical imaging applications, this can result in roughly 100 million bits, or 12.3 Mbytes of information stored in a file. If this file is to be centrally accessed, then it will take at least 10 sec to transfer it across an Ethernet network provided there is no other traffic, and there are no bridge/router boundaries to cross. The latter can introduce significant delays again. For an FDDI network, this transfer time is as little as just over 1 sec.

To keep response times to a minimum, and also to speed up the data transfer rates, FDDI or TPDDI can be employed, giving users a 100 Mbps bandwidth connection into the main server, which can be either on the main backbone (also at 100 Mbps) or on the same physical ring as the workstations. Due to FDDI's high loading tolerance, the impact on the overall network as a whole should be minimum.

Multimedia and Video Conferencing

LAN products that support multimedia services (mainly playback of video clips from file servers, or even video conferencing and interactive working) are rapidly appearing, to take advantage of the adoption of better sound and graphics capabilities within the standard desktop PC. Specific examples include Novell Netware Video, and IBM's LAN Server Ultimedia products. In Chapters 4 and 7 we looked at how FDDI can transport time-sensitive data using a synchronous data transmission service. Advances in data compression technology have allowed this synchronous facility to offer a reasonable service to the growing number of multimedia applications and video conferencing.

Though technologies such as FDDI 2 have been proposed for carrying such traffic, provided certain constraints can be met, then there is absolutely no reason why a user should have to migrate over to something like FDDI 2. ATM LAN networks will provide an overall better solution in the long term, so for now, an existing FDDI network can address many multimedia applications needs. The important technology area that makes multimedia and video transmissions possible over the LAN is data compression. When data is compressed, it means that it takes much less time to transmit the information over the LAN. What becomes important then is the data *latency* and *jitter*, i.e. the overall delay between the sending and receiving of the original uncompressed data, and the variance in the individual packet transmissions respectively. Latency is caused by the various compression and communication channel delays, whereas jitter can be caused by the variance in the LAN access times (due to token rotation variance, etc.). Though not a fully isochronous service, FDDI's synchronous facility handles this type of data well. In fact, data compression can desensitise the video or voice data from needing rigid time slots so well that standard asynchronous data services can also handle such data, provided the network is correctly load balanced.

Figure 9.6 illustrates time-critical data being transmitted between two end stations over a packet-oriented network versus an isochronous one. Basically, as long as the packets arrive within the allowed timeframe e.g. before the next frame is to be displayed on the receiving video conference console, the user sees no degradation in the service. If, however, the packet arrives too late, then the user may notice the effect

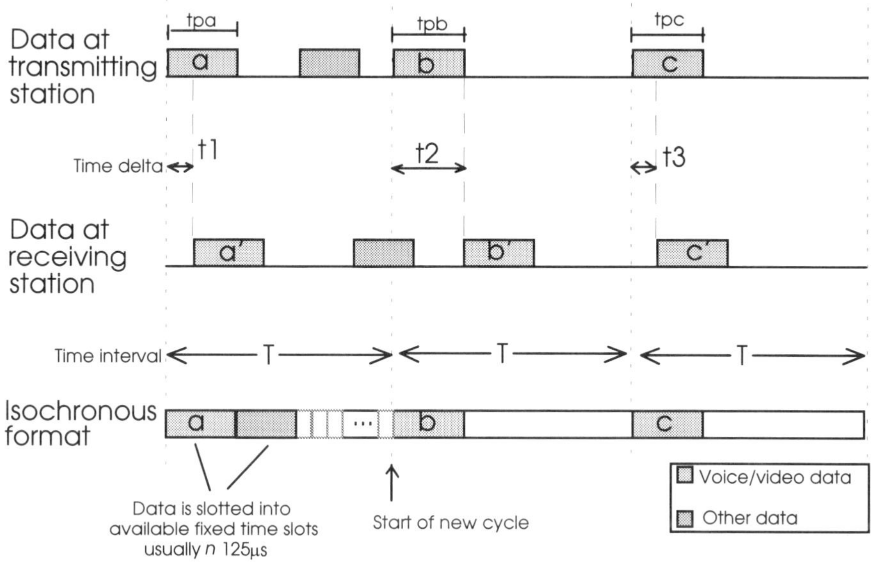

Figure 9.6 *Transmission delays, latency and jitter*

by a 'jumpy' picture, for example. Hence, so long as *t*1, *t*2 and *t*3 do not exceed *T*, the data rate is within an acceptable limit. This is basically the principle behind the synchronous payload and overhead calculations of Chapter 7. Figures taken from an IEEE paper which described the simulation of multimedia and video conferencing data across FDDI are detailed in Table 9.1. From these figures, we see that provided the overall latency and jitter is within acceptable limits (i.e. less than 100 msec for voice), an end user will not see any serious degradation in quality even though an isochronous scheme is not employed.

Data compression techniques vary according to the application. In the case of multimedia, the compression is usually something like MPEG, which is best suited to applications that require fast full-frame image decompression. Compression factors vary according to the original data, but on average image data can be compressed to around half its original size or more. Typical multimedia applications, such as educational training programs, include pulling a compressed video sequence live off a video server somewhere on the network as illustrated in Figure 7.7. Even as compressed data, this can be a 4–10 Mbps data stream, and hence, we are already getting out of Ethernet and Token Ring league.

For video conferencing applications, a different encoding scheme is used based on the ITU's H.261 standard (see Bibliography, ITU-T Blue book). Unlike the MPEG schemes, H.261 (or Px64Kbps), is more suited to the symmetrical requirements of bidirectional (as opposed to unidirectional) audiovisual data streams, and uses motion prediction to reduce overall bandwidth requirements. A typical audiovisual stream

Table 9.1 *Effects of latency on packet voice traffic on the human ear.*

One-way delay (msec)	Effect of delay
>600	Speech becomes incoherent and unintelligible
600	Speech is barely coherent
250	Annoying: conversation style has to be changed
100	Imperceptible if listener hears from network only and not off the air
50	Imperceptible even if the listener in same room and can hear naturally off the air and from the network

Source: Shah *et al.*, Multimedia over FDDI, *Proceedings of IEEE Local Computer Networks*, 1992.

requires 384 kbps of bandwidth, corresponding to a synchronous payload value of 6 and minimum frame size of 384 bytes (TTRT 8 msec) for FDDI as we saw in Chapter 7. Newer algorithms are being developed all the time, resulting in even lower bandwidth requirements, achieving, for example, data rates as low as 128 kbps for equivalent quality.

Shah *et al.* (1992) conclude in their simulation work with FDDI multimedia traffic that using typical token parameters and varying loading conditions, FDDI's synchronous channel provides a near constant, low latency service. The simulations ran a large number of simultaneous MPEG and Px64 sessions even when the network was overloaded, producing acceptable results. The results of the simulations are summarised in Table 9.2. A number of vendors have since produced FDDI adapter cards that support FDDI's synchronous mode in order to support such applications.

Cabling for Future Network Expansion

One of the most critical factors in cabling installations is ensuring support, wherever possible, for future standards. One example here is ATM. Most people associate FDDI with being solely a dual ring, hence wire the network accordingly. Unfortunately, this can lead to problems when upgrading your network to a newer networking technology later on. The best approach to wiring medium to large FDDI backbone or desktop networks is to use a concentrator tree wiring structure, implementing fault redundancy using backup or redundant links. Having said that, smaller desktop FDDI networks (a few 10 sec or less) can benefit from being wired in a dual ring as the cost of a concentrator or hub can be saved. One of the key advantages of ATM is its scalability, i.e. it has no fixed defined bandwidth ceiling as with FDDI, and hence can have data rates that run from anywhere between 10 Mbps up to 1.2 Gbps. It can also support

Table 9.2 *Multimedia traffic simulation results*

Traffic type and conditions	Latency for 99 per cent of video/voice traffic per loading and TTRT	Comments
Asynchronous only	15 msec 86% load. (TTRT 24 msec) 48 msec 90% load. 252 msec overloaded.	Large delays as network approached overload and beyond
Asynchronous traffic and Synchronous carrying voice/video	<24 msec for all loading (all TTRT used) <16 msec (TTRT 8 or 16 msec)	For typical usage, always achieved a 16 msec delay
Synchronous only voice/video	<7 msec (TTRT 26 msec)	70 Stations, ring latency of 122 msec, always within acceptable limits.

Source: Shah *et al.*, Multimedia over FDDI, *Proceedings of IEEE Local Computer Networks*, 1992.

virtual networks, allowing ease of user-segment configuration. ATM has in many ways become the goal for a new higher-speed networking standard. Until then, FDDI is a good intermediate step for those who need high-performance networking. A common transmission rate for ATM is 155 Mbps for backbone implementations seen today. At this speed, the same cabling and physical layer characteristics as FDDI apply. Hence, by structuring the FDDI cabling to be in a star-wired fashion utilising either datagrade category 5 unshielded twisted pair cabling for desktop or short inter-hub links, or of course fibre, then it is relatively easy to migrate over. The example in Figure 9.7 illustrates how ATM-capable hubs may be wired for a small number of hubs. By implementing the FDDI backbone using the same structure, then as ATM follows the same architecture, an ATM backbone may be later introduced without changing any wiring. Only end modules in the hubs and/or concentrators if these are standalone units need be changed, along with the end station adapters of course, thus preserving the cabling infrastructure. Many hubs today are 'ATM ready', making this evolution processes even easier.

Summary

FDDI's main application has been as a backbone network, linking many slower-speed LANs such as Ethernet and Token Ring. Its fault-redundant properties make it ideal for this application. It is also well suited to client/server applications, where a number of

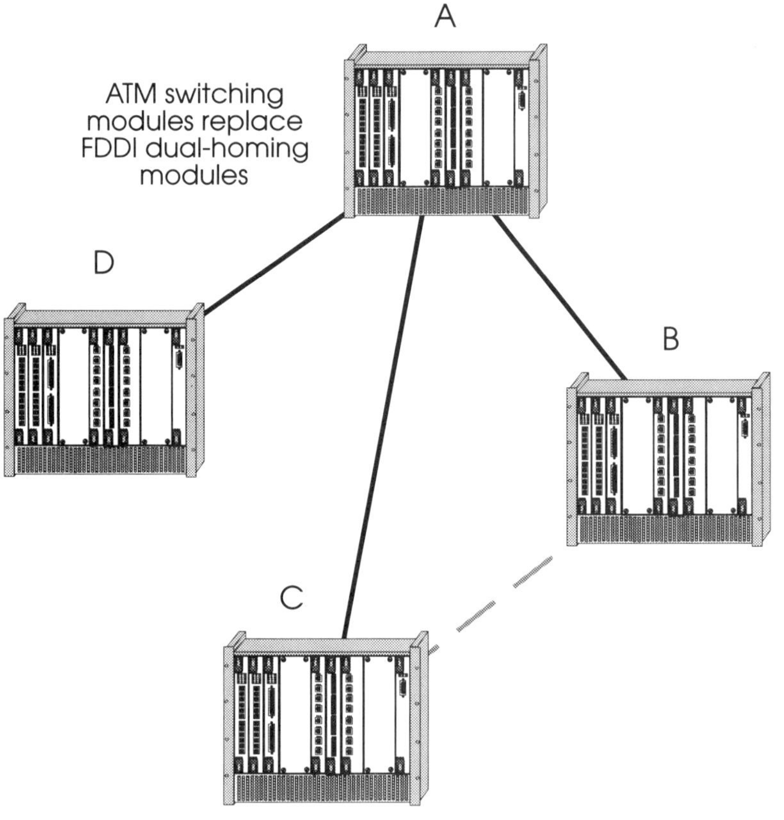

Figure 9.7 *Cabling structured for future ATM installation*

high-performance computers are clustered together to form a distributed server network, meeting the strict redundancy requirement of such a system.

FDDI's use as a desktop technology for directly linking workstations into a 100 Mbps network is increasing, especially with the introduction of lower-cost copper cabling that TP-PMD offers. Applications such as live video (compressed) playback and video conferencing are stimulating that growth.

Finally, when cabling an FDDI network, future standards such as ATM can be catered for, ensuring an easier migration when the time comes.

APPENDIX

FDDI SMT MIB Groups

Table A.1 *SMT object group attributes*

Attributes	
fddiSMTStationIdGrp	*Get*
fddiSMTStationId	Get
fddiSMTOpVersionId	Get
fddiSMTHiVersionId	Get
fddiSMTLoVersionId	Get
fddiSMTManufacturerData	Get
fddiSMTUserData	Get-replace
fddiSMTMIBVersionId	Get
fddiSMTStationConfigGrp	*Get*
fddiSMTMAC-Ct	Get
fddiSMTNonMaster-Ct	Get
fddiSMTMaster-Ct	Get
fddiSMTAvailablePaths	Get
fddiSMTConfigCapabilities	Get
fddiSMTConfigPolicy	Get-replace
fddiSMTConnectionPolicy	Get-replace
fddiSMTT-Notify	Get-replace
fddiSMTStatRptPolicy	Get-replace
fddiSMTTrace-MaxExpiration	Get-replace
fddiSMTPORTIndexes	Get
fddiSMTMACIndexes	Get
fddiSMTBypassPresent	Get
fddiSMTStatusGrp	*Get*
fddiSMTECMState	Get
fddiSMTCF-State	Get
fddiSMTHoldState	Get
fddiSMTRemoteDisconnectFlag	Get
fddiSMTStationStatus	Get
fddiSMTPeerWrapFlag	Get
fddiSMTMIBOperationGrp	Get
fddiSMTTimeStamp	Get
fddiSMTTransmitionTimeStamp	Get
fddiSMTSetCount	Get
fddiSMTLastSetStationId	Get

Table A.1 *SMT object group attributes (continued)*

Attributes (continued)	
NotGrouped	
fddiSMTVendorAttrib	Get-replace

Table A.2 *SMT object group actions*

Actions	
fddiSMTStationAction	PMF-Set
fddiSMTVendorAction	PMF-Set

Table A.3 *SMT object group notifications*

Notifications
fddiSMTHoldCondition
fddiSMTPeerWrapCondition
fddiSMTVendorNotification

Table A.4 *PATH object group attributes*

Attributes	
fddiPATHConfigGrp	*Get*
fddiPATHIndex	Get
fddiPATHRingLatency	Get-replace
fddiPATHTraceStatus	Get
fddiPATHSbaPayload	Get-replace
fddiPATHSbaOverhead	Get-replace
fddiPATHConfiguration	Get
fddiPATHT-Rmode	Get-replace
fddiPATHSbaAvailable	Get-replace
fddiPATHTVXLowerbound	Get-replace
fddiPATHT-MaxLowerBound	Get-replace
fddiPATHMaxT-Req	Get-replace
NotGrouped	
fddiPATHVendorAttrib	Get-replace

Table A.5 *PATH object group actions*

Actions	
fddiPATHVendorAction	PMF-Set

Table A.6 *PATH object group notifications*

Notifications
fddiPATHVendorNotification

Table A.7 *PORT object group attributes*

Attributes	
fddiPORTConfigGrp	*Get*
fddiPORTMy-Type	Get
fddiPORTNeighborType	Get
fddiPORTConnectionPolicies	Get-replace
fddiPORTMACIndicated	Get
fddiPORTCurrentPath	Get
fddiPORTRequestedPaths	Get-replace
fddiPORTMACPlacement	Get
fddiPORTAvailablePaths	Get
fddiPORTMACLoop-Time	Get-replace
fddiPORTPMDClass	Get
fddiPORTConnectionCapabilities	Get
fddiPORTIndex	Get
fddiPORTOperationGrp	*Get*
fddiPORTMaint-LS	Get-replace
fddiPORTBS-Flag	Get
fddiPORTPC-LS	Get
fddiPORTErrorCtrsGrp	*Get*
fddiPORTEBError-Ct	Get
fddiPORTLCTFail-Ct	Get
fddiPORTLerGrp	*Get*
fddiPORTLer-Estimate	Get
fddiPORTLem-Reject-Ct	Get
fddiPORTLem-Ct	Get
fddiPORTLer-Cutoff	Get-replace
fddiPORTLer-Alarm	Get-replace

Table A.7 *PORT object group attributes (continued)*

Attributes (continued)	
fddiPORTStatusGrp	*Get*
fddiPORTConnectState	Get
fddiPORTPCMState	Get
fddiPORTPC-Withhold	Get
fddiPORTLerFlag	Get
fddiPORTHardwarePresent	Get
NotGrouped	
fddiPORTVendorAttrib	Get-replace

Table A.8 *PORT object group actions*

Actions	
fddiPORTAction	PMF-Set
fddiPORTVendorAction	PMF-Set

Table A.9 *PORT object group notifications*

Notifications
fddiPORTLerCondition
fddiPORTUndersiredConnectionAttemptEvent
fddiPORTEBErrorCondition
fddiPORTPathChangeEvent
fddiPORTVendorNotification

Table A.10 *MAC object group attributes*

Attributes	
fddiMACCapabilitiesGrp	*Get*
fddiMACFrameStatusFunctions	Get
fddiMACBridgeFunctions	Get
fddiMACT-MaxCapability	Get
fddiMACTVXCapability	Get

Table A.10 *MAC object group attributes (continued)*

Attributes (continued)	
fddiMACConfigGrp	*Get*
fddiMACAvailablePaths	Get
fddiMACCurrentPath	Get
fddiMACUpstreamNbr	Get
fddiMACDownstreamNbr	Get
fddiMACOldUpstreamNbr	Get
fddiMACOldDownstreamNbr	Get
fddiMACDupAddressTest	Get
fddiMACRequestedPaths	Get-replace
fddiMACDownStreamPORTType	Get
fddiMACIndex	Get
fddiMACAddressGrp	*Get*
fddiMACSMTAddress	Get
fddiMACLongGrpAddress	Get
fddiMACShortGrpAddress	Get
fddiMACOperationGrp	*Get*
fddiMACT-Req	Get
fddiMACT-Neg	Get
fddiMACT-Max	Get
fddiMACT-TvxValue	Get
fddiMACT-Pri0	Get
fddiMACT-Pri1	Get
fddiMACT-Pri2	Get
fddiMACT-Pri3	Get
fddiMACT-Pri4	Get
fddiMACT-Pri5	Get
fddiMACT-Pri6	Get
fddiMACCountersGrp	*Get*
fddiMACFrame-Ct	Get
fddiMACCopied-Ct	Get
fddiMACTransmit-Ct	Get
fddiMACToken-Ct	Get
fddiMACError-Ct	Get
fddiMACLost-Ct	Get
fddiMACTvxExpired-Ct	Get
fddiMACNotCopied-Ct	Get
fddiMACLate-Ct	Get
fddiMACRingOp-Ct	Get
fddiMACFrameErrorConditionGrp	*Get*
fddiMACFrameErrorThreshold	Get-replace
fddiMACFrameErrorRatio	Get

Table A.10 *MAC object group attributes (continued)*

fddiMACnotCopiedConditionGrp	*Get*
fddiMACNotCopiedThreshold	Get-replace
fddiMACNotCopiedRatio	Get
fddiMACStatusGrp	*Get*
fddiMACRMTState	Get
fddiMACDA-Flag	Get
fddiMACUNDA-Flag	Get
fddiMACFrameErrorFlag	Get
fddiMACNotCopiedFlag	Get
fddiMACMA-UnitdataAvailable	Get
fddiMACHardwarePresent	Get
fddiMACMA-UnitdataEnable	Get
NotGrouped	
fddiMACVendorAttrib	Get-replace

Table A.11 *MAC object group actions*

Actions	
fddiMACVendorAction	PMF-Set

Table A.12 *MAC object group notifications*

Notifications
fddiMACDuplicateAddressCondition
fddiMACFrameErrorCondition
fddiMACFrameNotCopiedCondition
fddiMACNeighburChangeEvent
fddiMACPathChangeEvent
fddiMACVendorNotification

Glossary

ALS	active line state
ANSI	American National Standards Institute
ARP	address resolution protocol
ATM	asynchronous transfer mode
B-ISDN	broadband integrated services data network
CALM	consortium for advanced LAN management (founder members include Cabletron Systems, Inc., Crescendo Communications, Inc., Interphase Corp., ODC, Inc., SNMP Research, Inc. and XLNT Designs, Inc.)
CCE	configuration control element
CCITT	International Consultative Committee on Telegraphy and Telephony
CDDI	copper data distributed interface
CEM	configuration element management
CFM	configuration management
CMIP	common management information protocol
CMT	connection management
CRC	cyclic redundancy check
CSMA/CD	collision sense multiple access/collision detect
DA	destination address
DAC	dual attachment concentrator
DARPA	Defense Advanced Research Projects Agency
DAS	dual attachment station
DM-DAC	dual-MAC, dual attachment concentrator
DM-DAS	dual-MAC, dual attachment station
DMA	direct memory access
DNA	downstream neighbour address
EAC	error, address recognised, frame copied bits of FDDI frame ED field
ECF	echo frame
ECM	entity co-ordination management
ED	end delimiter

EIA/TIA	Electronics Industries Association/Telecommunications Industry Association
ESF	extended service frame
FC	frame control
FCC	Federal Communications Commission
FCS	frame check sequence
FDDI	fiber distributed data interface
FFOL	FDDI follow-on LAN
FS	frame status
FTP	file transfer protocol
HDLC	high-level entity management control
HLM	heterogeneous LAN management
HLS	halt line state
IAB	Internet Activities Board
ICMP	internet control message protocol
IEEE	Institute of Electrical and Electronic Engineers
IETF	Internet Engineering Task Force
ILS	idle line state
IP	internet protocol
ISDN	integrated services data network
ISO	International Organisation for Standardisation
ITU	International Telecommunications Union
LAN	local area network
LCF	low-cost fibre
LEM	link error monitor
LIPSTC	local, isolated, primary, secondary, thru and concatenated CFM configuration states
LLC	logical link control
LSU	line state unknown
MA	my address
MAC	medium access control
MAN	metropolitan area network
MASIC	management and security integrated circuit
MBONE	multicast backbone
MIB	management information base
MIC	media interface connector
MLS	master line state
MLT-3	multi-level transmission -3
MMF	multi-mode fibre
NAC	null attachment concentrator
NIF	neighbour information frame
NLS	noise line state
NRZ	non-return to zero
NRZI	non-return to zero invert

NSA	next station addressing
OSI	Open Systems Interconnection
OUI	organisational unique identifier
PA	preamble
PCM	physical connection management
PDU	protocol data unit
PHY	physical (OSI layer)
PMD	physical medium dependant (OSI sub-layer)
PMF	parameter management frame
QLS	quiet line state
RAF	resource allocation frame
RDF	request denied frame
RFC	request for comments
RMON	remote network monitoring
RMT	ring management
SA	source address
SAC	single attachment concentrator
SAP	service access point
SAS	single attachment station
SBA	synchronous bandwidth allocation
SD	start delimiter
SDU	service data unit
SIF	status information frame
SM-DAS	single MAC dual attachment stations
SMF	single-mode fibre
SMT	station management
SNMP	simple network management protocol
SPM	SONET physical layer mapping
SRF	status report frame
STP	shielded twisted pair
TBID	token rotation bid time carried within claim frame
TCP	transmission control protocol
THT	token holding timer
TNEG	current token rotation negotiated time (used during claim)
TOPR	TTRT operational time
TP-PMD	twisted pair - physical medium dependant (FDDI OSI sub-layer)
TPDDI	twisted pair distributed data interface
TREQ	requested token rotation time
TRT	token rotation timer
TTRT	target token rotation time
TVX	timer valid transmissions
UDP	user datagram protocol
ULS	unknown line state
UNA	upstream neighbour address

UTP	unshielded twisted pair
WAN	wide area network

Bibliography

Books

Baker, R. H. (1994) *Networking the Enterprise,* McGraw Hill, ISBN 0-07-005089-9.

Black, U. (1992) *TCP/IP and Related Protocols,* McGraw Hill, ISBN 0-07-005553-X.

De Prycker, M. (1993) *Asynchronous Transfer Mode,* 2nd edn, Prentice Hall, ISBN 0-13-178542-7.

Griffiths, J. M. (1990) *ISDN Explained,* Wiley, ISBN 0-471-92675.

Jain, R. (1994) *FDDI Handbook,* Addison Wesley, ISBN 0-201-56376-2.

Kessler, G. and Train, D. (1991) *Metropolitan Area Networks - Concepts, Standards and Services,* McGraw Hill, ISBN 0-07-034243-1.

Madron, T. W. (1990) *Local Area Networks: The Next Generation,* Wiley, ISBN 0-471-52250-3.

Miller, M. A. (1990) *LAN Protocol Handbook,* M&T Books, ISBN 1-55851-099-0.

Miller, M. A. (1991) *Internetworking: A Guide to Network Communications LAN to LAN; LAN to WAN,* M&T Books, ISBN 1-55851-143-1.

Mirchandani, S. and Khanna, R. (1993) *FDDI - Technology and Applications,* Wiley, ISBN 0-471-55896-6.

Ohta, N. (1994) *Packet Video - Modelling and Signal Processing,* Artech House, ISBN 0-89006-519-5.

Perlman, R. (1992) *Interconnections: Bridges and Routers,* Addison Wesley, ISBN 0-201-56332-0.

Rose, M. T. (1991) *The Simple Book - An Introduction to Management of TCP/IP based Internets,* Prentice Hall, ISBN 0-13-812611-9.

Sackett, G. C. (1993) *IBM's Token Ring Networking Handbook,* McGraw-Hill, ISBN 0-07-054418-2.

Shah, A. and Ramakrishnan, G. (1994) *FDDI - A High Speed Network,* Prentice Hall, ISBN 0-13-308388-8.

Stalling, W. (1990) *The Business Guide to Local Area Networks,* Howard W. Sams, ISBN 0-672-22728-2.

Stalling, W. (1993) *SNMP, SNMPv2, and CMIP: The Practical Guide to Network Management Standards,* Addison Wesley, ISBN 0-201-63331-0.

Tanenbaum, A. S. (1988) *Computer Networks,* 2nd edn, Prentice Hall, ISBN 0-13-162959.

Periodicals, Journals, Reports and Magazine Articles of Interest

Computer Technology (1991), *FDDI technology report*, 1st edn, Computer Technology Research Corp., April, ISBN 0-927695-70-7.

IDC (1994), '1993 PC Network Interface Card Market Review and Forecast', *IDC Market Analysis Report*, International Data Corporation, June 1994.

Johnson, M. J. (1987) 'Proof that timing requirements of the FDDI Token Ring protocol are satisfied', *IEEE Transactions on Communications*, vol. Com-35, No. 6, June.

LanQuest Labs (1993), 'Network Adapter Comparison – Executive Summary', LANQuest Labs (San Jose CA), July 1993.

Ovum (1993), *Networked multimedia: the business opportunity*, Ovum Ltd. (London) Market Report, 1993.

Roberts, D. (1992) 'The effect of local buffer memory size on FDDI throughput', Advanced Micro Devices publication 16294.

Shah, A., Staddon, D., Rubin, I. and Ratkovic, A. (1992) 'Multimedia over FDDI', *Proceedings of IEEE Local Computer Networks*, Minneapolis, 13-15 September.

Souza, R.J., Krishnakumar, P.G., Ozveren, C.M., Simcoe, R.J., Spinney, B.A., Thomas, R.E., Walsh, R.J. (1994) 'GIGAswitch: a high-performance packet switching platform', *Digital Equipment Corporation Technical Journal*, vol. 6, no. 1.

'Ethernet switches evaluated', *Data Communications International*, March 1994.

'FDDI adapters: a sure cure for the bandwidth blues', *Data Communications International*, July 1994.

'FDDI bridges and routers', *Data Communications International*, August 1993.

'How accurate is your LAN analyzer', *Data Communications International*, 21 January 1994.

'Special report on client server systems', *Data Communications International*, 21st May, 1994.

Standards and Specifications

ANSI X3.139-1987, *FDDI Token Ring Media Access Control (MAC)* Standard, 1987.

ANSI X3.148-1988, *FDDI Token Ring Physical Layer Protocol (PHY)* Standard, 1988.

ANSI X3.166-1990, *FDDI Token Ring Physical Layer Medium Dependent (PMD)* Standard, 1990.

ANSI X3T9.5 HRC (Draft) Rev 5.2, *FDDI Hybrid Ring Control* Specification, 23 April, 1990.

ANSI X3T9.5 LCF-PMD (Draft) Rev 1.3, *FDDI Low-cost Fibre Physical Layer Medium Dependent* Specification, 1 September, 1992.

ANSI X3T9.5 MAC-2 (Draft) Rev 3.3, *FDDI Media Access Control*, September, 1990.

ANSI X3T9.5 PHY-2 (Draft) Rev 5, *FDDI Physical Layer Protocol*, 17 June, 1992.

ANSI X3T9.5 SMF-PMD (Draft) Rev 4.2, *FDDI Single-mode Fiber Physical Layer Medium Dependent* Specification, 7 December, 1992

ANSI X3T9.5 SMT (Draft) v7.2, *FDDI Station Management* Specification, 25 June, 1992

ANSI X3T9.5 TP-PMD (Draft) Rev 2.1, *FDDI Twisted Pair Physical Layer Medium Dependent* Specification, 1 March, 1994.

EIA/TIA TSB 36 *Technical Systems Bulletin Additional Cable Specification for UTP Cables*, November 1991.

FDDI Synchronous Forum *Implementor's Agreement*, Rev 3, 19 April, 1994.

IBM Architecture Reference, *Token Ring Network*, IBM publication SC30-3374-02.

IBM/3-COM, *Heterogeneous LAN Management (HLM) Application Program Interface Technical Reference.*

IBM/3-COM, *Heterogeneous LAN Management (HLM) Architecture Reference.*

IEEE Draft Recommended Practice 802.1H, *Media Access Control (MAC) Bridging of Ethernet V2.0 in 802 Local Area Networks,* IEEE 802.1 Internetworking Task Group, January 1994 (unapproved at time of writing).

IEEE Std 802-1990, *IEEE Standard-Overview and Architecture,* IEEE, ISBN 1-55937-052-1.

IEEE Std 802.1B-1992, *LAN/MAN Management,* IEEE, ISBN 1-55937-263-X.

IEEE Std 802.1D-1990, *Media Access Control (MAC) Bridges* (includes 802.1i-1992 FDDI supplement), IEEE, ISBN 1-55937-055-6.

IEEE Std 802.1E-1990, *System Load Protocol,* IEEE, ISBN 1-55937-056-4.

IEEE Std 802.3I-1990 (supplement to ISO/IEC 8802-3), *System Considerations for Multisegment 10Mb/s Baseband Networks (Section 13). Twisted-pair Medium Attachment Unit (MAU) and Baseband Medium Type 10BASE-T (Section 14),* IEEE, ISBN 1-55937-070-X.

INTERNET DRAFT RTP, *A Transport Protocol for Real Time Applications*, Schulzrinne and Casner, Audio Visual Transport Working Group, October 1993.

ISO/IEC 8802-3 ANSI/IEEE Std 802.3 3rd edn, 1992, *Carrier Sense Multiple Access with Collision Detection (CSMA/CD) Access Method and Physical Layer Specifications,* IEEE, ISBN 1-55937-204-4.

ISO/IEC 8802-5 IEEE Std 802.5 1st edn, 1992, *Token Ring Access Method and Physical Specifications,* IEEE, ISBN 1-55937-205-2.

ITU-T (CCITT) Blue Book, Vol. III., Fascicle III.6, *Line Transmission of Non-telephone Signals, Transmission of Sound-programme and Television Signals,* Series H & J Recommendations.

RFC 1042, *A Standard for the Transmission of IP Datagrams over IEEE 802 Networks*, Postel & Reynolds, February 1988.

RFC 1122, *Requirements for Internet Hosts - Communication Layers*, Braden *et al.*, October 1989.

RFC 1188, *A Proposed Standard for the Transmission of IP Datagrams over FDDI Networks*, Katz, October 1990.

RFC 1285, *FDDI Management Information Base [SMT 6.2]*, Case, January 1992.

RFC 1286, *Definitions of Managed Objects for Bridges*, Decker *et al.*, December 1991.

RFC 1512, *FDDI Management Information Base [SMT 7.3]*, Case & Rijsinghani, September 1993.

Miscellaneous

AMD SUPERNET 2 Family for FDDI: 1994 World Network Data Book, Advanced Micro Devices, Sunnyvale, CA, publication 15502C

AMD SUPERNET Family for FDDI: Technical Manual (1989), Advanced Micro Devices, Sunnyvale, CA, publication 09779A

DEC *A Primer to FDDI: Fiber Distributed Data Interface*, Digital Equipment Corp.

XLNT Management and Security Integrated Circuit (MASIC) *User's Manual v1.1*, November 1993, XLNT Designs, Inc., San Diego, CA.

Index

—D—

—E—

—G—

—H—

—I—

—J—

—K—

—L—

—M—

—T—